Science, Faith, and Man

A volume
in
THE DOCUMENTARY HISTORY
of
WESTERN CIVILIZATION

SCIENCE, FAITH, AND MAN

European Thought Since 1914

edited by
W. WARREN WAGAR

MACMILLAN

London • Melbourne

1968

To
Franklin Le Van Baumer

Contents

Introduction

How MAY the historian characterize the *Zeitgeist* of the twentieth century? Is there, in fact, a distinctive spirit of the age? Is the twentieth century an "age" at all? For Egon Friedell, writing in the interwar years, the contemporary period marked the end of a sense of reality and certainty; man had lost his grip on truth. In *The Shape of Things to Come,* H. G. Wells's imaginary historian of the far future described the twentieth century as the Age of Confusion. W. H. Auden calls it an Age of Anxiety, Franz Alexander an Age of Unreason, Arthur Koestler an Age of Longing, Pitirim Sorokin an Age of Crisis, Morton White an Age of Analysis, Karl Mannheim an Age of Reconstruction. This is also the air age, the atomic age, the space age; the century of total war, of the common man, of totalitarianism. It is postmodern, or post-Christian, or even posthistoric.

Which labels, if any, will ultimately survive no one knows. It remains clear that the twentieth century, or at least that part of it which began with the "Great War" of 1914 and had not yet reached an obvious breaking-off point more than fifty years later, is an epoch in which advanced thought has had no spiritual center of gravity. Every effort to supply one has failed. Field theory, Freudian and Gestalt psychology, surrealism, logical positivism, existentialism, cyclical philosophy of history, Christian neo-orthodoxy, socialism, Nazi and Soviet millenarianism, all have had their moments of imposing strength; but the winds of change continue to blow, and no system of belief or interpretation seems destined to prevail. The orientation supplied to thought by Platonic and Aristotelian philosophy in antiquity, by Biblical and Augustinian faith in the Middle Ages, by the Newtonian world-picture in the Enlightenment, has no counterpart in the twentieth century.

This is not the first such period in Western thought. The immediate sources of contemporary pluralism—or chaos—may all be discovered in the nineteenth century. But the century most like

ours is perhaps the sixteenth. Consider just the first half of that
century. When Erasmus published *The Praise of Folly*, Jean
Texier had not yet begun the left spire of Chartres. Machiavelli's
The Prince, More's *Utopia*, Pomponazzi's refutation of the Christian doctrine of immortality, Luther's ninety-five theses, Matthias
Grünewald's "Temptation of Saint Anthony," Rabelais's *Panta-
gruel*, Copernicus's *De Revolutionibus Orbium Coelestium*, and
Calvin's *Institutes* were all completed within a few years of one
another (1513–36). The Middle Ages, the Renaissance, the Reformation, the Counter-Reformation, the Counter-Renaissance,
and the Scientific Revolution intersect in time. An intellectual
historian writing in 1550 would have found it no less difficult to
sort out the trends and identify the "spirit" of his century than we
do today, in contemplating the intellectual life of our own era.

But just as Thucydides regarded the Peloponnesian wars as the
greatest conflict in the history of mankind down to his own time,
so we are tempted to argue that the twentieth century poses the
greatest challenge to the human spirit since the beginning of civilization. Like Thucydides, we may possibly be right. In *The Courage to Be*, Paul Tillich identifies three kinds of anxiety, all of which
are present in our contemporary spiritual situation, as they were at
the end of antiquity and again at the end of the Middle Ages. The
first, ontic anxiety, is the fear of annihilation; the second, moral
anxiety, is the fear of condemnation that arises out of a sense of
guilt; and the third, spiritual anxiety, is the fear that life has no
meaning. In Tillich's judgment, ontic anxiety was dominant in late
antiquity, moral anxiety at the close of the Middle Ages, and
spiritual anxiety today. Modern man suffers most acutely from the
vertigo of meaninglessness; he has lost "a spiritual center . . . an
answer, however symbolic and indirect, to the question of the
meaning of existence." Yet even Tillich may underestimate the
gravity of our predicament. Twentieth-century man is assailed by
all three types of anxiety with a quite unprecedented fierceness.
Total war, total weaponry, and total government threaten him
with physical destruction or enslavement. The mass murder of
modern warfare, the affluence made possible by modern industry,
and the hectic tempo of socioeconomic change produce a sense of
guilt deeper than that which arose during the waning of the Middle
Ages and the era of the Reformation. The realization that we have
no common answer to the meaning of the existence that is about to

be wiped out, and no assurance that guilt and innocence are still terms with a cognitive content, only makes matters palpably worse.

A failure of nerve there may be, but not a failure of intellect or creative power. Despite fears of the "decline of the West" and the "passing of the European age," twentieth-century Europe has produced minds as remarkable as any in history; and not a few of the leading thinkers and artists resident in the Americas in this century have been exiles or immigrants from Europe, or their children. Nor is this, all things considered, a culturally lopsided century. Genius has flowered in virtually every department of higher culture: in literature and the theater, in music and the fine arts, in science, in philosophy, in theology, in sociological and historical thought, in economic thought, even (although one might have serious reservations here) in political thought. The universities have never been so full of teachers, students, and books. Concert halls, art galleries, and theaters have never flourished so well. No cities in world history have been more exciting than were Paris and Berlin in the 1920's, and an almost equally strong claim might be made for London in the 1950's and 1960's.

At the same time, it is almost impossible to see patterns emerging from the push and pull of conflicting tendencies in intellectual life. Theoretical physics, for example, has assailed the modern lay mind with relativity, field, quantum, and indeterminancy theory. The ferment of ideas is no less impressive than during the scientific revolution of the seventeenth century, but no coherent world-picture has developed—in fact, no picture at all. The reality of matter and cause-effect relationships can no longer be taken for granted. Some scientific thinkers return to organismic or teleological views of the cosmos, others feel more comfortable in a universe of random and discrete events from which no cosmological design can be inferred at all. The search for unity and purpose has not been abandoned. But it has remained a private search; each fresh "discovery," whether from Lecomte du Noüy, Teilhard de Chardin, Lancelot Law Whyte, or Einstein himself, fails to gain the general acceptance of the scientific community. Nor is there any assurance that a second Newtonian synthesis would decisively influence nonscientific thought, as the first did. The time when a large segment of the intelligentsia could be depended upon to turn to the natural sciences for light is long past.

The disunity of philosophy is even more spectacular. For some observers, especially in the Anglo-Saxon world, this is pre-eminently a century devoted to formal logical analysis. The positivist school descended from Mach and Russell and the linguistic school descended from Moore and Wittgenstein account, between them, for much of the best academic philosophical enterprise of the century. They claim to have abolished metaphysics, ethics, and aesthetics as branches of philosophy. But this is also the century of the phenomenological movement initiated by Husserl, which seeks to discern the essence of things through rigorously objective description of consciousness. It is the century of the existentialist movement, which has made extensive use of phenomenological techniques in returning in a radically new spirit to some of the ground questions of metaphysics and ethics. It is also the century of Bergson, Whitehead, and Teilhard, who have continued brilliantly in the biophilosophical tradition of nineteenth-century thought. It is the century, too, of a formalized Marxism, a liberalized Thomism, and a vulgarized Darwinism, the philosophies of Communists, Catholics, and Nazis, respectively. What is the common denominator that identifies these competing schools of thought as products of a single generation? Some are profoundly technical, some are frankly amateur. Some are analytical, some are synthetic, some are both. Some seek truth, others seek only clarification. Some treat the human condition, others ignore it. Some borrow concepts from science, others are antiscientific. All draw to some measurable extent on earlier traditions, all are to some degree revolutionary and destructive of tradition.

The difficulty experienced by the layman in finding relevance to his life in the exact sciences and in academic philosophy has contributed to the reversal of a trend established in the eighteenth and nineteenth centuries. At that time science and phiosophy were threatening to usurp the place of religion; in the twentieth century, it would almost seem that for a certain representative type of intellectual, religion is threatening to usurp the place of science and philosophy. Organized religion has fared poorly in Europe, but the demise of faith predicted by T. H. Huxley has failed to come to pass. The years since 1914 have been marked by a theological renaissance and a reawakening of sympathetic interest in the major world religions. The neo-orthodox theologies of Barth, Brunner, Adam, and Guardini, the existentialist theologies of Bultmann, Tillich, and Buber, and the pronouncements of such major ecclesiastical figures as Pius XI, Dean Inge, John XXIII, and, most recently, Bishop Robinson of Woolwich, have earned serious attention from the intelligentsia. Many more converts and favorably disposed spectators have been won for Christianity by the work of Toynbee, Eliot, Greene, C. S. Lewis, Maritain, Claudel, Bernanos, Mounier, Marcel, Schweitzer, Bonhoeffer, Voegelin, Berdyaev, and other writers both inside and outside the churches.

But it would be difficult to define with any degree of assurance the faith shared by these twentieth-century believers. Although contemporary religious thought has tended to back away from the immanentist, optimistic, pragmatic theology of the nineteenth century, it has backed away in several different directions. Some thinkers have sought to revive the essential doctrines of orthodox faith, others have reinterpreted them in terms of the categories of existentialist ontology. God is Wholly Other, or the second person singular in an I-thou dialogue, or dead, which is to say, withdrawn. Faith is essentially myth, but it must be "demythologized." For some the heart of the kerygma is all that matters, but one also hears the cry that Christianity must be "dekerygmatized." Much contemporary theology relies on the same sort of shock values as contemporary art. Each new voice labors under a compulsion to make a radically new utterance, to catapult the unsuspecting believer into a state of spiritual awareness as remote as possible from the familiar routines of conventional religious experience. Even orthodoxy must be studied under the rubric of neo-orthodoxy; it is much more (or less) than the original article.

Nor has every twentieth-century European mind made the leap forward to some form of faith. Most have felt the urge to do so, at one time or another in their lives. But the counterattack begun on traditional Christianity from the point of view of secular humanism during the Enlightenment has continued into this century. Freud, Shaw, Wells, Russell, Julian Huxley, Sartre, and Camus belong in the lineage of Comte, Marx, Spencer, and Nietzsche. The majority of avant-garde twentieth-century thinkers and artists have been, for all practical purposes, unbelievers. Much of the seemingly theatrical agony of Christian thinkers confronting the "death of God" in our time is wholly authentic. But again, the picture is confusing. Traditional faith has continued to wane in the twentieth century, and so, for that matter, has the buoyant humanism of the Enlightenment. At the same time there are enough great theologians and great humanists to make it possible for the historian to characterize the twentieth century as a second Reformation era, or, alternately, as the age of the maturation of agnostic humanism. We suffer, among other things, from an *embarras de richesse*.

Scholars in search of the *Zeitgeist* have sometimes attempted to discover the essence of twentieth-century thought in the vogue of psychology and psychoanalysis. Science, philosophy, and religion are as old as Western civilization itself, but psychology as a discipline and psychoanalysis as a technique and a *Weltanschauung* appear only in the present century, from origins late in the nineteenth. Above all, the function of the unconscious in life and thought, and the function of the sexual impulses, were largely unknown and unexamined until our century.

Sigmund Freud is not, however, our Augustine, our Newton, or even our Darwin. Modern art and literature owe much to psychoanalytic concepts. Psychology and psychiatry are firmly established as major disciplines, and no educated man can refrain from lacing his conversation at times with terms derived from the literatures of both. But this is not to say that most avant-garde thought in our time takes its basic inspiration or sense of direction from psychology. Even if it did, the question would remain: from which psychology? The same fundamental disunity of outlook exists here as in other departments of culture. Although Freud led the way, his chief disciples ultimately abandoned him for radically different points of view. Jung's world-outlook carried him back to some of the nuclear concepts of traditional religious faith. Adler, Rank, and Fromm parted company on other issues. The *Gestalt* psychology of Köhler and Koffka, the behaviorist school of Pavlov and Watson, and the existential psychology of Binswanger and May offer interpretations of man that rarely run parallel to the Freudian or to one another, and betray much much more the influence of science and philosophy on psychology than the influence of psychology on science and philosophy.

The historian must feel a special sense of embarrassment in trying to sum up the philosophy of history in twentieth-century thought. In nearly every earlier period in Western intellectual history, one well-defined understanding of the pattern of the past prevailed—or, at most, two opposed views struggled for the ascendancy. Advanced historical thought in this century is torn in at least five directions. Spengler's *Decline of the West* revived classical cyclical theory after the First World War; the earlier volumes of Toynbee's *Study of History* followed the basic Spenglerian pattern, but with a supernaturalist substructure that recalled Augustine. The later Toynbee has added a generous measure of Enlightenment progressivism, which, for that matter, lives on more or less intact in the thought of many humanists and in Soviet philosophy. Meanwhile, Christian writers on the philosophy of history have explicitly repudiated both the cyclical and the progressivist doctrines, either returning to the fundamental terms of the Christian hope or substituting for this a kind of mystical millenarianism, best illustrated by the thought of Teilhard, or embracing a radically existentialist conception of history as a continuum that can, at any instant, be punctured by the personal encounter of God and man, but which has no literal public end. Finally, a very considerable number of historians and philosophers of history side with the analytical philosophers in refusing to speculate at all. So far as we know, their argument runs, history is without any general meaning; it has no pattern, save what we give it; any effort to read a cosmic scheme into the human experience is nonsensical and a threat to freedom. Expectations of the future range from ecstatic optimism to black despair to a reasoned denial of man's prophetic powers.

In social and political thought the broad spectrum of views already available in the latter part of the nineteenth century has continued into the twentieth, supplemented by the ideologies of the totalitarian states: Fascism, National Socialism, and Leninism. Here again it would not be possible to single out, from the perspective of the 1960's, which conception of society, politics, and the state most fully expresses the spirit of the times. The struggles of liberalism and/or conservatism versus socialism, democracy versus totalitarianism, nationalism versus internationalism, fascism versus communism, and classical liberalism and/or socialism versus the eclecticism of the Welfare State, are all well-documented in the political history of our era. At times political commitment has been an active psychological substitute for religious or metaphysical belief, notably in the period between the outbreak of the Great Depression and the death of Stalin. But the 1920's, 1950's, and 1960's have been remarkable for the degree of disengagement from political issues practiced by the intelligentsia. There has also been less serious political philosophy than in any recent century, if one may distinguish between political philosophy and political ideas.

But it is in the arts that the confusion of the century asserts itself most spectacularly. The artist reflects his time; if the times are out of joint, they will give rise to a disorganized, promiscuous, and alienated art. The only universal attribute of twentieth-century art and literature has been an insatiable urge to experiment, to break with established canons of aesthetic value and start over again. No century has witnessed so many violent upheavals; no century has produced so many deeply personal and revolutionary artistic visions. Michelangelo, Shakespeare, and Mozart were simply the best of their kind. Picasso, Joyce, and Stravinsky are *sui generis*. What is one to make of a century that can encompass, for example, cubism, futurism, expressionism, Dada, surrealism, constructivism, socialist realism, abstract expressionism, and casualism? The loss of a center, even a provisionally valid center of reference, is strikingly clear. Equally meaningful is the almost random pillaging of past styles of art, music, and literature for fresh inspiration. Individually, the achievements of twentieth-century artists stun and dazzle. Collectively, they mirror the disintegration of Western civilization.

What, then, is the *Zeitgeist* of the twentieth century? Of what is it the "age"? Two possibilities suggest themselves. It is not inconceivable that the twentieth century lacks a unified spirit because we have reached the end of mentally unified epochs. Let us suppose that there are too many people, too many university graduates, too many well-established local and national cultures, too many spiritual and intellectual frontiers, that there is too much freedom and too little reverence for authority to expect a coherent cultural pattern throughout civilization. There may never again be such a pattern, given a continuation of modern affluence and freedom. This is one possibility. It cannot be dismissed out of hand.

The other is less remarkable, but in the nature of things more credible. One must apologize in advance for putting such a tired concept in harness again, but perhaps, after all, this is an "age of transition"; specifically, of transition from the continental civilizations of the last few thousand years, of which Europe and her progeny in America and Australasia are examples, to a new world civilization. It is difficult for a European historian to doubt that the thought and art of the West will loom larger in the coming planetary order than the thought and art of Africa, the Near East,

India, or East Asia. But one need not be concerned about the relative influence of the several civilizations destined for fusion. There is a certain rough justice in these matters; the compatible cultural values of each civilization that men find most vital will manage somehow to survive, and the life of Europe will stand or fall according to its merits.

No doubt the world civilization, if and when it arrives, will be qualitatively unlike past civilizations in many respects. Precisely because of the freedom and affluence and unlimited frontiers referred to above, it will be rather less unified and homogeneous than past societies. But it is unlikely to perpetuate the chaos of the twentieth century. The restoration of order at a new level and in a new spirit will exert a powerful formative influence on philosophy, religion, social thought, scholarship, the arts, and possibly even the exact sciences. An authentic planetary spirit will manifest itself, and intellectual historians may once again search for definitions of the *Zeitgeist* with at least some hope of success.

Meanwhile, there is every good reason to believe that the achievements of twentieth-century Western thought have not been wasted effort. They are the work of great minds, unsurpassed in the history of thought. They are also part of the ongoing development of ideas in each of the disciplines involved, and although much of the best thinking of our time will no doubt prove unacceptable in the next century, much more will endure. Even thought that lapses into extinction has its influence on later development, by provoking reactions against it in its decline. In the final analysis, history does nothing in vain.

The present volume does not pretend to sample every type of twentieth-century thought, nor to give fair representation to each country. In selecting documents, I have limited myself deliberately to what I should like to call "free spirits," thinkers who may or may not belong to a well-defined intellectual tradition, but who have felt free to express their innermost ideas and who stand—or have stood, in their time—at the frontiers of thought in their chosen fields. This is not a book of officially designated apologists; the reader will find no examples of government propaganda.

I have also focused on professions of belief or contributions to knowledge that have had a more or less universal impact on belief in our time. In so doing, I have neglected the internal development of many of the sciences, both natural and social. Some of the best work done by twentieth-century minds, which may very well outlast the type of thought represented in this volume, has been the work of specialists active in abstruse disciplines who have had little measurable influence in shaping the "spirit" of the age, such as it is. But it would take far more than a single volume to do anything like justice to the scope and variety of their enterprise. Our principal concern here is, rather, with attempts made by independent thinkers to supply their generation with large answers to large questions about the nature, meaning, and purpose of life. In short, this anthology is a contribution to intellectual history, or *Geistesgeschichte*, and not to the technical history of science, philosophy, theology, sociology, psychology, and the like.

Finally, a word about geography. All the documents reprinted here were first written in English, French, or German by thinkers resident in an English-, French-, or German-speaking country. This should not be taken to mean that thinkers writing in Spanish, Italian, Swedish, Polish, or Russian, for example, are unworthy of inclusion in such an anthology. But for a variety of reasons, the geographical center of thought in the twentieth century has been the northwestern quarter of Europe, as in every previous century since the seventeenth. To a greater degree than in the past, this intellectual leadership has been enhanced by the presence in northwestern Europe of émigrés and refugees from other parts of the continent. There are also signs, since 1945, that the United States is challenging northwestern Europe as the cultural center of Western civilization, if only because this country has been able to attract so many Europeans, permanently or temporarily, to its shores. But through the first five decades of the century, who can doubt that Britain, France, and the countries of the German-speaking world continued to hold the intellectual initiative they first seized in the era of the Reformation? Perhaps the day of *Untergang* is now finally at hand; or perhaps Europe is about to be absorbed into a higher synthesis of planetary proportions. Whatever happens, the cultural ascendancy of northwestern Europe down at least to the middle of the twentieth century seems incontrovertible.

I

Physics and Philosophy

Theoretical Physics

ALBERT EINSTEIN

Every modern century has its paragons, its culture-heroes, who fill the place once taken by saints and messiahs. For the first half of the twentieth century, outside the totalitarian states, the most celebrated paragons have been Gandhi, Schweitzer, and Einstein; and of these the most influential as a thinker was clearly Albert Einstein.

Born in Germany in 1879, Einstein became a Swiss citizen at the age of fifteen and earned his first academic post at Bern with the publication in 1905 of three papers in the *Annalen der Physik*, one of which laid the foundations of modern relativity theory. From Bern, he moved on to the universities of Zurich and Prague, and in 1914 to Berlin. After the accession to power of Hitler in 1933, Einstein emigrated to the United States, where he died in 1955. Almost alone, he is responsible for the general theory of relativity, one of the basic conceptions of twentieth-century physics. He also made major contributions to quantum and field theory.

Einstein belongs to what might be called the "right" wing of theoretical physicists: thinkers of "classical" views, who believe that the universe can be known, and that it obeys precise mathematical laws from which chance and chaos are excluded. Hence, although he helped to reveal a universe that seemed far less stable and intelligible than that of the nineteenth century, and although he unintentionally provided much intellectual ammunition for the prophets of ethical relativism, Einstein remained all his life a traditionalist on the central question of the orderliness of existence. In the following lecture, written in 1940, he reviews the progress of theoretical physics since Newton.

SOURCE: "Considerations Concerning the Fundaments of Theoretical Physics," by Albert Einstein, *Science*, XCI (May 24, 1940), 487–92. Reprinted by permission of the American Association for the Advancement of Science and of the Estate of Albert Einstein.

SCIENCE IS the attempt to make the chaotic diversity of our sense-experience correspond to a logically uniform system of thought. In this system single experiences must be correlated with the theoretic structure in such a way that the resulting coordination is unique and convincing.

The sense-experiences are the given subject-matter. But the theory that shall interpret them is man-made. It is the result of an extremely laborious process of adaptation: hypothetical, never completely final, always subject to question and doubt. The scientific way of forming concepts differs from that which we use in our daily life, not basically, but merely in the more precise definition of concepts and conclusions; more painstaking and systematic choice of experimental material; and greater logical economy. By this last we mean the effort to reduce all concepts and correlations to as few as possible logically independent basic concepts and axioms.

What we call physics comprises that group of natural sciences which base their concepts on measurements; and whose concepts and propositions lend themselves to mathematical formulation. Its realm is accordingly defined as that part of the sum total of our knowledge which is capable of being expressed in mathematical terms. With the progress of science, the realm of physics has so expanded that it seems to be limited only by the limitations of the method itself.

The larger part of physical research is devoted to the development of the various branches of physics, in each of which the object is the theoretical understanding of more or less restricted fields of experience, and in each of which the laws and concepts remain as closely as possible related to experience. It is this department of science, with its ever-growing specialization, which has revolutionized practical life in the last centuries, and given birth to the possibility that man may at last be freed from the burden of physical toil.

On the other hand, from the very beginning there has always been present the attempt to find a unifying theoretical basis for all these single sciences, consisting of a minimum of concepts and fundamental relationships, from which all the concepts and relationships of the single disciplines might be derived by logical process. This is what we mean by the search for a foundation of the whole of physics. The confident belief that this ultimate goal may be reached is the chief source of the passionate devotion which has always animated the researcher. It is in this sense that the following observations are devoted to the foundations of physics.

From what has been said it is clear that the word foundations in this connection does not mean something analogous in all respects to the foundations of a building. Logically considered, of course, the various single laws of physics rest upon this foundation. But whereas a building may be seriously damaged by a heavy storm or spring flood, yet its foundations remain intact, in science the logical foundation is always in greater peril from new experiences or new knowledge than are the branch disciplines with their closer experimental contacts. In the connection of the foundation with all the single parts lies its great significance, but likewise its greatest danger in face of any new factor. When we realize this, we are led to wonder why the so-called revolutionary epochs of the science of physics have not more often and more completely changed its foundation than has actually been the case.

The first attempt to lay a uniform theoretical foundation was the work of Newton. In his system everything is reduced to the following concepts: (1) Mass points with invariable mass; (2) action at a distance between any pair of mass points; (3) law of motion for the mass point. There was not, strictly speaking, any all-embracing foundation, because an explicit law was formulated only for the actions-at-a-distance of gravitation; while for other actions-at-a-distance nothing was established *a priori* except the law of equality of *actio* and *reactio*. Moreover, Newton himself fully realized that time and space were essential elements, as physically effective factors, of his system, if only by implication.

This Newtonian basis proved eminently fruitful and was regarded as final up to the end of the nineteenth century. It not only gave results for the movements of the heavenly bodies, down to the most minute details, but also furnished a theory of the mechanics of discrete and continuous masses, a simple explanation of the principle of the conservation of energy and a complete and brilliant theory of heat. The explanation of the facts of electrodynamics within the Newtonian system was more forced; least convincing of all, from the very beginning, was the theory of light.

It is not surprising that Newton would not listen to a wave theory of light; for such a theory was most unsuited to his theoretical foundation. The assumption that space was filled with a medium consisting of material points that propagated light waves without exhibiting any other mechanical properties must have seemed to him quite artificial. The strongest empirical arguments for the wave nature of light, fixed speeds of propagation, interference, diffraction, polarization were either unknown or else not known in any well-ordered synthesis. He was justified in sticking to his corpuscular theory of light.

During the nineteenth century the dispute was settled in favor of the wave theory. Yet no serious doubt of the mechanical foundation of physics arose, in the first place because nobody knew where to find a foundation of another sort. Only slowly, under the irresistible pressure of facts, there developed a new foundation of physics, field-physics.

From Newton's time on, the theory of action-at-a-distance was constantly found artificial. Efforts were not lacking to explain gravitation by a kinetic theory, that is, on the basis of collision forces of hypothetical mass particles. But the attempts were superficial and bore no fruit. The strange part played by space (or the inertial system) within the mechanical foundation was also clearly recognized, and criticized with especial clarity by Ernst Mach.

The great change was brought about by Faraday, Maxwell, and Hertz—as a matter of fact half-unconsciously and against their will. All three of them, throughout their lives, considered themselves adherents of the mechanical theory. Hertz had found the simplest form of the equations of the electromagnetic field, and declared that any theory leading to these equations was Maxwellian theory. Yet toward the end of his short life he wrote a paper in which he presented as the foundation of physics a mechanical theory freed from the force-concept.

For us, who took in Faraday's ideas so to speak with our mother's milk, it is hard to appreciate their greatness and audacity. Faraday must have grasped with unerring instinct the artificial nature of all attempts to refer electromagnetic phenomena to actions-at-a-distance between electric particles reacting on each other. How was each single iron filing among a lot scattered on a piece of paper to know of the single electric particles running round in a nearby conductor? All these electric particles together seemed to create in the surrounding space a condition which in turn produced a certain order in the filings. These spatial states, today called fields, if their geometrical structure and interdependent action were once rightly grasped, would, he was convinced, furnish the clue to the mysterious electromagnetic interactions. He conceived these fields as states of mechanical stress in a space-filling medium, similar to the states of stress in an elastically distended body. For at that time this was the only way one could conceive of states that were apparently continuously distributed in space. The peculiar type of mechanical interpretation of these fields remained in the background—a sort of placation of the scientific conscience in view of the mechanical tradition of Faraday's time. With the help of these new field concepts Faraday succeeded in forming a qualitative concept of the whole complex of electromagnetic effects discovered by him and his predecessors. The precise formulation of the time-space laws of those fields was the work of Maxwell. Imagine his feelings when the differential equations he had formulated proved to him that electromagnetic fields spread in the form of polarized waves and with the speed of light! To few men in the world has such an experience been vouchsafed. At that thrilling moment he surely never guessed that the riddling nature of light, apparently so completely solved, would continue to baffle succeeding generations. Meantime, it took physicists some decades to grasp the full significance of Maxwell's discovery, so bold was the leap that his genius forced upon the conceptions of his fellow-workers. Only after Hertz had demonstrated experimentally the existence of Maxwell's electromagnetic waves did resistance to the new theory break down.

But if the electromagnetic field could exist as a wave independent of the material source, then the electrostatic interaction could no longer be explained as action-at-a-distance. And what was true for electrical action could not be denied for gravitation. Everywhere Newton's actions-at-a-distance gave way to fields spreading with finite velocity.

Of Newton's foundation there now remained only the material mass points subject to the law of motion. But J. J. Thomson pointed out that an electrically charged body in motion must, according to Maxwell's theory, possess a magnetic field whose energy acted precisely as does an increase of kinetic energy to the body. If, then, a part of kinetic energy consists of field energy, might that not then be true of the whole of the kinetic energy? Perhaps the basic property of matter, its inertia, could be explained within the field theory? The question led to the problem of an interpretation of matter in terms of field theory, the solution of which would furnish an explanation of the atomic structure of matter. It was soon realized that Maxwell's theory could not accomplish such a program. Since then many scientists have zealously sought to complete the field theory by some generalization that should comprise a theory of matter; but so far such efforts have not been crowned with success. In order to construct a theory, it is not enough to have a clear conception of the goal. One must also have a formal point of view which will sufficiently restrict the unlimited variety of possibilities. So far this has not been found; accordingly the field theory has not succeeded in furnishing a foundation for the whole of physics.

For several decades most physicists clung to the conviction that a mechanical substructure would be found for Maxwell's theory. But the unsatisfactory results of their efforts led to gradual acceptance of the new field concepts as irreducible fundamentals—in other words, physicists resigned themselves to giving up the idea of a mechanical foundation.

Thus physicists held to a field-theory program. But it could not be called a foundation, since nobody could tell whether a consistent field theory could ever explain on the one hand gravitation, on the other hand the elementary components of matter. In this state of affairs it was necessary to think of material particles as mass points subject to Newton's laws of motion. This was the procedure of Lorentz in creating his electron theory and the theory of the electromagnetic phenomena of moving bodies.

Such was the point at which fundamental conceptions had arrived at the turn of the century. Immense progress was made in the theoretical penetration and understanding of whole groups of new phenomena; but the establishment of a unified foundation for physics seemed remote indeed. And this state of things has even been aggravated by subsequent developments. The development during the present century is characterized by two theoretical systems essentially independent of each other: the theory of relativity and the quantum theory. The two systems do not directly contradict each other; but they seem little adapted to fusion into one unified theory. We must briefly discuss the basic idea of these two systems.

The theory of relativity arose out of efforts to improve, with reference to logical economy, the foundation of physics as it existed at the turn of the century. The so-called special or restricted relativity theory is based on the fact that Maxwell's equations (and thus the law of propagation of light in empty space) are converted into equations of the same form, when they undergo Lorentz transformation. This formal property of the Maxwell equations is supplemented by our fairly secure empirical knowledge that the laws of physics are the same with respect to all inertial systems. This leads to the result that the Lorentz transformation—applied to space and time coordinates—must govern the transition from one inertial system to any other. The content of the restricted relativity theory can accordingly be summarized in one sentence: all natural laws must be so conditioned that they are covariant with respect to Lorentz transformations. From this it follows that the simultaneity of two distant events is not an invariant concept and that the dimensions of rigid bodies and the speed of clocks depend upon their state of motion. A further consequence was a modification of Newton's law of motion in cases where the speed of a given body was not small compared with the speed of light. There followed also the principle of the equivalence of mass and energy, with the laws of conservation of mass and energy becoming one and the same. Once it was shown that simultaneity was relative and depended on the frame of reference, every possibility of retaining actions-at-a-distance within the foundation of physics disappeared, since that concept presupposed the absolute character of simultaneity (it must be possible to state the location of the two interacting mass points "at the same time").

The general theory of relativity owes its origin to the attempt to explain a fact known since Galileo's and Newton's time but hitherto eluding all theoretical interpretation: the inertia and the weight of a body, in themselves two entirely distinct things, are measured by one and the same constant, the mass. From this correspondence follows that it is impossible to discover by experiment whether a given system of coordinates is accelerated, or whether its motion is straight and uniform and the observed effects are due to a gravitational field (this is the equivalence principle of the general relativity theory). It shatters the concepts of the inertial system, as soon as gravitation enters in. It may be remarked here that the inertial system is a weak point of the Galilean-Newtonian mechanics. For there is presupposed a mysterious property of physical space, conditioning the kind of coordinate-systems for which the law of inertia and the Newtonian law of motion hold good.

These difficulties can be avoided by the following postulate: natural laws are to be formulated in such a way that their form is identical for coordinate systems of any kind of states of motion. To accomplish this is the task of the general theory of relativity. On the other hand, we deduce from the restricted theory the existence of a Riemannian metric within the time-space continuum, which, according to the equivalence principle, describes both the gravitational field and the metric properties of space. Assuming that the field equations of gravitation are of the second differential order, the field law is clearly determined.

Aside from this result, the theory frees field physics from the disability it suffered from, in common with the Newtonian mechanics, of ascribing to space those independent physical properties which heretofore had been concealed by the use of an inertial system. But it cannot be claimed that those parts of the general relativity theory which can today be regarded as final have furnished physics with a complete and satisfactory foundation. In the first place, the total field appears in it to be composed of two logically unconnected parts, the gravitational and the electromagnetic. And in the second place, this theory, like the earlier field theories, has not up till now supplied an explanation of the atomistic structure of matter. This failure has probably some connection with the fact that so far it has contributed nothing to the understanding of quantum phenomena. To take in these phenomena, physicists have been driven to the adoption of entirely new methods, the basic characteristics of which we shall now discuss.

In the year nineteen hundred, in the course of a purely theoretic investigation, Max Planck made a very remarkable discovery: the law of radiation of bodies as a function of temperature could not be derived solely from the laws of Maxwellian electrodynamics. To arrive at results consistent with the relevant experiments, radiation of a given frequency had to be treated as though it consisted of energy atoms of the individual energy hv, where h is Planck's universal constant. During the years following, it was shown that light was everywhere produced and absorbed in such energy quanta. In particular Niels Bohr was able largely to understand the structure of the atom, on the assumption that atoms can have only discrete energy values, and that the discontinuous transitions be-

tween them are connected with the emission or absorption of such
an energy quantum. This threw some light on the fact that in their
gaseous state elements and their compounds radiate and absorb
only light of certain sharply defined frequencies. All this was quite
inexplicable within the frame of the hitherto existing theories. It
was clear that at least in the field of atomistic phenomena the
character of everything that happens is determined by discrete
states and by apparently discontinuous transitions between them,
Planck's constant h playing a decisive role.

The next step was taken by de Broglie. He asked himself how
the discrete states could be understood by the aid of the current
concepts, and hit on a parallel with stationary waves, as for
instance in the case of the proper frequencies of organ pipes and
strings in acoustics. True, wave actions of the kind here required
were unknown; but they could be constructed, and their mathematical laws formulated, employing Planck's constant h. De
Broglie conceived an electron revolving about the atomic nucleus
as being connected with such a hypothetical wave train, and made
intelligible to some extent the discrete character of Bohr's "permitted" paths by the stationary character of the corresponding
waves.

Now in mechanics the motion of material points is determined
by the forces or fields of force acting upon them. Hence it was to
be expected that those fields of force would also influence de
Broglie's wave fields in an analogous way. Erwin Schrödinger
showed how this influence was to be taken into account, re-in-
terpreting by an ingenious method certain formulations of classical
mechanics. He even succeeded in expanding the wave mechanical
theory to a point where without the introduction of any additional
hypotheses, it became applicable to any mechanical system consisting or an arbitrary number of mass points, that is to say possessing
an arbitrary number of degrees of freedom. This was possible
because a mechanical system consisting of n mass points is mathematically equivalent to a considerable degree to one single mass
point moving in a space of $3\,n$ dimensions.

On the basis of this theory there was obtained a surprisingly
good representation of an immense variety of facts which otherwise appeared entirely incomprehensible. But on one point, curi-
ously enough, there was failure: it proved impossible to associate
with these Schrödinger waves definite motions of the mass points—

and that, after all, had been the original purpose of the whole construction.

The difficulty appeared insurmountable, until it was overcome by Born in a way as simple as it was unexpected. The de Broglie-Schrödinger wave fields were not to be interpreted as a mathematical description of how an event actually takes place in time and space, though, of course, they have reference to such an event. Rather they are a mathematical description of what we can actually know about the system. They serve only to make statistical statements and predictions of the results of all measurements which we can carry out upon the system.

Let me illustrate these general features of quantum mechanics by means of a simple example: we shall consider a mass point kept inside a restricted region G by forces of finite strength. If the kinetic energy of the mass point is below a certain limit, then the mass point, according to classical mechanics, can never leave the region G. But according to quantum mechanics, the mass point, after a period not immediately predictable, is able to leave the region G, in an unpredictable direction, and escape into surrounding space. This case, according to Gamow, is a simplified model of radioactive disintegration.

The quantum theoretical treatment of this case is as follows: at the time t_0 we have a Schrödinger wave system entirely inside G. But from the time t_0 onwards, the waves leave the interior of G in all directions, in such a way that the amplitude of the outgoing wave is small compared to the initial amplitude of the wave system inside G. The further these outside waves spread, the more the amplitude of the waves inside G diminishes, and correspondingly the intensity of the later waves issuing from G. Only after infinite time has passed is the wave supply inside G exhausted, while the outside wave has spread over an ever-increasing space.

But what has this wave process to do with the first object of our interest, the particle originally enclosed in G? To answer this question, we must imagine some arrangement which will permit us to carry out measurements on the particle. For instance, let us imagine somewhere in the surrounding space a screen so made that the particle sticks to it on coming into contact with it. Then, from the intensity of the waves hitting the screen at some point, we draw conclusions as to the probability of the particle hitting the screen there at that time. As soon as the particle has hit any particular point of the screen, the whole wave field loses all its physical meaning; its only purpose was to make probability predictions as to the place and time of the particle hitting the screen (or, for instance, its momentum at the time when it hits the screen).

All other cases are analogous. The aim of the theory is to determine the probability of the results of measurement upon a system at a given time. On the other hand, it makes no attempt to give a mathematical representation of what is actually present or goes on in space and time. On this point the quantum theory of today differs fundamentally from all previous theories of physics, mechanistic as well as field theories. Instead of a model description of actual space-time events, it gives the probability distributions for possible measurements as functions of time.

It must be admitted that the new theoretical conception owes its origin not to any flight of fancy but to the compelling force of the facts of experience. All attempts to represent the particle and wave features displayed in the phenomena of light and matter, by direct recourse to a space-time model, have so far ended in failure. And Heisenberg has convincingly shown, from an empirical point of view, that any decision as to a rigorously deterministic structure of nature is definitely ruled out, because of the atomistic structure of our experimental apparatus. Thus it is probably out of the question that any future knowledge can compel physics again to relinquish our present statistical theoretical foundation in favor of a deterministic one which would deal directly with physical reality. Logically the problem seems to offer two possibilities, between which we are in principle given a choice. In the end the choice will be made according to which kind of description yields the formulation of the simplest foundation, logically speaking. At the present, we are quite without any deterministic theory directly describing the events themselves and in consonance with the facts.

For the time being, we have to admit that we do not possess any general theoretical basis for physics, which can be regarded as its logical foundation. The field theory, so far, has failed in the molecular sphere. It is agreed on all hands that the only principle which could serve as the basis of quantum theory would be one that constituted a translation of the field theory into the scheme of quantum statistics. Whether this will actually come about in a satisfactory manner, nobody can venture to say.

Some physicists, among them myself, cannot believe that we

must abandon, actually and forever, the idea of direct representation of physical reality in space and time; or that we must accept the view that events in nature are analogous to a game of chance. It is open to every man to choose the direction of his striving; and also every man may draw comfort from Lessing's fine saying, that the search for truth is more precious than its possession.

Science and Culture

WERNER HEISENBERG

If Einstein is the exemplar of "classical" physics in the twentieth century, Werner Heisenberg speaks for a younger and more radical school, which also includes the Danish physicist Niels Bohr. The new school is noted for its dependence on mathematical explanation and its opposition to mechanistic and deterministic theories in physics. The son of a distinguished German Byzantine scholar, Heisenberg writes that his early education in the humanities fortified him against the prevailing tendency in theoretical physics to rely on mechanical models as devices for representing the microcosm. His principle of indeterminancy or uncertainty, announced in 1927, argues that cause and effect relationships cannot be observed at the subatomic level. Subatomic particles are not like billiard balls, whose present position and velocity can be measured and whose future whereabouts can be accurately predicted. The best we can do is to work out statistical averages for the behavior of particles in large numbers.

Just as relativity theory has its illegitimate applications in ethics, so the principle of indeterminancy has sometimes been cited to support the idea that "free will" in the microcosm proves the existence of free will in man; alternatively, that the world is chaotic and all things happen by chance. In this passage from his *Physics and Philosophy*, Heisenberg inveighs against the dogmatism and naïve materialism of nineteenth-century thought, which, he feels, have been invalidated by recent physical theory.

IT HAS frequently been discussed among the historians whether the rise of natural science after the sixteenth century was in any way a natural consequence of earlier trends in human thinking. It may be

SOURCE: *Physics and Philosophy*, by Werner Heisenberg (Harper & Row, New York, 1958), pp. 194–206. Reprinted by permission of Harper & Row, Publishers, and George Allen and Unwin, Ltd. Copyright 1958 by Werner Heisenberg.

argued that certain trends in Christian philosophy led to a very abstract concept of God, that they put God so far above the world that one began to consider the world without at the same time also seeing God in the world. The Cartesian partition may be called a final step in this development. Or one may point out that all the theological controversies of the sixteenth century produced a general discontent about problems that could not really be settled by reason and were exposed to the political struggles of the time; that this discontent favored interest in problems which were entirely separated from the theological disputes. Or one may simply refer to the enormous activity, the new spirit that had come into the European societies through the Renaissance. In any case during this period a new authority appeared which was completely independent of Christian religion or philosophy or of the Church, the authority of experience, of the empirical fact. One may trace this authority back into older philosophical trends, for instance, into the philosophy of Occam and Duns Scotus, but it became a vital force of human activity only from the sixteenth century onward. Galileo did not only *think* about the mechanical motions, the pendulum and the falling stone; he tried out by experiments, quantitatively, how these motions took place. This new activity was in its beginning certainly not meant as a deviation from the traditional Christian religion. On the contrary, one spoke of two kinds of revelation of God. The one was written in the Bible and the other was to be found in the book of nature. The Holy Scripture had been written by man and was therefore subject to error, while nature was the immediate expression of God's intentions.

However, the emphasis on experience was connected with a slow and gradual change in the aspect of reality. While in the Middle Ages what we nowadays call the symbolic meaning of a thing was in some way its primary reality, the aspect of reality changed toward what we can perceive with our senses. What we can see and touch became primarily real. And this new concept of reality could be connected with a new activity: we can experiment and see how things really are. It was easily seen that this new attitude meant the departure of the human mind into an immense field of new possibilities, and it can be well understood that the Church saw in the new movement the dangers rather than the hopes. The famous trial of Galileo in connection with his views on the Copernican system marked the beginning of a struggle that went on for more than a century. In this controversy the representatives of natural science could argue that experience offers an undisputable truth, that it cannot be left to any human authority to decide about what really happens in nature, and that this decision is made by nature or in this sense by God. The representatives of the traditional religion, on the other hand, could argue that by paying too much attention to the material world, to what we perceive with our senses, we lose the connection with the essential values of human life, with just that part of reality which is beyond the material world. These two arguments do not meet, and therefore the problem could not be settled by any kind of agreement or decision.

In the meantime natural science proceeded to get a clearer and wider picture of the material world. In physics this picture was to be described by means of those concepts which we nowadays call the concepts of classical physics. The world consisted of things in space and time, the things consist of matter, and matter can produce and can be acted upon by forces. The events follow from the interplay between matter and forces; every event is the result and the cause of other events. At the same time the human attitude toward nature changed from a contemplative one to the pragmatic one. One was not so much interested in nature as it is; one rather asked what one could do with it. Therefore, natural science turned into technical science; every advancement of knowledge was connected with the question as to what practical use could be derived from it. This was true not only in physics; in chemistry and biology the attitude was essentially the same, and the success of the new methods in medicine or in agriculture contributed essentially to the propagation of the new tendencies.

In this way, finally, the nineteenth century developed an extremely rigid frame for natural science which formed not only science but also the general outlook of great masses of people. This frame was supported by the fundamental concepts of classical physics, space, time, matter and causality; the concept of reality applied to the things or events that we could perceive by our senses or that could be observed by means of the refined tools that technical science had provided. Matter was the primary reality. The progress of science was pictured as a crusade of conquest into the material world. Utility was the watchword of the time.

On the other hand, this frame was so narrow and rigid that it was difficult to find a place in it for many concepts of our language that had always belonged to its very substance, for instance, the concepts of mind, of the human soul or of life. Mind could be introduced into the general picture only as a kind of mirror of the material world; and when one studied the properties of this mirror in the science of psychology, the scientists were always tempted— if I may carry the comparison further—to pay more attention to its mechanical than to its optical properties. Even there one tried to apply the concepts of classical physics, primarily that of causality. In the same way life was to be explained as a physical and chemical process, governed by natural laws, completely determined by causality. Darwin's concept of evolution provided ample evidence for this interpretation. It was especially difficult to find in this framework room for those parts of reality that had been the object of the traditional religion and seemed now more or less only imaginary. Therefore, in those European countries in which one was wont to follow the ideas up to their extreme consequences, an open hostility of science toward religion developed, and even in the other countries there was an increasing tendency toward indifference toward such questions; only the ethical values of the Christian religion were excepted from this trend, at least for the time being. Confidence in the scientific method and in rational thinking replaced all other safeguards of the human mind.

Coming back now to the contributions of modern physics, one may say that the most important change brought about by its results consists in the dissolution of this rigid frame of concepts of the nineteenth century. Of course many attempts had been made before to get away from this rigid frame which seemed obviously too narrow for an understanding of the essential parts of reality. But it had not been possible to see what could be wrong with the fundamental concepts like matter, space, time and causality that had been so extremely successful in the history of science. Only experimental research itself, carried out with all the refined equipment that technical science could offer, and its mathematical interpretation, provided the basis for a critical analysis—or, one may say, enforced the critical analysis—of these concepts, and finally resulted in the dissolution of the rigid frame.

This dissolution took place in two distinct stages. The first was the discovery, through the theory of relativity, that even such fundamental concepts as space and time could be changed and in fact must be changed on account of new experience. This change did not concern the somewhat vague concepts of space and time in natural language; but it did concern their precise formulation in the scientific language of Newtonian mechanics, which had erroneously been accepted as final. The second stage was the discussion of the concept of matter enforced by the experimental results concerning the atomic structure. The idea of the reality of matter had probably been the strongest part in that rigid frame of concepts of the nineteenth century, and this idea had at least to be modified in connection with the new experience. Again the concepts so far as they belonged to the natural language remained untouched. There was no difficulty in speaking about matter or about facts or about reality when one had to describe the atomic experiments and their results. But the scientific extrapolation of these concepts into the smallest parts of matter could not be done in the simple way suggested by classical physics, though it had erroneously determined the general outlook on the problem of matter.

These new results had first of all to be considered as a serious warning against the somewhat forced application of scientific concepts in domains where they did not belong. The application of the concepts of classical physics, e.g., in chemistry, had been a mistake. Therefore, one will nowadays be less inclined to assume that the concepts of physics, even those of quantum theory, can certainly be applied everywhere in biology or other sciences. We will, on the contrary, try to keep the doors open for the entrance of new concepts even in those parts of science where the older concepts have been very useful for the understanding of the phenomena. Especially at those points where the application of the older concepts seems somewhat forced or appears not quite adequate to the problem we will try to avoid any rash conclusions.

Furthermore, one of the most important features of the development and the analysis of modern physics is the experience that the concepts of natural language, vaguely defined as they are, seem to be more stable in the expansion of knowledge than the precise terms of scientific language, derived as an idealization from only limited groups of phenomena. This is in fact not surprising since the concepts of natural language are formed by the immediate connection with reality; they represent reality. It is true that they are not very well defined and may therefore also undergo changes in the course of the centuries, just as reality itself did, but they never lose the immediate connection with reality. On the other hand, the scientific concepts are idealizations; they are derived from experience obtained by refined experimental tools, and are precisely defined through axioms and definitions. Only through these precise definitions is it possible to connect the concepts with a mathematical scheme and to derive mathematically the infinite variety of possible phenomena in this field. But through this process of idealization and precise definition the immediate connection with reality is lost. The concepts still correspond very closely to reality in that part of nature which had been the object of the research. But the correspondence may be lost in other parts containing other groups of phenomena.

Keeping in mind the intrinsic stability of the concepts of natural language in the process of scientific development, one sees that—after the experience of modern physics—our attitude toward concepts like mind or the human soul or life or God will be different from that of the nineteenth century, because these concepts belong to the natural language and have therefore immediate connection with reality. It is true that we will also realize that these concepts are not well defined in the scientific sense and that their application may lead to various contradictions, for the time being we may have to take the concepts, unanalyzed as they are; but still we know that they touch reality. It may be useful in this connection to remember that even in the most precise part of science, in mathematics, we cannot avoid using concepts that involve contradictions. For instance, it is well known that the concept of infinity leads to contradictions that have been analyzed, but it would be practically impossible to construct the main parts of mathematics without this concept.

The general trend of human thinking in the nineteenth century had been toward an increasing confidence in the scientific method and in precise rational terms, and had led to a general skepticism with regard to those concepts of natural language which do not fit into the closed frame of scientific thought—for instance, those of religion. Modern physics has in many ways increased this skepticism; but it has at the same time turned it against the overestimation of precise scientific concepts, against a too-optimistic view on progress in general, and finally against skepticism itself. The skepticism against precise scientific concepts does not mean that there should be a definite limitation for the application of rational thinking. On the contrary, one may say that the human ability to understand may be in a certain sense unlimited. But the existing scientific concepts cover always only a very limited part of reality, and the other part that has not yet been understood is infinite. Whenever we proceed from the known into the unknown we may hope to understand, but we may have to learn at the same time a new meaning of the word "understanding." We know that any understanding must be based finally upon the natural language because it is only there that we can be certain to touch reality, and hence we must be skeptical about any skepticism with regard to this natural language and its essential concepts. Therefore, we may use these concepts as they have been used at all times. In this way modern physics has perhaps opened the door to a wider outlook on the relation between the human mind and reality.

This modern science, then, penetrates in our time into other parts of the world where the cultural tradition has been entirely different from the European civilization. There the impact of this new activity in natural and technical science must make itself felt even more strongly than in Europe, since changes in the conditions of life that have taken two or three centuries in Europe will take place there within a few decades. One should expect that in many places this new activity must appear as a decline of the older culture, as a ruthless and barbarian attitude, that upsets the sensitive balance on which all human happiness rests. Such consequences cannot be avoided; they must be taken as one aspect of our time. But even there the openness of modern physics may help to some extent to reconcile the older traditions with the new trends of thought. For instance, the great scientific contribution in theoretical physics that has come from Japan since the last war may be an indication for a certain relationship between philosophical ideas in the tradition of the Far East and the philosophical substance of quantum theory. It may be easier to adapt oneself to the quantum-theoretical concept of reality when one has not gone through the naïve materialistic way of thinking that still prevailed in Europe in the first decades of this century.

Of course such remarks should not be misunderstood as an underestimation of the damage that may be done or has been done to old cultural traditions by the impact of technical progress. But since this whole development has for a long time passed far beyond any control by human forces, we have to accept it as one of the most essential features of our time and must try to connect it as much as possible with the human values that have been the aim of the older cultural and religious traditions. It may be allowed at this point to quote a story from the Hasidic religion: There was an old rabbi, a priest famous for his wisdom, to whom all people came for advice. A man visited him in despair over all the changes that went on around him, deploring all the harm done by so-called technical progress. "Isn't all this technical nuisance completely worthless," he exclaimed "if one considers the real values of life?" "This may be so," the rabbi replied, "but if one has the right attitude one can learn from everything." "No," the visitor rejoined, "from such foolish things as railway or telephone or telegraph one can learn nothing whatsoever." But the rabbi answered, "You are wrong. From the railway you can learn that you may by being one instant late miss everything. From the telegraph you can learn that every word counts. And from the telephone you can learn that what we say here can be heard there." The visitor understood what the rabbi meant and went away.

Finally, modern science penetrates into those large areas of our present world in which new doctrines were established only a few decades ago as foundations for new and powerful societies. There modern science is confronted both with the content of the doctrines, which go back to European philosophical ideas of the nineteenth century (Hegel and Marx), and with the phenomenon of uncompromising belief. Since modern physics must play a great role in these countries because of its practical applicability, it can scarcely be avoided that the narrowness of the doctrines is felt by those who have really understood modern physics and its philosophical meaning. Therefore, at this point an interaction between science and the general trend of thought may take place. Of course the influence of science should not be overrated; but it might be that the openness of modern science could make it easier even for larger groups of people to see that the doctrines are possibly not so important for the society as had been assumed before. In this way the influence of modern science may favor an attitude of tolerance and thereby may prove valuable.

On the other hand, the phenomenon of uncompromising belief carries much more weight than some special philosophical notions of the nineteenth century. We cannot close our eyes to the fact that the great majority of the people can scarcely have any well-founded judgment concerning the correctness of certain important general ideas or doctrines. Therefore, the word "belief" can for this majority not mean "perceiving the truth of something" but can only be understood as "taking this as the basis for life." One can easily understand that this second kind of belief is much firmer, is much more fixed than the first one, that it can persist even against immediate contradicting experience and can therefore not be shaken by added scientific knowledge. The history of the past two decades has shown by many examples that this second kind of belief can sometimes be upheld to a point where it seems completely absurd, and that it then ends only with the death of the believer. Science and history can teach us that this kind of belief may become a great danger for those who share it. But such knowledge is of no avail, since one cannot see how it could be avoided, and therefore such belief has always belonged to the great forces in human history. From the scientific tradition of the nineteenth century one would of course be inclined to hope that all belief should be based on a rational analysis of every argument, on careful deliberation; and that this other kind of belief, in which some real or apparent truth is simply taken as the basis for life, should not exist. It is true that cautious deliberation based on purely rational arguments can save us from many errors and dangers, since it allows readjustment to new situations, and this may be a necessary condition for life. But remembering our experience in modern physics it is easy to see that there must always be a fundamental complementarity between deliberation and decision. In the practical decisions of life it will scarcely ever be possible to go through all the arguments in favor of or against one possible decision, and one will therefore always have to act on insufficient evidence. The decision finally takes place by pushing away all the arguments—both those that have been understood and others that might come up through further deliberation—and by cutting off all further pondering. The decision may be the result of deliberation, but it is at the same time complementary to deliberation; it excludes deliberation. Even the most important decisions in life must always contain this inevitable element of irrationality. The decision itself is necessary, since there must be something to rely upon, some principle to guide our actions. Without such a firm stand our own actions would lose all force. Therefore, it cannot be avoided that some real or apparent truth form the basis of life; and this fact should be acknowledged with regard to those groups of people whose basis is different from our own.

Coming now to a conclusion from all that has been said about modern science, one may perhaps state that modern physics is just one, but a very characteristic, part of a general historical process that tends toward a unification and a widening of our present world. This process would in itself lead to a diminution of those cultural and political tensions that create the great danger of our time. But it is accompanied by another process which acts in the opposite direction. The fact that great masses of people become conscious of this process of unification leads to an instigation of all forces in the existing cultural communities that try to ensure for their traditional values the largest possible role in the final state of unification. Thereby the tensions increase and the two competing processes are so closely linked with each other that every intensification of the unifying process—for instance, by means of new technical progress—intensifies also the struggle for influence in the final state, and thereby adds to the instability of the transient state. Modern physics plays perhaps only a small role in this dangerous process of unification. But it helps at two very decisive points to guide the development into a calmer kind of evolution. First, it shows that the use of arms in the process would be disastrous and, second, through its openness for all kinds of concepts it raises the hope that in the final state of unification many different cultural traditions may live together and may combine different human endeavors into a new kind of balance between thought and deed, between activity and meditation.

The Impossibility of Metaphysics

A. J. AYER

The scientific revolution of the twentieth century has brought with it a revolution in philosophy, or rather a continuation of the revolution launched by the critical philosophies of Hume and Kant in the

SOURCE: "Demonstration of the Impossibility of Metaphysics," by A. J. Ayer, *Mind*, XLIII (July 1934), 335–45. Reprinted by permission of *Mind* and Professor A. J. Ayer.

eighteenth century and interrupted by the vogue of metaphysical and quasi-metaphysical systems in the nineteenth. Although confined principally to Vienna in the decades between the two wars and to Great Britain, the Lowlands, Scandinavia, and the United States, the school known as logical positivism or logical empiricism and its close and nowadays more fashionable relation, analytical philosophy, have exerted a considerable influence outside the ranks of the professional philosophers. Logical positivism, in particular, claims to be the philosophy of modern science, and maintains that the sole task of the philosopher in the modern world is to analyze and clarify empirical knowledge. The propositions of ethics, aesthetics, and metaphysics are seen as noncognitive, because empirically nonverifiable; the most the philosopher can do is subject them to rigorous logical analysis and elucidate their meaning.

Perhaps the most "scandalous" episode in the history of logical positivism has been its outspoken rejection of metaphysics as a philosophical discipline, beginning with Ludwig Wittgenstein's *Tractactus* in 1922 and leading to Rudolf Carnap's *The Logical Structure of the World* in 1928. The propositions of metaphysics are rejected, on the one hand, as meaningless, and on the other hand are applauded as a form of poetry expressing feelings toward life. The views of the Viennese positivists of the 1920's were first given wide publicity in Britain by A. J. Ayer, now Wykeham Professor of Logic at Oxford, in his book, *Language, Truth, and Logic* (1936), and in such articles as the one following, first published in *Mind* in 1934.

Foreword

THE VIEWS expressed in this paper are not original. The work of Wittgenstein inspired it. The arguments which it contains are for the most part such as have been used by writers in *Erkenntnis*, notably by Moritz Schlick in his *Positivismus und Realismus* and Rudolf Carnap in his *Überwindung der Metaphysik durch logische Analyse der Sprache*. But some may find my presentation of them the clearer. And I hope to convince others by whom the work of Wittgenstein and the Viennese school has so far been ignored or misunderstood.

Definition of Metaphysics

My purpose is to prove that any attempt to describe the nature or even to assert the existence of something lying beyond the reach of empirical observation must consist in the enunciation of pseudo-propositions, a pseudo-proposition being a series of words that may seem to have the structure of a sentence but is in fact meaningless. I call this a demonstration of the impossibility of metaphysics because I define a metaphysical enquiry as an enquiry into the nature of the reality underlying or transcending the phenomena which the special sciences are content to study. Accordingly if I succeed in showing that even to ask whether there is a reality underlying the world of phenomena is to formulate a bogus question, so that any assertion about the existence or nature of such a reality is a piece of nonsense, I shall have demonstrated the impossibility of metaphysics in the sense in which I am using the term. If anyone considers this an arbitrary definition, let him refer to any work which he would call metaphysical, and consider how it differs from an enquiry in one of the special sciences. He will find, not that the authors are merely using different means to derive from the same empirical premises the same sort of knowledge, but that they are seeking totally different types of knowledge. The metaphysician is concerned with a reality transcending the phenomena about which the scientist makes his generalisations. The metaphysician rejects the methods of the scientist, not because he believes them to be unfruitful in the field in which the scientist operates, but because he believes that by his own metaphysical methods he will be able to obtain knowledge in his own metaphysical field. It will be shown in this paper not that the metaphysician ought to use scientific methods to attain his end, but that the end itself is vain. Whatever form of reasoning he employs, he succeeds in saying nothing.

Comparison with Kant's Procedure

That the speculative reason falls into self-contradiction when it ventures out beyond the limits of experience is a proposition maintained by Kant. But by his formulation of the matter he is committed to a view different from that which will here be maintained. For he implies that there is a transcendent reality, but the constitution of our speculative reason is such that we cannot hope to gain knowledge of it: he should therefore find no absurdity in imagining that some other being, say a god, had knowledge of it, even though the existence of such a being could not be proved. Whereas on our view to say that there is or that there is not a transcendent reality is to utter a pseudo-proposition, a word-series empty of logical content: and no supposition about the knowledge of a higher reality possessed by a higher being is for us even a significant hypothesis. The difference between the two views is best expressed by saying that while Kant attempted to show that there were certain problems which the speculative reason was in virtue of its own nature incapable of solving, our aim is to show that these are not genuine problems.

No criticism of Kant's transcendental philosophy will be undertaken in this paper. But the method by which we demonstrate the impossibility of metaphysics, in the sense in which Kant too held it to be impossible, serves also to show that no knowledge is both synthetic and *a priori*. And this is enough to prove the impossibility of metaphysics, in the special sense which Kant reserved for the term, though it in no way discredits the excellent pieces of philosophical analysis which the *Critique of Pure Reason* contains.

Formulation of a Criterion of Significance

The method of achieving these results lies in the provision of a criterion by which the genuineness of all *prima facie* propositions may be tested. Having laid down the conditions which must be fulfilled by whatever is to be a significant proposition, we shall find that the propositions of metaphysics fail to satisfy the conditions and are therefore meaningless.

What is it, then, that we are asking when we ask what is the meaning of a proposition? I say "ask the meaning of a proposition" rather than "ask the meaning of a concept," because questions about the meaning of concepts reduce themselves to questions about the meanings of propositions. To discover the meaning of a concept we form its corresponding primary proposition, *i.e.* the simplest proposition in which it can significantly occur, and attempt to analyse this. I repeat "what is it that we are asking when we ask what is the meaning of a proposition?" There are various ways in which the correct answer can be formulated. One is to say that we are asking what are the propositions to which the proposition in question is reducible. For instance, if "being an amphisbæna" means "being a serpent with a head at both ends," then the proposition "X is an amphisbæna" is reducible to (or derivable from) the propositions "X is a serpent" and "X has a head at either end of its body". These propositions are in turn reducible to others until we reach the elementary propositions which are not descriptive at all but ostensive.[1] When the analysis reaches its furthest point the meaning of the proposition can no longer be defined in terms of other propositions but only pointed to or shown. It is to this process that those philosophers refer who say that philosophy is an activity and not a doctrine.

Alternatively the procedure of definition may be described by saying that to give the meaning of a proposition is to give the conditions under which it would be true and those under which it would be false. I understand a proposition if I know what observations I must make in order to establish its truth or falsity. This may be more succinctly expressed by saying that I understand a proposition when I know what facts would verify it. To indicate the situation which verifies a proposition is to indicate what the proposition means.

Application of the Criterion

Let us assume that some one says of my cat that it is corylous. I fail to understand him and enquire what circumstances would make it true to say that the cat was corylous. He replies "its having blue eyes". I conclude that in the sense in which he uses the word corylous "X is corylous" means "X has blue eyes". If he says that, although the fact that my cat has blue eyes and no other fact makes it true to say that it is corylous, nevertheless he means by "corylous" something more than "blue-eyed," we may infer that the use of the word "corylous" has for him a certain emotional value which is absent when he merely says "blue-eyed". But so long as its having blue eyes is all that is necessary to establish the truth of the proposition that something is corylous, and its having eyes of another colour all that is necessary to establish its falsehood, then "having blue eyes" is all that "being corylous" means.

In the case when something is called corylous and no description or indication can be given of the situation which verifies the proposition, we must conclude that the assertion is meaningless. If

[1] This article was written over a year ago; and I have since abandoned the view that there are elementary or purely ostensive propositions, for reasons which I have given in an article published in *Analysis*, Vol. I., No. 1. I have not troubled to alter this passage, because the reference to elementary propositions is wholly irrelevant to my main argument.

the speaker protests that he does mean something, but nothing that mere observation can establish, we allow that he has certain feelings which are in some way connected with the emission of the sound "corylous": and it may be a matter of interest to us that he should express these feelings. But he does not thereby make any assertion about the world. He utters a succession of words, but they do not form a genuine proposition. His sentence may provide good evidence of his feelings. In itself it has no sense.

So in every case where we have a series of words which seems to be a good grammatical sentence, and we wish to discover whether it really makes sense—*i.e.*, whether it expresses a genuine proposition—we must consider what are the circumstances in which the proposition apparently expressed would be called true or false: what difference in the world its truth or falsity would entail. And if those who have uttered it or profess to understand it are unable to describe what in the world would be different if it were true or false, or in any way to show how it could be verified, then we must conclude that nothing has been asserted. The series of words in question does not express a genuine proposition at all, but is as much a piece of nonsense as "the moon is the square root of three" or "Lenin or coffee how". The difference is merely that in some cases where a very slight transformation of the phrase, say the alteration of a single word, would turn it into a propositional sign, its senselessness is harder to detect.

Meaninglessness of every Metaphysical Assertion

In this way it can quickly be shown that any metaphysical assertion is nonsensical. It is not necessary to take a list of metaphysical terms such as the Absolute, the Unconditioned, the Ego, and so forth, and prove each of them to be meaningless: for it follows from the task metaphysics sets itself that all its assertions must be nonsense. For it is the aim of metaphysics to describe a reality lying beyond experience, and therefore any proposition which would be verified by empirical observation is *ipso facto* not metaphysical. But what no observation could verify is not a proposition. The fundamental postulate of metaphysics "There is a super- (or hinter-) phenomenal reality" is itself not a proposition. For there is no observation or series of observations we could conceivably make by which its truth or falsehood would be determined. It may seem to be a proposition, having the sensible form of a proposition. But nothing is asserted by it.

An example may make this clearer. The old conflict between Idealism and Realism is a fine instance of an illusory problem. Let us assume that a picture is unearthed, and that the finder suggests that it was painted by Goya. There are definite means of settling this question. The critics examine the picture and consider what points of resemblance it has to other works of Goya. They see if there is any contemporary or subsequent reference to the existence of such a work—and so on. Suppose now that two of the experts have also read philosophy and raise a further point of dispute. One says that the picture is a collection of ideas (his own or God's): the other that its colours are objectively real. What possible means have they of settling this question? Can either of them indicate any circumstances in which to the question "are those colours a collection of ideas?" or to the question "are those colours objective sensibilia?" the answer "yes" or "no" could be given? If they cannot then no such questions arise. And plainly they cannot. If it is raining now outside my window my observations are different from what they would be if it were fine. I assert that it rains and my proposition is verifiable. I can indicate the situation by which its truth or falsity is established. But if I ask "is the rain real or ideal?" this is a question which no observations enable me to answer. It is accordingly not a genuine question at all.

It is advisable here to remove a possible source of misunderstanding. I am not maintaining that if we wish to discover whether in a *prima facie* proposition anything is really being asserted, we must consider whether what seems to be asserted is practically verifiable. As Professor Schlick has pointed out, it makes perfectly good sense to say "there is a mountain 10,000 feet high on the other side of the moon," although this is a proposition which through practical disabilities we are not and may never be in a position to verify. But it is in principle verifiable. We know what sort of observations would verify or falsify it. If we got to the other side of the moon we should know how to settle the question. But the assertions of metaphysics are in principle unverifiable. We may take up any position in space and time that our imagination allows us to occupy, no observation that we can make therefrom makes it even probable in the least degree that any answer to a metaphysical question is correct. And therefore we conclude that there are no such questions.

Metaphysical Assertions not Hypotheses

So the conclusion is not that metaphysical assertions are uncertain or arbitrary or even false, but that they are nonsensical. They are not hypotheses, in the sense in which general propositions of law are hypotheses. It is true that assertions of such general propositions are not assertions of fact in the way that assertions of singular propositions are assertions of fact.[2] To that extent they are in no better case than metaphysical assertions. But variable hypotheticals (general propositions of law) make sense in a way in which metaphysical assertions do not. For a hypothesis has grounds. A certain sequence of events occurs and a hypothesis is formulated to account for it—i.e., on the strength of the hypothesis, when we make one such observation, we assume that we shall be able to make the others. It is the essence of a hypothesis that it admits of being used. In fact, the meaning of such general propositions is defined by reference to the situations in which they serve as rules for prediction, just as their truth is defined by reference to the accuracy of the predictions to which believing them gives rise. A so-called hypothesis which is not relevant to any situation is not a hypothesis at all. As a general proposition it is senseless. Now there is no situation in which belief in a metaphysical proposition bridges past and potential observations, in the way in which my belief in the poisonousness of arsenic connects my observation of a man's swallowing it with my expectation that he will shortly die. Therefore metaphysical propositions are not hypotheses. For they account for nothing.

[2] I now hold that all empirical propositions are hypotheses. And this means that none of them are conclusively verifiable. It follows that when we say that a proposition, other than a tautology, is significant if and only if it is empirically verifiable, we must be understood to be using the term "verifiable" in its "weakest" sense. In other words, the question we must ask about every putative proposition is not "What observations would make its truth or falsehood logically certain?" but simply "What observations are relevant to the determination of its truth or falsehood?" "What observations would lead us to allow or deny it a place in our system of accepted propositions pending the production of further evidence?" It is because no answer can be given to these questions, in the case of metaphysical assertions, that these assertions are held to be meaningless.

How Metaphysics has arisen. Defence against the
Objection from Piety

There may be some who find no flaw in our reasoning and yet
hesitate to accept the conclusion that all metaphysical assertions are
nonsensical. For such hesitation there appear to remain three
grounds. First, a failure to understand how, if they are unintentionally nonsensical, such assertions ever come to be made. Secondly, a doubt whether metaphysical assertions, if nonsensical,
could be made so often. Thirdly, a reluctance to admit that so
many men of great intellect could have made a number of what
they considered to be true and important statements, which were
in fact not statements at all. I proceed to answer these objections
in the order in which they have been stated.

(1) The fact that sentences may appear grammatically on a
level and yet have quite different logical forms makes it easy for
philosophers to formulate bogus questions. For example, "he
suffers from an imaginary illness" is grammatically on a par with
"he suffers from a severe illness". And philosophers are in consequence misled into asking what sort of being imaginary objects
have, on the ground that they must have some sort of being in
order to be imaginary, since what has no being can have no
property. But in fact, as a minority of distinguished philosophers
have seen, being imaginary is not a property like being severe; and
"his illness is imaginary" means "he is not ill although he thinks he
is". When the proposition is so formulated, the bogus question
"what is the ontological status of an imaginary illness?" does not
even seem to arise. The sentence "his illness is imaginary" is of a
type calculated to lead philosophers astray; but it is translatable
into a sentence wherein no such danger lies. The question "what
type of object is an imaginary object?" and the answer sometimes
given to it that "it is a subsistent entity" are both pieces of sheer
nonsense.

The case of the word "subsist" illustrates how words which have
meaning in a certain context are used by philosophers in a context
where they are meaningless. The sentence "he subsists on a small
income" makes perfectly good sense. "Subsists" here means "manages to exist," "keeps himself alive". Philosophers, falling into the
trap mentioned above, wish to assert that imaginary and illusory
objects have some sort of being. It seems a self-contradiction to say

that they exist. But somehow or other they "manage to keep alive". Therefore it is said that they subsist. But in this usage the word "subsist" is nonsense. It is a mere symbol of confusion.

There is a further class of words which are coined as a direct outcome of logical mistakes and possess no meaning from the outset. Such is the word "being" used as a substantive. This error originated with the Greeks. Because where X is an incomplete symbol it makes sense in some cases to say "X exists" (ἐστίν) and existence is wrongly assumed to be a property, it seems legitimate to talk about the being (οὐσία) of X, just as one may talk about the cleverness of X where it makes sense to say that X is clever. Once it is seen that "X exists" means not that a something X has a certain property "being" but merely that something is X-ish or is an X, the temptation to ask questions about "being" disappears.

I believe that these are the ways in which all metaphysical assertions that are not mere rhapsodical outpourings can be shown to arise.

(2) One reason for which men have persistently succumbed to the temptation to assert something metaphysical is that they are not content to make observations and generalisations and predictions but desire also to express their feelings about the world. Literature and the arts afford the most satisfactory medium for such expression. Metaphysics results when men attempt to extrapolate their emotions: they wish to present them not as feelings of their own, but somehow objectively as facts; therefore they express them in the form of argument and theory. But nothing is thereby asserted. All that has happened is that the form of a rational enquiry has been used for the expression of emotions which more commonly find their outlet in a work of literature or art.[3]

Another motive for the construction of metaphysical systems arises from a man's desire to unify his knowledge. In the natural sciences one is not content with the discovery of some uniform sequence of events: one seeks also to explain it, that is, to show its occurrence to have been predictable from knowledge of some more general principle. The metaphysician feels this impulse. But lacking either the patience or the ability to understand the propositions of natural science, being ignorant of the grounds on which

[3] For an elaboration of this point see my article on "the Genesis of Metaphysics" in *Analysis*, Vol. I., No. 3.

the scientist's hypotheses are based and the uses which they serve, he postulates a new and superior kind of knowledge, obtainable by his own ready method of intellectual intuition. And succeeds in knowing nothing.

(3) We need not go to the length of saying that all the great men who have written books of metaphysics are poets who have chosen what seems to us an unsuitable medium of expression. For, in many cases, once the work has been made to shed its metaphysical coating, pieces of genuine philosophising remain. For instance, Berkeley may be regarded not as one who denied the existence of matter, but as one who attempted to analyse the concept of a physical object. His merit is to have shown that when we make a proposition about a physical object we are giving some more complicated statement than the description of a single sense-datum. Similarly Locke, as Mr. Ryle has pointed out, deserves our gratitude for distinguishing our different types of enquiry, Leibnitz for maintaining that what is meant by a body's having a certain position in space is that it lies in certain spatial relations to other bodies, and so forth. Whereby it appears that the discovery that all metaphysical assertions are nonsensical is consistent with piety towards the great philosophers of the past.

Justification of our Procedure

In sum, as metaphysical propositions are by definition such as no possible experience could verify, and as the theoretical possibility of verification has been taken as our criterion of significance, there is no difficulty in concluding that metaphysical propositions are meaningless. There is no escape from this conclusion, provided that we can show that our criterion is correct. Can we do this?

If we assert that the meaning of a proposition consists in its method of verification, the proposition which this sentence would naturally be taken to assert would be a proposition about the meaning of the concept of meaning. So interpreted it would be an assertion about what was meant by the word "meaning" in one of its common uses; and as such a significant empirical proposition. Observation of the linguistic habits of the class of people whose use of the word "meaning" the proposition was about would show it to be true or false: and whatever their linguistic habits were, they might logically have been otherwise. But this is not the proposition which in formulating our criterion we intended to assert. In our criterion we have something that is presupposed in any enquiry into the meaning of meaning, or any other philosophical enquiry, and therefore cannot appear as the conclusion of such an enquiry. For the business of philosophy is to give definitions. And in setting out to define meaning or any other concept we must adopt some rule according to which we conduct our enquiry, and by reference to which we determine whether its conclusions are correct. In formulating our criterion we are attempting to show what this rule should be. We cannot do more.

It may be doubted by some whether we can even do as much. They would say that the *prima facie* proposition in which we formulated our criterion was itself nonsensical, and that it only seemed to be significant because we expressed it in sentences which, like the one given just above, would naturally be understood in a way other than we intended them to be. What we really mean was something that cannot be significantly said. To adopt this standpoint is to follow the example of Wittgenstein, who at the end of his *Tractatus Logico-Philosophicus* asserts that the propositions contained in it are nonsensical. They are a means for enabling the sympathetic reader to "see the world rightly". Having profited by them he must discard them. He must throw away the ladder after he has climbed up on it. But it is not a secure standpoint. Having said something which on your own showing no one can say, you attempt to save your face by pretending you really have not said it. But if you admit that your propositions are nonsensical, what ground have you given anybody for accepting the conclusions that you deduce from them? If we admit that the proposition in which we attempt to formulate our criterion of significance is nonsensical, does not our whole demonstration of the impossibility of metaphysics collapse? We may be able to *see* that metaphysical propositions are nonsensical and by making a special set of nonsensical utterances we may induce others to see it also: but for the rest we must do as Wittgenstein recommends: wait until some one says something metaphysical and then show him that he has used certain symbols to which no meaning can be attached; and this would only prove that one more attempt to assert a significant metaphysical proposition had been a failure, not that no attempt could ever be a success.

Fortunately we can assert all that we need without entering the realm of the unsayable. The proposition "the way to discover whether a *prima facie* proposition has meaning, and what its meaning is, is to consider what experience would verify it" is a significant empirical proposition. It asserts that certain discoveries, in fact those discoveries about the meaning of concepts which it is the business of philosophy to make, may be made and checked by using a certain criterion. We test the validity of the criterion by seeing if the results obtained by means of it are accurate. The difficulty is that in all doubtful cases, which means in very nearly all cases, we have recourse to the criterion to decide whether some suggested definition is correct. This procedure is obviously circular. What saves it from being wholly vicious is the possibility of determining psychologically in certain cases that a proposition is significant without it being necessary to apply the criterion. There are some *prima facie* propositions which by universal agreement are given as significant and some expressions which are agreed to be meaningless. Trusting our criterion if it accepts the former class and rejects the latter, we apply it to such doubtful cases as that of the propositions of metaphysics, and if they fail to satisfy it we pronounce them nonsensical. If we were to take as our criterion of significance the possibility of influencing action we should allow metaphysical propositions to be significant, but we should lose faith in our criterion when we found that it also admitted the significance of expressions which were universally agreed to be meaningless: since there is practically no limit to what can influence action.

If therefore a philosopher maintains that our criterion is too narrow and that metaphysical propositions are significant, it is for him to put forward a more liberal criterion: one that allows the significance of metaphysical propositions yet is not so liberal as to allow the significance of expressions such as "jealousy pronoun live" or "siffle hip brim" which are agreed by all parties to be meaningless. Until he can do this, he has no right to object to our procedure and no means of escaping our conclusions.

II

Faith and Morals

The Righteousness of God

KARL BARTH

Theology in the nineteenth century was characterized by an openness to philosophical and scientific thought. Under the influence first
of Hegel and later of Darwin, theologians argued that God was not so
much a transcendent being as an immanent force, unfolding and
realizing itself in time. Each fresh advance of humanity became a new
step in the self-realization of the Divine.

The first major movement of reaction away from this "liberal"
theology of the nineteenth century, back to a more pessimistic anthropology and a more orthodox view of God, came in the years immediately after the First World War, under the leadership of the
Swiss preacher and theologian Karl Barth. In more recent years, Barth
has written what amounts to a Protestant *Summa Theologica*, his
Church Dogmatics in twelve volumes. But at the beginning of his
career he was a preacher of the Word, gifted with the uncompromising eloquence of the great Reformers, a quality that reveals itself
quite clearly in the sermon that follows, first delivered at the town
church of Aarau, near Zurich, in 1916. In the red light of war, modern
civilization is disclosed to Barth as a tower of Babel ready to topple.
Man has listened only to himself; now, he must listen to the Word of
God.

"THE VOICE of him that crieth in the wilderness, Prepare ye the way
of the Lord, make straight in the desert a highway for our God.
Every valley shall be exalted, and every mountain and hill shall be

SOURCE: *The Word of God and the Word of Man*, by Karl Barth, trans.
Douglas Horton (The Pilgrim Press, Boston, 1928), pp. 9–27. Reprinted by
permission of Harper & Row, Publishers. Copyright 1928 by Sidney A.
Weston. Copyright 1956, 1957 by Douglas Horton.

made low; and the crooked shall be made straight, and the rough places plain; and the glory of the Lord shall be revealed!" This is the voice of our conscience, telling us of the righteousness of God. And since conscience is the perfect interpreter of life, what it tells us is no question, no riddle, no problem, but a fact—the deepest, innermost, surest fact of life: God is righteous. Our only question is what attitude toward the fact we ought to take.

We shall hardly approach the fact with our critical reason. The reason sees the small and the larger but not the large. It sees the preliminary but not the final, the derived but not the original, the complex but not the simple. It sees what is human but not what is divine.

We shall hardly be taught this fact by men. One man may speak about it to another, to be sure. One man may perhaps provoke another to reflect upon "the righteousness of God." But no man may bring another to the peculiar, immediate, penetrating certainty which lies behind the phrase. We must first learn again to speak to each other with authority and not as the scribes. For the present we are all much too clever and unchildlike to be of real mutual help.

We must let conscience speak, for it tells of the righteousness of God in such a way that that righteousness becomes a certainty. Conscience, as everybody knows, may be reduced almost to silence or crushed into oblivion; it may be led astray to the point of folly and wrongdoing; but it remains forever the place, the only place between heaven and earth, in which God's righteousness is manifest. As with a blare of trumpets from another world it interrupts one's reflections concerning himself and his life, concerning his duties to family, calling, and country. It interrupts even the cultivation of his religious thoughts and feelings! It comes with its message, now as a bitter, pressing accusation, now as a quiet, firm assertion, now as an imperious task set for the will, now as an obstruction opposing against you an inexorable No, now as a curse and condemnation which crushes you to earth, now as a holy joy which lifts you above yourself and all that is—but always awaking and agitating in you fundamentally the same thought, pointing you in the same direction. In every chance and change of experience it convinces you that all your living and learning have a goal. In every coming and going of sensation, joyful or painful, it speaks of an existence higher than joy and deeper than pain. In every rise and fall of the sincerity, strength, and purity of the will, it speaks of a will which remains true to itself. And that is the righteousness of God.

What delight to discover a will which seems to be clear and constant in itself, free from caprice and fickleness, possessing a dominant and inflexible idea! And now the conscience tells us that the last and deepest essence of all things is such a will—that God is righteous. We live by knowing this. We forget it often, to be sure; we overlook it; we spurn it. And yet we could not even keep on living, did we not profoundly know that God is righteous.

For we suffer from unrighteousness. We dread it. All that is within us revolts against it. We know more about it, it is true, than we do about righteousness. We have constantly before us, in the great and small occurrences of life, in our own conduct and in that of others, another kind of will, a will which knows no dominant and inflexible idea but is grounded upon caprice, vagary, and self-seeking—a will without faithfulness, logic, or correlation, disunited and distraught within itself. The more sharply we look, the more clearly we see it. Of such are we, of such is life, of such is the world. The critical reason may come and prove to us that it has always been so and always must be so. But we have before our eyes the consequences of this unrighteous will—disquiet, disorder, and distress in forms minute and gross, obscure and evident. We have before us the fiendishness of business competition and the world war, passion and wrongdoing, antagonism between classes and moral depravity within them, economic tyranny above and the slave spirit below. We may indeed argue about these things and prove to ourselves and others quite shrewdly that they all have their necessary reasons. We may imagine ourselves thus becoming inwardly free from them. But we do not escape the simple fact that we suffer from them. The unjust will which imbues and rules our life makes of it, with or without our sanction, a weltering inferno. How heavily it lies upon us! How unendurably! We live in the shadow. We may temporarily deceive ourselves about it. We may temporarily come to an understanding with it. Obviously it will never do so with us. For the unrighteous will is by nature the unendurable, the impossible. We live by knowing that there is really something else in the world.

But many times the fearful apprehension seizes us that unrighteousness may triumph in the end. The frightful fancy comes, that the unrighteous will which now persecutes and tortures us may be the only, the profoundest, will in life. And the impossible resolve suggests itself—make peace with it! Surrender yourself to the thought that the world is a hell, and conform! There seems nothing else to do.

But now into the midst of this sense of need and apprehension, as resistless and unbroken as the theme of a Bach fugue, comes the assurance of conscience—No, it is not true! There is above this warped and weakened will of yours and mine, above this absurd and senseless will of the world, another which is straight and pure, and which, when it once prevails, must have other, wholly other, issues than these we see today. Out of this will, when it is recognized, another life must grow. Out of this will, when it emerges, a new world will arise. Our home is where this will prevails; we have wandered away, but we can return. There is a will of God which is righteous.

As a drowning man grasps at a straw, all that is within us reaches out for the certainty which the conscience gives. If only we might stand in the shining presence of the other will, not doubtfully but with assurance! If only, instead of merely guessing at it as men who can only hope and wish, we might contemplate it quietly and take enjoyment in it! If only we might approach it, come to know it, and have it for our own! The deepest longing in us is born of the deepest need: oh that Thou wouldest rend the heavens, that thou wouldest come down! Oppressed and afflicted by his own unrighteousness and the unrighteousness of others, man—every man—lifts up from the depths of his nature the cry for righteousness, the righteousness of God. Whoever understands him at this point, understands him wholly. Whoever can reach a hand to him here, can really help him. This is the reason that such prophets as Moses, Jeremiah, and John the Baptist are figures never to be erased from the memory of humanity. They uncovered to men their deepest need; they made articulate their conscience within them; they wakened and kept awake the longing within them for the righteousness of God. They prepared the way of the Lord.

But now comes a remarkable turn in our relation with the righteousness of God. The trumpet of conscience sounds; we start with apprehension; we feel the touch of holiness upon us—but at first we do not dream of appealing beyond ourselves for help in our need and anxiety. Quite the opposite. "They said one to another, Go to, let us make brick, and burn them throughly. Let us build us a city and a tower whose top may reach unto heaven; and let us make a name, lest we be scattered abroad upon the face of the whole earth!" We come to our own rescue and build the tower of Babel. In what haste we are to soothe within us the stormy desire for the righteousness of God! And to soothe means, unfortunately, to cover up, to bring to silence. It is as if we could not long endure our own perfervid cry. It is as if we were afraid of a too real and complete fulfillment of our longing. The conscience speaks; we hear; something must be done! But we do not let conscience speak to the end. We hear the alarm and rush out sleepily before we have found out what is really the matter and what must first be done if anything else is to be done.

We stand here before the really tragic, the most fundamental, error of mankind. We long for the righteousness of God, and yet we do not let it enter our lives and our world—cannot let it enter because the entrance has long since been obstructed. We know what the one thing needful for us really is, but long ago we set it aside or put it off till later "better times"—in the meanwhile making ourselves sicker and sicker with substitutes. We go off and build the pitiable tower at the Babel of our human righteousness, human consequence, human significance. Our answer to the call of conscience is one great makeshift, extending over the whole of life, a single gigantic "as if" (als ob)! And because and as long as we are willing to think, speak, and act "as if"—*as if* our tower were important, as if something were happening, as if we were doing something in obedience to the conscience—the reality of the righteousness after which we hunger and thirst will elude us.

Shall we call this pride on our part? There is, as a matter of fact, something of pride in it. We are inwardly resentful that the righteousness we pant after is God's and can come to us only from God. We should like to take the mighty thing into our own hands and under our own management, as we have done with so many other things. It seems quite desirable that the righteousness without which we cannot exist should be controlled by our own will, whatever kind of will that may really be. We arrogate to ourselves, unquestioningly, the right to take up the tumultuous question, What shall we *do?* as if that were in any case the first and most pressing problem. Only let us be quick to put our hand to reform, sanitation, methods, cultural and religious endeavors of all sorts! Only to do "real work"! And before we know it, the trumpet blast of conscience has lost its disturbing tone. The anxiety in which we found ourselves when confronted by the dominant world-will has been gently changed into a prosperous sense of normality, and we have arrived again at reflection, criticism, construction, and organization. The longing for a new world has lost all its bitterness, sharpness, and restlessness, has become the joy of development, and now blossoms sweetly and surely in orations, donor's tablets, committee meetings, reviews, annual reports, twenty-five-year anniversaries, and countless mutual bows. The righteousness of God itself has slowly changed from being the surest of facts into being the highest among various high ideals, and is now at all events our very own affair. This is evident in our ability now to hang it gaily out of the window and now to roll it up again, somewhat like a flag. *Eritis sicut Deus*! You may act as if you were God, you may with ease take his righteousness under your own management. This is certainly pride.

One might equally well, however, call it despair. And it is singular that in our relations with God these two contrasted qualities always keep each other company. We are fundamentally fearful of the stream of God's righteousness which seeks entrance into our life and our world. The safe citizen is startled enough when he hears of tuberculosis, the general strike, or war; but it is far more painful to him to think of that radical overturn of life which God might send to make an end not only of such results of unrighteousness but of unrighteousness itself. The same happy gentleman of culture who today drives up so briskly in his little car of progress and so cheerfully displays the pennants of his various ideals, will tell you apprehensively tomorrow, if the matter comes up, that men are small and imperfect and that one may not indeed desire and expect too much from them—that one may not be too decided about it, anyway. This will be his thought if he has once conceived or conjectured that, apart from the righteousness of God there is nothing to reflect upon, to reform, or to aim at; that, apart from the righteousness of God, all clever newspaper articles and well-attended conventions are completely insignificant; that the primary matter is a very decided Yes or No to a whole new world of life. We are apprehensive of the righteousness of God because we feel much too small and too human for anything different and new to begin in us and among us. This is our despair.

And because we are so proud and so despairing, we build a tower at Babel. The righteousness of God which we have looked upon and our hands have handled changes under our awkward touch into all kinds of human righteousness.

I think of the righteousness of our morality, of the good will which we all, I trust, develop and exemplify in certain excellent principles and virtues. The world is full of morality, but where have we really got with it? It is always an exceptional condition—I had almost said, an artificial dislocation of our will. It is no new will. Steadily or intermittently we apply ourselves to our morality —to our thrift, let us say, to thought for our family, to efficiency in our vocation, to our patriotism—and through it we lift ourselves above our own real level and that of our fellow men. We tear ourselves loose from the general unrighteousness and build ourselves a pleasant home in the suburbs apart—seemingly apart! But what has really happened? Is the unrighteous, self-seeking, capricious, world-will really struck at, much less overcome, by our withdrawing with our morality—seemingly—a little to one side? Is it not our very morality which prevents our discerning that at a hundred other points we are the more firmly fettered to that will? Does it not make us blind and impenitent toward the deep real needs of existence? Is it not remarkable that the greatest atrocities of life—I think of the capitalistic order and of the war—can justify themselves on purely moral principles? The devil may also make use of morality. He laughs at the tower of Babel which we erect to him.

The righteousness of the state and of the law. A wonderful tower! A most necessary and useful substitute to protect us in some measure from certain unpleasant results of our unrighteous will! Very suitable for quieting the conscience! But what does the state really do for us? It can order and organize the self-seeking and capricious vagaries of the human will. It can oppose certain hindrances to this will by its regulations and intimidations. It can set up certain institutions—schools, for instance—for the refining and ennobling of it. A vast amount of respectable work goes into all of this; for the building of this one tower of the state, millions of valuable lives are offered and consumed—to what end? The righteousness of the state, for all its variety of form, fails to touch the inner character of the world-will at any point. By this will it is indeed dominated. The war again provides the striking illustration: were it really possible for the state to make men out of wild animals, would the state find it necessary by a thousand arts to make wild animals out of men? The devil may laugh at this tower of Babel, also.

Religious righteousness! There seem to be no surer means of rescuing us from the alarm cry of conscience than religion and Christianity. Religion gives us the chance, beside and above the vexations of business, politics, and private and social life, to cele- brate solemn hours of devotion—to take flight to Christianity as to an eternally green island in the gray sea of the everyday. There comes over us a wonderful sense of safety and security from the unrighteousness whose might we everywhere feel. It is a wonderful illusion, if we can comfort ourselves with it, that in our Europe— in the midst of capitalism, prostitution, the housing problem, alco- holism, tax evasion, and militarism—the church's preaching, the church's morality, and the "religious life" go their uninterrupted way. And we are Christians! Our nation is a Christian nation! A wonderful illusion, but an illusion, a self-deception! We should above all be honest and ask ourselves far more frankly what we really gain from religion. *Cui bono?* What is the use of all the preaching, baptizing, confirming, bell-ringing, and organ-playing, of all the religious moods and modes, the counsels of "applied religion" "for the guidance of parents" (den Eheleuten zum Geleite), the community houses with or without motion-picture equipment, the efforts to enliven church singing, the unspeakably tame and stupid monthly church papers, and whatever else may belong to the equipment of modern ecclesiasticism? Will some- thing different eventuate from all this in our relation to the righteousness of God? Are we even expecting something different from it? Are we hoping that something may happen? Are we not rather hoping by our very activity to conceal in the most subtle way the fact that the critical event that ought to happen has not yet done so and probably never will? Are we not, with our religious righteousness, acting "as if"—in order not to have to deal with reality? Is not our religious righteousness a product of our pride and our despair, a tower of Babel, at which the devil laughs more loudly than at all the others?

We are fixed firmly, very firmly, in human righteousness. We are alarmed by the cry of conscience, but we have gone no further

than to play sleepily with shadow pictures of the divine righteousness. It, itself, is too great and too high for us. And therefore
the need and anxiety caused by unrighteousness still remain with
us. Conscience within us continues to call. Our deepest longing is
unstilled.

This then is the inner situation in which we come upon the quite
pointless question whether God is righteous. The righteousness of
God becomes preposterously a problem and a subject for discussion. In the war it has become a "real question" again. There is now
hardly a community in all the country round in which, noisily or
quietly, roughly or delicately, this question is not mooted; and it is
mooted, fundamentally, in us all: If God were righteous, could he
then "permit" all that is now happening in the world?

A pointless question? Absolutely so, if it refers to God, the
living God. For the living God never for a moment manifests
himself in our conscience except as a righteous God. When we see
him as he is and when he asks us to recognize and accept him as he
is, is it not pointless to ask, Art Thou righteous? A very pointed
and correct and weighty question it is, however, when we refer it
to the god to whom in our pride and despair we have erected the
tower of Babel; to the great personal or impersonal, mystical,
philosophical, or naïve Background and Patron Saint of our human
righteousness, morality, state, civilization, or religion. If it is he we
mean, we are quite right in asking, Is God righteous? For the
answer is soon given. It is our calamity, a calamity from which
there is no possibility of rescue or release, that with a thousand arts
we have made ourselves a god in our own image and must now
own him—a god to whom one must put such comfortless questions
and receive such comfortless answers. In the question, Is God
righteous? our whole tower of Babel falls to pieces. In this now
burning question it becomes evident that we are looking for a
righteousness without God, that we are looking, in truth, for a god
without God and against God—and that our quest is hopeless. It is
clear that such a god is not God. He is not even righteous. He
cannot prevent his worshipers, all the distinguished European and
American apostles of civilization, welfare, and progress, all zealous
citizens and pious Christians, from falling upon one another with
fire and sword to the amazement and derision of the poor heathen
in India and Africa. This god is really an unrighteous god, and it is

high time for us to declare ourselves thorough-going doubters, sceptics, scoffers and atheists in regard to him. It is high time for us to confess freely and gladly: this god, to whom we have built the tower of Babel, is not God. He is an idol. He is dead.

God himself, the real, the living God, and his love which comes in glory! These provide the solution. We have not yet begun to listen quietly to what the conscience asks when it reminds us, in our need and anxiety, of the righteousness of God. We have been much too eager to do something ourselves. Much too quickly we have made ourselves comfortable in temporary structures. We have mistaken our tent for our home; the moratorium for the normal course of things. We have prayed, Thy will be done! and meant by it, Thy will be done not just now! We have believed in an eternal life, but what we took for eternal life and satisfied ourselves upon was really only temporary. And for this reason we have remained the same as we were. And unrighteousness has remained. And the righteousness of God has disappeared from our eyes. And God himself has become to us dubious, for in his place there has stood the questionable figment of our own thoughts.

There is a fundamentally different way to come into relation with the righteousness of God. This *other* way we enter not by speech nor reflection nor reason, but by being still, by listening to and not silencing the conscience when we have hardly begun to hear its voice. When we let conscience speak to the end, it tells us not only that there is something else, a righteousness above unrighteousness, but also—and more important—that this something else for which we long and which we need is God. He is right and not we! His righteousness is an eternal righteousness! This is difficult for us to hear. We must take the trouble to go far enough off to hear it again. We make a veritable uproar with our morality and culture and religion. But we may presently be brought to silence, and with that will begin our true redemption.

It will then be, above all, a matter of our recognizing God once more as God. It is easy to say recognize. But recognizing is an ability won only in fierce inner personal conflict. It is a task beside which all cultural, moral, and patriotic duties, all efforts in "applied religion," are child's play. For here one must give himself up in order to give himself over to God, that God's will may be done. To do his will, however, means to begin with him anew. His will is not a corrected continuation of our own. It approaches ours as a

Wholly Other. There is nothing for our will except a basic re-
creation. Not a reformation but a re-creation and re-growth. For
the will to which the conscience points is purity, goodness, truth,
and brotherhood as the perfect will of God. It is a will which
knows no subterfuges, reservations, nor preliminary compromises.
It is a will with character, a will blessed and holy through and
through. It is the righteousness of God. In its presence the first
need is for humility. Have we enough humility? May we take it
for granted and go on to tower-building of various sorts? In taking
it for granted, have we yet begun to practice it?

And then a second consideration: in place of despair a childlike
joyfulness will come; a joy that God is so much greater than we
thought. Joy that his righteousness has far more depth and meaning
than we had allowed ourselves to dream. Joy that from God much
more is to be expected for our poor, perplexed, and burdened life
than with our idealism, our principles, and our Christianity we had
dared to hope. More to be *expected!* We ought not to scatter our
emotions as we do to every wind. We ought not so gratuitously to
confuse our hearts by the continual building of towers of Babel.
We ought not to waste our faith on these things—only to convince
ourselves and others of our want of faith. We ought not to put our
most fruitful moments to second-best uses in the belief that it is the
way of piety and wisdom to pursue men's thoughts rather than
God's. We ought to apply ourselves with all our strength to expect
more from God, to let grow within us that which he will in fact
cause to grow, to accept what indeed he constantly offers us,
watching and praying that we may respond to his originative
touch. As children to take joy in the great God and his righteousness, and to trust all to him! *Have* we joy enough? Are the springs
which might be flowing really flowing so abundantly? Have we
barely yet begun to feel the true creative joy of God's presence?

In the Bible this humility and this joy are called—faith. Faith
means seeking not noise but quiet, and letting God speak within—
the righteous God, for there is no other. And then God works in
us. Then begins in us, as from a seed, but an unfailing seed, the new
basic something which overcomes unrighteousness. Where faith is,
in the midst of the old world of war and money and death, there is
born a new spirit out of which grows a new world, the world of
the righteousness of God. The need and anxiety in which we live
are done away when this new beginning comes. The old fetters are

broken, the false idols begin to totter. For now something real has happened—the only real thing that can happen: God has now taken his own work in hand. "I beheld Satan as lightning fall from heaven." Life receives its meaning again—your own life and life as a whole. Lights of God rise in the darkness, and powers of God become real in weakness. Real love, real sincerity, real progress become possible; morality and culture, state and nation, even religion and the church now become possible—now for the first time! One is taken with the vision of an immortality or even of a future life here on earth in which the righteous will of God breaks forth, prevails, and is done as it is done in heaven. In such wise the righteousness of God, far, strange, high, becomes our own possession and our great hope.

The inner way, the way of simple faith, is the way of Christ. A greater than Moses and a greater than John the Baptist is here. He is the love of God, glorified before the world was and forever glorified. Can one say that humanity has exhausted the possibilities of his way? We have received from Jesus many different truths. But the simplest of them all we have the least comprehended—that he was the Son of God and that we, if we will, may go with him the way wherein one simply believes that the Father's will is truth and must be done. One may object that this method of squaring the circle is childlike and inadequate. I grant it. But this childlike and inadequate solution is the beginning of the vast plan of God. It remains to be seen whether the quaking of the tower of Babel which we are now experiencing will be violent enough to bring us somewhat nearer to the way of *faith*. Opportunity offers. We may take the new way. Or we may not. Sooner or later we shall. There is no other.

Christian Humanism

JACQUES MARITAIN

The counterpart of Barth in Catholic thought is the French Thomist philosopher Jacques Maritain. Born in 1882, Maritain was raised a Protestant, but became a convert to Catholicism in 1906 and taught

SOURCE: *The Range of Reason*, by Jacques Maritain (Charles Scribner's Sons, New York, 1952), pp. 185–99. Reprinted by permission of Charles Scribner's Sons and Geoffrey Bles, Ltd. Copyright 1952 by Jacques Maritain.

philosophy at the Institut Catholique in Paris from 1913 down to 1940. Between 1948 and 1953 he was a professor of philosophy at Princeton.

In company with most other leading Catholic thinkers of the twentieth century, Maritain has sought to revive the teachings of St. Thomas Aquinas, which afford a somewhat less drastic view of the gulf between God and man than Barth's neo-Calvinism, but recall man to an awareness of his need for divine grace. Modern civilization, writes Maritain, is in crisis because it has allowed itself to become severed from its spiritual roots. True humanism is Christian humanism, a full and integral belief in man both as a natural being and as a child of God who can achieve temporal progress only with the help of eternal power. Maritain offers in this essay, written during the Second World War, the vision of a new Christendom, qualitatively different from medieval Christendom, and yet sharing its love of God and its evangelical inspiration.

I. The Secularization of the Christian Image of Man

EVERY GREAT period of civilization is dominated by a certain peculiar idea that man fashions of man. Our behavior depends on this image as much as on our very nature—an image which appears with striking brilliance in the minds of some particularly representative thinkers, and which, more or less unconscious in the human mass, is none the less strong enough to mold after its own pattern the social and political formations that are characteristic of a given cultural epoch.

In broad outline, the image of man which reigned over medieval Christendom depended upon St. Paul and St. Augustine. This image was to disintegrate from the time of the Renaissance and the Reformation—torn between an utter Christian pessimism which despaired of human nature and an utter Christian optimism which counted on human endeavor more than on divine grace. The image of man which reigned over modern times depended upon Descartes, John Locke, the Enlightenment, and Jean-Jacques Rousseau.

Here we are confronted with the process of secularization of the Christian man which took place from the sixteenth century on. Let's not be deceived by the merely philosophical appearance of such a process. In reality the man of Cartesian Rationalism was a pure mind conceived after an angelistic pattern. The man of Natural Religion was a Christian gentleman who did not need grace, miracle, or revelation, and was made virtuous and just by his own good nature. The man of Jean-Jacques Rousseau was, in a much more profound and significant manner, the very man of St.

Paul transferred to the plane of pure nature—innocent as Adam before the fall, longing for a state of divine freedom and bliss, corrupted by social life and civilization as the sons of Adam by the original sin. He was to be redeemed and set free, not by Christ, but by the essential goodness of human nature, which must be restored by means of an education without constraint and must reveal itself in the City of Man of coming centuries, in that form of state in which "everyone obeying all, will nevertheless continue to obey only himself."

This process was not at all a merely rational process. It was a process of secularization of something consecrated, elevated above nature by God, called to a divine perfection, and living a divine life in a fragile and wounded vessel—the man of Christianity, the man of the Incarnation. All that meant simply bringing back this man into the realm of man himself ("anthropocentric humanism"), keeping a Christian façade while replacing the Gospel by human Reason or human Goodness, and expecting from Human Nature what had been expected from the virtue of God giving Himself to His creatures. Enormous promises, divine promises were made to man at the dawn of modern times. Science, it was believed, would liberate man and make him master and possessor of all nature. An automatic and necessary progress would lead him to the earthly realm of peace, to that blessed Jerusalem which our hands would build by transforming social and political life, and which would be the Kingdom of Man, and in which we would become the supreme rulers of our own history, and whose radiance has awakened the hope and energy of the great modern revolutionaries.

II. The Modern Man

If I were to try now to disentangle the ultimate results of this vast process of secularization, I should have to describe the progressive loss, in modern ideology, of all the certitudes, coming either from metaphysical insight or from religious faith, which had given foundation and granted reality to the image of Man in the Christian system. The historical misfortune has been the failure of philosophic Reason which, while taking charge of the old theological heritage in order to appropriate it, found itself unable even to maintain its own metaphysical pretense, its own justification of its secularized Christian man, and was obliged to decline toward a

positivist denial of this very justification. Human Reason lost its
grasp of Being, and became available only for the mathematical
reading of sensory phenomena, and for the building up of corresponding material techniques—a field in which any absolute
reality, any absolute truth, and any absolute value is of course
forbidden.

Let us therefore say as briefly as possible: As regards man
himself, modern man (I mean that man who seemed himself to be
modern, and who starts now entering into the past) modern man
knew truths—without *the* Truth; he was capable of the relative
and changing truths of science, incapable and afraid of any supra-
temporal truth reached by Reason's metaphysical effort or of the
divine Truth given by the Word of God. Modern man claimed
human rights and dignity—without God, for his ideology
grounded human rights and human dignity on a godlike, infinite
autonomy of human will, which any rule or measurement received
from Another would offend and destroy. Modern man trusted in
peace and fraternity—without Christ, for he did not need a Redeemer, he was to save himself by himself alone, and his love for
mankind did not need to be founded in divine charity. Modern
man constantly progressed toward good and toward the possession
of the earth—without having to face evil on earth, for he did not
believe in the existence of evil; evil was only an imperfected stage
in evolution, which a further stage was naturally and necessarily to
transcend. Modern man enjoyed human life and worshipped human life as having an infinite value—without possessing a soul or
knowing the gift of oneself, for the soul was an unscientific
concept, inherited from the dreams of primitive men. And if a man
does not give his soul to the one he loves, what can he give? He can
give money, not himself.

As concerns civilization, modern man had in the bourgeois state
a social and political life, a life in common without common good
or common work, for the aim of common life consisted only of
preserving everyone's freedom to enjoy private ownership, acquire
wealth, and seek his own pleasure. Modern man believed in liberty
—without the mastery of self or moral responsibility, for free will
was incompatible with scientific determinism; and he believed in
equality—without justice, for justice too was a metaphysical idea
that lost any rational foundation and lacked any criterion in our
modern biological and sociological outlook. Modern man placed

his hope in machinism, in technique, and in mechanical or industrial civilization—without wisdom to dominate them and put them at the service of human good and freedom; for he expected freedom from the development of external techniques themselves, not from any ascetic effort toward the internal possession of self. And how can one who does not possess the standards of human life, which are metaphysical, apply them to our use of the machine? The law of the machine, which is the law of matter, will apply itself to him, and enslave him.

As regards, lastly, the internal dynamism of human life, modern man looked for happiness—without any final end to be aimed at, or any rational pattern to which to adhere; the most natural concept and motive power, that of happiness, was thus warped by the loss of the concept and the sense of purpose or finality (for finality is but one with desirability, and desirability but one with happiness). Happiness became the movement itself toward happiness, a movement at once limitless and increasingly lower, more and more stagnant. And modern man looked for democracy—without any heroic task of justice to be performed and without brotherly love from which to get inspiration. The most significant political improvement of modern times, the concept of, and the devotion to, the rights of the human person and the rights of the people, was thus warped by the same loss of the concept and the sense of purpose or finality, and by the repudiation of the evangelical ferment acting in human history; democracy tended to become an embodiment of the sovereign will of the people in the machinery of a bureaucratic state more and more irresponsible and more and more asleep.

III. The Crisis of Our Civilization

I have spoken just now of the infinite promises made to man at the dawn of modern times. The great undertaking of secularized Christian man has achieved splendid results for everyone but man himself; in what concerns man himself things have turned out badly—and this is not surprising.

The process of secularization of the Christian man concerns above all the idea of man and the philosophy of life which developed in the modern age. In the concrete reality of human history, a process of growth occurred at the same time, great human conquests were achieved, owing to the natural movement of civilization and to the primitive impulse, the evangelical one, toward the democratic ideal. At least the civilization of the nineteenth century remained Christian in its real though forgotten or disregarded principles, in the secularized remnants involved in its very idea of man and civilization; in the religious freedom—thwarted as this may have been at certain moments and in certain countries—that it willingly or unwillingly preserved; even in the very emphasis on reason and human grandeur which its freethinkers used as a weapon against Christianity; and finally in the secularized feeling which inspired, despite a wrong ideology, its social and political improvements, and its great hopes.

But the split had progressively increased between the real behavior of this secularized Christian world and the moral and spiritual principles which had given it its meaning and its internal consistency, and which it came to ignore. Thus this world seemed emptied of its own principles; it tended to become a universe of words, a nominalistic universe, a dough without leaven. It lived and endured by habit and by force acquired from the past, not by its own power; it was pushed forward by a *vis a tergo,* not by an internal dynamism. It was utilitarian, its supreme rule was utility. Yet utility which is not a means toward a goal is of no use at all. It was capitalistic (in the nineteenth-century sense of this word, which is the genuine and unmitigated sense), and capitalist civilization enabled the initiatives of the individual to achieve tremendous conquests over material nature. Yet, as Werner Sombart observed, the man of this age was neither "ontologic" nor "erotic"; that is to say, he had lost the sense of Being because he lived in signs and by signs, and he had lost the sense of Love because he did not enjoy the life of a person dealing with other persons, but he underwent the hard labor of enrichment for the sake of enrichment.

Despite the wrong ideology I have just described, and the disfigured image of man which is linked to it, our civilization bears in its very substance the sacred heritage of human and divine values which depends on the struggle of our forefathers for freedom, on Judaeo-Christian tradition, and on classical antiquity, and which has been sadly weakened in its efficiency but not at all destroyed in its potential reserves.

The most alarming symptom in the present crisis is that, while engaged in a death struggle for the defense of these values, we have

too often lost faith and confidence in the principles on which what
we are defending is founded, because we have more often than not
forgotten the true and authentic principles and because, at the same
time, we feel more or less consciously the weakness of the insub-
stantial ideology which has preyed upon them like a parasite.

IV. Marxist and Racist Delusions

The great revolutionary movements which reacted against our
secularized Christian world were to aggravate the evil and bring it
to a peak. For they developed toward a definitive break with
Christian values. Here it is a question both of a doctrinal opposition
to Christianity and of an existential opposition to the presence and
action of Christ at the core of human history.

A first development continued and climaxed the trend of secularized reason, the "anthropocentric humanism," in the direction
which it followed from its origin, in the direction of rationalistic
hopes, now no longer constituted solely as philosophical ideology
but as a lived religion. This development arises from the unfolding
of all the consequences of the principle that man alone, and
through himself alone, works out his salvation.

The purest case of this tendency is that of Marxism. No matter
how strong some of the pessimistic aspects of Marxism may be, it
remains attached to this postulate. Marxist materialism remained
rationalistic, so much so that for it the movement proper to matter
is a *dialectical* movement.

If man alone and through himself alone works out his salvation,
then this salvation is purely and exclusively temporal, and must be
accomplished without God, and even against God—I mean against
whatever in man and the human world bears the likeness of God,
that is to say, from the Marxist point of view, the likeness of
"alienation" and enslavement; this salvation demands the giving up
of personality, and the organization of collective man into one
single body whose supreme destiny is to gain dominion over matter
and human history. What becomes then of the image of man? Man
is no longer the creature and image of God, a personality which
implies free will and is responsible for an eternal destiny, a being
which possesses rights and is called to the conquest of freedom and
to a self-achievement consisting of love and charity. He is a particle
of the social whole and lives on the collective consciousness of the

whole, and his happiness and liberty lie in serving the work of the whole. This whole itself is an economic and industrial whole, its essential and primordial work consists of the industrial domination of nature, for the sake of the very whole which alone presents absolute value, and has nothing above itself. There is here a thirst for communion, but communion is sought in economic activity, in pure productivity, which, being regarded as the paradise and only genuine goal of human endeavor, is but the world of a beheaded reason, no longer cut out for truth, but engulfed in a demiurgic task of fabrication and domination over things. The human person is sacrificed to industry's titanism, which is the god of the merely industrial community.

Rationalistic reason winds up in intoxication with matter. By the same token it enters a process of self-degradation. Thus it is that in the vision of the world offered by Marxist materialism, rationalistic overoptimism comes to coincide, in many respects, with another development, depending upon a quite opposite trend of mind, which may be described as an utter reaction against any kind of rationalism and humanism. The roots of this other development are pessimistic, it corresponds to a process of animalization of the image of man, in which a formless metaphysics avails itself of every misconception of scientific or sociological data to satisfy a hidden resentment against Reason and human dignity. According to this trend of mind the human species is only a branch which sprouted by chance on the genealogical tree of the monkeys; all our systems of ideas and values are only an epiphenomenon of the social evolution of the primitive clan; or an ideological superstructure determined by, and masking the struggle for life of class interests and imperialistic ambitions. All our seemingly rational and free behavior is only an illusory appearance, emerging from the inferno of our unconscious and of instinct. All our seemingly spiritual feelings and activities, poetic creation, human pity and devotion, religious faith, contemplative love, are only the sublimation of sexual libido or an outgrowth of matter. Man is unmasked, the countenance of the beast appears. The human specificity, which rationalism had caused to vanish into pure spirit, now vanishes in animality.

Yet the development of which I am speaking has its real sources in something much more profound, which began to reveal itself from the second half of the last century on: anguish and despair, as exemplified in Dostoevski's *Possessed*. A deeper abyss than ani-

mality appears in the unmasking of man. Having given up God so
as to be self-sufficient, man has lost track of his soul. He looks in
vain for himself; he turns the universe upside down trying to find
himself; he finds masks and, behind the masks, death.

Then was to be witnessed the spectacle of a tidal wave of
irrationality, of hatred of intelligence, the awakening of a tragic
opposition between life and spirit. To overcome despair, Nietzsche
proclaimed the advent of the superman of the will to power, the
death of truth, the death of God. More terrific voices, the voices of
a base multitude whose baseness itself appears as an apocalyptic
sign, cry out: We have had enough of lying optimism and illusory
morality, enough of freedom and personal dignity and justice and
peace and faithfulness and goodness which made us mad with
distress. Let us give ground to the infinite promises of evil, and of
swarming death, and of blessed enslavement, and of triumphant
despair!

The purest case of this tendency was Nazi racism. It was
grounded not in an idolatry of reason ending in the hate of every
transcendent value, but in a mysticism of instinct and life ending in
the hatred of reason. Intelligence for it was of use only to develop
techniques of destruction and to pervert the function of language.
Its demonic religiosity tried to pervert the very nature of God, to
make of God Himself an idol. It invoked God, but as a spirit
protector attached to the glory of a people or a state, or as a demon
of the race. A god who will end by being identified with an
invincible force at work in the blood was set up against the God of
Sinai and against the God of Calvary, against the One Whose law
rules nature and human conscience, against the Word Which was
at the beginning, against the God of Whom it is said that He is
Love.

Here, too, man is no longer the creature and image of God; a
person animated by a spiritual soul and endowed with free will,
and responsible for an eternal destiny, who possesses rights and is
called to the conquest of freedom and to a self-achievement consisting of love and charity. And now this disfigured image of man is
rooted in a warring pessimism. Man is a particle of the political
whole, and lives by the *Volksgeist*, yet for this collective whole
there is even no longer any decoy of happiness and liberty and of
universal emancipation, but only power and self-realization
through violence. Communion is sought in the glorification of the

race and in a common hatred of some enemy, in animal blood, which, separated from the spirit, is no more than a biological inferno. The human person is sacrificed to the demon of the blood, which is the god of the community of blood.

There is nothing but human despair to be expected either from Communism or Racism. On the one hand, Racism, on its irrational and biological basis, rejects all universalism and breaks even the natural unity of the human race, so as to impose the hegemony of a so-called higher racial essence. On the other hand, if it is true that in the dialectic of culture, Communism is the final state of anthropocentric rationalism, it follows that by virtue of the universality inherent in reason—even in reason gone mad—Communism dreams of an all-embracing emancipation and pretends to substitute for the universalism of Christianity its own earthly universalism—the universalism of the good tidings of Deception and Terror, and of the immolation of man to the blind god of History.

V. The Idea of a New Christian Civilization

If the description which I outlined above is accurate, it appears that the only way of regeneration for the human community is a rediscovery of the true image of man and a definite attempt toward a new Christian civilization, a new Christendom. Modern times have sought many good things along wrong tracks. The question now is to seek these good things along right tracks, and to save the human values and achievements aimed at by our forefathers and endangered by the false philosophy of life of the last century, and to have for that purpose the courage and audacity of proposing to ourselves the biggest task of renewal, of internal and external transformation. A coward flees backward, away from new things. The man of courage flees forward, in the midst of new things.

Christians find themselves today, in the order of temporal civilization, facing problems similar to those which their forefathers met in the sixteenth and seventeenth centuries. At that time modern physics and astronomy in the making were at one with the philosophical systems set up against Christian tradition. The defenders of the latter did not know how to make the necessary distinction; they took a stand both against that which was to become modern science and against the philosophical errors which at the outset preyed upon this science as parasites. Three centuries were needed to get away from this misunderstanding, if it be true that a better philosophical outlook has actually caused us to get away from it. It would be disastrous to fall once again into similar errors today in the field of the philosophy of civilization. The true substance of the nineteenth century's aspirations, as well as the human gains it achieved, must be saved, from its own errors and from the aggression of totalitarian barbarism. A world of genuine humanism and Christian inspiration must be built.

In the eyes of the observer of historical evolution, a new Christian civilization is going to be quite different from medieval civilization, though in both cases Christianity is at the root. For the historical climate of the Middle Ages and that of modern times are utterly diverse. Briefly, medieval civilization, whose historical ideal was the Holy Empire, constituted a "sacral" Christian civilization, in which temporal things, philosophical and scientific reason, and the reigning powers, were subservient organs or instruments of spiritual things, of religious faith, and of the Church. In the course of the following centuries temporal things gained a position of autonomy, and this was in itself a normal process. The misfortune has been that this process became warped, and instead of being a process of distinction for a better form of union, progressively severed earthly civilization from evangelical inspiration.

A new age of Christendom, if it is to come, will be an age of reconciliation of that which was disjoined, the age of a "secular" Christian civilization, in which temporal things, philosophical and scientific reason, and civil society, will enjoy their autonomy and at the same time recognize the quickening and inspiring role that spiritual things, religious faith, and the Church play from their higher plane. Then a Christian philosophy of life would guide a community vitally, not decoratively Christian, a community of human rights and of the dignity of the human person, in which men belonging to diverse racial stocks and to diverse spiritual lineages would work at a temporal common task which was truly human and progressive.

In the last analysis, I would say that from the end of the Middle Ages—a moment at which the human creature, while awakening to itself, felt itself oppressed and crushed in its loneliness—modern times have longed for a rehabilitation of the human creature. They sought this rehabilitation in a separation from God. It was to be sought in God. The human creature claims the right to be loved; it can be really and efficaciously loved only in God. It must be respected in its very connection with God and because it receives everything—and its very dignity—from Him. After the great disillusionment of "anthropocentric humanism" and the atrocious experience of the anti-humanism of our day, what the world needs is a new humanism, a "theocentric" or integral humanism which would consider man in all his natural grandeur and weakness, in the entirety of his wounded being inhabited by God, in the full reality of nature, sin, and sainthood. Such a humanism would recognize all that is irrational in man, in order to tame it to reason, and all that is suprarational, in order to have reason vivified by it and to open man to the descent of the divine into him. Its main work would be to cause the Gospel leaven and inspiration to penetrate the secular structures of life—a work of sanctification of the temporal order.

This "humanism of the Incarnation" would care for the masses, for their right to a temporal condition worthy of man and to spiritual life, and for the movement which carries labor toward the social responsibility of its coming of age. It would tend to substitute for materialistic-individualistic civilization, and for an economic system based on the fecundity of money, not a collectivistic economy but a "Christian-personalistic" democracy. This task is joined to today's crucial effort to preserve freedom from totalitarian aggression, and to a simultaneous work of reconstruction which requires no less vigor. It is also joined to a thorough awakening of the religious conscience. One of the worst diseases of the modern world, as I pointed out in an earlier essay,[1] is its dualism, the dissociation between the things of God and the things of the world. The latter, the things of the social, economic, and political life, have been abandoned to their own carnal law, removed from the exigencies of the Gospel. The result is that it has become more and more impossible to live with them. At the same time, Christian ethics, not really permeating the social life of people, became in this connection—I do not mean in itself or in the Church, I mean in the world, in the general cultural behavior—a universe of formulas and words; and this universe of formulas and

[1] *Scholasticism and Politics*, 1940, Chapter I, page 22.

words was in effect made subservient in practical cultural behavior
to the real energies of this same temporal world existentially
detached from Christ.

In addition, modern civilization, which pays dearly today for the
past, seems as if it were pushed by the self-contradiction and blind
compulsions suffered by it, toward contrasting forms of misery and
intensified materialism. To rise above these blind compulsions we
need an awakening of liberty and of its creative forces, of which
man does not become capable by the grace of the state or any
party pedagogy, but by that love which fixes the center of his life
infinitely above the world and temporal history. In particular, the
general paganization of our civilization has resulted in man's
placing his hope in force alone and in the efficacy of hate, whereas
in the eyes of an integral humanism a political ideal of justice and
civic friendship, requiring political strength and technical equipment, but inspired by love, is alone able to direct the work of social
regeneration.

VI. The True Image of Man

The image of man involved in integral humanism is that of a being
made of matter and spirit, whose body may have emerged from the
historical evolution of animal forms, but whose immortal soul
directly proceeds from divine creation. He is made for truth,
capable of knowing God as the Cause of Being, by his reason, and
of knowing Him in his intimate life, by the gift of faith. Man's
dignity is that of an image of God, his rights derive as well as his
duties from natural law, whose requirements express in the creature
the eternal plan of creative Wisdom. Wounded by sin and death
from the first sin of his race, whose burden weighs upon all of us,
he is caused by Christ to become of the race and lineage of God,
living by divine life, and called upon to enter by suffering and love
into Christ's very work of redemption. Called upon by his nature,
on the other hand, to unfold historically his internal potentialities
by achieving little by little reason's domination over his own
animality and the material universe, his progress on earth is not
automatic or merely natural, but accomplished in step with freedom and together with the inner help of God, and constantly
thwarted by the power of evil, which is the power of created
spirits to inject nothingness into being, and which unceasingly

tends to degrade human history, while unceasingly and with greater force the creative energies of reason and love revitalize and raise up this same history.

Our natural love for God and for the human being is fragile; charity alone received from God as a participation in His own life, makes man efficaciously love God above everything, and each human person in God. Thus brotherly love brings to earth, through the heart of man, the fire of eternal life, which is the true peacemaker, and it must vitalize from within that natural virtue of friendship, disregarded by so many fools, which is the very soul of social communities. Man's blood is at once of infinite value and must be shed all along mankind's roads "to redeem the blood of man." On the one hand, nothing in the world is more precious than one single human person. On the other hand, man exposes nothing more willingly than his own being to all kinds of danger and waste—and this condition is normal. The meaning of that paradox is that man knows very well that death is not an end, but a beginning. If I think of the perishable life of man, it is something naturally sacred, yet many things are still more precious: Man can be required to sacrifice it by devotion to his neighbor or by his duty to his country. Moreover a single word is more precious than human life if in uttering this word a man braves a tyrant for the sake of truth or liberty. If I think of the imperishable life of man, of that life which makes him "a god by participation" and, beginning here below, will consist in seeing God face to face, nothing in the world is more precious than human life. And the more a man gives himself, the more he makes this life intense within him. Every self-sacrifice, every gift of oneself involves, be it in the smallest way, a dying for the one we love. The man who knows that "after all, death is only an episode," is ready to give himself with humility, and nothing is more human and more divine than the gift of oneself, for "it is more blessed to give than to receive."

As concerns civilization, the man of Christian humanism knows that political life aims at a common good which is superior to a mere collection of the individual's goods and yet must flow back upon human persons. He knows that the common work must tend above all toward the improvement of human life itself, enabling everyone to exist on earth as a free man and to enjoy the fruits of culture and the spirit. He knows that the authority of those who are in charge of the common good, and who are, in a community of free men, designated by the people, and accountable to the people, originates in the Author of Nature and is therefore binding in conscience, and is binding in conscience on condition that it be just. The man of Christian humanism cherishes freedom as something he must be worthy of; he realizes his essential equality with other men in terms of respect and fellowship, and sees in justice the force of preservation of the political community and the prerequisite which, "bringing unequals to equality," enables civic friendship to spring forth. He is aware both of the tremendous ordeal which the advent of machinism imposes on human history, and of the marvelous power of liberation it offers to man, if the brute instinct of domination does not avail itself of the techniques of machinism, and of science itself, in order to enslave mankind; and if reason and wisdom are strong enough to turn them to the service of truly human aims and apply to them the standards of human life. The man of Christian humanism does not look for a merely industrial civilization, but for a civilization integrally human (industrial as it may be as to its material conditions) and of evangelical inspiration.

VII. The Vertical Movement and the Horizontal Movement in Man's Life

As regards, finally, the internal dynamism of human life, the man of Christian humanism has an ultimate end, God to be seen and possessed—and he tends toward self-perfection, which is the chief element of that imperfect happiness which is accessible to him in earthly existence. Thus life has meaning and a direction for him, and he is able to grow up on the way, without turning and wavering and without remaining spiritually a child. This perfection toward which he tends is not perfection of some stoic athleticism wherein a man would make himself impeccable, but rather the perfection of love, of love toward Another whom he loves more than himself, and whom he craves above all to join and love even more, even though in the process he carries with him imperfections and weaknesses. In such an evangelical perfection lies perfect freedom, which is to be conquered by ascetic effort but which is finally given by the very One Who is loved, and Who was the first to love us.

But this vertical movement toward divine union and self-perfection is not the only movement involved in the internal dynamism of human life. The second one, the horizontal movement, concerns the evolution of mankind and progressively reveals the substance and creative forces of man in history. The horizontal movement of civilization, when directed toward its authentic temporal aims, helps the vertical movement of souls. And without the movement of souls toward their eternal aim, the movement of civilization would lose the charge of spiritual energy, human pressure, and creative radiance which animates it toward its temporal accomplishment. For the man of Christian humanism history has a meaning and a direction. The progressive integration of humanity is also a progressive emancipation from human servitude and misery as well as from the constraints of material nature. The supreme ideal which the political and social work in mankind has to aim at is thus the inauguration of a brotherly city, which does not imply the hope that all men will someday be perfect on earth and love each other fraternally, but the hope that the existential *state* of human life and the structures of civilization will draw nearer to their perfection, the standard of which is justice and friendship—and what aim, if not perfection, is to be aimed at? This supreme ideal is the very one of a genuine democracy, of the new democracy we are expecting. It requires not only the development of powerful technical equipment and of a firm and rational politico-social organization in human communities, but also a heroic philosophy of life, and the quickening inner ferment of evangelical inspiration. It is in order to advance toward such an ideal that the community must be strong. The inauguration of a common life which responds to the truth of our nature, freedom to be achieved, and friendship to be set up at the core of a civilization vitalized by virtues higher than civic virtues, all these define the historical ideal for which men can be asked to work, fight, and die. Against the deceptive myths raised by the powers of illusion, a vaster and greater hope must rise up, a bolder promise must be made to the human race. The truth of God's image, as it is naturally impressed upon us, freedom, and fraternity are not dead. If our civilization struggles with death, the reason is not that it dares too much, and that it proposes too much to men. It is that it does not dare enough or propose enough to them. It shall revive, a new civilization shall come to life, on condition that it hope for, and will, and love truly and heroically truth, freedom, and fraternity.

Faith and Myth

Rudolf Bultmann

In the past quarter-century Protestant thinkers have shifted their attention from the neo-orthodoxy of Karl Barth and Emil Brunner to the existentialist theologies of Paul Tillich and Rudolf Bultmann. In one sense this represents a real *bouleversement* in theological thinking, a capitulation to philosophical influence and a return to liberalism. But neither Tillich nor Bultmann is, in fact, a religious liberal of the old school. Bultmann, in particular, owes little to nineteenth-century liberal theology, which he condemns as an abandonment of the essential message of the Christian faith in favor of man-made values. On the other hand, he agrees with the liberals that the gospels must be "demythologized"—stripped of their mythic integuments—and reinterpreted in terms that make sense to contemporary minds. For Bultmann, the terms are provided by the philosophy of Martin Heidegger. The eschatological myth in the New Testament, for example, can best be seen as a statement of the simple truth, also stressed by Heidegger, that the individual man is at all times threatened with extinction and that one day the threat will be carried out. The good Christian life is equated with the Heideggerian "authentic" life, the life that is self-determined in the realization of its finitude. But Bultmann adds that the possibility of right decision comes from divine grace as mediated by Christ. At every moment we have the opportunity of "dying to the world" and being reborn in faith. This is the essence of the Christian message, and, to believe it, one need no longer also believe in a literal Resurrection or a literal Second Coming.

Born in 1884, Bultmann was for thirty years professor of New Testament studies at Marburg University. The following excerpt is the opening section of his theological manifesto on the need for demythologization, "New Testament and Mythology," originally published in 1941.

A. The Problem

1. THE MYTHICAL VIEW OF THE WORLD AND THE MYTHICAL EVENT OF REDEMPTION

THE COSMOLOGY of the New Testament is essentially mythical in character. The world is viewed as a three-storied structure, with

SOURCE: *Kerygma and Myth*, by Rudolf Bultmann, trans. Reginald H. Fuller (Harper & Row, New York, 1961), pp. 1–16. Reprinted by permission of Harper & Row, Publishers, and the Society for Promoting Christian Knowledge.

the earth in the centre, the heaven above, and the underworld
beneath. Heaven is the abode of God and of celestial beings—
the angels. The underworld is hell, the place of torment. Even the
earth is more than the scene of natural, everyday events, of the
trivial round and common task. It is the scene of the supernatural
activity of God and his angels on the one hand, and of Satan and
his daemons on the other. These supernatural forces intervene in
the course of nature and in all that men think and will and do.
Miracles are by no means rare. Man is not in control of his own
life. Evil spirits may take possession of him. Satan may inspire him
with evil thoughts. Alternatively, God may inspire his thought and
guide his purposes. He may grant him heavenly visions. He may
allow him to hear his word of succour or demand. He may give
him the supernatural power of his Spirit. History does not follow a
smooth unbroken course; it is set in motion and controlled by these
supernatural powers. This aeon is held in bondage by Satan, sin,
and death (for "powers" is precisely what they are), and hastens
towards its end. That end will come very soon, and will take the
form of a cosmic catastrophe. It will be inaugurated by the "woes"
of the last time. Then the Judge will come from heaven, the dead
will rise, the last judgement will take place, and men will enter into
eternal salvation or damnation.

*This then is the mythical view of the world which the New
Testament presupposes when it presents the event of redemption
which is the subject of its preaching.* It proclaims in the language
of mythology that the last time has now come. "In the fulness of
time" God sent forth his Son, a pre-existent divine Being, who
appears on earth as a man.[1] He dies the death of a sinner[2] on the
cross and makes atonement for the sins of men.[3] His resurrection
marks the beginning of the cosmic catastrophe. Death, the consequence of Adam's sin, is abolished,[4] and the daemonic forces are
deprived of their power.[5] The risen Christ is exalted to the right
hand of God in heaven[6] and made "Lord" and "King".[7] He will
come again on the clouds of heaven to complete the work of
redemption, and the resurrection and judgement of men will fol-

[1] Gal. 4. 4; Phil. 2. 6 ff.; 2 Cor. 8. 9; John 1. 14, etc.
[2] 2 Cor. 5. 21; Rom. 8. 3.
[3] Rom. 3. 23–26; 4. 25; 8. 3; 2 Cor. 5. 14, 19; John 1. 29; I John 2. 2, etc.
[4] 1 Cor. 15. 21 f.; Rom. 5. 12 ff.
[5] 1 Cor. 2. 6; Col. 2. 15; Rev. 12. 7 ff., etc.
[6] Acts 1. 6 f.; 2. 33; Rom. 8. 34, etc.
[7] Phil. 2. 9–11; 1 Cor. 15. 25.

low.[8] Sin, suffering and death will then be finally abolished.[9] All this is to happen very soon; indeed, St Paul thinks that he himself will live to see it.[10]

All who belong to Christ's Church and are joined to the Lord by Baptism and the Eucharist are certain of resurrection to salvation,[11] unless they forfeit it by unworthy behaviour. Christian believers already enjoy the first instalment of salvation, for the Spirit[12] is at work within them, bearing witness to their adoption as sons of God,[13] and guaranteeing their final resurrection.[14]

2. THE MYTHOLOGICAL VIEW OF THE WORLD OBSOLETE

All this is the language of mythology, and the origin of the various themes can be easily traced in the contemporary mythology of Jewish Apocalyptic and in the redemption myths of Gnosticism. To this extent *the kerygma is incredible to modern man, for he is convinced that the mythical view of the world is obsolete.* We are therefore bound to ask whether, when we preach the Gospel today, we expect our converts to accept not only the Gospel message, but also the mythical view of the world in which it is set. If not, does the New Testament embody a truth which is quite independent of its mythical setting? If it does, theology must undertake the task of stripping the Kerygma from its mythical framework, of "demythologizing" it.

Can Christian preaching expect modern man *to accept the mythical view of the world as true?* To do so would be both senseless and impossible. It would be senseless, because there is nothing specifically Christian in the mythical view of the world as such. It is simply the cosmology of a pre-scientific age. Again, it would be impossible, because no man can adopt a view of the world by his own volition—it is already determined for him by his place in history. Of course such a view is not absolutely unalterable, and the individual may even contribute to its change. But he can do so only when he is faced by a new set of facts so compelling as to make his previous view of the world untenable. He has then no alternative but to modify his view of the world or produce a new

[8] 1 Cor. 15. 23 f., 50 ff., etc.
[9] Rev. 21. 4, etc.
[10] 1 Thess. 4. 15 ff.; 1 Cor. 15. 51 f.; cf. Mark 9. 1.
[11] Rom. 5. 12 ff.; 1 Cor. 15. 21 ff., 44b, ff.
[12] Ἀπαρχή: Rom. 8. 23, ἀρραβών: 2 Cor. 1. 22; 5. 5.
[13] Rom. 8. 15; Gal. 4. 6.
[14] Rom. 8. 11.

one. The discoveries of Copernicus and the atomic theory are instances of this, and so was romanticism, with its discovery that the human subject is richer and more complex than enlightenment or idealism had allowed, and nationalism, with its new realization of the importance of history and the tradition of peoples.

It may equally well happen that truths which a shallow enlightenment had failed to perceive are later rediscovered in ancient myths. Theologians are perfectly justified in asking whether this is not exactly what has happened with the New Testament. At the same time it is impossible to revive an obsolete view of the world by a mere fiat, and certainly not a mythical view. For all our thinking to-day is shaped irrevocably by modern science. A blind acceptance of the New Testament mythology would be arbitrary, and to press for its acceptance as an article of faith would be to reduce faith to works. Wilhelm Herrmann pointed this out, and one would have thought that his demonstration was conclusive. It would involve a sacrifice of the intellect which could have only one result—a curious form of schizophrenia and insincerity. It would mean accepting a view of the world in our faith and religion which we should deny in our everyday life. Modern thought as we have inherited it brings with it criticism of *the New Testament view of the world*.

Man's knowledge and mastery of the world have advanced to such an extent through science and technology that it is no longer possible for anyone seriously to hold the New Testament view of the world—in fact, there is no one who does. What meaning, for instance, can we attach to such phrases in the creed as "descended into hell" or "ascended into heaven"? We no longer believe in the three-storied universe which the creeds take for granted. The only honest way of reciting the creeds is to strip the mythological framework from the truth they enshrine—that is, assuming that they contain any truth at all, which is just the question that theology has to ask. No one who is old enough to think for himself supposes that God lives in a local heaven. There is no longer any heaven in the traditional sense of the word. The same applies to hell in the sense of a mythical underworld beneath our feet. And if this is so, the story of Christ's descent into hell and of his Ascension into heaven is done with. We can no longer look for the return of the Son of Man on the clouds of heaven or hope that the faithful will meet him in the air (I Thess. 4. 15 ff.).

Now that the forces and the laws of nature have been discovered, we can no longer believe in *spirits, whether good or evil*. We know that the stars are physical bodies whose motions are controlled by the laws of the universe, and not daemonic beings which enslave mankind to their service. Any influence they may have over human life must be explicable in terms of the ordinary laws of nature; it cannot in any way be attributed to their malevolence. Sickness and the cure of disease are likewise attributable to natural causation; they are not the result of daemonic activity or of evil spells.[15] The *miracles of the New Testament* have ceased to be miraculous, and to defend their historicity by recourse to nervous disorders or hypnotic effects only serves to underline the fact. And if we are still left with certain physiological and psychological phenomena which we can only assign to mysterious and enigmatic causes, we are still assigning them to causes, and thus far are trying to make them scientifically intelligible. Even occultism pretends to be a science.

It is impossible to use electric light and the wireless and to avail ourselves of modern medical and surgical discoveries, and at the same time to believe in the New Testament world of spirits and miracles.[16] We may think we can manage it in our own lives, but to expect others to do so is to make the Christian faith unintelligible and unacceptable to the modern world.

The mythical eschatology is untenable for the simple reason that the parousia of Christ never took place as the New Testament expected. History did not come to an end, and, as every schoolboy knows, it will continue to run its course. Even if we believe that the world as we know it will come to an end in time, we expect the end to take the form of a natural catastrophe, not of a mythical

[15] It may of course be argued that there are people alive to-day whose confidence in the traditional scientific view of the world has been shaken, and others who are primitive enough to qualify for an age of mythical thought. And there are also many varieties of superstition. But when belief in spirits and miracles has degenerated into superstition, it has become something entirely different from what it was when it was genuine faith. The various impressions and speculations which influence credulous people here and there are of little importance, nor does it matter to what extent cheap slogans have spread an atmosphere inimical to science. What matters is the world view which men imbibe from their environment, and it is science which determines that view of the world through the school, the press, the wireless, the cinema, and all the other fruits of technical progress.

[16] Cp. the observations of Paul Schütz on the decay of mythical religion in the East through the introduction of modern hygiene and medicine.

event such as the New Testament expects. And if we explain the parousia in terms of modern scientific theory, we are applying criticism to the New Testament, albeit unconsciously.

But natural science is not the only challenge which the mythology of the New Testament has to face. There is the still more serious challenge presented by *modern man's understanding of himself*.

Modern man is confronted by a curious dilemma. He may regard himself as pure nature, or as pure spirit. In the latter case he distinguishes the essential part of his being from nature. In either case, however, *man is essentially a unity*. He bears the sole responsibility for his own feeling, thinking, and willing.[17] He is not, as the New Testament regards him, the victim of a strange dichotomy which exposes him to the interference of powers outside himself. If his exterior behaviour and his interior condition are in perfect harmony, it is something he has achieved himself, and if other people think their interior unity is torn asunder by daemonic or divine interference, he calls it schizophrenia.

Although biology and psychology recognize that man is a highly dependent being, that does not mean that he has been handed over to powers outside of and distinct from himself. This dependence is inseparable from human nature, and he needs only to understand it in order to recover his self-mastery and organize his life on a rational basis. If he regards himself as spirit, he knows that he is permanently conditioned by the physical, bodily part of his being, but he distinguishes his true self from it, and knows that he is independent and responsible for his mastery over nature.

In either case he finds *what the New Testament has to say about the "Spirit"* (πνεῦμα) *and the sacraments utterly strange and incomprehensible*. Biological man cannot see how a supernatural entity like the πνεῦμα can penetrate within the close texture of his natural powers and set to work within him. Nor can the idealist understand how a πνεῦμα working like a natural power can touch and influence his mind and spirit. Conscious as he is of his own moral responsibility, he cannot conceive how baptism in water can convey a mysterious something which is henceforth the agent of all his decisions and actions. He cannot see how physical food can convey spiritual strength, and how the unworthy receiving of the Eucharist

[17] Cp. Gerhardt Krüger, *Einsicht und Leidenschaft, Das Wesen des platonischen Denkens*, Frankfort, 1939, p. 11 f.

can result in physical sickness and death (I Cor. 11. 30). The only possible explanation is that it is due to suggestion. He cannot understand how anyone can be baptized for the dead (I Cor. 15. 29).

We need not examine in detail the various forms of modern *Weltanschauung*, whether idealist or naturalist. For the only criticism of the New Testament which is theologically relevant is that which arises *necessarily* out of the situation of modern man. The biological *Weltanschauung* does not, for instance, arise necessarily out of the contemporary situation. We are still free to adopt it or not as we choose. The only relevant question for the theologian is the basic assumption on which the adoption of a biological as of every other *Weltanschauung* rests, and that assumption is the view of the world which has been moulded by modern science and the modern conception of human nature as a self-subsistent unity immune from the interference of supernatural powers.

Again, the biblical doctrine that *death is the punishment of sin* is equally abhorrent to naturalism and idealism, since they both regard death as a simple and necessary process of nature. To the naturalist death is no problem at all, and to the idealist it is a problem for that very reason, for so far from arising out of man's essential spiritual being it actually destroys it. The idealist is faced with a paradox. On the one hand man is a spiritual being, and therefore essentially different from plants and animals, and on the other hand he is the prisoner of nature, whose birth, life, and death are just the same as those of the animals. Death may present him with a problem, but he cannot see how it can be a punishment for sin. Human beings are subject to death even before they have committed any sin. And to attribute human mortality to the fall of Adam is sheer nonsense, for guilt implies personal responsibility, and the idea of original sin as an inherited infection is sub-ethical, irrational, and absurd.

The same objections apply to *the doctrine of the atonement*. How can the guilt of one man be expiated by the death of another who is sinless—if indeed one may speak of a sinless man at all? What primitive notions of guilt and righteousness does this imply? And what primitive idea of God? The rationale of sacrifice in general may of course throw some light on the theory of the atonement, but even so, what a primitive mythology it is, that a divine Being should become incarnate, and atone for the sins of men through his own blood! Or again, one might adopt an analogy from the law courts, and explain the death of Christ as a transaction between God and man through which God's claims on man were satisfied. But that would make sin a juridical matter; it would be no more than an external transgression of a commandment, and it would make nonsense of all our ethical standards. Moreover, if the Christ who died such a death was the pre-existent Son of God, what could death mean for him? Obviously very little, if he knew that he would rise again in three days!

The *resurrection of Jesus* is just as difficult for modern man, if it means an event whereby a living supernatural power is released which can henceforth be appropriated through the sacraments. To the biologist such language is meaningless, for he does not regard death as a problem at all. The idealist would not object to the idea of a life immune from death, but he could not believe that such a life is made available by the resuscitation of a dead person. If that is the way God makes life available for man, his action is inextricably involved in a nature miracle. Such a notion he finds incomprehensible, for he can see God at work only in the reality of his personal life and in his transformation. But, quite apart from the incredibility of such a miracle, he cannot see how an event like this could be the act of God, or how it could affect his own life.

Gnostic influence suggests that this Christ, who died and rose again, was not a mere human being but a God-man. His death and resurrection were not isolated facts which concerned him alone, but a cosmic event in which we are all involved.[18] It is only with effort that modern man can think himself back into such an intellectual atmosphere, and even then he could never accept it himself, because it regards man's essential being as nature and redemption as a process of nature. And as for the pre-existence of Christ, with its corollary of man's translation into a celestial realm of light, and the clothing of the human personality in heavenly robes and a spiritual body—all this is not only irrational but utterly meaningless. Why should salvation take this particular form? Why should this be the fulfilment of human life and the realization of man's true being?

B. The Task before Us

1. NOT SELECTION OR SUBTRACTION

Does this drastic criticism of the New Testament mythology mean the complete elimination of the kerygma?

[18] Rom. 5. 12 ff.; 1 Cor. 15. 21 ff., 44b.

Whatever else may be true, we cannot save the kerygma by selecting some of its features and subtracting others, and thus reduce the amount of mythology in it. For instance, it is impossible to dismiss St Paul's teaching about the unworthy reception of Holy Communion or about baptism for the dead, and yet cling to the belief that physical eating and drinking can have a spiritual effect. If we accept *one* idea, we must accept everything which the New Testament has to say about Baptism and Holy Communion, and it is just this one idea which we cannot accept.

It may of course be argued that some features of the New Testament mythology are given greater prominence than others: not all of them appear with the same regularity in the various books. There is for example only one occurrence of the legends of the Virgin birth and the Ascension; St Paul and St John appear to be totally unaware of them. But, even if we take them to be later accretions, it does not affect the mythical character of the event of redemption as a whole. And if we once start subtracting from the kerygma, where are we to draw the line? The mythical view of the world must be accepted or rejected in its entirety.

At this point absolute clarity and ruthless honesty are essential both for the academic theologian and for the parish priest. It is a duty they owe to themselves, to the Church they serve, and to those whom they seek to win for the Church. They must make it quite clear what their hearers are expected to accept and what they are not. At all costs the preacher must not leave his people in the dark about what he secretly eliminates, nor must he be in the dark about it himself. In Karl Barth's book *The Resurrection of the Dead* the cosmic eschatology in the sense of "chronologically final history" is eliminated in favour of what he intends to be a non-mythological "ultimate history". He is able to delude himself into thinking that this is exegesis of St Paul and of the New Testament generally only because he gets rid of everything mythological in I Corinthians by subjecting it to an interpretation which does violence to its meaning. But that is an impossible procedure.

If the truth of the New Testament proclamation is to be preserved, the only way is to demythologize it. But our motive in so doing must not be to make the New Testament relevant to the modern world at all costs. The question is simply whether the New Testament message consists exclusively of mythology, or whether it actually demands the elimination of myth if it is to be understood as it is meant to be. This question is forced upon us from two sides. First there is the nature of myth in general, and then there is the New Testament itself.

2. THE NATURE OF MYTH

The real purpose of myth is not to present an objective picture of the world as it is, but to express man's understanding of himself in the world in which he lives. Myth should be interpreted not cosmologically, but anthropologically, or better still, existentially.[19] Myth speaks of the power or the powers which man supposes he experiences as the ground and limit of his world and of his own activity and suffering. He describes these powers in terms derived from the visible world, with its tangible objects and forces, and from human life, with its feelings, motives, and potentialities. He may, for instance, explain the origin of the world by speaking of a world egg or a world tree. Similarly he may account for the present state and order of the world by speaking of a primeval war between the gods. He speaks of the other world in terms of this world, and of the gods in terms derived from human life.[20]

Myth is an expression of man's conviction that the origin and purpose of the world in which he lives are to be sought not within it but beyond it—that is, beyond the realm of known and tangible reality—and that this realm is perpetually dominated and menaced by those mysterious powers which are its source and limit. Myth is also an expression of man's awareness that he is not lord of his own being. It expresses his sense of dependence not only within the visible world, but more especially on those forces which hold sway beyond the confines of the known. Finally, myth expresses man's belief that in this state of dependence he can be delivered from the forces within the visible world.

Thus myth contains elements which demand its own criticism—namely, its imagery with its apparent claim to objective validity.

[19] Cp. Gerhardt Krüger, *Einsicht und Leidenschaft,* esp. p. 17 f., 56 f.
[20] Myth is here used in the sense popularized by the "History of Religions" school. Mythology is the use of imagery to express the other worldly in terms of this world and the divine in terms of human life, the other side in terms of this side. For instance, divine transcendence is expressed as spatial distance. It is a mode of expression which makes it easy to understand the cultus as an action in which material means are used to convey immaterial power. Myth is not used in that modern sense, according to which it is practically equivalent to ideology.

The real purpose of myth is to speak of a transcendent power which controls the world and man, but that purpose is impeded and obscured by the terms in which it is expressed.

Hence the importance of the New Testament mythology lies not in its imagery but in the understanding of existence which it enshrines. The real question is whether this understanding of existence is true. Faith claims that it is, and faith ought not to be tied down to the imagery of New Testament mythology.

3. THE NEW TESTAMENT ITSELF

The New Testament itself invites this kind of criticism. Not only are there rough edges in its mythology, but some of its features are actually contradictory. For example, the death of Christ is sometimes a sacrifice and sometimes a cosmic event. Sometimes his person is interpreted as the Messiah and sometimes as the Second Adam. The kenosis of the pre-existent Son (Phil. 2. 6 ff.) is incompatible with the miracle narratives as proofs of his messianic claims. The Virgin birth is inconsistent with the assertion of his pre-existence. The doctrine of the Creation is incompatible with the conception of the "rulers of this world" (I Cor. 2. 6 ff.), the "god of this world" (2 Cor. 4. 4) and the "elements of this world" στοιχεῖα τοῦ κόσμου, Gal. 4. 3). It is impossible to square the belief that the law was given by God with the theory that it comes from the angels (Gal. 3. 19 f.).

But the principal demand for the criticism of mythology comes from a curious contradiction which runs right through the New Testament. Sometimes we are told that human life is determined by cosmic forces, at others we are challenged to a decision. Side by side with the Pauline indicative stands the Pauline imperative. In short, man is sometimes regarded as a cosmic being, sometimes as an independent "I" for whom decision is a matter of life or death. Incidentally, this explains why so many sayings in the New Testament speak directly to modern man's condition while others remain enigmatic and obscure. Finally, attempts at demythologization are sometimes made even within the New Testament itself. But more will be said on this point later.

4. PREVIOUS ATTEMPTS AT DEMYTHOLOGIZING

How then is the mythology of the New Testament to be reinterpreted? This is not the first time that theologians have approached this task. Indeed, all we have said so far might have been said in much the same way thirty or forty years ago, and it is a sign of the bankruptcy of contemporary theology that it has been necessary to go all over the same ground again. The reason for this is not far to seek. The liberal theologians of the last century were working on the wrong lines. They threw away not only the mythology but also the kerygma itself. Were they right? Is that the treatment the New Testament itself required? That is the question we must face to-day. The last twenty years have witnessed a movement away from criticism and a return to a naïve acceptance of the kerygma. The danger both for theological scholarship and for the Church is that this uncritical resuscitation of the New Testament mythology may make the Gospel message unintelligible to the modern world. We cannot dismiss the critical labours of earlier generations without further ado. We must take them up and put them to constructive use. Failure to do so will mean that the old battles between orthodoxy and liberalism will have to be fought out all over again, that is assuming that there will be any Church or any theologians to fight them at all! Perhaps we may put it schematically like this: whereas the older liberals used criticism to *eliminate* the mythology of the New Testament, our task to-day is to use criticism to *interpret* it. Of course it may still be necessary to eliminate mythology here and there. But the criterion adopted must be taken not from modern thought, but from the understanding of human existence which the New Testament itself enshrines.[21]

To begin with, let us review some of these earlier attempts at demythologizing. We need only mention briefly the allegorical interpretation of the New Testament which has dogged the Church throughout its history. This method spiritualizes the mythical events so that they become symbols of processes going on in the soul. This is certainly the most comfortable way of avoiding the critical question. The literal meaning is allowed to stand and is dispensed with only for the individual believer, who can escape into the realm of the soul.

It was characteristic of the older liberal theologians that they regarded mythology as relative and temporary. Hence they thought they could safely eliminate it altogether, and retain only

[21] As an illustration of this critical re-interpretation of myth cf. Hans Jonas, *Augustin und das paulinische Freiheitsproblem*, 1930, pp. 66–76.

the broad, basic principles of religion and ethics. They distinguished between what they took to be the essence of religion and
the temporary garb which it assumed. Listen to what Harnack has
to say about the essence of Jesus' preaching of the Kingdom of
God and its coming: "The kingdom has a triple meaning. Firstly, it
is something supernatural, a gift from above, not a product of
ordinary life. Secondly, it is a purely religious blessing, the inner
link with the living God; thirdly, it is the most important experience that a man can have, that on which everything else depends; it
permeates and dominates his whole existence, because sin is for-
given and misery banished." Note how completely the mythology
is eliminated: "The kingdom of God comes by coming to the
individual, by entering into his *soul* and laying hold of it."[22]

It will be noticed how Harnack reduces the kerygma to a few
basic principles of religion and ethics. Unfortunately this means
that *the kerygma has ceased to be kerygma:* it is no longer the
proclamation of the decisive act of God in Christ. For the liberals
the great truths of religion and ethics are timeless and eternal,
though it is only within human history that they are realized, and
only in concrete historical processes that they are given clear
expression. But the apprehension and acceptance of these principles
does not depend on the knowledge and acceptance of the age in
which they first took shape, or of the historical persons who first
discovered them. We are all capable of verifying them in our own
experience at whatever period we happen to live. History may be
of academic interest, but never of paramount importance for
religion.

But the New Testament speaks of an *event* through which God
has wrought man's redemption. For it, Jesus is not primarily the
teacher, who certainly had extremely important things to say and
will always be honoured for saying them, but whose person in the
last analysis is immaterial for those who have assimilated his teaching. On the contrary, his person is just what the New Testament
proclaims as the decisive event of redemption. It speaks of this
person in mythological terms, but does this mean that we can reject
the kerygma altogether on the ground that it is nothing more than
mythology? That is the question.

Next came the History of Religions school. Its representatives

22 *What is Christianity?* Williams and Norgate, 1904, pp. 63–4 and 57.

were the first to discover the extent to which the New Testament is permeated by mythology. The importance of the New Testament, they saw, lay not in its teaching about religion and ethics but in its actual religion and piety; in comparison with that all the dogma it contains, and therefore all the mythological imagery with its apparent objectivity, was of secondary importance or completely negligible. The essence of the New Testament lay in the religious life it portrayed; its high-watermark was the experience of mystical union with Christ, in whom God took symbolic form.

These critics grasped one important truth. Christian faith is not the same as religious idealism; the Christian life does not consist in developing the individual personality, in the improvement of society, or in making the world a better place. The Christian life means a turning away from the world, a detachment from it. But the critics of the History of Religions school failed to see that in the New Testament this detachment is essentially eschatological and not mystical. Religion for them was an expression of the human yearning to rise above the world and transcend it: it was the discovery of a supramundane sphere where the soul could detach itself from all earthly care and find its rest. Hence the supreme manifestation of religion was to be found not in personal ethics or in social idealism but in the cultus regarded as an end in itself. This was just the kind of religious life portrayed in the New Testament, not only as a model and pattern, but as a challenge and inspiration. The New Testament was thus the abiding source of power which enabled man to realize the true life of religion, and Christ was the eternal symbol for the cultus of the Christian Church.[23] It will be noticed how the Church is here defined exclusively as a worshipping community, and this represents a great advance on the older liberalism. This school rediscovered the Church as a *religious* institution. For the idealist there was really no place for the Church at all. But did they succeed in recovering the meaning of the Ecclesia in the full, New Testament sense of the word? For in the New Testament the Ecclesia is invariably a phenomenon of salvation history and eschatology.

Moreover, if the History of Religions school is right, the kerygma has once more ceased to be kerygma. Like the liberals,

[23] Cp. e.g. Troeltsch, *Die Bedeutung der Geschichtlichkeit Jesu für den Glauben*, Tübingen, 1911.

they are silent about a decisive act of God in Christ proclaimed as the event of redemption. So we are still left with the question whether this event and the person of Jesus, both of which are described in the New Testament in mythological terms, are nothing more than mythology. Can the kerygma be interpreted apart from mythology? Can we recover the truth of the kerygma for men who do not think in mythological terms without forfeiting its character as kerygma?

5. AN EXISTENTIALIST INTERPRETATION THE ONLY SOLUTION

The theological work which such an interpretation involves can be sketched only in the broadest outline and with only a few examples. We must avoid the impression that this is a light and easy task, as if all we have to do is to discover the right formula and finish the job on the spot. It is much more formidable than that. It cannot be done single-handed. It will tax the time and strength of a whole theological generation.

The mythology of the New Testament is in essence that of Jewish apocalyptic and the Gnostic redemption myths. A common feature of them both is their basic dualism, according to which the present world and its human inhabitants are under the control of daemonic, satanic powers, and stand in need of redemption. Man cannot achieve this redemption by his own efforts; it must come as a gift through a divine intervention. Both types of mythology speak of such an intervention: Jewish apocalyptic of an imminent world crisis in which this present aeon will be brought to an end and the new aeon ushered in by the coming of the Messiah, and Gnosticism of a Son of God sent down from the realm of light, entering into this world in the guise of a man, and by his fate and teaching delivering the elect and opening up the way for their return to their heavenly home.

The meaning of these two types of mythology lies once more not in their imagery with its apparent objectivity but in the understanding of human existence which both are trying to express. In other words, they need to be interpreted existentially. A good example of such treatment is to be found in Hans Jonas's book on Gnosticism.[24]

Our task is to produce an existentialist interpretation of the dualistic mythology of the New Testament along similar lines.

---

[24] *Gnosis und spätantiker Geist.* I. *Die mythologische Gnosis,* 1934.

When, for instance, we read of daemonic powers ruling the world and holding mankind in bondage, does the understanding of human existence which underlies such language offer a solution to the riddle of human life which will be acceptable even to the non-mythological mind of to-day? Of course we must not take this to imply that the New Testament presents us with an anthropology like that which modern science can give us. It cannot be proved by logic or demonstrated by an appeal to factual evidence. Scientific anthropologies always take for granted a definite understanding of existence, which is invariably the consequence of a deliberate decision of the scientist, whether he makes it consciously or not. And that is why we have to discover whether the New Testament offers man an understanding of himself which will challenge him to a genuine existential decision.

Evolutionary Humanism

SIR JULIAN HUXLEY

Few families have produced more distinguished thinkers than the Huxleys. T. H. Huxley was the foremost man of science in England after the death of his intellectual hero Charles Darwin. His son Leonard was a prominent editor. Leonard's two sons, Aldous and Sir Julian, have been numbered among the leading intellectual forces in the English-speaking world since the 1920's, Aldous as novelist and critic, Sir Julian as biologist, popularizer of science, and scientific humanist.

The next excerpt defines "evolutionary humanism," which Sir Julian offers as a comprehensive philosophy of life to those who cannot accept any of the positive religions but who look to the sciences for orientation and feel the need for a "religion without revelation" that can give meaning and direction to their lives.

Scientific humanism is, in essence, a nineteenth-century philosophy adapted to twentieth-century needs. It finds its chief adherents in Britain, Scandinavia, the Netherlands, and North America, where the confident, freethinking, rationalist positivism of the nineteenth century has survived with the greatest success into the twentieth. Other major figures in the movement, all British, include C. H. Waddington, Morris Ginsberg, and J. Bronowski.

SOURCE: "The Humanist Frame," by Sir Julian Huxley, in *The Humanist Frame,* ed. Sir Julian Huxley (Harper & Row, New York, 1961), pp. 38–48. Reprinted by permission of George Allen and Unwin, Ltd.

ALL THEISTIC religions are based on the God hypothesis (or, to use Ralph Turner's more inclusive term, the daimonic hypothesis)—the belief that there exist supernatural beings of a personal or super-personal nature, capable of influencing natural events, including events in human minds. This is a dualistic theory, for it implies the existence of a basic and essential cleavage between natural and supernatural realms of being.

Early theologies are all polytheistic. Christian theology calls itself monotheistic, but permits itself a partial polytheism in the doctrine of the Trinity, while the position ascribed to the Virgin, the Angels and the Saints in Catholicism and to a lesser degree in other sects, gives full rein to polydaimonism. Christian theology bases itself on revelation and on belief in the historical reality of supernatural events such as the incarnation and resurrection of Jesus as the Son of God. It also maintains the reality of miracles.

A theological system incorporating such beliefs has a number of consequences which Humanists find undesirable. The belief in supernatural beings capable of affecting human destiny leads to petitionary rather than aspirational prayer, and to all kinds of propitiatory practices, from the use of incense to the bequeathing of rich gifts, from asceticism to penitential sacrifice. Belief in a supernatural after-life leads to concentration on attaining salvation in the other world and to a lack of concern for life in this world and its possible improvement. Belief in the fall of man and the necessity of redemption through an incarnate divine Saviour has led to the cruel (and untrue) doctrines of Original Sin and Damnation for unbelievers, as well as to a belief in the guilt and inherent inferiority of the female sex. Belief in the value of orthodox Christian beliefs and practices as the sole or main means of achieving salvation leads to the rejection or playing down of other ideas as to what constitutes 'salvation', and of other methods of transcending selfhood. Belief in the Bible as the inspired word of God, and in the Church and its representatives as the sole source of correct doctrine, leads to a regrettable dogmatism and to the rejection or playing down of secular knowledge and scientific method.

Belief in a supernatural Ruler, endowed with absolute wisdom and the capacity of issuing absolute moral edicts, coupled with an ignorance of the workings of the unconscious as revealed by modern psychology, permits would-be dictators, fanatical moralists and other power-hungry men to believe that their subjective feelings of internal certainty are 'really' the voice of an objective and external God and to claim divine guidance and sanction as a convenient disguise for their amibitions, and enables them with a good conscience to project their own guilt and resentful inferiority on to their enemies, and to canalize their repressed sadism on to their victims. How unfortunate for mankind that the Lord is reported by Holy Writ as having said 'Vengeance is mine!'

Belief in the efficacy of ritual practices for ensuring salvation or other kinds of religious advancement has a deadening effect on the religious and moral life. Belief in supernaturalism and the miraculous and magical elements which go with it always leads to gross superstition, and usually to its financial exploitation. Think of the cult of relics, the complete repudiation of any scientific approach shown by the promulgation of doctrines like the bodily assumption of the Virgin Mary, by the proclamation of the miracle of Fatima, or by highly profitable pilgrimages to sites of 'miraculous' cures like Lourdes.

Such theistically-based beliefs in various combinations can lead to a materialistic degradation of religion, sometimes silly, sometimes serious and sometimes horrible, as seen in the prayer-wheels of Tibetan Buddhism, the scandal of indulgences which started off the Reformation, or the human sacrifices of the Aztecs and the Carthaginians.

Above all, belief in an omnipotent, omniscient and omnibenevolent God leads to a frustrating dilemma at the very heart of our approach to reality. For many thinking people, it is incompatible with our knowledge of nature and history and with the facts of evil, suffering, and human misery. Even when, as in some modernist versions of Christian theology, the idea of a personal God is watered down and transmogrified into some abstract principle or supposed Absolute behind phenomena, and the Deity is removed farther and farther from any possibility of active interference in natural or human events, the dilemma remains. The human mind and spirit is not interested in such a Pickwickian God, and refuses to be fobbed off by assertions as to our inherent incapacity to understand Him. The theologian's assertion of divine incomprehensibility does not satisfy man in his modern world any more than Humpty Dumpty's remark, 'Impenetrability, that's what I say,' satisfied Alice in her Wonderland.

To sum up, any belief in supernatural creators, rulers, or influ-

encers of natural or human process introduces an irreparable split
into the universe, and prevents us from grasping its real unity. Any
belief in Absolutes, whether the absolute validity of moral commandments, of authority of revelation, of inner certitude, or of
divine inspiration, erects a formidable barrier against progress and
the possibility of improvement, moral, rational, or religious. And
the all-too-frequent combination of the two constitutes a grave
brake on human advance, and, by obfuscating all the major problems of existence, prevents the attainment of a full and comprehensive vision of human destiny.

All this merely spells out the consequences of the fact that
theistic religions, with their inescapable basis of divine revelations
and dogmatic theologies, are today not merely incompatible with
human progress and the advance of human knowledge but are
obstacles to the emergence of new types of religion which could be
compatible with our knowledge and capable of promoting our
future progress.

Although destructive criticism of established religious systems,
such as that of orthodox Christianity by militant Rationalism
around the turn of the nineteenth century, may be necessary at
certain periods, the time for negative activities is now past. It was
not for nothing that Goethe made the Devil proclaim himself as
der Geist der stets verneint.

What the world now needs is not merely a rationalist denial of
the old but a religious affirmation of something new. However, it is
harder to affirm, at least to affirm anything of lasting value, than to
deny. It is harder for the same reason that, as the world has
experienced on a gigantic scale, it is easier to destroy than to
construct, easier to smash a cathedral, a city or a statue than to
create one.

Construction needs a positive plan of some sort to work to and
cooperative effort for its execution, and this demands intelligence,
imagination, goodwill, and above all vision.

One of the main things needed by the world today is a new
single religious system to replace the multiplicity of conflicting and
incompatible religious systems that are now competing for the
spirit of man. Our new vision of the universe and man's role in it is
beginning to indicate the lines of its construction.

All religions, as I pointed out earlier, are psychosocial organs of
evolving man: their function is to help him to cope with the

problems of his destiny. They themselves evolve. But they always involve the emotion of sacred mystery experienced by men confronted with what Otto calls the numinous, the *mysterium tremendum;* the sense of right and wrong; and feelings of guilt, shame, or sin. They are always concerned in some way or another with the relation between the individual and the community, and with the possibility of his escaping from the prisoning immediacies of space, time, and selfhood by relating himself to some broader frame of reference, or in some self-transcending experience of union or communion with a larger reality.

They always possess what we may broadly call an ideology, a morality, and a ritual—an intellectual framework of beliefs, myths, and theological principles, an ethical framework of moral codes and injunctions, and an expressive framework of actions expressing or enhancing religious emotion.

As I have set forth at greater length in my *Religion Without Revelation,*[1] the raw materials out of which religions are formed consist of actual religious experiences, numinous or holy, mystical or transcendent. But the particular form which they take is primarily the result of their ideological framework of belief: I have given various examples of how the morality and the ritual expressions of a religion are determined by its beliefs to a much greater extent than its beliefs are determined by its morality or ritual.

Let us look at some of the major ideas which our new vision will contribute or dictate to the new belief-system. In the first place we have a totally different view of the mysterious. With the advance of scientific knowledge, many phenomena which once appeared wholly mysterious can now be described or explained in rationally intelligible or naturalistic terms. This applies not only to physical phenomena like rainbows and eclipses, pestilences and earthquakes, but also to biological phenomena like reproduction and sex, heredity and evolution, and to psychological phenomena such as obsession and possession, insanity and inspiration.

The clear light of science, we are often told, has abolished mystery, leaving only logic and reason. This is quite untrue. Science has removed the obscuring veil of mystery from many phenomena, much to the benefit of the human race: but it confronts us with a basic and universal mystery—the mystery of

[1] *Religion Without Revelation*, London: Parrish, 1957.

existence in general, and of the existence of mind in particular. Why does the world exist? Why is the world-stuff what it is? Why does it have mental or subjective aspects as well as material or objective ones? We do not know. All we can do is to admit the facts.

This means that, as Margaret Fuller said, we accept the universe. In spite of Carlyle's comment, 'Gad, she'd better', this is not easy: there is great resistance to such acceptance. Initially, the universe reveals itself as too vast and varied to be accepted as a unitary whole by our small human minds; many of its components are apparently incommensurable with human thought and feeling, and in many of its aspects it appears alien and even hostile to human aspiration and endeavour. But we must learn to accept it, and to accept its and our existence as the one basic mystery.

Accordingly, any new emergent religion must have a background of reverence and awe in its belief-system, and must seek to keep alive man's sense of wonder, strangeness and challenge in all his particular dealings with the general problem of existence.

But though all we can do about the universe in its total existence is to discover it as an irreducible mystery, to be humanly assimilated only by wonder and free acceptance, yet the details of its phenomenal working and the relations of its operative parts can be profitably clarified by human intellectual and imaginative effort. And this applies to religion as well as to science or to art. In all of them the ecological approach is essential.

Religion can be usefully regarded as applied spiritual ecology. The relations with which a religion must attempt to deal are the relations of mankind with the rest of external nature, the relation of man's individualized self with the rest of his internal nature, and the relation of individual men and women with other men and women and with their communities.

All these can be much clarified by our new humanist vision. In its light the universe is seen as a unitary and evolutionary process. Man is part and a product of the process, but a very peculiar part, capable of affecting its further course on earth and perhaps elsewhere. But he is only able to affect the process constructively by understanding its workings.

The rightness of relation he must aim at has two aspects. One is a relation of right position in an integrated and harmonious pattern; the other (and this is the major novelty introduced by the new vision) is a relation of right direction with the whole process. Man's religious aim must therefore be to achieve not a static but a dynamic spiritual equilibrium. And his emergent religion must therefore learn how to be an open and self-correcting system, like that of his science.

All religions provide for some ceremonial sanctification of life, especially of events like birth, marriage and death, and those marking the transition from one stage of life to another, like initiation or the taking of a degree: his new emergent religion must continue to do this, though it must translate the ceremonials into terms that are relevant to the new vision and the new circumstances of his life.

This reformulation of traditional religious concepts and beliefs and ceremonies, their translation into a new terminology and a new framework of ideas, is a major task for Humanism.

Man makes his concepts. He constructs them out of the raw material of his experience, immediate and accumulated, with the aid of his psychological machinery of reason and imagination.

This is true not only of religious concepts but of scientific concepts like the atom or natural selection today, or the four elements or the inheritance of acquired characters in earlier times.

But whereas science is constantly and willingly improving its terminology and reformulating its concepts, even scrapping them and constructing quite new ones, religion on the whole resists any such transformation.

Religious concepts like God, incarnation, the soul, salvation, original sin, grace, atonement, all have a basis in man's experiences of phenomenal reality. It is necessary now to analyze that basis of reality into its component parts, and then to reassemble these elements, together with any new factors that have come to light, into concepts which correspond more closely to reality and are more relevant to present circumstances.

Thus, if I may over-simplify the matter, *God* appears to be a semantic symbol denoting what Matthew Arnold called 'the power not ourselves', or rather the various powers felt to be greater than our narrow selves, whether the forces of external nature or the forces imminent in our own nature, all bound together in the concept of a personal or super-personal sacred being in some way capable of affecting or guiding or interfering in the course of events. The forces are real enough: what we have done is, quite illegitimately, to project the god concept into them. And in so doing we have distorted their true significance, and effectively altered the course of history.[2]

Once this is realized, it should be possible to reformulate such ideas as Divine Law, obedience to God's will, or union with the mind of God, in an evolutionary terminology consonant with existing scientific knowledge.

Again, Christian ethics (to which the world owes a great debt) is based on the doctrine of Original Sin resulting from the Fall of Man. This attempts to give an intelligible intrepretation of such general and wellnigh universal phenomena as our sense of guilt, our search for atonement, our authoritarian consciences, our rigorous sense of right and wrong, our consequent persecution of those who deviate from what we feel is the right path.

As Professor Waddington points out [in his contribution to *The Humanist Frame*] and reinforces with a wealth of supporting argument in his admirable book, *The Ethical Animal*,[3] psychology and evolutionary biology between them are now indicating a rational and coherent explanation for these facts.

Psychosocial life is based on the transmission of accumulated experience in the form of tradition. And this, Waddington makes clear, cannot be effective unless the human infant is genetically equipped as an 'authority-acceptor': he is constructed so as to accept what he is told by his parents as authoritative, in the same sort of way as baby birds are equipped with an imprinting mechanism which makes them accept any moving object within certain limits of size as a parent.

This 'proto-ethical mechanism' involves the internalization of external authority in the baby's primitive conscience, a process accompanied by all-or-nothing repression of impulses of hate for the authority who is also the loved parent. As a result, a quality of absoluteness becomes attached to the baby's sense of rightness and wrongness, together with an ambivalent attitude to authority in general: his morality is burdened with a load of guilt, and his feelings towards authority become impregnated with ambivalence.

All this happens before he is old enough to verify his ideas by

[2] For a valuable discussion of the semantic, symbolic and functional aspects of religion, see Raymond Firth's Huxley Memorial Lecture for 1959 (*J. Roy. Anthrop. Inst.*, 89, 129).

[3] *The Ethical Animal*, London: Allen & Unwin, 1960.

experience. During his later development he will modify and rectify the content and authoritarianism of what he has accepted, but will generally retain a great deal of both. The aim of the Humanist must be, not to destroy the inner authority of conscience, but to help the growing individual to escape from the shackles of an imposed authority-system into the supporting arms of one freely and consciously built up. And this will involve a thorough reformulation of the ethical aspects of religion.

Reformulation—even reappraisal—is perhaps most necessary in regard to man's inner life and what, for want of a better terminology, is called spiritual development.

Religious experiences such as those of communion with some higher reality, or inspiration from outside the personality, or a sense of transcendent power or glory, or sudden conversion, or apparently supernormal beauty or ineffable sacredness, or the healing power of prayer or repentant adoration, or, above all, the deep sense of inner peace and assurance in spite of disorder and suffering, can no longer be interpreted in the traditional terms of communication with a personal God or with a supernatural realm of being. But neither can they be denied or explained away by over-zealous rationalism as merely illusory products. They are the outcome of human minds in their strange commerce with outer reality and in the still stranger and often unconscious internal struggle between their components. But they are none the less real[4] and they can be of great importance to the individual who experiences them: but further, as the Churches well know, they need to be examined and disciplined.

Religious experiences often are or appear to be ineffable in the literal sense of the word, which makes their discussion very difficult. But their significance is a matter both high and deep (as I am in all humility aware); and they certainly need re-examination and reappraisal if their great potential value is to be realized.

Further, experiential religion should enlist the aid of psychological science in a radical study of man's actual and potential spiritual resources. Such a study would, of course, have to start from the presuppositions that 'man' is a new type of organism consisting of individual mind-bodies interacting with a superindividual and con-

[4] Besides William James's famous book, there are many valuable descriptions and studies of the varieties of religious experience, a number of which I have cited and discussed in my *Religion Without Revelation*.

tinuing system of ideas and beliefs, whose destiny is to actualize
more and more of his possibilities for greater fulfilment during
further evolution; and that 'religion' is an organ of man primarily
concerned with what is felt and believed to be sacred in that
destiny.

But our new vision illuminates our existence and our destiny in a
new way, and necessitates a new approach to their problems. In its
light we see at once that the reappraisal of religious experience
must be a part of something much larger—a thorough investigation
of man's inner world, a great project of 'Mind Exploration' which
could and should rival and surpass 'Space Exploration' in interest
and importance. This would open up a new realm of being for
colonization and fruitful occupation by man, a realm of mental
realities, built on but transcending the realm of material realities, a
world of satisfactions transcending physical satisfactions, in some
way felt as more absolute and more perfect. Ordinary men and
women obtain occasional glimpses of it through falling in love, or
through overwhelming experiences of ecstasy, beauty or awe. And
we have the reports of the occasional mental explorers, poets,
thinkers, scientists and mystics who have penetrated into its interior. Think of St Teresa, or of Blake as the Mental Traveller, or
of Wordsworth anticipating Freud by revealing in us the 'high
instincts before which our mortal nature Doth tremble like a guilty
thief surprised'.

No concerted effort has yet been made towards its exploration
or adequate mapping. There is as yet no proper terminology for its
discussion. In describing its workings and results, ordinary language falls back on terms like *rapture* and *inspiration, magical* and
heavenly, bewitching and *divine*, while the first attempts at scientific terminology, like *repression* and *sublimation, id* and *superego*,
deal only with its fringes.

From the specifically religious point of view, the desirable direction of evolution might be defined as the divinization of existence—
but for this to have operative significance, we must frame a new
definition of 'the divine', free from all connotations of external
supernatural beings.

Religion today is imprisoned in a theistic frame of ideas, compelled to operate in the unrealities of a dualistic world. In the
unitary Humanist frame it acquires a new look and a new freedom.
With the aid of our new vision, it has the opportunity of escaping

from the theistic impasse, and of playing its proper role in the real world of unitary existence.

This brings me back to where I started—to our new and revolutionary vision of reality. Like all true visions it is prophetic; by enabling us to understand the present condition of life in terms of its extraordinary past, it helps us not only to envisage an equally extraordinary future, but to inject planned purpose into its course.

In its light, fulfilment and enrichment of life are seen as the overriding aims of existence, to be achieved by the realization of life's inherent possibilities. Thus the development of man's vast potential of realizable possibility provides the prime motive for collective action—the only motive on which all men or nations could agree, the only basis for transcending conflicting ideologies. It makes it possible to heal the splits between religion and science and art by enlisting man's religious and scientific and artistic capacities in a new common enterprise. It prescribes an agenda for the world's discussions of that enterprise and suggests the practical methods to be employed in running it.

It indicates the urgent need for survey and research in all fields of human development. This includes the promotion of what I may call a psychosocial technology, including the production of ideological machine-tools like concepts and beliefs for the better processing of experience.

We also need to develop a new ecology, an ecology of the human evolutionary enterprise. This means thinking out a new pattern of our relations with each other and with the rest of our environment, including the mental environment which we both create and inhabit.

Psychosocial ecology must aim at a right balance between different values, between continuity and change, and between the evolutionary process for whose guidance we have responsibility and the resources with which we have to operate. Those resources are of two kinds—material and quantitative, for maintenance and utility, and psychological and qualitative, for enjoyment and fulfilment—such things as food, and energy, mines and industrial plants on the one hand; solitude, landscape beauty, marine and mountain adventure, the wonder and interest of wild life on the other. Planned human ecology must balance and where possible reconcile the two kinds of resource.

What is the place of the individual in all this? At first sight the individual human being appears as a little, temporary, and insignificant creature, of no account in the vast enterprise of mankind as a whole. But in Evolutionary Humanism, unlike some other ideologies, the human individual has high significance. Quite apart from the practical function which he performs in society and its collective enterprises, he can help in fulfilling human destiny by the fuller realization of his own personal possibilities. A strong and rich personality is the individual's unique and wonderful contribution to the psychosocial process.

Santayana has come close to the central idea of Evolutionary Humanism in sane and splendid words. 'There is only one world, the natural world, and only one truth about it; but this world has a spiritual life in it, which looks not to another world but to the beauty and perfection that this world suggests, approaches and misses.'

If we aspire to realize this potential beauty and perfection more fully, we shall have to utilize all the resources available—not only those of the external world, but those internal resources of our own nature—wonder and intelligence, creative freedom and love, imagination and belief. The central belief of Evolutionary Humanism is that existence can be improved, that vast untapped possibilities can be increasingly realized, that greater fulfilment can replace frustration. This belief is now firmly grounded in knowledge: it could become in turn the firm ground for action.

Marriage and Morals

BERTRAND RUSSELL

In a productive career spanning more than seventy years, Bertrand Russell has written scores of books on everything from mathematics to politics. He is also the best possible example of the modern positivist philosopher who rejects absolutism in ethics and at the same time responds to Nietzsche's plea for value-makers. In his self-appointed role as conscience of his age, Russell has dispensed formulas for education, government, and world peace; and he has also helped lead the

SOURCE: *Marriage and Morals,* by Bertrand Russell (Liveright, New York, 1929), pp. 303–20. Reprinted by permission of the Liveright Publishing Corporation and George Allen and Unwin, Ltd.

way to the modern sexual revolution with his still widely read book, *Marriage and Morals*, first published in 1929.

Like most other liberal moralists, Russell insists that freedom, humanized by love, must be the supreme principle in sexual ethics. The petty tyrannies of Judeo-Christian morality obstruct the full flow of life, deny nature, and convert marriage into bondage. At the center of the sexual revolution, in Russell's treatment of it, and in the literature of sexual liberalism generally, stands the conviction derived ultimately from Freud that sexual impulses are not inherently wicked but a natural part of life that must accommodate to the equally natural demands of love and reason, but cannot be repressed without the most serious consequences to mental and spiritual health. The "new morality" of the radical theology of the 1960's reaches much the same conclusion.

IN THE course of our discussion we have been led to certain conclusions, some historical, some ethical. Historically, we found that sexual morality, as it exists in civilized societies, has been derived from two quite different sources, on the one hand desire for certainty as to fatherhood, on the other an ascetic belief that sex is wicked, except in so far as it is necessary for propagation. Morality in pre-Christian times, and in the Far East down to the present time, had only the former source, except in India and Persia, which are the centres from which asceticism appears to have spread. The desire to make sure of paternity does not, of course, exist in those backward races which are ignorant of the fact that the male has any part in generation. Among them, although masculine jealousy places certain limitations upon female licence, women are on the whole much freer than in early patriarchal societies. It is clear that in the transition there must have been considerable friction, and the restraints upon women's freedom were doubtless considered necessary by men who took an interest in being the fathers of their own children. At this stage, sexual morality existed only for women. A man might not commit adultery with a married woman, but otherwise he was free.

With Christianity, the new motive of avoidance of sin enters in, and the moral standard becomes in theory the same for men as for women, though in practice the difficulty of enforcing it upon men has always led to a greater toleration of their failings than of those of women. Early sexual morality had a plain biological purpose, namely to ensure that the young should have the protection of two parents during their early years and not only of one. The purpose was lost sight of in Christian theory, though not in Christian practice.

In quite modern times there have been signs that both the Christian and the pre-Christian parts of sexual morality are undergoing modification. The Christian part has not the hold that it formerly had, because of the decay of religious orthodoxy and the diminishing intensity of belief even among those who still believe. Men and women born during the present century, although their unconscious is apt to retain the old attitudes, do not, for the most part, consciously believe that fornication as such is sin. As for the pre-Christian elements in sexual ethics, these have been modified by one factor, and are in process of being modified by yet another. The first of these factors is the use of contraceptives, which are making it increasingly possible to prevent sexual intercourse from leading to pregnancy, and are therefore enabling women, if unmarried, to avoid children altogether, and if married, to have children only by their husbands, without in either case finding it necessary to be chaste. This process is not yet complete, because contraceptives are not yet wholly reliable, but one may, I think, assume that before very long they will become so. In that case, assurance of paternity will become possible without the insistence that women shall have no sexual intercourse outside marriage. It may be said that women could deceive their husbands on the point, but after all it has been possible from the earliest times for women to deceive their husbands, and the motive for deception is much less strong when the question is merely who shall be the father than when it is whether there shall be intercourse with a person who may be passionately loved. One may, therefore, assume that deceit as to paternity, though it may occasionally occur, will be less frequent than deceit as to adultery has been in the past. It is also by no means impossible that the jealousy of husbands should, by a new convention, adapt itself to the new situation, and arise only when wives propose to choose some other man as the father of their children. In the East, men have always tolerated liberties on the part of eunuchs which most European husbands would resent. They have tolerated them because they introduce no doubt as to paternity. The same kind of toleration might easily be extended to liberties accompanied by the use of contraceptives.

The bi-parental family may, therefore, survive in the future without making such great demands upon the continence of women as it had to make in the past. A second factor, however, in the change which is coming over sexual morals, is liable to have more far-reaching effects. This is the increasing participation of the State in the maintenance and education of children. This factor, so far, operates in Europe more than in America, and affects mainly the wage-earning classes, but they, after all, are a majority of the population, and it is quite likely that the substitution of the State for the father, which is gradually taking place where they are concerned, will ultimately extend to the whole population. The part of the father, in animal families as with the human family, has been to provide protection and maintenance, but in civilized communities protection is provided by the police, and maintenance may come to be provided wholly by the State, so far, at any rate, as the poorer sections of the population are concerned. If that were so, the father would cease to serve any obvious purpose. With regard to the mother, there are two possibilities. She may continue her ordinary work and have her children cared for in institutions, or she may, if the law so decides, be paid by the State to care for her children while they are young. If the latter course is adopted, it may be used for a while to bolster up traditional morality, since a woman who is not virtuous may be deprived of payment. But if she is deprived of payment she will be unable to support her children unless she goes to work, and it will, therefore, be necessary to put her children in some institution. It would seem probable, therefore, that the operation of economic forces may lead to the elimination of the father, and even to a great extent of the mother, in the care of children whose parents are not rich. If so, all the traditional reasons for traditional morality will have disappeared, and new reasons will have to be found for a new morality.

The break-up of the family, if it comes about, will not be, to my mind, a matter for rejoicing. The affection of parents is important to children, and institutions, if they exist on a large scale, are sure to become very official and rather harsh. There will be a terrible degree of uniformity when the differentiating influence of different home environments is removed. And unless an international government is previously established, the children of different countries will be taught a virulent form of patriotism which will make it nearly certain that they will exterminate each other when grown up. The necessity for an international government arises also in regard to population, since in its absence nationalists have a motive for encouraging a greater increase of numbers than is desirable, and, with the progress of medicine and hygiene, the only remaining method of disposing of excessive numbers will be war.

While the sociological questions are often difficult and complicated, the personal questions are, to my mind, quite simple. The doctrine that there is something sinful about sex is one which has done untold harm to individual character—a harm beginning in early childhood and continuing throughout life. By keeping sex love in a prison, conventional morality has done much to imprison all other forms of friendly feeling, and to make men less generous, less kindly, more self-assertive and more cruel. Whatever sexual ethic may come to be ultimately accepted must be free from superstition and must have recognizable and demonstrable grounds in its favour. Sex cannot dispense with an ethic, any more than business or sport or scientific research or any other branch of human activity. But it can dispense with an ethic based solely upon ancient prohibitions propounded by uneducated people in a society wholly unlike our own. In sex, as in economics and in politics, our ethic is still dominated by fears which modern discoveries have made irrational, and the benefit to be derived from those discoveries is largely lost through failure of psychological adaptation to them.

It is true that the transition from the old system to the new has its own difficulties, as all transitions have. These who advocate any ethical innovation are invariably accused, like Socrates, of being corrupters of youth; nor is this accusation always wholly unfounded, even when in fact the new ethic which they preach would, if accepted in its entirety, lead to a better life than the old ethic which they seek to amend. Every one who knows the Mahometan East asserts that those who have ceased to think it necessary to pray five times a day have also ceased to respect other moral rules which we consider more important. The man who proposes any change in sexual morality is especially liable to be misinterpreted in this way, and I am conscious myself of having said things which some readers may have misinterpreted.

The general principle upon which the newer morality differs from the traditional morality of puritanism is this: we believe that instinct should be trained rather than thwarted. Put in these general terms, the view is one which would win very wide acceptance among modern men and women, but it is one which is fully valid only when accepted with its full implications and applied from the earliest years. If in childhood instinct is thwarted rather than trained, the result may be that it has to be to some extent thwarted throughout later life, because it will have taken on highly undesirable forms as a result of thwarting in early years. The morality which I should advocate does not consist simply of saying to grown-up people or to adolescents: "Follow your impulses and do as you like." There has to be consistency in life; there has to be continuous effort directed to ends that are not immediately beneficial and not at every moment attractive; there has to be consideration for others; and there should be certain standards of rectitude. I should not, however, regard self-control as an end in itself, and I should wish our institutions and our moral conventions to be such as to make the need for self-control a minimum rather than a maximum. The use of self-control is like the use of brakes on a train. It is useful when you find yourself going in the wrong direction, but merely harmful when the direction is right. No one would maintain that a train ought always to be run with the brakes on, yet the habit of difficult self-control has a very similar injurious effect upon the energies available for useful activity. Self-control causes these energies to be largely wasted on internal friction instead of external activity; and on this account it is always regrettable, though sometimes necessary.

The degree to which self-control is necessary in life depends upon the early treatment of instinct. Instincts, as they exist in children, may lead to useful activities or harmful ones, just as the steam in a locomotive may take it toward its destination or into a siding where it is smashed by an accident. The function of education is to guide instinct into the directions in which it will develop useful rather than harmful activities. If this task has been adequately performed in early years, a man or woman will, as a rule, be able to live a useful life without the need of severe self-control, except, perhaps, at a few rare crises. If on the other hand early education has consisted in a mere thwarting of instinct, the acts to which instinct prompts in later life will be partly harmful, and will therefore have to be continually restrained by self-control.

These general considerations apply with peculiar force to sexual impulses, both because of their great strength and because of the fact that traditional morality has made them its peculiar concern. Most traditional moralists appear to think that, if our sexual impulses were not severely checked, they would become trivial, anarchic and gross. I believe this view to be derived from observation of those who have acquired the usual inhibitions from their early years and have subsequently attempted to ignore them. But in such men the early prohibitions are still operative even when they do not succeed in prohibiting. What is called conscience, that is to say the unreasoning and more or less unconscious acceptance of precepts learnt in early youth, causes men still to feel that whatever the conventions prohibit is wrong, and this feeling may persist in spite of intellectual convictions to the contrary. It thus produces a personality divided against itself, one in which instinct and reason no longer go hand in hand, but instinct has become trivial and reason has become anaemic. One finds in the modern world various different degrees of revolt against conventional teaching. The commonest of all is the revolt of the man who intellectually acknowledges the ethical truth of the morality he was taught in youth, but confesses, with a more or less unreal regret, that he is not sufficiently heroic to live up to it. For such a man there is little to be said. It would be better that he should alter either his practice or his beliefs in such a way as to bring harmony between them. Next comes the man whose conscious reason has rejected much that he learnt in the nursery, but whose unconscious still accepts it in its entirety. Such a man will suddenly change his line of conduct under the stress of any strong emotion, especially fear. A serious illness or an earthquake may cause him to repent and to abandon his intellectual convictions as the result of an uprush of infantile beliefs. Even at ordinary times his behaviour will be inhibited, and the inhibitions may take an undesirable form. They will prevent him from acting in ways that are condemned by traditional morals, but they will prevent him from doing so in a whole-hearted way, and will thus eliminate from his actions some of the elements that would have given them value. The substitution of a new moral code for the old one can never be completely satisfactory unless the new one is accepted with the whole personality, not only with that top layer which constitutes our conscious thought. To most people this is very difficult if throughout their early years they have been exposed to the old morality. It is therefore impossible to judge a new morality fairly until it has been applied in early education.

Sex morality has to be derived from certain general principles, as to which there is perhaps a fairly wide measure of agreement, in spite of the wide disagreement as to the consequences to be drawn from them. The first thing to be secured is that there should be as much as possible of that deep, serious love between man and woman which embraces the whole personality of both and leads to a fusion by which each is enriched and enhanced. The second thing of importance is that there should be adequate care of children, physical and psychological. Neither of these principles in itself can be considered in any way shocking, yet it is as a consequence of these two principles that I should advocate certain modifications of the conventional code. Most men and women, as things stand, are incapable of being as whole-hearted and as generous in the love that they bring to marriage as they would be if their early years had been less hedged about with taboos. They either lack the necessary experience, or they have gained it in furtive and undesirable ways. Moreover, since jealousy has the sanction of moralists, they feel justified in keeping each other in a mutual prison. It is, of course, a very good thing when a husband and wife love each other so completely that neither is ever tempted to unfaithfulness; it is not, however, a good thing that unfaithfulness, if it does occur, should be treated as something terrible, nor is it desirable to go so far as to make all friendship with persons of the other sex impossible. A good life cannot be founded upon fear, prohibition, and mutual interference with freedom. Where faithfulness is achieved without these, it is good, but where all this is necessary it may well be that too high a price has been paid, and that a little mutual toleration of occasional lapses would be better. There can be no doubt that mutual jealousy, even where there is physical faithfulness, often causes more unhappiness in a marriage than would be caused if there were more confidence in the ultimate strength of a deep and permanent affection.

The obligations of parents toward children are treated far more lightly than seems to me right by many persons who consider themselves virtuous. Given the present system of the bi-parental family, as soon as there are children it is the duty of both parties to a marriage to do everything that they can to preserve harmonious relations, even if this requires considerable self-control. But the control required is not merely, as conventional moralists pretend, that involved in restraining every impulse to unfaithfulness; it is just as important to control impulses to jealousy, ill-temper, masterfulness, and so on. There can be no doubt that serious quarrels between parents are a very frequent cause of nervous disorders in children; therefore whatever can be done to prevent such quarrels should be done. At the same time, where one or both parties have not sufficient self-control to prevent disagreements from coming to the knowledge of the children, it may well be better that the marriage should be dissolved. It is by no means the case that the dissolution of a marriage is invariably the worst thing possible from the point of view of the children; indeed it is not nearly so bad as the spectacle of raised voices, furious accusations, perhaps even violence, to which many children are exposed in bad homes.

It must not be supposed that the sort of thing which a sane advocate of greater freedom desires is to be achieved at once by leaving adults, or even adolescents, who have been brought up under the old severe restrictive maxims, to the unaided promptings of the damaged impulses which are all the moralists have left to them. This is a necessary stage, since otherwise they will bring up their children as badly as they were brought up; but it is no more than a stage. Sane freedom must be learnt from the earliest years, since otherwise the only freedom possible will be a frivolous, superficial freedom, not freedom of the whole personality. Trivial impulses will lead to physical excesses, while the spirit remains in fetters. Instinct rightly trained from the first can produce something much better than what results from an education inspired by a Calvinistic belief in original sin, but when such an education has been allowed to do its evil work, it is exceedingly difficult to undo the effect in later years. One of the most important benefits which psycho-analysis has conferred upon the world is its discovery of the bad effects of prohibitions and threats in early childhood; to undo this effect may require all the time and technique of a psycho-analytic treatment. This is true not only of those obvious neurotics who have suffered damage visible to every one; it is true also of most apparently normal people. I believe that nine out of ten of those who have had a conventional upbringing in their early years have become in some degree incapable of a decent and sane attitude toward marriage and sex generally. The kind of attitude and behaviour that I should regard as the best has been rendered impossible for such people; the best that can be done is to make them aware of the damage that they have sustained and to persuade them to abstain from maiming their children in the same way in which they have been maimed.

The doctrine that I wish to preach is not one of licence; it involves exactly as much self-control as is involved in the conventional doctrine. But self-control will be applied more to abstaining from interference with the freedom of others than to restraining one's own freedom. It may, I think, be hoped that with the right education from the start this respect for the personality and freedom of others may become comparatively easy; but for those of us who have been brought up to believe that we have a right to place a veto upon the actions of others in the name of virtue, it is undoubtedly difficult to forego the exercise of this agreeable form of persecution. It may even be impossible. But it is not to be inferred that it would be impossible to those who had been taught from the first a less restrictive morality. The essence of a good marriage is respect for each other's personality combined with that deep intimacy, physical, mental, and spiritual, which makes a serious love between man and woman the most fructifying of all human experiences. Such love, like everything that is great and precious, demands its own morality, and frequently entails a sacrifice of the less to the greater; but such sacrifice must be voluntary, for, where it is not, it will destroy the very basis of the love for the sake of which it is made.

III

Existentialism

What Is Metaphysics?

MARTIN HEIDEGGER

Although metaphysics has been rejected as a field of philosophical inquiry by the logical positivists, its legitimacy has been strongly reaffirmed by the founders of German existential philosophy, notably Martin Heidegger. For Heidegger the problem of being is still, and more than ever, the central problem of philosophy. In this essay, his inaugural lecture in 1929 at the University of Freiburg, he takes up being in its relationship to nothingness. What it means to be, the to-be-ness of the world, cannot be perceived, he writes, until we have first experienced nothingness, through the metaphysical dread that grips the reflective mind when it confronts the threat of nonbeing existentially. In the end, being and nothingness are found to be integral to each other, rather than opposites. Metaphysics itself begins when we ask ourselves what it means to be and not to be; it is therefore the most basic and serious of disciplines, and the most natural to man.

In a civilization constantly menaced with annihilation, such themes as these have taken on new urgency, which helps to explain the broad influence of existentialist thought, not only in academic philosophy, but also in theology, psychology, and imaginative literature. But see also Rudolf Carnap's article, "The Elimination of Metaphysics," in A. J. Ayer, ed., *Logical Positivism* (1959). Carnap holds up Heidegger's essay as a prime example of the meaninglessness of metaphysical argument as cognitive discourse.

"WHAT IS metaphysics?" The question leads one to expect a discussion about metaphysics. Such is not our intention. Instead, we

SOURCE: *Existence and Being*, by Martin Heidegger, trans. R. F. C. Hull and Alan Crick (Regnery, Chicago, 1949), pp. 355–80. Reprinted by permission of the Henry Regnery Company and Vision Press, Ltd.

shall discuss a definite metaphysical question, thus, as it will appear, landing ourselves straight into metaphysics. Only in this way can we make it really possible for metaphysics to speak for itself.

Our project begins with the presentation of a metaphysical question, then goes on to its development and ends with its answer.

The Presentation of a Metaphysical Question

Seen from the point of view of sound common sense, Philosophy, according to Hegel, is the "world stood on its head." Hence the peculiar nature of our task calls for some preliminary definition. This arises out of the dual nature of metaphysical questioning.

Firstly, every metaphysical question always covers the whole range of metaphysical problems. In every case it is itself the whole. Secondly, every metaphysical question can only be put in such a way that the questioner as such is by his very questioning involved in the question.

From this we derive the following pointer: metaphysical questioning has to be put as a whole and has always to be based on the essential situation of existence, which puts the question. We question here and now, on our own account. Our existence—a community of scientists, teachers and students—is ruled by science. What essential things are happening to us in the foundations of our existence, now that science has become our passion?

The fields of the sciences lie far apart. Their methodologies are fundamentally different. This disrupted multiplicity of disciplines is today only held together by the technical organisation of the Universities and their faculties, and maintained as a unit of meaning by the practical aims of those faculties. As against this, however, the root of the sciences in their essential ground has atrophied.

And yet—insofar as we follow their most specific intentions—in all the sciences we are related to what-is. Precisely from the point of view of the sciences no field takes precedence over another, neither Nature over History nor vice versa. No one methodology is superior to another. Mathematical knowledge is no stricter than philological or historical knowledge. It has merely the characteristic of "exactness," which is not to be identified with strictness. To demand exactitude of history would be to offend against the idea of the kind of strictness that pertains to the humanistic sciences. The world-relationship which runs through all the sciences as such constrains them to seek what-is *in itself*, with a view to rendering it, according to its quiddity (*Wasgehalt*) and its modality (*Seinsart*), an object of investigation and basic definition. What the sciences accomplish, ideally speaking, is an approximation to the essential nature of all things.

This distinct world-relationship to what-is in itself is sustained and guided by a freely chosen attitude on the part of our human existence. It is true that the pre-scientific and extra-scientific activities of man also relate to what-is. But the distinction of science lies in the fact that, in an altogether specific manner, it and it alone explicitly allows the object itself the first and last word. In this objectivity of questioning, definition and proof there is a certain limited submission to what-is, so that this may reveal itself. This submissive attitude taken up by scientific theory becomes the basis of a possibility: the possibility of science acquiring a leadership of its own, albeit limited, in the whole field of human existence. The world-relationship of science and the attitude of man responsible for it can, of course, only be fully understood when we see and understand what is going on in the world-relationship so maintained. Man—one entity (*Seiendes*) among others—"pursues" science. In this "pursuit" what is happening is nothing less than the irruption of a particular entity called "Man" into the whole of what-is, in such a way that in and through this irruption what-is manifests itself *as* and *how* it is. The manner in which the revelatory irruption occurs is the chief thing that helps what-is to become what it is.

This triple process of world-relationship, attitude, and irruption —a radical unity—introduces something of the inspiring simplicity and intensity of *Da-sein* [human existence] into scientific existence. If we now explicitly take possession of scientific *Da-sein* as clarified by us, we must necessarily say:

That to which the world-relationship refers is what is—and nothing else.

That by which every attitude is moulded is what-is—and nothing more.

That with which scientific exposition effects its "irruption" is what-is—and beyond that, nothing.

But is it not remarkable that precisely at that point where scientific man makes sure of his surest possession he should speak of something else? What is to be investigated is what-is—and nothing else; only what-is—and nothing more; simply and solely what-is—and beyond that, nothing.

But what about this "nothing"? Is it only an accident that we speak like that quite naturally? Is it only a manner of speaking—and nothing more?

But why worry about this Nothing? "Nothing" is absolutely rejected by science and abandoned as null and void (*das Nichtige*). But if we abandon Nothing in this way are we not, by that act, really admitting it? Can we, though, speak of an admission when we admit Nothing? But perhaps this sort of cross-talk is already degenerating into an empty wrangling about words.

Science, on the other hand, has to assert its soberness and seriousness afresh and declare that it is concerned solely with what-is. Nothing—how can it be for science anything other than a horror and a phantasm? If science is right then one thing stands firm: science wishes to know nothing of Nothing. Such is after all the strictly scientific approach to Nothing. We know it by wishing to know nothing of Nothing.

Science wishes to know nothing of Nothing. Even so the fact remains that at the very point where science tries to put its own essence in words it invokes the aid of Nothing. It has recourse to the very thing it rejects. What sort of schizophrenia is this?

A consideration of our momentary existence as one ruled by science has landed us in the thick of an argument. In the course of this argument a question has already presented itself. The question only requires putting specifically: What about Nothing?

The Development of the Question

The development of our enquiry into Nothing is bound to lead us to a position where either the answer will prove possible or the impossibility of an answer will become evident. "Nothing" is admitted. Science, by adopting an attitude of superior indifference, abandons it as that which "is not."

All the same we shall endeavour to enquire into Nothing. What is Nothing? Even the initial approach to this question shows us something out of the ordinary. So questioning, we postulate Nothing as something that somehow or other "is"—as an entity (*Seiendes*). But it is nothing of the sort. The question as to the what and wherefore of Nothing turns the thing questioned into its opposite. The question deprives itself of its own object.

Accordingly, every answer to this question is impossible from the start. For it necessarily moves in the form that Nothing "is" this, that or the other. Question and answer are equally nonsensical in themselves where Nothing is concerned.

Hence even the rejection by science is superfluous. The commonly cited basic rule of all thinking—the proposition that contradiction must be avoided—and common "logic" rule out the question. For thinking, which is essentially always thinking about something, would, in thinking of Nothing, be forced to act against its own nature.

Because we continually meet with failure as soon as we try to turn Nothing into a subject, our enquiry into Nothing is already at an end—always assuming, of course, that in this enquiry "logic" is the highest court of appeal, that reason is the means and thinking the way to an original comprehension of Nothing and its possible revelation.

But, it may be asked, can the law of "logic" be assailed? Is not reason indeed the master in this enquiry into Nothing? It is in fact only with reason's help that we can define Nothing in the first place and postulate it as a problem—though a problem that consumes only itself. For Nothing is the negation (*Verneinung*) of the totality of what-is: that which is absolutely not. But at this point we bring Nothing into the higher category of the Negative (*Nichthaftes*) and therefore of what is negated. But according to the overriding and unassailable teachings of "logic" negation is a specific act of reason. How, then, in our enquiry into Nothing and into the very possibility of holding such an enquiry can we dismiss reason? Yet is it so sure just what we are postulating? Does the Not (*das Nicht*), the state of being negated (*die Verneintheit*) and hence negation itself (*Verneinung*), in fact represent that higher category under which Nothing takes its place as a special kind of thing negated? Does Nothing "exist" only because the Not, i.e. negation exists? Or is it the other way about? Does negation and the Not exist only because Nothing exists? This has not been decided—indeed, it has not even been explicitly asked. We assert: "Nothing" is more original than the Not and negation.

If this thesis is correct then the very possibility of negation as an act of reason, and consequently reason itself, are somehow dependent on Nothing. How, then, can reason attempt to decide this issue? May not the apparent nonsensicality of the question and answer where Nothing is concerned only rest, perhaps, on the blind obstinacy of the roving intellect?

If, however, we refuse to be led astray by the formal impossibility of an enquiry into Nothing and still continue to enquire in the face of it, we must at least satisfy what remains the fundamental pre-requisite for the full pursuit of any enquiry. If Nothing as such is still to be enquired into, it follows that it must be "given" in advance. We must be able to encounter it.

Where shall we seek Nothing? Where shall we find Nothing? In order to find something must we not know beforehand that it is there? Indeed we must! First and foremost we can only look if we have presupposed the presence of a thing to be looked for. But here the thing we are looking for is Nothing. Is there after all a seeking without pre-supposition, a seeking complemented by a pure finding?

However that may be, we do know "Nothing" if only as a term we bandy about every day. This ordinary hackneyed Nothing, so completely taken for granted and rolling off our tongue so casually —we can even give an off-hand "definition" of it:

Nothing is the complete negation of the totality of what-is.

Does not this characteristic of Nothing point, after all, in the direction from which alone it may meet us?

The totality of what-is must be given beforehand so as to succumb as such to the negation from which Nothing is then bound to emerge.

But, even apart from the questionableness of this relationship between negation and Nothing, how are we, as finite beings, to render the whole of what-is in its totality accessible *in itself*—let alone to ourselves? We can, at a pinch, think of the whole of what-is as an "idea" and then negate what we have thus imagined in our thoughts and "think" it negated. In this way we arrive at the formal concept of an imaginary Nothing, but never Nothing itself. But Nothing is nothing, and between the imaginary and the "authentic" (*eigentlich*) Nothing no difference can obtain, if Nothing represents complete lack of differentiation. But the "authentic" Nothing—is this not once again that latent and nonsensical idea of a Nothing that "is"? Once again and for the last time rational objections have tried to hold up our search, whose legitimacy can only be attested by a searching experience of Nothing.

As certainly as we shall never comprehend absolutely the totality of what-is, it is equally certain that we find ourselves placed in the midst of what-is and that this is somehow revealed in totality. Ultimately there is an essential difference between comprehending the totality of what-is and finding ourselves in the midst of what-is-in-totality. The former is absolutely impossible. The latter is going on in existence all the time.

Naturally enough it looks as if, in our everyday activities, we were always holding on to this or that actuality (*Seiendes*), as if we were lost in this or that region of what-is. However fragmentary the daily round may appear it still maintains what-is, in however shadowy a fashion, within the unity of a "whole." Even when, or rather, precisely when we are not absorbed in things or in our own selves, this "wholeness" comes over us—for example, in real boredom. Real boredom is still far off when this book or that play, this activity or that stretch of idleness merely bores us. Real boredom comes when "one is bored." This profound boredom, drifting hither and thither in the abysses of existence like a mute fog, draws all things, all men and oneself along with them, together in a queer kind of indifference. This boredom reveals what-is in totality.

There is another possibility of such revelation, and this is in the joy we feel in the presence of the being—not merely the person—of someone we love.

Because of these moods in which, as we say, we "are" this or that (i.e. bored, happy, etc.) we find ourselves (*befinden uns*) in the midst of what-is-in-totality, wholly pervaded by it. The affective state in which we find ourselves not only discloses, according to the mood we are in, what-is in totality, but this disclosure is at the same time far from being a mere chance occurrence and is the ground-phenomenon of our *Da-sein*.

Our "feelings," as we call them, are not just the fleeting concomitant of our mental or volitional behaviour, nor are they simply the cause and occasion of such behaviour, nor yet a state that is merely "there" and in which we come to some kind of understanding with ourselves.

Yet, at the very moment when our moods thus bring us face to face with what-is-in-totality they hide the Nothing we are seeking.

We are now less than ever of the opinion that mere negation of
what-is-in-totality as revealed by these moods of ours can in fact
lead us to Nothing. This could only happen in the first place in a
mood so peculiarly revelatory in its import as to reveal Nothing
itself.

Does there ever occur in human existence a mood of this kind,
through which we are brought face to face with Nothing itself?

This may and actually does occur, albeit rather seldom and for
moments only, in the key-mood of dread (*Angst*). By "dread" we
do not mean "anxiety" (*Aengstlichkeit*), which is common enough
and is akin to nervousness (*Furchtsamkeit*)—a mood that comes
over us only too easily. Dread differs absolutely from fear
(*Furcht*). We are always *afraid* of this or that definite thing, which
threatens us in this or that definite way. "Fear of" is generally
"fear about" something. Since fear has this characteristic limitation—"of" and "about"—the man who is afraid, the nervous man,
is always bound by the thing he is afraid of or by the state in which
he finds himself. In his efforts to save himself from this "something" he becomes uncertain in relation to other things; in fact, he
"loses his bearings" generally.

In dread no such confusion can occur. It would be truer to say
that dread is pervaded by a peculiar kind of peace. And although
dread is always "dread of," it is not dread of this or that. "Dread
of" is always a dreadful feeling "about"—but not about this or
that. The indefiniteness of *what* we dread is not just lack of
definition: it represents the essential impossibility of defining the
"what." The indefiniteness is brought out in an illustration familiar
to everybody.

In dread, as we say, "one feels something uncanny." What is this
"something" (*es*) and this "one"? We are unable to say what gives
"one" that uncanny feeling. "One" just feels it generally (*im
Ganzen*). All things, and we with them, sink into a sort of indifference. But not in the sense that everything simply disappears; rather,
in the very act of drawing away from us everything turns towards
us. This withdrawal of what-is-in-totality, which then crowds
round us in dread, this is what oppresses us. There is nothing to
hold on to. The only thing that remains and overwhelms us whilst
what-is slips away, is this "nothing."

Dread reveals Nothing.

In dread we are "in suspense" (*wir schweben*). Or, to put it more precisely, dread holds us in suspense because it makes what-is-in-totality slip away from us. Hence we too, as existents in the midst of what-is, slip away from ourselves along with it. For this reason it is not "you" or "I" that has the uncanny feeling, but "one." In the trepidation of this suspense where there is nothing to hold on to, pure *Da-sein* is all that remains.

Dread strikes us dumb. Because what-is-in-totality slips away and thus forces Nothing to the fore, all affirmation (lit. "Is"-saying: *"Ist"-Sagen*) fails in the face of it. The fact that when we are caught in the uncanniness of dread we often try to break the empty silence by words spoken at random, only proves the presence of Nothing. We ourselves confirm that dread reveals Nothing —when we have got over our dread. In the lucid vision which supervenes while yet the experience is fresh in our memory we must needs say that what we were afraid of was "actually" (*eigentlich:* also "authentic") *Nothing.* And indeed Nothing itself, Nothing as such, was there.

With this key-mood of dread, therefore, we have reached that event in our *Da-sein* which reveals Nothing, and which must therefore be the starting-point of our enquiry.

What about Nothing?

The Answer to the Question

The answer which alone is important for our purpose has already been found if we take care to ensure that we really do keep to the problem of Nothing. This necessitates changing man into his *Da-sein*—a change always occasioned in us by dread—so that we may apprehend Nothing as and how it reveals itself in dread. At the same time we have finally to dismiss those characteristics of Nothing which have not emerged as a result of our enquiry.

"Nothing" is revealed in dread, but not as something that "is." Neither can it be taken as an object. Dread is not an appehension of Nothing. All the same, Nothing is revealed in and through dread, yet not, again, in the sense that Nothing appears as if detached and apart from what-is-in-totality when we have that "uncanny" feeling. We would say rather: in dread Nothing functions as if *at one with* what-is-in-totality. What do we mean by "at one with"?

In dread what-is-in-totality becomes untenable (*hinfällig*).

How? What-is is not annihilated (*vernichtet*) by dread, so as to leave Nothing over. How could it, seeing that dread finds itself completely powerless in face of what-is-in-totality! What rather happens is that Nothing shows itself as essentially belonging to what-is while this is slipping away in totality.

In dread there is no annihilation of the whole of what-is in itself; but equally we cannot negate what-is-in-totality in order to reach Nothing. Apart from the fact that the explicitness of a negative statement is foreign to the nature of dread as such, we would always come too late with any such negation intended to demonstrate Nothing. For Nothing is anterior to it. As we said, Nothing is "at one with" what-is as this slips away in totality.

In dread there is a retreat from something, though it is not so much a flight as a spell-bound (*gebannt*) peace. This "retreat from" has its source in Nothing. The latter does not attract: its nature is to repel. This "repelling from itself" is essentially an "expelling into": a conscious gradual relegation to the vanishing what-is-in-totality (*das entgleitenlassende Verweisen auf das versinkende Seiende im Ganzen*). And this total relegation to the vanishing what-is-in-totality—such being the form in which Nothing crowds round us in dread—is the essence of Nothing: nihilation. Nihilation is neither an annihilation (*Vernichtung*) of what-is, nor does it spring from negation (*Verneinung*). Nihilation cannot be reckoned in terms of annihilation or negation at all. Nothing "nihilates" (*nichtet*) of itself.

Nihilation is not a fortuitous event; but understood as the relegation to the vanishing what-is-in-totality, it reveals the latter in all its till now undisclosed strangeness as the pure "Other"—contrasted with Nothing.

Only in the clear night of dread's Nothingness is what-is as such revealed in all its original overtness (*Offenheit*): that it "is" and is not Nothing. This verbal appendix "and not Nothing" is, however, not an *a posteriori* explanation but an *a priori* which alone makes possible any revelation of what-is. The essence of Nothing as original nihilation lies in this: that it alone brings *Da-sein* face to face with what-is as such.

Only on the basis of the original manifestness of Nothing can our human *Da-sein* advance towards and enter into what-is. But insofar as *Da-sein* naturally relates to what-is, as that which it is not and which itself is, Da-sein *qua Da-sein* always proceeds from Nothing as manifest.

Da-sein means *being projected into* Nothing (*Hineingehalten-heit in das Nichts*).

Projecting into Nothing, *Da-sein* is already beyond what-is-in-totality. This "being beyond" (*Hinaussein*) what-is we call Transcendence. Were *Da-sein* not, in its essential basis, transcendent, that is to say, were it not projected from the start into Nothing, it could never relate to what-is, hence could have no self-relationship.

Without the original manifest character of Nothing there is no self-hood and no freedom.

Here we have the answer to our question about Nothing. Nothing is neither an object nor anything that "is" at all. Nothing occurs neither by itself nor "apart from" what-is, as a sort of adjunct. Nothing is that which makes the revelation of what-is as such possible for our human existence. Nothing not merely provides the conceptual opposite of what-is but is also an original part of essence (*Wesen*). It is in the Being (*Sein*) of what-is that the nihilation of Nothing (*das Nichten des Nichts*) occurs.

But now we must voice a suspicion which has been withheld far too long already. If it is only through "projecting into Nothing" that our *Da-sein* relates to what-is, in other words, has any existence, and if Nothing is only made manifest originally in dread, should we not have to be in a continual suspense of dread in order to exist at all? Have we not, however, ourselves admitted that this original dread is a rare thing? But above all, we all exist and are related to actualities which we ourselves are not and which we ourselves are—without this dread. Is not this dread, therefore, an arbitrary invention and the Nothing attributed to it an exaggeration?

Yet what do we mean when we say that this original dread only occurs in rare moments? Nothing but this: that as far as we are concerned and, indeed, generally speaking, Nothing is always distorted out of its original state. By what? By the fact that in one way or another we completely lose ourselves in what-is. The more we turn to what-is in our dealings the less we allow it to slip away, and the more we turn aside from Nothing. But all the more certainly do we thrust ourselves into the open superficies of existence.

And yet this perpetual if ambiguous aversion from Nothing accords, within certain limits, with the essential meaning of Nothing. It—Nothing in the sense of nihilation—relegates us to what-is. Nothing "nihilates" unceasingly, without our really knowing what is happening—at least, not with our everyday knowledge.

What could provide more telling evidence of the perpetual, far-reaching and yet ever-dissimulated overtness of Nothing in our existence, than negation? This is supposed to belong to the very nature of human thought. But negation cannot by any stretch of imagination produce the Not out of itself as a means of distinguishing and contrasting given things, thrusting this Not between them, as it were. How indeed could negation produce the Not out of itself, seeing that it can only negate when something is there to be negated? But how can a thing that is or ought to be negated be seen as something negative (*nichthaft*) unless all thinking as such is on the look-out for the Not? But the Not can only manifest itself when its source—the nihilation of Nothing and hence Nothing itself—is drawn out of concealment. The Not does not come into being through negation, but negation is based on the Not, which derives from the nihilation of Nothing. Nor is negation only a mode of nihilating behaviour, i.e. behaviour based *a priori* on the nihilation of Nothing.

Herewith we have proved the above thesis in all essentials: Nothing is the source of negation, not the other way about. If this breaks the sovereignty of reason in the field of enquiry into Nothing and Being, then the fate of the rule of "logic" in philosophy is also decided. The very idea of "logic" disintegrates in the vortex of a more original questioning.

However often and however variously negation—whether explicit or not—permeates all thinking, it cannot *of itself* be a completely valid witness to the manifestation of Nothing as an essential part of *Da-sein*. For negation cannot be cited either as the sole or even the chief mode of nihilation, with which, because of the nihilation of Nothing, *Da-sein* is saturated. More abysmal than the mere propriety of rational negation is the harshness of opposition and the violence of loathing. More responsible the pain of refusal and the mercilessness of an interdict. More oppressive the bitterness of renunciation.

These possible modes of nihilating behaviour, through which our *Da-sein* endures, even if it does not master, the fact of our being thrown upon the world are not modes of negation merely. That does not prevent them from expressing themselves in and through negation. Indeed, it is only then that the empty expanse of negation is really revealed. The permeation of *Da-sein* by nihilating modes of behaviour points to the perpetual, ever-dissimulated manifestness of Nothing, which only dread reveals in all its originality. Here, of course, we have the reason why original dread is generally repressed in *Da-sein*. Dread is there, but sleeping. All *Da-sein* quivers with its breathing: the pulsation is slightest in beings that are timorous, and is imperceptible in the "Yea, yea!" and "Nay, nay!" of busy people; it is readiest in the reserved, and surest of all in the courageous. But this last pulsation only occurs for the sake of that for which it expends itself, so as to safeguard the supreme greatness of *Da-sein*.

The dread felt by the courageous cannot be contrasted with the joy or even the comfortable enjoyment of a peaceable life. It stands—on the hither side of all such contrasts—in secret union with the serenity and gentleness of creative longing.

Original dread can be awakened in *Da-sein* at any time. It need not be awakened by any unusual occurrence. Its action corresponds in depth to the shallowness of its possible cause. It is always on the brink, yet only seldom does it take the leap and drag us with it into the state of suspense.

Because our *Da-sein* projects into Nothing on this basis of hidden dread, man becomes the "stand-in" (*Platzhalter*) for Nothing. So finite are we that we cannot, of our own resolution and will, bring ourselves originally face to face with Nothing. So bottomlessly does finalisation (*Verendlichung*) dig into existence that our freedom's peculiar and profoundest finality fails.

This projection into Nothing on the basis of hidden dread is the overcoming of what-is-in-totality: Transcendence.

Our enquiry into Nothing will, we said, lead us straight to metaphysics. The name "metaphysics" derives from the Greek τὰ μετὰ τὰ φυσικά. This quaint title was later interpreted as characterising the sort of enquiry which goes μετά—trans, beyond—what-is as such.

Metaphysics is an enquiry over and above what-is, with a view to winning it back again as such and in totality for our understanding.

In our quest for Nothing there is similar "going beyond" what-is, conceived as what-is-in-totality. It therefore turns out to be a "metaphysical" question. We said in the beginning that such questioning had a double characteristic: every metaphysical question at once embraces the whole of metaphysics, and in every question the being (*Da-sein*) that questions is himself caught up in the question.

To what extent does the question about Nothing span and pervade the whole of metaphysics?

Since ancient times metaphysics has expressed itself on the subject of Nothing in the highly ambiguous proposition: *ex nihilo nihil fit*—nothing comes from nothing. Even though the proposition as argued never made Nothing itself the real problem, it nevertheless brought out very explicitly, from the prevailing notions about Nothing, the over-riding fundamental concept of what-is.

Classical metaphysics conceives Nothing as signifying Not-being (*Nichtseiendes*), that is to say, unformed matter which is powerless to form itself into "being" and cannot therefore present an appearance (εἶδος). What has "being" is the self-creating product (*Gebilde*) which presents itself as such in an image (*Bild*), i.e. something seen (*Anblick*). The origin, law and limits of this ontological concept are discussed as little as Nothing itself.

Christian dogma, on the other hand, denies the truth of the proposition *ex nihilo nihil fit* and gives a twist to the meaning of Nothing, so that it now comes to mean the absolute absence of all "being" outside God: *ex nihilo fit—ens creatum:* The created being is made out of nothing. "Nothing" is now the conceptual opposite of what truly and authentically (*eigentlich*) "is"; it becomes the *summum ens*, God as *ens increatum*. Here, too, the interpretation of Nothing points to the fundamental concept of what-is. Metaphysical discussion of what-is, however, moves on the same plane as the enquiry into Nothing. In both cases the questions concerning Being (*Sein*) and Nothing as such remain unasked. Hence we need not be worried by the difficulty that if God creates "out of nothing" he above all must be able to relate himself to Nothing. But if God is God he cannot know Nothing, assuming that the "Absolute" excludes from itself all nullity (*Nichtigkeit*).

This crude historical reminder shows Nothing as the conceptual opposite of what truly and authentically "is," i.e. as the negation of it. But once Nothing is somehow made a problem this contrast not only undergoes clearer definition but also arouses the true and authentic metaphysical question regarding the Being of what-is. Nothing ceases to be the vague opposite of what-is: it now reveals itself as integral to the Being of what-is.

"Pure Being and pure Nothing are thus one and the same." This proposition of Hegel's ("The Science of Logic," I, WW III, p. 74) is correct. Being and Nothing hang together, but not because the two things—from the point of view of the Hegelian concept of thought—are one in their indefiniteness and immediateness, but because Being itself is finite in essence and is only revealed in the Transcendence of *Da-sein* as projected into Nothing.

If indeed the question of Being as such is the all-embracing question of metaphysics, then the question of Nothing proves to be such as to span the whole metaphysical field. But at the same time the question of Nothing pervades the whole of metaphysics only because it forces us to face the problem of the origin of negation, that is to say, forces a decision about the legitimacy of the rule of "logic" in metaphysics.

The old proposition *ex nihilo nihil fit* will then acquire a different meaning, and one appropriate to the problem of Being itself, so as to run: *ex nihilo omne ens qua ens fit*: every being, so far as it is a being, is made out of nothing. Only in the Nothingness of *Da-sein* can what-is-in-totality—and this in accordance with its peculiar possibilities, i.e. in a finite manner—come to itself. To what extent, then, has the enquiry into Nothing, if indeed it be a metaphysical one, included our own questing *Da-sein*?

Our *Da-sein*, as experienced here and now is, we said, ruled by science. If our *Da-sein*, so ruled, is put into this question concerning Nothing, then it follows that it must itself have been put in question by this question.

The simplicity and intensity of scientific *Da-sein* consist in this: that it relates in a special manner to what-is and to this alone. Science would like to abandon Nothing with a superior gesture. But now, in this question of Nothing, it becomes evident that scientific *Da-sein* is only possible when projected into Nothing at the outset. Science can only come to terms with itself when it does not abandon Nothing. The alleged soberness and superiority of science becomes ridiculous if it fails to take Nothing seriously. Only because Nothing is obvious can science turn what-is into an object of investigation. Only when science proceeds from metaphysics can it conquer its essential task ever afresh, which consists not in the accumulation and classification of knowledge but in the perpetual discovery of the whole realm of truth, whether of Nature or of History.

Only because Nothing is revealed in the very basis of our *Da-sein* is it possible for the utter strangeness of what-is to dawn on us. Only when the strangeness of what-is forces itself upon us does it awaken and invite our wonder. Only because of wonder, that is to say, the revelation of Nothing, does the "Why?" spring to our lips. Only because this "Why?" is possible as such can we seek for reasons and proofs in a definite way. Only because we can ask and prove are we fated to become enquirers in this life.

The enquiry into Nothing puts us, the enquirers, ourselves in question. It is a metaphysical one.

Man's *Da-sein* can only relate to what-is by projecting into Nothing. Going beyond what-is is of the essence of *Da-sein*. But this "going beyond" is metaphysics itself. That is why metaphysics belongs to the nature of man. It is neither a department of scholastic philosophy nor a field of chance ideas. Metaphysics is the ground-phenomenon of *Da-sein*. It is *Da-sein* itself. Because the truth of metaphysics is so unfathomable there is always the lurking danger of profoundest error. Hence no scientific discipline can hope to equal the seriousness of metaphysics. Philosophy can never be measured with the yard-stick of the idea of science.

Once the question we have developed as to the nature of Nothing is really asked by and among our own selves, then we are not bringing in metaphysics from the outside. Nor are we simply "transporting" ourselves into it. It is completely out of our power to transport ourselves into metaphysics because, in so far as we exist, we are already there. Φύσει γὰρ ὦ φίλει, ἔνεστί τις φιλοσοφία τῇ τοῦ ἀνδρὸς διανοίᾳ (Plato: Phaedrus 279a). While man exists there will be philosophising of some sort. Philosophy, as we call it, is the setting in motion of metaphysics; and in metaphysics philosophy comes to itself and sets about its explicit tasks. Philosophy is only set in motion by leaping with all its being, as only it can, into the ground-possibilities of being as a whole. For this leap the following things are of crucial importance: firstly, leaving room for what-is-in-totality; secondly, letting oneself go into Nothing, that is to say, freeing oneself from the idols we all have and to which we are wont to go cringing; lastly, letting this "suspense" range where it will, so that it may continually swing back again to the ground-question of metaphysics, which is wrested from Nothing itself:

Why is there any Being at all—why not far rather Nothing?

Existential Ethics

KARL JASPERS

Although less highly regarded by professional philosophers than Heidegger, Karl Jaspers is a major force in the existentialist movement, not only for his contributions to existentialist metaphysics, theory of knowledge, and ethics, but also for his analyses of modern civilization and his writings on history, religion, and the history of philosophy. Born six years before Heidegger, in 1883, Jaspers came to philosophy relatively late in life, after a promising beginning as a psychiatrist and student of psychological theory. He has taught at the universities of Heidelberg and Basel.

The difference between Heidegger and Jaspers as thinkers is easily seen. Heidegger is fundamentally a mystic, self-absorbed and withdrawn; Jaspers is the man of the world, liberal, humanistic, cosmopolitan, an existentialist Voltaire who lays great stress on the importance of communication and writes with an obvious concern to be understood. Not surprisingly, the Nazi regime deprived Jaspers of his chair at Heidelberg in 1938, whereas Heidegger stayed on at Freiburg all through the Hitler period and was dismissed for alleged pro-Nazi sympathies in 1945. In the postwar era, from his headquarters in Basel, Jaspers has plunged into many controversies—such as the well-documented debate with Bultmann on demythologization—whereas Heidegger has maintained himself in inscrutable retirement in his village in the Schwarzwald.

The essay below was written as a contribution to a symposium on ethics, but it also contains a brief summary of Jaspers's general philosophical position.

THE QUESTION posed in this chapter is whether ethics is derivable from nature or whether it has some other origin. In either case there exists the further question: What is our ethical relation to nature; what could it be; and what should it be?

SOURCE: "Nature and Ethics," by Karl Jaspers, trans. Eugene T. Gadol, in *Moral Principles of Action*, ed. Ruth Nanda Anshen (Harper & Row, New York, 1952), pp. 48–61. Reprinted by permission of Harper & Row, Publishers. Copyright 1952 by Harper & Row, Publishers.

I. What Is the Meaning of Nature?

We speak about nature in various senses.

Nature passes for the *encompassing Being*, which is all, and from which all is (Spinoza: *Deus sive Natura*); it is the total life to which we ourselves belong completely; or nature is assumed to be the *Given*, the Other, as contrasted to ourselves; it is the unconscious, that which is merely occurring without freedom, without choice.

Ethics has consequently a radically different origin if it derives its meaning from nature to which we ourselves belong, or if it derives its meaning from the Self which we juxtapose to nature.

The sense in which we speak of nature has yet another polarity. Nature is taken to be the *actual occurrence* as it streams forth in its fullness through time, or nature passes for the *Eternal Being* or *Gestalten* (the forms of the inanimate, the animate, and of man) and of the timeless laws of temporal events.

Ethics, therefore, is inclined to comprehend itself as emerging from the stream of Becoming and to see Truth, ever-changing, only in historically concrete particularity; or ethics comprehends itself in terms of the universal and permanent character of a Being or of a Law.

Such polarities, seemingly in radical conflict with one another, nevertheless do not exclude each other; but this is so only if in each case both sides are limited to their respective meanings and do not become absolutized.

Clarity in ethical thought would be reached if we knew, in the daily situations of our lives, what is given as nature and what we may accomplish by virtue of our own freedom; but only on condition that in each case we would bring both elements to a decisive unity in our practice; in other words, that we would realize the two original sources from which in fact we draw our lives as separate influences, even as we unite them in the building-up of every determinate being that is human.

Then we are dealing with that part of nature which is ourselves, the nature of man, and with that part which is the *Other*, i.e., nature which surrounds us as the world. Toward both and in relation to both we realize and actualize ourselves.

II. The Nature of Man

The nature of man may be understood in a three-fold sense:

Human nature as the *empirical existence* of man which becomes the subject of scientific inquiry, and which reveals itself in the findings of anthropology, psychology, and sociology;

Human nature as the *essence* of Man, as the innate, the eternal, which may indeed become buried in Time, but which at any moment can be set free; i.e., man as the image of God;

Human nature as man's *limitless possibility;* he not only is, he not only becomes, he may yet create himself; there is no eternal essence of being, but only an infinity of possibilities.

On each of these three approaches we gain a peculiar kind of self-consciousness, a consciousness through which we experience insights as to how we may cope with ourselves.

1. We know ourselves as the *empirical existence of a psycho-physical life* together with the rules of its development. For example, we experience bodily fatigue, its causes, its course; we experience recuperation, or memory, or our ability to memorize; we experience reproduction and its conditions. We know of individually varying natural predispositions, e.g., color-blindness and other specific characteristics. We know of many psycho-physical processes and anomalies. Inasmuch as we use such knowledge as means we may, by taking the appropriate measures, increase our working capacity; we may clear the ground in the light of our talents for correct judgments concerning what profession to choose; we may in short gain the means for the correction of all sorts of defects. In all such cases we are dealing with ourselves as tools, never with our Selves. Insofar as it is real, critically limited, and purified, all such knowledge is useful.

What is of essentially ethical import is that we learn to distinguish first of all what we are as psychological instruments and what we can be purely for our Selves; and secondly that we learn, by means of a critique of that knowledge which is obtained through scientific channels, not to take our real Selves for our instrumental selves, and consequently not to surrender our Selves to illusory knowledge. Thus modern tests are immensely useful whenever indispensable matters of fact are to be determined, as, for example,

color-blindness, which disqualifies one from ever becoming a locomotive engineer. Yet it is equally clear that overestimation of the
value of such tests may lead to erroneous judgments concerning
men, judgments that may severely and detrimentally curtail the
possibilities some individuals might actualize. Even in the domain of
technical efficiency, it is on the whole not possible to form absolutely certain judgments based upon tests. An aviator who, on the
strength of examination results, was rejected as unfit but who
stubbornly persisted, finally succeeded in his efforts and proved
through his extraordinary exertions the radical error of the original
test procedure. If it is true that such uncertainty reigns in the
domain of purely practical capabilities, and an advantageous selection can as a rule be made only statistically, discounting many
errors in individual cases, how much more does this hold for all
that men will do and create in the realm of the mind and spirit.
Here life is verified only in its total process—through the test of
situations—a verification predictable by no one. The worst of
students become ingenious scientists and inventors, useless and
eccentric men turn into irreplaceable poets and sages.

When we are employing psychological science, it is a demand of
ethics to look steadily for the boundaries which divide real knowledge from illusory knowledge, the certain from the possible, the
probable from the improbable. At the same time, it is ethically
imperative not to circumvent this body of real knowledge, if there
exists some purpose for which it may become useful.

A knowledge of man, obtainable through science, especially that
part of psychological knowledge which leads to a knowing of
myself as a psychological instrument, possesses something ethically
liberating. I become lord over that within me which, although I
accept it as inescapably belonging to me, is nevertheless not my
own Self.

An axiom underlying all science is: Man is infinitely and essentially more than he can ever know himself to be.

2. The nature of man is thought to be the *essence of man*. It is
not an object of science but of illumination. It is conceived in terms
of symbols. It becomes lucid in moral demands such as the Ten
Commandments. It entails the unconditional claim of the inviola-
bility of man's dignity, every man's, qua man. It was Kant who said
that no man shall be used as if he were only a means. Brought to

consciousness, the knowledge of the eternal nature of man gives rise to the concept of "crimes against humanity."

Here, in its traffic with the nature of man as eternal essence, ethos becomes the self-subjugation of man's existence to the universally valid. The point in question here is that upon which all men can agree, if it is brought to full consciousness. The self-examination as to whether or not my act is moral rests, according to Kant's formulation, upon the question: Can you will that there be a world in which every man does what you yourself are now doing, i.e., that the principle of your action be a universal law of this world? Or, to put it differently: Accept the responsibility as if, through the manner of your acts, you were co-creator of the world!

The limitation of this ethics lies in the fact that not all actions of man can be grasped as true by means of subsuming them under a universal principle. Exceptions may always arise from every unique historical situation. But such an exception can never justify itself by a universal principle, for in that case it would not be an exception, and it must submit itself to the universal principle which it violates according to its own conscience.

This is the reason for the insufficiency of every ethos, for the unrest which remains. In the face of the exception, this unrest permits neither the existence of a clear conscience obeying the universally valid principle, the moral law springing from the essence of man, nor—in the face of the universally valid principle—a clear conscience and consciousness of the exception as the true origin of the ethos. The ethical path of man is not toward the absolute, the perfected in itself, but rather lies in need of completion. Only the vault above, symbolizing the transcendence of God, gives him purpose and strength.

3. The nature of man is conceived *as that which is in no sense determined*. His nature is neither finally valid as an object of science nor perfected as an eternal essence in the Idea. Moreover, man's nature is not as yet, but still remains to be, completed in such a way that the task of completion is itself as yet undetermined, and in many ways presents a domain of limitless possibilities. Mankind's nature consists in aspiration and daring to choose and to enter paths none of which is the only prescribed or valid one. Man can fall or rise, but not in a uniquely determined manner. It is as though man

were yet to become, to actualize himself, out of mere possibility, out of that which is still non-being. He is, as Nietzsche said, the "indeterminate animal." Pico della Mirandola had pronounced it as early as the fifteenth century: "God created man without bestowing upon him anything special (as He did upon all animals); in His own all-uniting image, He put him in the middle of the world. . . . 'You alone are limited nowhere, you can take or choose to be whatever you decide to be according to your own will. Not heavenly, not earthly, not mortal, not immortal, did I create you. For you yourself shall be your own master and builder and creator according to your own will and for your own honor. So you are free to sink to the lowest level of the animal kingdom. But you may also soar into the highest spheres of divinity. . . .' Beasts possess from the time of birth all that they will ever possess. Only in man at his birth, has God poured forth the semen of all deeds and sown the seeds for all ways of life."

The boundlessness of this daring and aspiration consists in the fact that it does not come from "nothingness." The freedom of the possible is fulfilled due to the origins of its own willing, origins which are not analogous to anything in the world.

That which is attained through these origins is further bound to the empirically given, natural existence, and to the universally valid principle that springs from the essence of man.

In no way can one speak of man's self-creation out of nothing, but one may indeed raise the question of his freedom within the limits of the encompassing world, a freedom which seems to call out to man: It lies with you what will become of you—you not only are what you are now, but you become during the period of your existence whatever you decide through your daily deeds.

III. Nature as World

We find ourselves in the midst of an environment whose nature determines our nature and which we reciprocally bring to full appearance and expression.

Nature, once she confronts us, has a two-fold character: She is material to be used, to be consumed, and to be made; she is the object of our rule. But she is also self-sufficient essence out of the depth of being.

Accordingly she is either a task for the idea of mechanization, for the gratification of our needs; or she presents to us the task of transforming her into a language for us, to which we, surrendering ourselves, are listening.

In the first case, the goal is a transformation of the earth into a world-factory, permitting our existence to be swallowed up in the functioning of this factory through which we remain alive. In the second case, the goal is to grasp the surrounding world in the infinite manifold of its possible *Gestalten*, its totality, to envisage the earth and to let it flourish in the fullness of its engaging cultural scenes borne out by history.

The first road leads to the destruction of the landscape's soul, it leads to its transformation into a field of uncontrollable catastrophes of drought and floods, and in the end it leads to the transformation of the earth into some kind of wasteland, be it either that of lifelessness or of monotony. Finally, the first road leads to the possible destruction of the earth, due to the consequence of what one day may still become possible by means of the atomic bomb.

The second approach leads to the idea of forming the earth into the perfect environment, the House of Man, in which infinite nature is preserved and in which nature also becomes the lucid and intelligible language for man. The earth thus becomes a constantly changing entity—but nevertheless proves itself in and through its historical continuity. It becomes an entity that no one can fully survey and plan, and that is not impoverished, but rather enriched by man.

Examples of the phenomena revealed through either approach are, on the one hand, the dump-yards of industrial areas, the slum sections of big cities, the modern battlefields. On the other hand, there is Chinese landscaping, which arose in rationalized forms because of a sense for the historically-determined and beautiful environment, adapted to the natural scene; there are also the European landscapes as an expression of European culture.

In relation to nature there exists therefore a two-fold ethos. If nature becomes nothing but material for exploitation, the will is thrown exclusively in the direction of the quantitative: always more human beings; always more foodstuffs, more houses, more clothing; the mere size determines man's loveless conduct in his intoxicating conquest of nature. The impoverishment of man's soul is the result of his lust for quantity.

If, however, the claims of nature remain audible, then he feels that in violating nature man violates himself, that in destroying her he finally destroys himself.

The wayfarer who with his stick beheads flowers along the edge of the road displays his alienation from and his disloyalty to nature. The farmer who with his scythe transforms the growth into fodder for his animals acts close to and in conformity with nature.

Love for nature sees everything in its individual "Gestalt"—its organic totality—this tree, that landscape. Love, so to say, achieves a dialogue with the genus of places; it permits everything that is formed to actualize itself, and at the same time to become a member of the human environment.

This love knows the sorrows of nature's necessity; not merely the sorrows of the farmer but also those of all creation, which as it produces, also destroys, and which while letting the garden landscape grow, must constantly prune and trim it. This love must do without some beloved individual trees, it must mourn the loss of freedom and wilderness, must witness the death of animals and plants. Love for all organic matter will try to avoid the total extinction or destruction of natural forms, of certain animal species, because the forms life has created never return once the genus has been destroyed. However much man can do—he can not recreate animal species once it has been lost! Where the loss has occurred, he can only see with amazement mummies, skeletons, and reproductions stored in his museums for a short time.

Ethos, in its interaction with external nature, is capable of an as yet unimagined deepening, even after the first steps toward a meaningful forming of the earth by older cultures have been almost forgotten. Today new and powerful possibilities come into being with dangers equally as great as the opportunities which they harbor. Initial trials and great enterprises are already searching for ways of salvation.

IV. Outer and Inner Action

Our ethos realizes itself in the interaction with nature within us and outside of us. We live in a schism, because we oppose ourselves to nature. We live in the becoming-one-with, or the regaining of, the origin, when we bind nature and self-being into one out of the all-embracing oneness. This we can do, however, only by way of the schism, because the approach we must take is that of consciousness and will, i.e., of clarity and becoming clear ad infinitum; it is not solely the road of an unconscious doing and becoming, which may indeed remain an area not to be planned and which we do in fact accept, but which is nonetheless not our being qua being human itself.

Ethics demands: What ought we to do? This question already lies within the schism. For it treats the problem as standing juxtaposed to us. We wish to hear how a craftsman, how a technician, how a cook performs his work; in short, how anything ought to be done. An answer to this question is possible in many domains. We possess an abundance of knowledge and prescriptions telling us what needs to be done if certain ends are to be reached.

But such ends must themselves already be determined and finally must be something opposed to us; and the further and decisive question, namely, which end we ought to seek, still remains. All thought and communication concerning what we ought to do abides in the antechamber of the ethos. For nowhere does objective thinking meet with an ultimate and unconditioned principle.

It is therefore easily possible to doubt every pronounced and determined "ought," for an "ought" is determined by ends, and ends are not unconditionally established. It is possible to investigate historically all that has been demanded by men, what claims, commandments, and taboos have appeared, what diverse answers have been given to the question: What ought we to do? What answers have, in fact, been accepted, what rejected? Moreover, one can continue to construct future possibilities.

Therefore, it is decisive for our ethical consciousness to emerge from the antechamber and enter the temple itself. This, however, is not possible through customary, objective thinking alone. That is why here, concurrent with the essential, the real difficulty of the intellect begins. Here there are no longer prescriptions and programs, but there is only a becoming aware of something which is and remains intangible as Object. It may appear that nothing is asserted just where the essential is touched upon. Let us try to fix our attention on what really constitutes the crux of the matter.

Our action is of a two-fold kind. We stand opposed to something other than ourselves, which we manipulate and out of which we make something according to plan and purpose; or we ourselves are the object of our actions. Through doing, something happens *in* us, something that is not confronting us, something moreover that only happens because we ourselves are in it, identically with ourselves.

Whether I affect objects outside of me through actions, or whether I affect my body and my consciousness through such actions—viz., be it technical action in the world or be it psycho-therapeutic in reference to my soul—in both actions there is the common element, namely, that I myself remain unaffected, in contradistinction to the objects affected. The outer action is essentially different from the inner action. The inner act takes place not through will tending toward an object, but through conscience tending toward myself, within myself.

The external act coerces its object through work, the inner act is presented with its object, i.e., the decision, through the seriousness of its intent. Opposed to the Doing stands the Letting-mature; opposed to the Continuity of producing there is the Suddenness of Revelation. Ruling over something other than myself is distinguished from the being-present to myself. In external acts I remain at a distance and hold myself in untouchable reserve, internally I spend myself without reserve as mere Existence. Externally I may enter danger, perhaps to the extent of risking my own physical life; internally I risk my Self *in toto*, utterly and entirely.

In external acts, in those extending only to natural objects, directed at what is to be mastered, we descend to the level of despair because at the end of our aimless fury, during which we hold ourselves in constant reserve as a presumably lasting Self, there remains a Self to which the Other is always opposed, never united. The Self, that never surrenders, causes a radical concealment of its own Self, in spite of all the clarity it may have achieved concerning matters of fact.

We oppose ourselves to nature in our external acts because of the impulse of our will to dominate; a will which desires to dispose of nature according to its own ends. The internal act is already present as a momentum when our dedicated contemplation becomes our driving force; because of this contemplation we enlarge our Selves through the re-cognition of our essence in nature. Only in so far as we possess in our consciousness a vision of fulfillment of being does it become clear to us what we are and what we may become.

External actions are distinguished and comprehended as right and wrong, good and evil. The inner act cannot be grasped and remains incomprehensible. To an ethics of the will, which formulates norms and laws, commandments and taboos, there corresponds an ethics of existence, which illuminates, but does not point the way.

The meaning of an inner act may be shown by an example Kierkegaard cites in one of his aphorisms: "Woman becomes more beautiful as time goes by." This means: In youth beauty is vital and radiant, then changes rapidly, keeping its greatest magic for only a brief transitory period, may still be prolonged for a few decades with the help of hygienic and artificial means, but finally perishes. It is an event of life common to man and beast. But underneath it lies a spiritual essence which out of its depths radiates great beauty; a spiritual essence which is not by itself already present in nature, but which can be there only because of the original primordial possession in each individual of that potential being qua being. This essence is internally active in the daily modes of experience, the modes of answering, of accepting, and of rejecting; it is active in life's crises whenever decisions of vital importance arise. Vital beauty itself is incorporated into the way of life. Woman does not subjugate herself to beauty; rather she takes beauty in her stride while she is building her life with others—fully cognizant of beauty's frailty and corruption—in order to make beauty a vessel of profoundest bliss, a symbol of immutable truth. Thus the change of woman's beauty is such that in the waning of her mere vitality there follows ever so much clearer the radiance of her essence, shining through her eyes and finding expression in a face grown old and wrinkled. An aged actress can play Juliet—as Kierkegaard shows—as she never was able to do in her youth, because her essence now knows human depths, as they are only known in the inner acts, in renunciation and creation, in loyalty and continuity.

That is why man's age is the result of a lifetime of ethos. The vital passage of life's phases, in their ascent and decline, is only vaulted by a process of existence itself; an existence which is capable of growing independently, even during very old age, because of the inner life's seriousness, which finds its expression even in an external appearance. Man comes from an origin which accepts his vital existence—bound as he is to it in the succession of life's phases, in sickness and death—to be formed and to be animated, and which is allowed to become the organ of his essential appearance. But this takes place not of necessity as does the natural event of growing old; rather it is a possibility of man's freedom, which may also fail.

V. Science of Nature

Nature is known through the natural sciences. Our relation to nature is determined by our knowledge of her. Knowledge is possible within limits only and remains capable of improvement ad infinitum. Man, however, must act—and sometimes immediately; he cannot wait until all that can be known is known in fact. His actions themselves become the source of new experience and consequently of new knowledge; they are like experiments whose failure is as instructive as their success.

Man is only at the beginning in the natural sciences. Even in the face of tremendous accomplishments there prevails in great scientists the fundamental attitude, formulated by Newton: "I feel like a child who has found some shells on the shore of the sea."

We would commit a serious error if we were to transcend the limitations and believe that on the basis of natural knowledge all acts are sufficiently justified through planning, and that we are now in a position to accomplish everything. Correct action on the whole is not to be calculated by means of formulas, neither in dealing with nature external to us, nor within the human being. All planned action is in need of limitation by means of a critique of our knowledge and abilities, if absurd disaster is to be avoided. Planning has for its limits—so to say—the planning of not-planning. The origin of seriousness in every man is not replaceable by rules and regulations, nor by calculations, although for particular ends everywhere the use of rules and regulations is not only meaningful but indispensable.

What is the cause of a planning that desires to transcend the limitation imposed by itself, of a wanting that desires to accomplish all, even the making of man himself, of the new creative man? The reason is solely this: Man wants to escape from his freedom. He chooses under cover of this flight—a flight which is capable of masking itself under the guise of the wildest desires—such rationally pronounceable views as justify and at the same time camouflage his escape.

In this category also belongs the alleged all-inclusive knowledge of nature to which Man surrenders himself in so far as he brings it out into the open. A superstitious belief in science seduces him to forget himself and to expect salvation from the sciences and pseudo-sciences. For example: instead of expecting scientifically well-founded help only in those cases of disease where such help is possible and relevant, he wants to be treated in every case, even where such help is scientifically unjustified. In addition to the great and genuine cures discovered by modern science, man is in need of an endless chain of fake treatments, which are the combined product of the patient's fear and the fancy of an unbridled enter-prising medical spirit. Instead of earnestly becoming himself, this man, in flight from freedom, permits psychoanalytic diggings and probings into his unconscious foundations. In the end he believes he can have his uncomfortable "complexes" extracted in a manner not unlike the extraction of his bad teeth. Instead of participating daily in the ethos of his community through reason, the setting of a good example, and the displaying of a responsible personality, he expects all solutions to be brought about through institutions and through his own obedience; but even then only with the secret proviso that he does not deny himself any possible advantage obtained by means of trickery.

Clarity about the nature of natural knowledge which is to be used, a critique of the limitations of natural knowledge, a maturing into a genuinely scientific attitude, to promote all this is a funda-mental characteristic of our ethos and becomes a condition for the realization of the ethical conscience.

VI. The Road Between Two Abysses: The Surrender into Unconscious Nature and the Making of Everything Through Will

Outer and inner actions are indeed inseparable. Possessing an exist-ence which is to be objectively investigated by means of laws, we are more than nature, and nature outside of us is not exhausted in such scientific objectifications. We do not reach the meaning of our humanity, of our being human, if we remain only nature. Man is an artificial being; he is, as far as his physical nature is concerned, not without history and tradition. He is what he is, in no way by virtue of heredity, as are the beasts. Being human begins with the violent subjugation of nature in and outside himself. Man establishes taboos which he conceives as posited by a higher power; he becomes enmeshed in distortions of his appearance because of his suppressions and dishonesties. But it is of small avail to him to desire simply to become pure nature. Even this drive to become natural is a resolution not natural by itself, and he has to learn that there is no such thing as a natural state of man, closed in itself and clear, given through his essence.

Man goes his way between two abysses: the one consists in the allegedly simple, natural state of his being-thus-and-so; and the other in his alleged power to accomplish anything, i.e., he goes between what he is and what he wishes to be; between being lost in nature and being lost in the corruption of nature.

On the one side he slips into the stream of mere natural events, abandoning himself as a being unto himself; he is, in the end, indifferent toward life and death and in the steady becoming of the other self he is arrested by the momentary Now and by an empty infinitude of nature. On the other hand he slips into the convulsions of desire, into the vainglorious belief that he can plan and do everything; he is now arrested by the will and believes that he gains his fortunes through manipulations from without, that he becomes master of himself and of the world through mere morality; but will alone leads him to endless self-deceptions and inevitably to his destruction.

In the first case man wastes away—instead of spending his existence in the light of the transcendent Truth, in an effort to achieve Self-being. In the first case he excludes himself from his origin by the fact that he includes himself in mere reason, a reason which attempts to master everything and in this attempt permits his unwitting descent into a realm where all his passions under the guise of reason are directed in fact against reason; where all evil spirits thrive and Hell is brewing. Man thus wastes away, instead of erecting the substructure of his possibilities in terms of ends which at last have been determined reasonably and meaningfully under the guidance of the Idea of his relation to nature, and of Self-being.

The attitude of man toward nature, as it manifests itself in him and in the environment, forms the foundation of what he becomes. No coercion can prove helpful in man's helplessness as he oscillates back and forth from mere nature to purposive doing and in reverse again from doing to allegedly pure nature. Nor can concealing be of any help. Desperation must drive him on and on; desperation which teaches him to acknowledge that for him there is neither pure nature nor pure doing.

Desperation can call him to deeper reason. Man cannot find in himself alone the road to becoming a Self through freedom. Here we come upon a limit which, binding us to our theme, we cannot cross. Another mode of thought becomes necessary when the question is raised of man's becoming free only in the light of transcendent Truth, which he possesses in his freedom. In other words, there can be no ethos, no ethics, without God.

Freedom and Nothingness

JEAN-PAUL SARTRE

Both Heidegger and Jaspers are ontologists, students of the science of being, who locate human existence in a universe that itself possesses existence, out of which man exists. He suffers from anxiety and alienation, but he is nonetheless in and of Being. The more recent French school of existentialism, headed by Jean-Paul Sartre, takes the opposite view, that man is alone in an alien cosmos, from which he is shut off by an incomprehensible fate. To allow oneself to fall unresistingly into the power of that outer world is to cease to be human. The passage that follows is taken from Sartre's novel *The Reprieve*, published in 1945. All the action in the novel takes place in Paris during the week of the Sudetenland crisis in September, 1938. Sartre's spokesman, the young philosophy professor Mathieu Delarue, reflects on freedom, suicide, and the opacity of the universe while crossing the Pont-Neuf.

OUTSIDE. Everything is outside: the trees on the quay, the two houses by the bridge that lend a pink flush to the darkness, the petrified gallop of Henri IV above my head—solid objects, all of them. Inside, nothing, not even a puff of smoke, there is no *inside*, there is nothing. Myself: nothing. I am free, he said to himself, and his mouth was dry.

Halfway across the Pont-Neuf he stopped and began to laugh:

SOURCE: *The Reprieve*, by Jean-Paul Sartre, trans. Eric Sutton (Knopf, New York, 1947), pp. 362–65. Reprinted by permission of Alfred A. Knopf, Inc., and Hamish Hamilton, Ltd. Copyright 1947 by Eric Sutton.

liberty—I sought it far away; it was so near that I couldn't touch it, that I can't touch it; it is, in fact, myself. I am my own freedom. He had hoped that one day he would be filled with joy, transfixed by a lightning-flash. But there was neither lightning-flash nor joy: only a sense of desolation, a void blurred by its own aspect, an anguish so transparent as to be utterly unseeable. He reached out his hands and slid them slowly over the stone parapet, it was wrinkled and furrowed, like a petrified sponge, and still warm from the afternoon sun. There it lay, vast and massive, enclosing in itself the crushed silence, the compressed shadows that are the inside of objects. There it lay: a plenitude. He longed to clutch to that stone and melt into it, to fill himself with its opaqueness and repose. But it could not help him: it was outside, and forever. There lay his hands on the white parapet: bronze hands, they seemed, as he looked at them. But just because he could look at them, they were no longer his, they were the hands of another, they were outside, like the trees, like the reflections shimmering in the Seine—severed hands. He closed his eyes and they became his own again: there was nothing in contact with the stone save a faintly acid and familiar flavor, a whiff of formic acid. My hands: the inappreciable distance that reveals things to me and sets me apart from them forever. I am nothing; I possess nothing. As inseparable from the world as light, and yet exiled, gliding like light over the surface of stones and water, but nothing can ever grasp me or absorb me. Outside the world, outside the past, outside myself: freedom is exile, and I am condemned to be free.

He walked on a few steps, stopped again, sat down on the parapet, and watched the water flowing past. What shall I do with all this freedom? What shall I do with myself? His future lay marked out by definite tasks: the railway station, the Nancy train, the barracks, and the manual of arms. Nothing was any longer his: war seamed the earth, but it was not *his* war. He was alone on this bridge, alone in the world, accountable to no man. "I am free *for nothing*," he reflected wearily. Not a sign in the sky, nor on the earth, the things of this world were too utterly immersed in the war that was theirs, they turned their manifold heads towards the east. Mathieu was moving swiftly over the surface of things un- conscious of his presence. He was forgotten: by the bridge that indifferently held him up, by the roads that sped towards the frontier, by that city which rose slowly upwards to look at that

fire on the horizon which did not concern him. Forgotten, unknown, and utterly alone: a defaulter; all mobilized men had gone
two days ago, he had now no business to be here. Shall I take the
train? What did it matter?—go, or stay, or run away—acts of that
kind would not call his freedom into play. And yet he must risk that
freedom. He clutched the stone with both hands and leaned over
the water. A plunge, and the water would engulf him, his freedom
would be transmuted into water. Rest at last—and why not? This
obscure suicide would *also* be an absolute, a law, a choice, and a
morality, all of them complete. A unique, unmatchable act, a
lightning-flash would light up the bridge and the Seine. He need
only lean a little farther over, and he would have made his choice
for all eternity. He leaned over, but his hands still clutched the
stone and bore the whole weight of his body. Why not? He had no
special reason for letting himself drop, nor any reason for not
doing so. And the act was there, before him, on the black water, a
presentment of his future. All hawsers cut, nothing now could hold
him back: here was his freedom, and how horrible it was! Deep
down within him he felt his heart throbbing wildly; one gesture,
the mere unclasping of his hands, and *I would have been* Mathieu.
Dizziness rose softly over the river; sky and bridge dissolved:
nothing remained but himself and the water; it heaved up to him
and rippled round his dangling legs. The water, where his future
lay. At the moment *it is true*, I'm going to kill myself. Suddenly he
decided not to do it. He decided: it shall merely be a trial. Then he
was again upon his feet and walking on, gliding over the crest of a
dead star. Next time, perhaps.

The Rebel

ALBERT CAMUS

The powerful ethical emphasis of French existentialism is also clearly
exhibited in the work of the late Albert Camus. Just as Sartre constantly exhorts his readers to a life of commitment, to overcoming the
downward pull of the outer world through active use of freedom, so

SOURCE: *The Rebel*, by Albert Camus, trans. Anthony Bower (Knopf, New
York, 1956), pp. 3–10. Reprinted by permission of Alfred A. Knopf, Inc.,
and Hamish Hamilton, Ltd. Copyright 1956 by Alfred A. Knopf, Inc.

Camus sees authentic man as the perpetual rebel, who struggles as hopelessly but also as perseveringly as Sisyphus against the silence of the universe and refuses to surrender his autonomy.

The essay presented here is the introduction to Camus's *The Rebel*, originally published in 1951, which continues a discussion begun in *The Myth of Sisyphus* in 1942. The "absurdist" view to which Camus refers is the essentially Sartrean position that the outer world makes no sense to man, says nothing to him, and gives him no values. If man must make his own life in confrontation with the brute fact of this external absurdity, Camus concluded in his earlier study, suicide was not a valid choice, because it ended the confrontation. In *The Rebel*, he goes further, to invalidate murder and to attack the various totalitarian ideological systems of modern times, which have elevated murder to a political principle. Camus's philosophy has had considerable appeal to postwar young people because it manages successfully to combine a refutation of the exhausted faiths and ideologies of the twentieth century with a refutation of nihilism.

THERE ARE crimes of passion and crimes of logic. The boundary between them is not clearly defined. But the Penal Code makes the convenient distinction of premeditation. We are living in the era of premeditation and the perfect crime. Our criminals are no longer helpless children who could plead love as their excuse. On the contrary, they are adults and they have a perfect alibi: philosophy, which can be used for any purpose—even for transforming murderers into judges.

Heathcliff, in *Wuthering Heights*, would kill everybody on earth in order to possess Cathy, but it would never occur to him to say that murder is reasonable or theoretically defensible. He would commit it, and there his convictions end. This implies the power of love, and also strength of character. Since intense love is rare, murder remains an exception and preserves its aspect of infraction. But as soon as a man, through lack of character, takes refuge in doctrine, as soon as crime reasons about itself, it multiplies like reason itself and assumes all the aspects of the syllogism. Once crime was as solitary as a cry of protest; now it is as universal as science. Yesterday it was put on trial; today it determines the law.

This is not the place for indignation. The purpose of this essay is once again to face the reality of the present, which is logical crime, and to examine meticulously the arguments by which it is justified; it is an attempt to understand the times in which we live. One might think that a period which, in a space of fifty years, uproots, enslaves, or kills seventy million human beings should be condemned out of hand. But its culpability must still be understood. In more ingenuous times, when the tyrant razed cities for his own greater glory, when the slave chained to the conqueror's chariot was dragged through the rejoicing streets, when enemies were thrown to the wild beasts in front of the assembled people, the mind did not reel before such unabashed crimes, and judgment remained unclouded. But slave camps under the flag of freedom, massacres justified by philanthropy or by a taste for the super-human, in one sense cripple judgment. On the day when crime dons the apparel of innocence—through a curious transposition peculiar to our times—it is innocence that is called upon to justify itself. The ambition of this essay is to accept and examine this strange challenge.

Our purpose is to find out whether innocence, the moment it becomes involved in action, can avoid committing murder. We can act only in terms of our own time, among the people who surround us. We shall know nothing until we know whether we have the right to kill our fellow men, or the right to let them be killed. In that every action today leads to murder, direct or indirect, we cannot act until we know whether or why we have the right to kill.

The important thing, therefore, is not, as yet, to go to the root of things, but, the world being what it is, to know how to live in it. In the age of negation, it was of some avail to examine one's position concerning suicide. In the age of ideologies, we must examine our position in relation to murder. If murder has rational foundations, then our period and we ourselves are rationally conse-quent. If it has no rational foundations, then we are insane and there is no alternative but to find some justification or to avert our faces. It is incumbent upon us, at all events, to give a definite answer to the question implicit in the blood and strife of this century. For we are being put to the rack. Thirty years ago, before reaching a decision to kill, people denied many things, to the point of denying themselves by suicide. God is deceitful; the whole world (myself included) is deceitful; therefore I choose to die: suicide was the problem then. Ideology today is concerned only with the denial of other human beings, who alone bear the respon-sibility of deceit. It is then that we kill. Each day at dawn, assassins in judges' robes slip into some cell: murder is the problem today.

The two arguments are inextricably bound together. Or rather they bind us, and so firmly that we can no longer choose our own problems. They choose us, one after another, and we have no alternative but to accept their choice. This essay proposes, in the face of murder and rebellion, to pursue a train of thought which began with suicide and the idea of the absurd.

But, for the moment, this train of thought yields only one concept: that of the absurd. And the concept of the absurd leads only to a contradiction as far as the problem of murder is concerned. Awareness of the absurd, when we first claim to deduce a rule of behavior from it, makes murder seem a matter of indifference, to say the least, and hence possible. If we believe in nothing, if nothing has any meaning and if we can affirm no values whatsoever, then everything is possible and nothing has any importance. There is no pro or con: the murder is neither right nor wrong. We are free to stoke the crematory fires or to devote ourselves to the care of lepers. Evil and virtue are mere chance or caprice.

We shall then decide not to act at all, which amounts to at least accepting the murder of others, with perhaps certain mild reservations about the imperfection of the human race. Again we may decide to substitute tragic dilettantism for action, and in this case human lives become counters in a game. Finally, we may propose to embark on some course of action which is not entirely gratuitous. In the latter case, in that we have no higher values to guide our behavior, our aim will be immediate efficacy. Since nothing is either true or false, good or bad, our guiding principle will be to demonstrate that we are the most efficient—in other words, the strongest. Then the world will no longer be divided into the just and the unjust, but into masters and slaves. Thus, whichever way we turn, in our abyss of negation and nihilism, murder has its privileged position.

Hence, if we claim to adopt the absurdist attitude, we must prepare ourselves to commit murder, thus admitting that logic is more important than scruples that we consider illusory. Of course, we must have some predisposition to murder. But, on the whole, less than might be supposed, to judge from experience. Moreover, it is always possible, as we can so often observe, to delegate murder. Everything would then be made to conform to logic—if logic could really be satisfied in this way.

But logic cannot be satisfied by an attitude which first demonstrates that murder is possible and then that it is impossible. For after having proved that the act of murder is at least a matter of indifference, absurdist analysis, in its most important deduction, finally condemns murder. The final conclusion of absurdist reasoning is, in fact, the repudiation of suicide and the acceptance of the desperate encounter between human inquiry and the silence of the universe. Suicide would mean the end of this encounter, and absurdist reasoning considers that it could not consent to this without negating its own premises. According to absurdist reasoning, such a solution would be the equivalent of flight or deliverance. But it is obvious that absurdism hereby admits that human life is the only necessary good since it is precisely life that makes this encounter possible and since, without life, the absurdist wager would have no basis. To say that life is absurd, the conscience must be alive. How is it possible, without making remarkable concessions to one's desire for comfort, to preserve exclusively for oneself the benefits of such a process of reasoning? From the moment that life is recognized as good, it becomes good for all men. Murder cannot be made coherent when suicide is not considered coherent. A mind imbued with the idea of the absurd will undoubtedly accept fatalistic murder; but it would never accept calculated murder. In terms of the encounter between human inquiry and the silence of the universe, murder and suicide are one and the same thing, and must be accepted or rejected together.

Equally, absolute nihilism, which accepts suicide as legitimate, leads, even more easily, to logical murder. If our age admits, with equanimity, that murder has its justifications, it is because of this indifference to life which is the mark of nihilism. Of course there have been periods of history in which the passion for life was so strong that it burst forth in criminal excesses. But these excesses were like the searing flame of a terrible delight. They were not this monotonous order of things established by an impoverished logic in whose eyes everything is equal. This logic has carried the values of suicide, on which our age has been nurtured, to their extreme logical consequence, which is legalized murder. It culminates, at the same time, in mass suicide. The most striking demonstration of this was provided by the Hitlerian apocalypse of 1945. Self-destruction meant nothing to those madmen, in their bomb-shelters, who were preparing for their own death and apotheosis. All that mattered was not to destroy oneself alone and to drag a whole world with one. In a way, the man who kills himself in solitude still preserves certain values since he, apparently, claims no rights over the lives of others. The proof of this is that he never makes use, in order to

dominate others, of the enormous power and freedom of action
which his decision to die gives him. Every solitary suicide, when it
is not an act of resentment, is, in some way, either generous or
contemptuous. But one feels contemptuous in the name of something. If the world is a matter of indifference to the man who
commits suicide, it is because he has an idea of something that is not
or could not be indifferent to him. He believes that he is destroying
everything or taking everything with him; but from this act of self-
destruction itself a value arises which, perhaps, might have made it
worth while to live. Absolute negation is therefore not consummated by suicide. It can only be consummated by absolute destruction, of oneself and of others. Or, at least, it can only be lived by
striving toward that delectable end. Here suicide and murder are
two aspects of a single system, the system of a misguided intelligence that prefers, to the suffering imposed by a limited situation,
the dark victory in which heaven and earth are annihilated.

By the same token, if we deny that there are reasons for suicide,
we cannot claim that there are grounds for murder. There are no
half-measures about nihilism. Absurdist reasoning cannot defend
the continued existence of its spokesman and, simultaneously, accept the sacrifice of others' lives. The moment that we recognize
the impossibility of absolute negation—and merely to be alive is to
recognize this—the very first thing that cannot be denied is the
right of others to live. Thus the same idea which allowed us to
believe that murder was a matter of indifference now proceeds to
deprive it of any justification; and we return to the untenable
position from which we were trying to escape. In actual fact, this
form of reasoning assures us at the same time that we can kill and
that we cannot kill. It abandons us in this contradiction with no
grounds either for preventing or for justifying murder, menacing
and menaced, swept along with a whole generation intoxicated by
nihilism, and yet lost in loneliness, with weapons in our hands and
a lump in our throats.

This basic contradiction, however, cannot fail to be accompanied by a host of others from the moment that we claim to
remain firmly in the absurdist position and ignore the real nature of
the absurd, which is that it is an experience to be lived through, a
point of departure, the equivalent, in existence, of Descartes's
methodical doubt. The absurd is, in itself, contradiction.

It is contradictory in its content because, in wanting to uphold life, it excludes all value judgments, when to live is, in itself, a value judgment. To breathe is to judge. Perhaps it is untrue to say that life is a perpetual choice. But it is true that it is impossible to imagine a life deprived of all choice. From this simplified point of view, the absurdist position, translated into action, is inconceivable. It is equally inconceivable when translated into expression. Simply by being expressed, it gives a minimum of coherence to incoherence, and introduces consequence where, according to its own tenets, there is none. Speaking itself is restorative. The only coherent attitude based on non-signification would be silence—if silence, in its turn, were not significant. The absurd, in its purest form, attempts to remain dumb. If it finds its voice, it is because it has become complacent or, as we shall see, because it considers itself provisional. This complacency is an excellent indication of the profound ambiguity of the absurdist position. In a certain way, the absurd, which claims to express man in his solitude, really makes him live in front of a mirror. And then the initial anguish runs the risk of turning to comfort. The wound that is scratched with such solicitude ends by giving pleasure.

Great explorers in the realm of absurdity have not been lacking. But, in the last analysis, their greatness is measured by the extent to which they have rejected the complacencies of absurdism in order to accept its exigencies. They destroy as much, not as little, as they can. "My enemies," says Nietzsche, "are those who want to destroy without creating their own selves." He himself destroys, but in order to try to create. He extols integrity and castigates the "hog-faced" pleasure-seekers. To escape complacency, absurdist reasoning then discovers renunciation. It refuses to be sidetracked and emerges into a position of arbitrary barrenness—a determination to be silent—which is expressed in the strange asceticism of rebellion. Rimbaud, who extols "crime puling prettily in the mud of the streets," runs away to Harrar only to complain about having to live there without his family. Life for him was "a farce for the whole world to perform." But on the day of his death, he cries out to his sister: "I shall lie beneath the ground but you, you will walk in sun!"

The absurd, considered as a rule of life, is therefore contradictory. What is astonishing about the fact that it does not provide us with values which will enable us to decide whether murder is legitimate or not? Moreover, it is obviously impossible to formulate an attitude on the basis of a specially selected emotion. The perception of the absurd is one perception among many. That it has colored so many thoughts and actions between the two wars only proves its power and its validity. But the intensity of a perception does not necessarily mean that it is universal. The error of a whole period of history has been to enunciate—or to suppose already enunciated—general rules of action founded on emotions of despair whose inevitable course, in that they are emotions, is continually to exceed themselves. Great suffering and great happiness may be found at the beginning of any process of reasoning. They are intermediaries. But it is impossible to rediscover or sustain them throughout the entire process. Therefore, if it was legitimate to take absurdist sensibility into account, to make a diagnosis of a malady to be found in ourselves and in others, it is nevertheless impossible to see in this sensibility, and in the nihilism it presupposes, anything but a point of departure, a criticism brought to life—the equivalent, in the plane of existence, of systematic doubt. After this, the mirror, with its fixed stare, must be broken and we are, perforce, caught up in the irresistible movement by which the absurd exceeds itself.

Once the mirror is broken, nothing remains which can help us to answer the questions of our time. Absurdism, like methodical doubt, has wiped the slate clean. It leaves us in a blind alley. But, like methodical doubt, it can, by returning upon itself, open up a new field of investigation, and the process of reasoning then pursues the same course. I proclaim that I believe in nothing and that everything is absurd, but I cannot doubt the validity of my proclamation and I must at least believe in my protest. The first and only evidence that is supplied me, within the terms of the absurdist experience, is rebellion. Deprived of all knowledge, incited to murder or to consent to murder, all I have at my disposal is this single piece of evidence, which is only reaffirmed by the anguish I suffer. Rebellion is born of the spectacle of irrationality, confronted with an unjust and incomprehensible condition. But its blind impulse is to demand order in the midst of chaos, and unity in the very heart of the ephemeral. It protests, it demands, it insists that the outrage be brought to an end, and that what has up to now been built upon shifting sands should henceforth be founded on rock. Its preoccupation is to transform. But to transform is to act, and to act will be, tomorrow, to kill, and it still does not know whether murder is legitimate. Rebellion engenders exactly the actions it is asked to legitimate. Therefore it is absolutely necessary that rebellion find its reasons within itself, since it cannot find them elsewhere. It must consent to examine itself in order to learn how to act.

* * *

In any event, the reasons for rebellion cannot be explained except in terms of an inquiry into its attitudes, pretensions, and conquests. Perhaps we may discover in its achievements the rule of action that the absurd has not been able to give us; an indication, at least, about the right or the duty to kill and, finally, hope for a new creation. Man is the only creature who refuses to be what he is. The problem is to know whether this refusal can only lead to the destruction of himself and of others, whether all rebellion must end in the justification of universal murder, or whether, on the contrary, without laying claim to an innocence that is impossible, it can discover the principle of reasonable culpability.

IV

Psychoanalysis and Civilization

The Disillusionment of the War

SIGMUND FREUD

One of the most forceful shocks administered in our time to the belief in human goodness and progress has come from the revelations of psychoanalysis, and especially those of Dr. Sigmund Freud of Vienna. Although in later life he elaborated a whole philosophy of history and civilization, Freud was first a physician, who earned his M.D. at the University of Vienna as long ago as 1881, and based his understanding of human nature on thousands of hours of professional consultations with mentally disturbed patients. Beneath the rational man of the Enlightenment and the passional man of Romanticism he discovered the still vigorously thriving animal man of prehistory. Even the "innocence of childhood" was demolished by Freud's inquiries. It follows that he was better equipped than many of the leading thinkers of his generation to explain the psychological significance of the world war that broke out in 1914.

The essay below is the first of two studies of the war published in 1915 under the general title of "Thoughts for the Times on War and Death." The second piece, not reprinted here, shows how the war changed men's attitudes toward death, bringing them closer to the primitive point of view. The war "strips us of the later accretions of civilization, and lays bare the primal man in each of us. It constrains us once more to be heroes who cannot believe in their own death; it

SOURCE: "Thoughts for the Times on War and Death," by Sigmund Freud, in *The Standard Edition of the Complete Psychological Works of Sigmund Freud*, translated from the German under the general editorship of James Strachey, Vol. XIV (Hogarth Press, London, 1957), pp. 275–88. Also published, in the translation by E. Colburn Mayne, in *The Collected Papers of Sigmund Freud*, Vol. IV (Basic Books, New York, 1959), pp. 288–304. Reprinted by permission of Basic Books, Inc.; Sigmund Freud Copyrights, Ltd.; James Strachey; and The Hogarth Press, Ltd.

stamps the alien as the enemy, whose death is to be brought about or desired; it counsels us to rise above the death of those we love." But Freud was also a prophet of the same scientific rationalism that his psychoanalytical discoveries apparently undermined, and in the essay which follows he concludes on a note of typically cautious optimism. As he wrote years later, in *The Future of an Illusion:* "The voice of the intellect is a soft one, but it does not rest until it has gained a hearing. Ultimately, after endlessly repeated rebuffs, it succeeds. . . . The primacy of the intellect certainly lies in the far, far, but still not infinite, distance."

IN THE confusion of wartime in which we are caught up, relying as we must on one-sided information, standing too close to the great changes that have already taken place or are beginning to, and without a glimmering of the future that is being shaped, we ourselves are at a loss as to the significance of the impressions which press in upon us and as to the value of the judgements which we form. We cannot but feel that no event has ever destroyed so much that is precious in the common possessions of humanity, confused so many of the clearest intelligences, or so thoroughly debased what is highest. Science herself has lost her passionless impartiality; her deeply embittered servants seek for weapons from her with which to contribute towards the struggle with the enemy. Anthropologists feel driven to declare him inferior and degenerate, psychiatrists issue a diagnosis of his disease of mind or spirit. Probably, however, our sense of these immediate evils is disproportionately strong, and we are not entitled to compare them with the evils of other times which we have not experienced.

The individual who is not himself a combatant—and so a cog in the gigantic machine of war—feels bewildered in his orientation, and inhibited in his powers and activities. I believe that he will welcome any indication, however slight, which will make it easier for him to find his bearings within himself at least. I propose to pick out two among the factors which are responsible for the mental distress felt by non-combatants, against which it is such a heavy task to struggle, and to treat of them here: the disillusionment which this war has evoked, and the altered attitude towards death which this—like every other war—forces upon us.

When I speak of disillusionment, everyone will know at once what I mean. One need not be a sentimentalist; one may perceive the biological and psychological necessity for suffering in the economy of human life, and yet condemn war both in its means and ends and long for the cessation of all wars. We have told ourselves, no doubt, that wars can never cease so long as nations live under such widely differing conditions, so long as the value of individual life is so variously assessed among them, and so long as the animosities which divide them represent such powerful motive forces in the mind. We were prepared to find that wars between the primitive and the civilized peoples, between the races who are divided by the colour of their skin—wars, even, against and among the nationalities of Europe whose civilization is little developed or has been lost—would occupy mankind for some time to come. But we permitted ourselves to have other hopes. We had expected the great world-dominating nations of white race upon whom the leadership of the human species has fallen, who were known to have world-wide interests as their concern, to whose creative powers were due not only our technical advances towards the control of nature but the artistic and scientific standards of civiliza-tion—we had expected these peoples to succeed in discovering another way of settling misunderstandings and conflicts of interest. Within each of these nations high norms of moral conduct were laid down for the individual, to which his manner of life was bound to conform if he desired to take part in a civilized com-munity. These ordinances, often too stringent, demanded a great deal of him—much self-restraint, much renunciation of instinctual satisfaction. He was above all forbidden to make use of the im-mense advantages to be gained by the practice of lying and decep-tion in the competition with his fellow-men. The civilized states regarded these moral standards as the basis of their existence. They took serious steps if anyone ventured to tamper with them, and often declared it improper even to subject them to examination by a critical intelligence. It was to be assumed, therefore, that the state itself would respect them, and would not think of undertaking anything against them which would contradict the basis of its own existence. Observation showed, to be sure, that embedded in these civilized states there were remnants of certain other peoples, which were universally unpopular and had therefore been only reluc-tantly, and even so not fully, admitted to participation in the common work of civilization, for which they had shown them-selves suitable enough. But the great nations themselves, it might have been supposed, would have acquired so much comprehension of what they had in common, and so much tolerance for their differences, that 'foreigner' and 'enemy' could no longer be merged, as they still were in classical antiquity, into a single concept.

Relying on this unity among the civilized peoples, countless men and women have exchanged their native home for a foreign one, and made their existence dependent on the intercommunications between friendly nations. Moreover anyone who was not by stress of circumstance confined to one spot could create for himself out of all the advantages and attractions of these civilized countries a new and wider fatherland, in which he could move about without hindrance or suspicion. In this way he enjoyed the blue sea and the grey; the beauty of snow-covered mountains and of green meadow lands; the magic of northern forests and the splendour of southern vegetation; the mood evoked by landscapes that recall great historical events, and the silence of untouched nature. This new fatherland was a museum for him, too, filled with all the treasures which the artists of civilized humanity had in the successive centuries created and left behind. As he wandered from one gallery to another in this museum, he could recognize with impartial appreciation what varied types of perfection a mixture of blood, the course of history, and the special quality of their mother-earth had produced among his compatriots in this wider sense. Here he would find cool, inflexible energy developed to the highest point; there, the graceful art of beautifying existence; elsewhere, the feeling for orderliness and law, or others among the qualities which have made mankind the lords of the earth.

Nor must we forget that each of these citizens of the civilized world had created for himself a 'Parnassus' and a 'School of Athens' of his own. From among the great thinkers, writers and artists of all nations he had chosen those to whom he considered he owed the best of what he had been able to achieve in enjoyment and understanding of life, and he had venerated them along with the immortal ancients as well as with the familiar masters of his own tongue. None of these great men had seemed to him foreign because they spoke another language—neither the incomparable explorer of human passions, nor the intoxicated worshipper of beauty, nor the powerful and menacing prophet, nor the subtle satirist; and he never reproached himself on that account for being a renegade towards his own nation and his beloved mother-tongue.

The enjoyment of this common civilization was disturbed from time to time by warning voices, which declared that old traditional differences made wars inevitable, even among the members of a community such as this. We refused to believe it; but if such a war were to happen, how did we picture it? We saw it as an opportunity for demonstrating the progress of comity among men since the era when the Greek Amphictyonic Council proclaimed that no city of the league might be destroyed, nor its olive-groves cut down, nor its water-supply stopped; we pictured it as a chivalrous passage of arms, which would limit itself to establishing the superiority of one side in the struggle, while as far as possible avoiding acute suffering that could contribute nothing to the decision, and granting complete immunity for the wounded who had to withdraw from the contest, as well as for the doctors and nurses who devoted themselves to their recovery. There would, of course, be the utmost consideration for the non-combatant classes of the population—for women who take no part in war-work, and for the children who, when they are grown up, should become on both sides one another's friends and helpers. And again, all the international undertakings and institutions in which the common civilization of peace-time had been embodied would be maintained.

Even a war like this would have produced enough horror and suffering; but it would not have interrupted the development of ethical relations between the collective individuals of mankind— the peoples and states.

Then the war in which we had refused to believe broke out, and it brought—disillusionment. Not only is it more bloody and more destructive than any war of other days, because of the enormously increased perfection of weapons of attack and defence; it is at least as cruel, as embittered, as implacable as any that has preceded it. It disregards all the restrictions known as International Law, which in peace-time the states had bound themselves to observe; it ignores the prerogatives of the wounded and the medical service, the distinction between civil and military sections of the population, the claims of private property. It tramples in blind fury on all that comes in its way, as though there were to be no future and no peace among men after it is over. It cuts all the common bonds between the contending peoples, and threatens to leave a legacy of embitterment that will make any renewal of those bonds impossible for a long time to come.

Moreover, it has brought to light an almost incredible phenomenon: the civilized nations know and understand one another so little that one can turn against the other with hate and loathing. Indeed, one of the great civilized nations is so universally unpopular that the attempt can actually be made to exclude it from the civilized community as 'barbaric', although it has long proved its fi ness by the magnificent contributions to that community which it l as made. We live in hopes that the pages of an impartial history will prove that that nation, in whose language we write and for whose victory our dear ones are fighting, has been precisely the one which has least transgressed the laws of civilization. But at such a time who dares to set himself up as judge in his own cause?

Peoples are more or less represented by the states which they form, and these states by the governments which rule them. The individual citizen can with horror convince himself in this war of what would occasionally cross his mind in peace-time—that the state has forbidden to the individual the practice of wrong-doing, not because it desires to abolish it, but because it desires to monopolize it, like salt and tobacco. A belligerent state permits itself every such misdeed, every such act of violence, as would disgrace the individual. It makes use against the enemy not only of the accepted *ruses de guerre*, but of deliberate lying and deception as well—and to a degree which seems to exceed the usage of former wars. The state exacts the utmost degree of obedience and sacrifice from its citizens, but at the same time it treats them like children by an excess of secrecy and a censorship upon news and expressions of opinion which leaves the spirits of those whose intellects it thus suppresses defenceless against every unfavourable turn of events and every sinister rumour. It absolves itself from the guarantees and treaties by which it was bound to other states, and confesses shamelessly to its own rapacity and lust for power, which the private individual has then to sanction in the name of patriotism.

It should not be objected that the state cannot refrain from wrong-doing, since that would place it at a disadvantage. It is no less disadvantageous, as a general rule, for the individual man to conform to the standards of morality and refrain from brutal and arbitrary conduct; and the state seldom proves able to indemnify him for the sacrifices it exacts. Nor should it be a matter for surprise that this relaxation of all the moral ties between the collective individuals of mankind should have had repercussions on the morality of individuals; for our conscience is not the inflexible judge that ethical teachers declare it, but in its origin is 'social anxiety' and nothing else. When the community no longer raises objections, there is an end, too, to the suppression of evil passions, and men perpetrate deeds of cruelty, fraud, treachery and barbarity so incompatible with their level of civilization that one would have thought them impossible.

Well may the citizen of the civilized world of whom I have spoken stand helpless in a world that has grown strange to him—his great fatherland disintegrated, its common estates laid waste, his fellow-citizens divided and debased!

There is something to be said, however, in criticism of his disappointment. Strictly speaking it is not justified, for it consists in the destruction of an illusion. We welcome illusions because they spare us unpleasurable feelings, and enable us to enjoy satisfactions instead. We must not complain, then, if now and again they come into collision with some portion of reality, and are shattered against it.

Two things in this war have aroused our sense of disillusionment: the low morality shown externally by states which in their internal relations pose as the guardians of moral standards, and the brutality shown by individuals whom, as participants in the highest human civilization, one would not have thought capable of such behaviour.

Let us begin with the second point and try to formulate, in a few brief words, the point of view that we wish to criticize. How, in point of fact, do we imagine the process by which an individual rises to a comparatively high plane of morality? The first answer will no doubt simply be that he is virtuous and noble from birth—from the very start. We shall not consider this view any further here. A second answer will suggest that we are concerned with a developmental process, and will probably assume that the development consists in eradicating his evil human tendencies and, under the influence of education and a civilized environment, replacing them by good ones. If so, it is nevertheless surprising that evil should re-emerge with such force in anyone who has been brought up in this way.

But this answer also contains the thesis which we propose to contradict. In reality, there is no such thing as 'eradicating' evil. Psychological—or, more strictly speaking, psycho-analytic—investigation shows instead that the deepest essence of human nature consists of instinctual impulses which are of an elementary nature, which are similar in all men and which aim at the satisfaction of certain primal needs. These impulses in themselves are neither good nor bad. We classify them and their expressions in that way, according to their relation to the needs and demands of the human community. It must be granted that all the impulses which society condemns as evil—let us take as representative the selfish and the cruel ones—are of this primitive kind.

These primitive impulses undergo a lengthy process of development before they are allowed to become active in the adult. They are inhibited, directed towards other aims and fields, become commingled, alter their objects, and are to some extent turned back upon their possessor. Reaction-formations against certain instincts take the deceptive form of a change in their content, as though egoism had changed into altruism, or cruelty into pity. These reaction-formations are facilitated by the circumstance that some instinctual impulses make their appearance almost from the first in pairs of opposites—a very remarkable phenomenon, and one strange to the lay public, which is termed 'ambivalence of feeling'. The most easily observed and comprehensible instance of this is the fact that intense love and intense hatred are so often to be found together in the same person. Psycho-analysis adds that the two opposed feelings not infrequently have the same person for their object.

It is not until all these "instinctual vicissitudes' have been surmounted that what we call a person's character is formed, and this, as we know, can only very inadequately be classified as 'good' or 'bad'. A human being is seldom altogether good or bad; he is usually 'good' in one relation and 'bad' in another, or 'good' in certain external circumstances and in others decidedly 'bad'. It is interesting to find that the pre-existence of strong 'bad' impulses in infancy is often the actual condition for an unmistakable inclination towards 'good' in the adult. Those who as children have been the most pronounced egoists may well become the most helpful and self-sacrificing members of the community; most of our sentimentalists, friends of humanity and protectors of animals have been evolved from little sadists and animal-tormentors.

The transformation of 'bad' instincts is brought about by two factors working in the same direction, an internal and an external one. The internal factor consists in the influence exercised on the bad (let us say, the egoistic) instincts by erotism—that is, by the human need for love, taken in its widest sense. By the admixture of *erotic* components the egoistic instincts are transformed into *social* ones. We learn to value being loved as an advantage for which we are willing to sacrifice other advantages. The external factor is the force exercised by upbringing, which represents the claims of our cultural environment, and this is continued later by the direct pressure of that environment. Civilization has been attained through the renunciation of instinctual satisfaction, and it demands the same renunciation from each newcomer in turn. Throughout an individual's life there is a constant replacement of external by internal compulsion. The influences of civilization cause an ever-increasing transformation of egoistic trends into altruistic and social ones by an admixture of erotic elements. In the last resort it may be assumed that every internal compulsion which makes itself felt in the development of human beings was originally—that is, in the *history of mankind*—only an external one. Those who are born to-day bring with them as an inherited organization some degree of tendency (disposition) towards the transformation of egoistic into social instincts, and this disposition is easily stimulated into bringing about that result. A further portion of this instinctual transformation has to be accomplished during the life of the individual himself. So the human being is subject not only to the pressure of his immediate cultural environment, but also to the influence of the cultural history of his ancestors.

If we give the name of 'susceptibility to culture' to a man's personal capacity for the transformation of the egoistic impulses under the influence of erotism, we may further affirm that this susceptibility is made up of two parts, one innate and the other acquired in the course of life, and that the relation of the two to each other and to that portion of the instinctual life which remains untransformed is a very variable one.

Generally speaking, we are apt to attach too much importance to the innate part, and in addition to this we run the risk of over-estimating the total susceptibility to culture in comparison with the portion of instinctual life which has remained primitive—that is, we are misled into regarding men as 'better' than they actually are. For there is yet another element which obscures our judgement and falsifies the issue in a favourable sense.

The instinctual impulses of other people are of course hidden from our observation. We infer them from their actions and behaviour, which we trace back to *motives* arising from their instinctual life. Such an inference is bound to be erroneous in many cases. This or that action which is 'good' from the cultural point of view may in one instance originate from a 'noble' motive, in another not. Ethical theorists class as 'good' actions only those which are the outcome of good impulses; to the others they refuse recognition. But society, which is practical in its aims, is not on the whole troubled by this distinction; it is content if a man regulates his behaviour and actions by the precepts of civilization, and is little concerned with his motives.

We have learned that the *external compulsion* exercised on a human being by his upbringing and environment produces a further transformation towards good in his instinctual life—a further turning from egoism towards altruism. But this is not the regular or necessary effect of the external compulsion. Upbringing and environment not only offer benefits in the way of love, but also employ other kinds of incentive, namely, rewards and punishments. In this way their effect may turn out to be that a person who is subjected to their influence will choose to behave well in the cultural sense of the phrase, although no ennoblement of instinct, no transformation of egoistic into altruistic inclinations, has taken place in him. The result will, roughly speaking, be the same; only a particular concatenation of circumstances will reveal that one man always acts in a good way because his instinctual inclinations compel him to, and the other is good only in so far and for so long as such cultural behaviour is advantageous for his own selfish purposes. But superficial acquaintance with an individual will not enable us to distinguish between the two cases, and we are certainly misled by our optimism into grossly exaggerating the number of human beings who have been transformed in a cultural sense.

Civilized society, which demands good conduct and does not trouble itself about the instinctual basis of this conduct, has thus won over to obedience a great many people who are not in this following their own natures. Encouraged by this success, society has allowed itself to be misled into tightening the moral standard to the greatest possible degree, and it has thus forced its members into a yet greater estrangement from their instinctual disposition. They are consequently subject to an unceasing suppression of instinct,

SIGMUND FREUD   161

and the resulting tension betrays itself in the most remarkable
phenomena of reaction and compensation. In the domain of sexuality, where such suppression is most difficult to carry out, the
result is seen in the reactive phenomena of neurotic disorders.
Elsewhere the pressure of civilization brings in its train no pathological results, it is true, but is shown in malformations of character, and in the perpetual readiness of the inhibited instincts to break
through to satisfaction at any suitable opportunity. Anyone thus
compelled to act continually in accordance with precepts which
are not the expression of his instinctual inclinations, is living, psychologically speaking, beyond his means, and may objectively be
described as a hypocrite, whether he is clearly aware of the
incongruity or not. It is undeniable that our contemporary civilization favours the production of this form of hypocrisy to an extraordinary extent. One might venture to say that it is built up on
such hypocrisy, and that it would have to submit to far-reaching
modifications if people were to undertake to live in accordance
with psychological truth. Thus there are very many more cultural
hypocrites than truly civilized men—indeed, it is a debatable point
whether a certain degree of cultural hypocrisy is not indispensable
for the maintenance of civilization, because the susceptibility to
culture which has hitherto been organized in the minds of present-
day men would perhaps not prove sufficient for the task. On the
other hand, the maintenance of civilization even on so dubious a
basis offers the prospect of paving the way in each new generation
for a more far-reaching transformation of instinct which shall be
the vehicle of a better civilization.

We may already derive one consolation from this discussion: our
mortification and our painful disillusionment on account of the
uncivilized behaviour of our fellow-citizens of the world during
this war were unjustified. They were based on an illusion to which
we had given way. In reality our fellow-citizens have not sunk so
low as we feared, because they had never risen so high as we
believed. The fact that the collective individuals of mankind, the
peoples and states, mutually abrogated their moral restraints naturally prompted these individual citizens to withdraw for a while
from the constant pressure of civilization and to grant a temporary
satisfaction to the instincts which they had been holding in check.
This probably involved no breach in their relative morality within
their own nations.

We may, however, obtain a deeper insight than this into the change brought about by the war in our former compatriots, and at the same time receive a warning against doing them an injustice. For the development of the mind shows a peculiarity which is present in no other developmental process. When a village grows into a town or a child into a man, the village and the child become lost in the town and the man. Memory alone can trace the old features in the new picture; and in fact the old materials or forms have been got rid of and replaced by new ones. It is otherwise with the development of the mind. Here one can describe the state of affairs, which has nothing to compare with it, only by saying that in this case every earlier stage of development persists alongside the later stage which has arisen from it; here succession also involves co-existence, although it is to the same materials that the whole series of transformations has applied. The earlier mental state may not have manifested itself for years, but none the less it is so far present that it may at any time again become the mode of expression of the forces in the mind, and indeed the only one, as though all later developments had been annulled or undone. This extraordinary plasticity of mental developments is not unrestricted as regards direction; it may be described as a special capacity for involution— for regression—since it may well happen that a later and higher stage of development, once abandoned, cannot be reached again. But the primitive stages can always be re-established; the primitive mind is, in the fullest meaning of the word, imperishable.

What are called mental diseases inevitably produce an impression in the layman that intellectual and mental life have been destroyed. In reality, the destruction only applies to later acquisitions and developments. The essence of mental disease lies in a return to earlier states of affective life and of functioning. An excellent example of the plasticity of mental life is afforded by the state of sleep, which is our goal every night. Since we have learnt to interpret even absurd and confused dreams, we know that whenever we go to sleep we throw off our hard-won morality like a garment, and put it on again next morning. This stripping of ourselves is not, of course, dangerous, because we are paralysed, condemned to inactivity, by the state of sleep. It is only dreams that can tell us about the regression of our emotional life to one of the earliest stages of development. For instance, it is noteworthy that all our dreams are governed by purely egoistic motives.[1] One of my English friends put forward this thesis at a scientific meeting in America, whereupon a lady who was present remarked that that might be the case in Austria, but she could assert as regards herself and her friends that *they* were altruistic even in their dreams. My friend, although himself of English race, was obliged to contradict the lady emphatically on the ground of his personal experience in dream-analysis, and to declare that in their dreams high-minded American ladies were quite as egoistic as the Austrians.

Thus the transformation of instinct, on which our susceptibility to culture is based, may also be permanently or temporarily undone by the impacts of life. The influences of war are undoubtedly among the forces that can bring about such involution; so we need not deny susceptibility to culture to all who are at the present time behaving in an uncivilized way, and we may anticipate that the ennoblement of their instincts will be restored in more peaceful times.

There is, however, another symptom in our fellow-citizens of the world which has perhaps astonished and shocked us no less than the descent from their ethical heights which has given us so much pain. What I have in mind is the want of insight shown by the best intellects, their obduracy, their inacessibility to the most forcible arguments and their uncritical credulity towards the most disputable assertions. This indeed presents a lamentable picture, and I wish to say emphatically that in this I am by no means a blind partisan who finds all the intellectual shortcomings on one side. But this phenomenon is much easier to account for and much less disquieting than the one we have just considered. Students of human nature and philosophers have long taught us that we are mistaken in regarding our intelligence as an independent force and in overlooking its dependence on emotional life. Our intellect, they teach us, can function reliably only when it is removed from the influences of strong emotional impulses; otherwise it behaves merely as an instrument of the will and delivers the inference which the will requires. Thus, in their view, logical arguments are

[1] [Freud later qualified this view in an addition made in 1925 to a footnote to *The Interpretation of Dreams* (*Standard Ed.*, 4, 270–1) where he also tells the anecdote which follows. The 'English friend', as is there made plain, was Dr. Ernest Jones.—*Trans.* and *ed.*]

impotent against affective interests, and that is why disputes backed by reasons, which in Falstaff's phrase are 'as plenty as blackberries', are so unfruitful in the world of interests. Psycho-analytic experience has, if possible, further confirmed this statement. It can show every day that the shrewdest people will all of a sudden behave without insight, like imbeciles, as soon as the necessary insight is confronted by an emotional resistance, but that they will completely regain their understanding once that resistance has been overcome. The logical bedazzlement which this war has conjured up in our fellow-citizens, many of them the best of their kind, is therefore a secondary phenomenon, a consequence of emotional excitement, and is bound, we may hope, to disappear with it.

Having in this way once more come to understand our fellow-citizens who are now alienated from us, we shall much more easily endure the disappointment which the nations, the collective individuals of mankind, have caused us, for the demands we make upon these should be far more modest. Perhaps they are recapitulating the course of individual development, and to-day still represent very primitive phases in organization and in the formation of higher unities. It is in agreement with this that the educative factor of an external compulsion towards morality, which we found was so effective in individuals, is as yet barely discernible in them. We had hoped, certainly, that the extensive community of interests established by commerce and production would constitute the germ of such a compulsion, but it would seem that nations still obey their passions far more readily than their interests. Their interests serve them, at most, as *rationalizations* for their passions; they put forward their interests in order to be able to give reasons for satisfying their passions. It is, to be sure, a mystery why the collective individuals should in fact despise, hate and detest one another—every nation against every other—and even in times of peace. I cannot tell why that is so. It is just as though when it becomes a question of a number of people, not to say millions, all individual moral acquisitions are obliterated, and only the most primitive, the oldest, the crudest mental attitudes are left. It may be that only later stages in development will be able to make some change in this regrettable state of affairs. But a little more truthfulness and honesty on all sides—in the relations of men to one another and between them and their rulers—should also smooth the way for this transformation.

The Spiritual Problem of Modern Man

CARL GUSTAV JUNG

Although the Freudian school is still pre-eminent in psychoanalytical circles, some of Freud's best disciples deserted their master in early or middle life to found rival schools. "The private history of the psychoanalytic movement," writes A. W. Levi in *Philosophy and the Modern World*, "is a record of misunderstandings, comedies of errors, schisms, heresies, and deviations within the interpretation of the sacred doctrines." The secessions of Adler, Jung, and Rank struck "old Jacob" to the heart: "it is family tragedy—with Biblical overtones."

Especially in the case of Carl Gustav Jung, the parting of ways resulted from much more than a disagreement over analytical techniques or even Freud's often criticized emphasis on the function of sexuality in human behavior. If Freud was at bottom a child of the Enlightenment and a believer in the healing powers of reason, Jung was fundamentally a mystic. The sickness of the twentieth century, he felt, originated not in reversions to animality but in modern man's self-imposed alienation from the constructive, life-giving resources of the "collective unconscious," the racial spirit, on which all the world's religions have drawn for their symbols and myths. Freudian therapy might benefit certain younger people, but the need of the mature man was for a sense of the meaningfulness of life, which he could find only through re-establishing contact with the collective unconscious. Jung did not recommend any particular religion; each had its own special virtues. But he broke decisively with Freud on the question of the therapeutic value of rational self-understanding. Whereas Freud saw religions as narcotic systems of illusion, Jung saw them as aids to mental health. It is hardly surprising that Jung has been taken up with great interest by liberal clergymen and religious writers, while Freud in these same quarters is regarded as "old-fashioned" and "narrow-minded."

But master and disciple alike agreed on at least one point: modern civilization is suffering from one or another form of mass insanity. The essay reprinted here was originally published in German in 1931 and revised by the author for its first appearance in English in 1933.

THE SPIRITUAL problem of modern man is one of those questions which belong so intimately to the present in which we are living

SOURCE: *Modern Man in Search of a Soul*, by Carl Gustav Jung, trans. W. S. Dell and Cary F. Baynes (Harcourt, Brace, New York, 1933), pp. 226–54. Reprinted by permission of Harcourt, Brace and World, Inc., and Routledge and Kegan Paul, Ltd.

that we cannot judge of them fully. The modern man is a newly formed human being; a modern problem is a question which has just arisen and whose answer lies in the future. In speaking, therefore, of the spiritual problem of modern man we can at most state a question—and we should perhaps put this statement in different terms if we had but the faintest inkling of the answer. The question, moreover, seems rather vague; but the truth is that it has to do with something so universal that it exceeds the grasp of any single human being. We have reason enough, therefore, to approach such a problem with true moderation and with the greatest caution. I am deeply convinced of this, and wish it stressed the more because it is just such problems which tempt us to use high-sounding words—and because I shall myself be forced to say certain things which may sound immoderate and incautious.

To begin at once with an example of such apparent lack of caution, I must say that the man we call modern, the man who is aware of the immediate present, is by no means the average man. He is rather the man who stands upon a peak, or at the very edge of the world, the abyss of the future before him, above him the heavens, and below him the whole of mankind with a history that disappears in primeval mists. The modern man—or, let us say again, the man of the immediate present—is rarely met with. There are few who live up to the name, for they must be conscious to a superlative degree. Since to be wholly of the present means to be fully conscious of one's existence as a man, it requires the most intensive and extensive consciousness, with a minimum of unconsciousness. It must be clearly understood that the mere fact of living in the present does not make a man modern, for in that case everyone at present alive would be so. He alone is modern who is fully conscious of the present.

The man whom we can with justice call "modern" is solitary. He is so of necessity and at all times, for every step towards a fuller consciousness of the present removes him further from his original *"participation mystique"* with the mass of men—from submersion in a common unconsciousness. Every step forward means an act of tearing himself loose from that all-embracing, pristine unconsciousness which claims the bulk of mankind almost entirely. Even in our civilizations the people who form, psychologically speaking, the lowest stratum, live almost as unconsciously as primitive races. Those of the succeeding stratum manifest a level of consciousness which corresponds to the beginnings of human culture, while those of the highest stratum have a consciousness capable of keeping step with the life of the last few centuries. Only the man who is modern in our meaning of the term really lives in the present; he alone has a present-day consciousness, and he alone finds that the ways of life which correspond to earlier levels pall upon him. The values and strivings of those past worlds no longer interest him save from the historical standpoint. Thus he has become "unhistorical" in the deepest sense and has estranged himself from the mass of men who live entirely within the bounds of tradition. Indeed, he is completely modern only when he has come to the very edge of the world, leaving behind him all that has been discarded and outgrown, and acknowledging that he stands before a void out of which all things may grow.

These words may be thought to be but empty sound, and their meaning reduced to mere banality. Nothing is easier than to affect a consciousness of the present. As a matter of fact, a great horde of worthless people give themselves the air of being modern by overleaping the various stages of development and the tasks of life they represent. They appear suddenly by the side of the truly modern man as uprooted human beings, bloodsucking ghosts, whose emptiness is taken for the unenviable loneliness of the modern man and casts discredit upon him. He and his kind, few in number as they are, are hidden from the undiscerning eyes of mass-men by those clouds of ghosts, the pseudo-moderns. It cannot be helped; the "modern" man is questionable and suspect, and has always been so, even in the past.

An honest profession of modernity means voluntarily declaring bankruptcy, taking the vows of poverty and chastity in a new sense, and—what is still more painful—renouncing the halo which history bestows as a mark of its sanction. To be "unhistorical" is the Promethean sin, and in this sense modern man lives in sin. A higher level of consciousness is like a burden of guilt. But, as I have said, only the man who has outgrown the stages of consciousness belonging to the past and has amply fulfilled the duties appointed for him by his world, can achieve a full consciousness of the present. To do this he must be sound and proficient in the best sense—a man who has achieved as much as other people, and even a little more. It is these qualities which enable him to gain the next highest level of consciousness.

I know that the idea of proficiency is especially repugnant to the pseudo-moderns, for it reminds them unpleasantly of their deceits. This, however, cannot prevent us from taking it as our criterion of the modern man. We are even forced to do so, for unless he is proficient, the man who claims to be modern is nothing but an unscrupulous gambler. He must be proficient in the highest degree, for unless he can atone by creative ability for his break with tradition, he is merely disloyal to the past. It is sheer juggling to look upon a denial of the past as the same thing as consciousness of the present. "Today" stands between "yesterday" and "tomorrow", and forms a link between past and future; it has no other meaning. The present represents a process of transition, and that man may account himself modern who is conscious of it in this sense.

Many people call themselves modern—especially the pseudo-moderns. Therefore the really modern man is often to be found among those who call themselves old-fashioned. He takes this stand for sufficient reasons. On the one hand he emphasizes the past in order to hold the scales against his break with tradition and that effect of guilt of which I have spoken. On the other hand he wishes to avoid being taken for a pseudo-modern.

Every good quality has its bad side, and nothing that is good can come into the world without directly producing a corresponding evil. This is a painful fact. Now there is the danger that consciousness of the present may lead to an elation based upon illusion: the illusion, namely, that we are the culmination of the history of mankind, the fulfilment and the end-product of countless centuries. If we grant this, we should understand that it is no more than the proud acknowledgement of our destitution: we are also the disappointment of the hopes and expectations of the ages. Think of nearly two thousand years of Christian ideals followed, instead of by the return of the Messiah and the heavenly millennium, by the World War among Christian nations and its barbed-wire and poison-gas. What a catastrophe in heaven and on earth!

In the face of such a picture we may well grow humble again. It is true that modern man is a culmination, but tomorrow he will be surpassed; he is indeed the end-product of an age-old development, but he is at the same time the worst conceivable disappointment of the hopes of humankind. The modern man is aware of this. He has seen how beneficent are science, technology and organization, but also how catastrophic they can be. He has likewise seen that well-meaning governments have so thoroughly paved the way for peace on the principle "in time of peace prepare for war", that Europe has nearly gone to rack and ruin. And as for ideals, the Christian church, the brotherhood of man, international social democracy and the "solidarity" of economic interests have all failed to stand the baptism of fire—the test of reality. Today, fifteen years after the war, we observe once more the same optimism, the same organization, the same political aspirations, the same phrases and catch-words at work. How can we but fear that they will inevitably lead to further catastrophes? Agreements to outlaw war leave us sceptical, even while we wish them all possible success. At bottom, behind every such palliative measure, there is a gnawing doubt. On the whole, I believe I am not exaggerating when I say that modern man has suffered an almost fatal shock, psychologically speaking, and as a result has fallen into profound uncertainty.

These statements, I believe, make it clear enough that my being a physician has coloured my views. A doctor always spies out diseases, and I cannot cease to be a doctor. But it is essential to the physician's art that he should not discover diseases where none exists. I will therefore not make the assertion that the white races in general, and occidental nations in particular, are diseased, or that the Western world is on the verge of collapse. I am in no way competent to pass such a judgement.

It is of course only from my own experience with other persons and with myself that I draw my knowledge of the spiritual problem of modern man. I know something of the intimate psychic life of many hundreds of educated persons, both sick and healthy, coming from every quarter of the civilized, white world; and upon this experience I base my statements. No doubt I can draw only a one-sided picture, for the things I have observed are events of psychic life; they lie within us—on the *inner side*, if I may use the expression. I must point out that this is not always true of psychic life; the psyche is not always and everywhere to be found on the inner side. It is to be found on the *outside* in whole races or periods of history which take no account of psychic life as such. As examples we may choose any of the ancient cultures, but especially that of Egypt with its imposing objectivity and its naïve confession of sins that have not been committed.[1] We can no more feel the Pyramids and the Apis tombs of Sakkara to be expressions of personal problems or personal emotions, than we can feel this of the music of Bach.

Whenever there is established an external form, be it ritual or spiritual, by which all the yearnings and hopes of the soul are adequately expressed—as for instance in some living religion—then we may say that the psyche is outside, and no spiritual problem, strictly speaking, exists. In consonance with this truth, the development of psychology falls entirely within the last decades, although long before that man was introspective and intelligent enough to recognize the facts that are the subject-matter of psychology. The same was the case with technical knowledge. The Romans were familiar with all the mechanical principles and physical facts on the basis of which they could have constructed the steam-engine, but all that came of it was the toy made by Hero of Alexandria. There was no urgent necessity to go further. It was the division of labour and specialization in the nineteenth century which gave rise to the need to apply all available knowledge. So also a spiritual need has produced in our time our "discovery" of psychology. There has never, of course, been a time when the psyche did not manifest itself, but formerly it attracted no attention—no one noticed it. People got along without heeding it. But today we can no longer get along unless we give our best attention to the ways of the psyche.

It was men of the medical profession who were the first to notice this; for the priest is concerned only to establish an undisturbed functioning of the psyche within a recognized system of belief. As long as this system gives true expression to life, psychology can be nothing but a technical adjuvant to healthy living, and the psyche cannot be regarded as a problem in itself. While man still lives as a herd-being he has no "things of the spirit" of his own; nor does he need any, save the usual belief in the immortality of the soul. But as soon as he has outgrown whatever local form of religion he was born to—as soon as this religion can no longer embrace his life in all its fulness—then the psyche becomes something in its own right which cannot be dealt with by the measures of the Church alone.

[1] [According to Egyptian tradition, when the dead man meets his judges in the underworld, he makes a detailed confession of the crimes he has *not* committed, but leaves unmentioned his actual sins—*Trans.*]

It is for this reason that we of today have a psychology founded on experience, and not upon articles of faith or the postulates of any philosophical system. The very fact that we have such a psychology is to me symptomatic of a profound convulsion of spiritual life. Disruption in the spiritual life of an age shows the same pattern as radical change in an individual. As long as all goes well and psychic energy finds its application in adequate and well-regulated ways, we are disturbed by nothing from within. No uncertainty or doubt besets us, and we *cannot* be divided against ourselves. But no sooner are one or two of the channels of psychic activity blocked, than we are reminded of a stream that is dammed up. The current flows backward to its source; the inner man wants something which the visible man does not want, and we are at war with ourselves. Only then, in this distress, do we discover the psyche; or, more precisely, we come upon something which thwarts our will, which is strange and even hostile to us, or which is incompatible with our conscious standpoint. Freud's psychoanalytic labours show this process in the clearest way. The very first thing he discovered was the existence of sexually perverse and criminal fantasies which at their face value are wholly incompatible with the conscious outlook of a civilized man. A person who was activated by them would be nothing less than a mutineer, a criminal or a madman.

We cannot suppose that this aspect of the unconscious or of the hinterland of man's mind is something totally new. Probably it has always been there, in every culture. Each culture gave birth to its destructive opposite, but no culture or civilization before our own was ever forced to take these psychic undercurrents in deadly earnest. Psychic life always found expression in a metaphysical system of some sort. But the conscious, modern man, despite his strenuous and dogged efforts to do so, can no longer refrain from acknowledging the might of psychic forces. This distinguishes our time from all others. We can no longer deny that the dark stirrings of the unconscious are effective powers—that psychic forces exist which cannot, for the present at least, be fitted in with our rational world-order. We have even enlarged our study of these forces to a science—one more proof of the earnest attention we bring to them. Previous centuries could throw them aside unnoticed; for us they are a shirt of Nessus which we cannot strip off.

The revolution in our conscious outlook, brought about by the catastrophic results of the World War, shows itself in our inner life by the shattering of our faith in ourselves and our own worth. We used to regard foreigners—the other side—as political and moral reprobates; but the modern man is forced to recognize that he is politically and morally just like anyone else. Whereas I formerly believed it to be my bounden duty to call other persons to order, I now admit that I need calling to order myself. I admit this the more readily because I realize only too well that I am losing my faith in the possibility of a rational organization of the world, that old dream of the millennium, in which peace and harmony should rule, has grown pale. The modern man's scepticism regarding all such matters has chilled his enthusiasm for politics and world-reform; more than that, it does not favour any smooth application of psychic energies to the outer world. Through his scepticism the modern man is thrown back upon himself; his energies flow towards their source and wash to the surface those psychic contents which are at all times there, but lie hidden in the silt as long as the stream flows smoothly in its course. How totally different did the world appear to mediæval man! For him the earth was eternally fixed and at rest in the centre of the universe, encircled by the course of a sun that solicitously bestowed its warmth. Men were all children of God under the loving care of the Most High, who prepared them for eternal blessedness; and all knew exactly what they should do and how they should conduct themselves in order to rise from a corruptible world to an incorruptible and joyous existence. Such a life no longer seems real to us, even in our dreams. Natural science has long ago torn this lovely veil to shreds. That age lies as far behind as childhood, when one's own father was unquestionably the handsomest and strongest man on earth.

The modern man has lost all the metaphysical certainties of his mediæval brother, and set up in their place the ideals of material security, general welfare and humaneness. But it takes more than an ordinary dose of optimism to make it appear that these ideals are still unshaken. Material security, even, has gone by the board, for the modern man begins to see that every step in material "progress" adds just so much force to the threat of a more stupendous catastrophe. The very picture terrorizes the imagination. What are we to imagine when cities today perfect measures of defence against poison-gas attacks and practise them in "dress rehearsals"?

We cannot but suppose that such attacks have been planned and provided for—again on the principle "in time of peace prepare for war". Let man but accumulate his materials of destruction and the devil within him will soon be unable to resist putting them to their fated use. It is well known that fire-arms go off of themselves if only enough of them are together.

An intimation of the law that governs blind contingency, which Heraclitus called the rule of *enantiodromia* (conversion into the opposite), now steals upon the modern man through the by-ways of his mind, chilling him with fear and paralysing his faith in the lasting effectiveness of social and political measures in the face of these monstrous forces. If he turns away from the terrifying prospect of a blind world in which building and destroying successively tip the scale, and if he then turns his gaze inward upon the recesses of his own mind, he will discover a chaos and a darkness there which he would gladly ignore. Science has destroyed even the refuge of the inner life. What was once a sheltering haven has become a place of terror.

And yet it is almost a relief for us to come upon so much evil in the depths of our own minds. We are able to believe, at least, that we have discovered the root of the evil in mankind. Even though we are shocked and disillusioned at first, we yet feel, because these things are manifestations of our own minds, that we hold them more or less in our own hands and can therefore correct or at least effectively suppress them. We like to assume that, if we succeeded in this, we should have rooted out some fraction of the evil in the world. We like to think that, on the basis of a widespread knowledge of the unconscious and its ways, no one could be deceived by a statesman who was unaware of his own bad motives; the very newspapers would pull him up: "Please have yourself analysed; you are suffering from a repressed father-complex."

I have purposely chosen this grotesque example to show to what absurdities we are led by the illusion that because something is psychic it is under our control. It is, however, true that much of the evil in the world is due to the fact that man in general is hopelessly unconscious, as it is also true that with increasing insight we can combat this evil at its source in ourselves. As science enables us to deal with injuries inflicted from without, so it helps us to treat those arising from within.

The rapid and world-wide growth of a "psychological" interest over the last two decades shows unmistakably that modern man has to some extent turned his attention from material things to his own subjective processes. Should we call this mere curiosity? At any rate, art has a way of anticipating future changes in man's fundamental outlook, and expressionist art has taken this subjective turn well in advance of the more general change.

This "psychological" interest of the present time shows that man expects something from psychic life which he has not received from the outer world: something which our religions, doubtless, ought to contain, but no longer do contain—at least for the modern man. The various forms of religion no longer appear to the modern man to come from within—to be expressions of his own psychic life; for him they are to be classed with the things of the outer world. He is vouchsafed no revelation of a spirit that is not of this world; but he tries on a number of religions and convictions as if they were Sunday attire, only to lay them aside again like worn-out clothes.

Yet he is somehow fascinated by the almost pathological manifestations of the unconscious mind. We must admit the fact, however difficult it is for us to understand that something which previous ages have discarded should suddenly command our attention. That there is a general interest in these matters is a truth which cannot be denied, their offence to good taste notwithstanding. I am not thinking merely of the interest taken in psychology as a science, or of the still narrower interest in the psychoanalysis of Freud, but of the widespread interest in all sorts of psychic phenomena as manifested in the growth of spiritualism, astrology, theosophy, and so forth. The world has seen nothing like it since the end of the seventeenth century. We can compare it only to the flowering of Gnostic thought in the first and second centuries after Christ. The spiritual currents of the present have, in fact, a deep affinity with Gnosticism. There is even a Gnostic church in France today, and I know of two schools in Germany which openly declare themselves Gnostic. The modern movement which is numerically most impressive is undoubtedly Theosophy, together with its continental sister, Anthroposophy; these are pure Gnosticism in a Hindu dress. Compared with these movements the interest in scientific psychology is negligible. What is striking about Gnostic systems is that they are based exclusively upon the manifestations of the unconscious, and that their moral teachings do not baulk at the shadow-side of life. Even in the form of its European revival, the Hindu *Kundalini-Yoga* shows this clearly. And as every person informed on the subject of occultism will testify, the statement holds true in this field as well.

The passionate interest in these movements arises undoubtedly from psychic energy which can no longer be invested in obsolete forms of religion. For this reason such movements have a truly religious character, even when they pretend to be scientific. It changes nothing when Rudolf Steiner calls his Anthroposophy "spiritual science", or Mrs. Eddy discovers a "Christian Science". These attempts at concealment merely show that religion has grown suspect—almost as suspect as politics and world-reform.

I do not believe that I am going too far when I say that modern man, in contrast to his nineteenth-century brother, turns his attention to the psyche with very great expectations; and that he does so without reference to any traditional creed, but rather in the Gnostic sense of religious experience. We should be wrong in seeing mere caricature or masquerade when the movements already mentioned try to give themselves scientific airs; their doing so is rather an indication that they are actually pursuing "science" or knowledge instead of the *faith* which is the essence of Western religions. The modern man abhors dogmatic postulates taken on faith and the religions based upon them. He holds them valid only in so far as their knowledge-content seems to accord with his own experience of the deeps of psychic life. He wants to know—to experience for himself. Dean Inge of St. Paul's has called attention to a movement in the Anglican Church with similar objectives.

The age of discovery has only just come to a close in our day when no part of the earth remains unexplored; it began when men would no longer *believe* that the Hyperboreans inhabited the land of eternal sunshine, but wanted to find out and to see with their own eyes what existed beyond the boundaries of the known world. Our age is apparently bent on discovering what exists in the psyche outside of consciousness. The question asked in every spiritualistic circle is: What happens when the medium has lost consciousness? Every Theosophist asks: What shall I experience at higher levels of consciousness? The question which every astrologer puts is this: What are the effective forces and determinants of my fate beyond the reach of my conscious intention? And every psychoanalyst wants to know: What are the unconscious drives behind the neurosis?

Our age wishes to have actual experiences in psychic life. It wants to experience for itself, and not to make assumptions based on the experience of other ages. Yet this does not preclude its trying anything in a hypothetical way—for instance, the recognized religions and the genuine sciences. The European of yesterday will feel a slight shudder run down his spine when he gazes at all deeply into these delvings. Not only does he consider the subject of this research all too obscure and uncanny, but even the methods employed seem to him a shocking misuse of man's finest intellectual attainments. What can we expect an astronomer to say when he is told that at least a thousand horoscopes are drawn today to one three hundred years ago? What will the educator and the advocate of philosophical enlightenment say to the fact that the world has not been freed of one single superstition since Greek antiquity? Freud himself, the founder of psychoanalysis, has thrown a glaring light upon the dirt, darkness and evil of the psychic hinterland, and has presented these things as so much refuse and slag; he has thus taken the utmost pains to discourage people from seeking anything behind them. He did not succeed, and his warning has even brought about the very thing he wished to prevent: it has awakened in many people an admiration for all this filth. We are tempted to call this sheer perversity; and we could hardly explain it save on the ground that it is not a love of dirt, but the fascination of the psyche, which draws these people.

There can be no doubt that from the beginning of the nineteenth century—from the memorable years of the French Revolution onwards—man has given a more and more prominent place to the psyche, his increasing attentiveness to it being the measure of its growing attraction for him. The enthronement of the Goddess of Reason in Notre Dame seems to have been a symbolic gesture of great significance to the Western world—rather like the hewing down of Wotan's oak by the Christian missionaries. For then, as at the Revolution, no avenging bolt from heaven struck the blasphemer down.

It is certainly more than an amusing coincidence that just at that time a Frenchman, Anquetil du Perron, was living in India, and, in the early eighteen-hundreds, brought back with him a translation of the *Oupnek'hat*—a collection of fifty *Upanishads*—which gave the Western world its first deep insight into the baffling mind of the East. To the historian this is mere chance without any factors of cause and effect. But in view of my medical experience I cannot take it as accident. It seems to me rather to satisfy a psychological law whose validity in personal life, at least, is complete. For every piece of conscious life that loses its importance and value—so runs the law—there arises a compensation in the unconscious. We may see in this an analogy to the conservation of energy in the physical world, for our psychic processes have a quantitative aspect also. No psychic value can disappear without being replaced by another of equivalent intensity. This is a rule which finds its pragmatic sanction in the daily practice of the psychotherapist; it is repeatedly verified and never fails. Now the doctor in me refuses point blank to consider the life of a people as something that does not conform to psychological law. A people, in the doctor's eyes, presents only a somewhat more complex picture of psychic life than the individual. Moreover, taking it the other way round, has not a poet spoken of the "nations" of his soul? And quite correctly, as it seems to me, for in one of its aspects the psyche is not individual, but is derived from the nation, from collectivity, or from humanity even. In some way or other we are part of an all-embracing psychic life, of a single "greatest" man, to quote Swedenborg.

And so we can draw a parallel: just as in me, a single human being, the darkness calls forth the helpful light, so does it also in the psychic life of a people. In the crowds that poured into Notre Dame, bent on destruction, dark and nameless forces were at work that swept the individual off his feet; these forces worked also upon Anquetil du Perron, and provoked an answer which has come down in history. For he brought the Eastern mind to the West, and its influence upon us we cannot as yet measure. Let us beware of underestimating it! So far, indeed, there is little of it to be seen in Europe on the intellectual surface: some orientalists, one or two Buddhist enthusiasts, and a few sombre celebrities like Madame Blavatsky and Annie Besant. These manifestations make us think of tiny, scattered islands in the ocean of mankind; in reality they are like the peaks of submarine mountain-ranges of considerable size. The Philistine believed until recently that astrology had been disposed of long since, and was something that could be safely laughed at. But today, rising out of the social deeps, it knocks at the doors of the universities from which it was banished some three hundred years ago. The same is true of the thought of the East; it takes root in the lower social levels and slowly grows to the surface. Where did the five or six million Swiss francs for the Anthroposophist temple at Dornach come from? Certainly not from one individual. Unfortunately there are no statistics to tell us the exact number of avowed Theosophists today, not to mention the unavowed. But we can be sure that there are several millions of them. To this number we must add a few million Spiritualists of Christian or Theosophic leanings.

Great innovations never come from above; they come invariably from below; just as trees never grow from the sky downward, but upward from the earth, however true it is that their seeds have fallen from above. The upheaval of our world and the upheaval in consciousness is one and the same. Everything becomes relative and therefore doubtful. And while man, hesitant and questioning, contemplates a world that is distracted with treaties of peace and pacts of friendship, democracy and dictatorship, capitalism and Bolshevism, his spirit yearns for an answer that will allay the turmoil of doubt and uncertainty. And it is just people of the lower social levels who follow the unconscious forces of the psyche; it is the much-derided, silent folk of the land—those who are less infected with academic prejudices than great celebrities are wont to be. All these people, looked at from above, present mostly a dreary or laughable comedy; and yet they are as impressively simple as those Galileans who were once called blessed. Is it not touching to see the refuse of man's psyche gathered together in compendia a foot thick? We find recorded in *Anthropophyteia* with scrupulous care the merest babblings, the most absurd actions and the wildest fantasies, while men like Havelock Ellis and Freud have dealt with the like matters in serious treatises which have been accorded all scientific honours. Their reading public is scattered over the breadth of the civilized, white world. How are we to explain this zeal, this almost fanatical worship of repellent things? In this way: the repellent things belong to the psyche, they are of the substance of the psyche and therefore as precious as fragments of manuscript salvaged from ancient ruins. Even the secret and noisome things of the inner life are valuable to modern man because they serve his purpose. But what purpose?

Freud has prefixed to his *Interpretation of Dreams* the citation: *Flectere si nequeo superos Acheronta movebo*—"If I cannot bend the gods on high, I will at least set Acheron in uproar". But to what purpose?

The gods whom *we* are called to dethrone are the idolized values of our conscious world. It is well known that it was the love-scandals of the ancient deities which contributed most to their discredit; and now history is repeating itself. People are laying bare the dubious foundations of our belauded virtues and incomparable ideals, and are calling out to us in triumph: "There are your man-made gods, mere snares and delusions tainted with human base-ness—whited sepulchres full of dead men's bones and of all un-cleanness". We recognize a familiar strain, and the Gospel words, which we never could make our own, now come to life again.

I am deeply convinced that these are not vague analogies. There are too many persons to whom Freudian psychology is dearer than the Gospels, and to whom the Russian Terror means more than civic virtue. And yet all these people are our brothers, and in each of us there is at least *one* voice which seconds them—for in the end there is a psychic life which embraces us all.

The unexpected result of this spiritual change is that an uglier face is put upon the world. It becomes so ugly that no one can love it any longer—we cannot even love ourselves—and in the end there is nothing in the outer world to draw us away from the reality of the life within. Here, no doubt, we have the true significance of this spiritual change. After all, what does Theosophy, with its doctrines of *karma* and reincarnation, seek to teach except that this world of appearance is but a temporary health-resort for the morally unperfected? It depreciates the present-day world no less radically than does the modern outlook, but with the help of a different technique; it does not vilify our world, but grants it only a relative meaning in that it promises other and higher worlds. The result is in either case the same.

I grant that all these ideas are extremely "unacademic," the truth being that they touch modern man on the side where he is least conscious. Is it again a mere coincidence that modern thought has had to come to terms with Einstein's relativity theory and with ideas about the structure of the atom which lead us away from determinism and visual representation? Even physics volatilizes our material world. It is no wonder, then, in my opinion, if the modern man falls back upon the reality of psychic life and expects from it that certainty which the world denies him.

But spiritually the Western world is in a precarious situation— and the danger is greater the more we blind ourselves to the merciless truth with illusions about our beauty of soul. The Occidental burns incense to himself, and his own countenance is veiled from him in the smoke. But how do we strike men of another colour? What do China and India think of us? What feelings do we arouse in the black man? And what is the opinion of all those whom we deprive of their lands and exterminate with rum and venereal disease?

I have a Red Indian friend who is the governor of a pueblo. When we were once speaking confidentially about the white man, he said to me: "We don't understand the whites; they are always wanting something—always restless—always looking for something. What is it? We don't know. We can't understand them. They have such sharp noses, such thin, cruel lips, such lines in their faces. We think they are all crazy".

My friend had recognized, without being able to name it, the Aryan bird of prey with his insatiable lust to lord it in every land— even those that concern him not at all. And he had also noted that megalomania of ours which leads us to suppose, among other things, that Christianity is the only truth, and the white Christ the only Redeemer. After setting the whole East in turmoil with our science and technology, and exacting tribute from it, we send our missionaries even to China. The stamping out of polygamy by the African missions has given rise to prostitution on such a scale that in Uganda alone twenty thousand pounds sterling is spent yearly on preventatives of venereal infection, not to speak of the moral consequences, which have been of the worst. And the good European pays his missionaries for these edifying achievements! No need to mention also the story of suffering in Polynesia and the blessings of the opium trade.

That is how the European looks when he is extricated from the cloud of his own moral incense. No wonder that to unearth buried fragments of psychic life we have first to drain a miasmal swamp. Only a great idealist like Freud could devote a lifetime to the unclean work. This is the beginning of our psychology. For us acquaintance with the realities of psychic life could start only at this end, with all that repels us and that we do not wish to see.

But if the psyche consisted for us only of evil and worthless things, no power in the world could induce a normal man to pretend to find it attractive. This is why people who see in Theosophy nothing but regrettable intellectual superficiality, and in Freudian psychology nothing but sensationalism, prophesy an early and inglorious end for these movements. They overlook the fact that they derive their force from the fascination of psychic life. No doubt the passionate interest that is aroused by them may find other expressions; but it will certainly show itself in these forms until they are replaced by something better. Superstition and perversity are after all one and the same. They are transitional or embryonic stages from which new and riper forms will emerge.

Whether from the intellectual, the moral or the æsthetic viewpoint, the undercurrents of the psychic life of the West present an uninviting picture. We have built a monumental world round about us, and have slaved for it with unequalled energy. But it is so imposing only because we have spent upon the outside all that is imposing in our natures—and what we find when we look within must necessarily be as it is, shabby and insufficient.

I am aware that in saying this I somewhat anticipate the actual growth of consciousness. There is as yet no general insight into these facts of psychic life. Westerners are only on the way to a recognition of these facts, and for quite understandable reasons they struggle violently against it. Of course Spengler's pessimism has exerted some influence, but this has been safely confined to academic circles. As for psychological insight, it always trespasses upon personal life, and therefore meets with personal resistances and denials. I am far from considering these resistances meaningless; on the contrary I see in them a healthy reaction to something which threatens destruction. Whenever relativism is taken as a fundamental and final principle it has a destructive effect. When, therefore, I call attention to the dismal undercurrents of the psyche, it is not in order to sound a pessimistic note; I wish rather to emphasize the fact that the unconscious has a strong attraction not only for the sick, but for healthy, constructive minds as well—and this in spite of its alarming aspect. The psychic depths are nature, and nature is creative life. It is true that nature tears down what she has herself built up—yet she builds it once again. Whatever values in the visible world are destroyed by modern relativism, the psyche will produce their equivalents. At first we cannot see beyond the path that leads downward to dark and hateful things—but no light or beauty will ever come from the man who cannot bear this sight. Light is always born of darkness, and the sun never yet stood still in heaven to satisfy man's longing or to still his fears. Does not the example of Anquetil du Perron show us how psychic life survives its own eclipse? China hardly believes that European science and technology are preparing her ruin. Why should we believe that we must be destroyed by the secret, spiritual influence of the East?

But I forget that we do not yet realize that while we are turning upside down the material world of the East with our technical proficiency, the East with its psychic proficiency is throwing our spiritual world into confusion. We have never yet hit upon the thought that while we are overpowering the Orient from without, it may be fastening its hold upon us from within. Such an idea strikes us as almost insane, because we have eyes only for gross material connections, and fail to see that we must lay the blame for the intellectual confusion of our middle class at the doors of Max Müller, Oldenberg, Neumann, Deussen, Wilhelm and others like them. What does the example of the Roman Empire teach us? After the conquest of Asia Minor, Rome became Asiatic; even Europe was infected by Asia, and remains so today. Out of Cilicia came the Mithraic cult—the religion of the Roman army—and it spread from Egypt to fog-bound Britain. Need I point to the Asiatic origin of Christianity?

We have not yet clearly grasped the fact that Western Theosophy is an amateurish imitation of the East. We are just taking up astrology again, and that to the Oriental is his daily bread. Our studies of sexual life, originating in Vienna and in England, are matched or surpassed by Hindu teachings on this subject. Oriental texts ten centuries old introduce us to philosophical relativism, while the idea of indetermination, newly broached in the West, furnishes the very basis of Chinese science. Richard Wilhelm has even shown me that certain complicated processes discovered by analytical psychology are recognizably described in ancient Chinese texts. Psychoanalysis itself and the lines of thought to which it gives rise—surely a distinctly Western development—are only a beginner's attempt compared to what is an immemorial art in the East. It should be mentioned that the parallels between psychoanalysis and yoga have already been traced by Oskar A. H. Schmitz.

The Theosophists have an amusing idea that certain Mahatmas, seated somewhere in the Himalayas or Tibet, inspire or direct every mind in the world. So strong, in fact, can be the influence of the Eastern belief in magic upon Europeans of a sound mind, that some of them have assured me that I am unwittingly inspired by the Mahatmas with every good thing I say, my own inspirations being of no account whatever. This myth of the Mahatmas, widely circulated and firmly believed in the West, far from being nonsense, is—like every myth—an important psychological truth. It seems to be quite true that the East is at the bottom of the spiritual change we are passing through today. Only this East is not a Tibetan monastery full of Mahatmas, but in a sense lies within us. It is from the depths of our own psychic life that new spiritual forms will rise; they will be expressions of psychic forces which may help to subdue the boundless lust for prey of Aryan man. We shall perhaps come to know something of that circumscription of life which has grown in the East into a dubious quietism; also something of that stability which human existence acquires when the claims of the spirit become as imperative as the necessities of social life. Yet in this age of Americanization we are still far from anything of the sort, and it seems to me that we are only at the threshold of a new spiritual epoch. I do not wish to pass myself off as a prophet, but I cannot outline the spiritual problem of modern man without giving emphasis to the yearning for rest that arises in a period of unrest, or to the longing for security that is bred of insecurity. It is from needs and distress that new forms of life take their rise, and not from mere wishes or from the requirements of our ideals.

To me, the crux of the spiritual problem of today is to be found in the fascination which psychic life exerts upon modern man. If we are pessimists, we shall call it a sign of decadence; if we are optimistically inclined, we shall see in it the promise of a far-reaching spiritual change in the Western world. At all events, it is a significant manifestation. It is the more noteworthy because it shows itself in broad sections of every people; and it is the more important because it is a matter of those imponderable psychic forces which transform human life in ways that are unforeseen and—as history shows—unforeseeable. These are the forces, still invisible to many persons today, which are at the bottom of the present "psychological" interest. When the attractive power of psychic life is so strong that man is neither repelled nor dismayed by what he is sure to find, then it has nothing of sickliness or perversion about it.

Along the great highroads of the world everything seems desolate and outworn. Instinctively the modern man leaves the trodden ways to explore the by-paths and lanes, just as the man of the Græco-Roman world cast off his defunct Olympian gods and turned to the mystery-cults of Asia. The force within us that impels us to the search, turning outward, annexes Eastern Theosophy and magic; but it also turns inward and leads us to give our thoughtful attention to the unconscious psyche. It inspires in us the selfsame scepticism and relentlessness with which a Buddha swept aside his two million gods that he might come to the pristine experience which alone is convincing.

And now we must ask a final question. Is what I have said of the modern man really true, or is it perhaps the result of an optical illusion? There can be no doubt whatever that the facts I have cited are wholly irrelevant contingencies in the eyes of many millions of Westerners, and seem only regrettable errors to a large number of educated persons. But I may ask: What did a cultivated Roman think of Christianity when he saw it spreading among the people of the lowest classes? The biblical God is still a living person in the Western world—as living as Allah beyond the Mediterranean. One kind of believer holds the other an ignoble heretic, to be pitied and tolerated if he cannot be changed. What is more, a clever European is convinced that religion and such things are good enough for the masses and for women, but are of little weight compared to economic and political affairs.

So I am refuted all along the line, like a man who predicts a thunderstorm when there is not a cloud in the sky. Perhaps it is a storm beneath the horizon that he senses—and it may never reach us. But what is significant in psychic life is always below the horizon of consciousness, and when we speak of the spiritual problem of modern man we are dealing with things that are barely visible—with the most intimate and fragile things—with flowers that open only in the night. In daylight everything is clear and tangible; but the night lasts as long as the day, and we live in the night-time also. There are persons who have bad dreams which even spoil their days for them. And the day's life is for many people such a bad dream that they long for the night when the spirit awakes. I even believe that there are nowadays a great many such people, and this is why I maintain that the spiritual problem of modern man is much as I have presented it. I must plead guilty, indeed, to the charge of one-sidedness, for I have not mentioned the modern spirit of commitment to a practical world about which everyone has much to say because it lies in such full view. We find it in the ideal of internationalism or supernationalism which is embodied in the League of Nations and the like; and we find it also in sport and, very expressively, in the cinema and in jazz music.

These are certainly characteristic symptoms of our time; they show unmistakably how the ideal of humanism is made to embrace the body also. Sport represents an exceptional valuation of the human body, as does also modern dancing. The cinema, on the other hand, like the detective story, makes it possible to experience without danger all the excitement, passion and desirousness which must be repressed in a humanitarian ordering of life. It is not difficult to see how these symptoms are connected with the psychic situation. The attractive power of the psyche brings about a new self-estimation—a re-estimation of the basic facts of human nature. We can hardly be surprised if this leads to the rediscovery of the body after its long depreciation in the name of the spirit. We are even tempted to speak of the body's revenge upon the spirit. When Keyserling sarcastically singles out the chauffeur as the culture-hero of our time, he has struck, as he often does, close to the mark. The body lays claim to equal recognition; like the psyche, it also exerts a fascination. If we are still caught by the old idea of an antithesis between mind and matter, the present state of affairs means an unbearable contradiction; it may even divide us against ourselves. But if we can reconcile ourselves with the mysterious truth that spirit is the living body seen from within, and the body the outer manifestation of the living spirit—the two being really one—then we can understand why it is that the attempt to transcend the present level of consciousness must give its due to the body. We shall also see that belief in the body cannot tolerate an outlook that denies the body in the name of the spirit. These claims of physical and psychic life are so pressing compared to similar claims in the past, that we may be tempted to see in this a sign of decadence. Yet it may also signify a rejuvenation, for as Hölderlin says:

> Danger itself
> Fosters the rescuing power.[2]

What we actually see is that the Western world strikes up a still more rapid tempo—the American tempo—the very opposite of quietism and resigned aloofness. An enormous tension arises between the opposite poles of outer and inner life, between objective and subjective reality. Perhaps it is a final race between ageing Europe and young America; perhaps it is a desperate or a wholesome effort of conscious man to cheat the laws of nature of their hidden might and to wrest a yet greater, more heroic victory from the sleep of the nations. This is a question which history will answer.

In coming to a close after so many bold assertions, I would like to return to the promise made at the outset to be mindful of the need for moderation and caution. Indeed, I do not forget that my voice is but one voice, my experience a mere drop in the sea, my knowledge no greater than the visual field in a microscope, my mind's eye a mirror that reflects a small corner of the world, and my ideas—a subjective confession.

[2] *Wo Gefahr ist,*
Wächst das Rettende auch. (Hölderlin.)

V

Theories of Art

Lecture on Dada

TRISTAN TZARA

The twentieth century has given rise to a confusing array of movements in the fine arts, from the cubism of the 1900's to the aleatoric
and pop art of the 1960's. Some of these movements have hinged their
efforts on theories of form that find underlying order in the prevailing
chaos of modern life. Others have proclaimed that chaos alone is real
and have dedicated themselves to an irreverent assault on reason,
religion, and modern civilization in general. The most extreme example
of irrationalism in literature and the arts is Dadaism, which originated
in 1916 in Switzerland and commanded much public attention in the
early postwar years, numbering among its exponents Hugo Ball,
George Grosz, Hans Arp, and André Breton. After the demise of
Dada, some of the Dadaists went on to found the surrealist movement;
but a good deal of the avant-garde art and poetry of the 1950's and
1960's strongly calls to mind the jeering nihilism of Dada in its original
form. The chief manifesto-writer of the Dadaists, Tristan Tzara, was a
Rumanian by birth, a Parisian by adoption. His most conventionally
intelligible effort to explain the antiphilosophy of Dada is perhaps this
lecture, given in 1922.

LADIES AND GENTLEMEN:

I don't have to tell you that for the general public and for you,
the refined public, a Dadaist is the equivalent of a leper. But that is
only a manner of speaking. When these same people get close to us,
they treat us with that remnant of elegance that comes from their

SOURCE: "Lecture on Dada, 1922," by Tristan Tzara, trans. Ralph Manheim,
in *The Dada Painters and Poets: An Anthology*, ed. Robert Motherwell
(Wittenborn, New York, 1951), pp. 246–48 and 250–51. Reprinted by permission of George Wittenborn, Inc., New York, N.Y., 10021.

old habit of belief in progress. At ten yards distance, hatred begins again. If you ask me why, I won't be able to tell you.

Another characteristic of Dada is the continuous breaking off of our friends. They are always breaking off and resigning. The first to tender his resignation from the Dada movement *was myself*. Everybody knows that Dada is nothing. I broke away from Dada and from myself as soon as I understood the implications of *nothing*.

If I continue to do something, it is because it amuses me, or rather because I have a need for activity which I use up and satisfy wherever I can. Basically, the true Dadas have always been separate from Dada. Those who acted as if Dada were important enough to resign from with a big noise have been motivated by a desire for personal publicity, proving that counterfeiters have always wriggled like unclean worms in and out of the purest and most radiant religions.

I know that you have come here today to hear explanations. Well, don't expect to hear any explanations about Dada. You explain to me why you exist. You haven't the faintest idea. You will say: I exist to make my children happy. But in your hearts you know that isn't so. You will say: I exist to guard my country against barbarian invasions. That's a fine reason. You will say: I exist because God wills. That's a fairy tale for children. You will never be able to tell me why you exist but you will always be ready to maintain a serious attitude about life. You will never understand that life is a pun, for you will never be alone enough to reject hatred, judgments, all these things that require such an effort, in favor of a calm and level state of mind that makes everything equal and without importance.

Dada is not at all modern. It is more in the nature of a return to an almost Buddhist religion of indifference. Dada covers things with an artificial gentleness, a snow of butterflies released from the head of a prestidigitator. Dada is immobility and does not comprehend the passions. You will call this a paradox, since Dada is manifested only in violent acts. Yes, the reactions of individuals contaminated by *destruction* are rather violent, but when these reactions are exhausted, annihilated by the Satanic insistence of a continuous and progressive "What for?" what remains, what dominates is *indifference*. But with the same note of conviction I might maintain the contrary.

I admit that my friends do not approve this point of view. But the *Nothing* can be uttered only as the reflection of an individual. And that is why it will be valid for everyone, since everyone is important only for the individual who is expressing himself.—I am speaking of myself. Even that is too much for me. How can I be expected to speak of all men at once, and satisfy them too?

Nothing is more delightful than to confuse and upset people. People one doesn't like. What's the use of giving them explanations that are merely food for curiosity? The truth is that people love nothing but themselves and their little possessions, their income, their dog. This state of affairs derives from a false conception of property. If one is poor in spirit, one possesses a sure and indomitable intelligence, a savage logic, a point of view that can not be shaken. Try to be empty and fill your brain cells with a petty happiness. Always destroy what you have in you. On random walks. Then you will be able to understand many things. You are not more intelligent than we, and we are not more intelligent than you.

Intelligence is an organization like any other, the organization of society, the organization of a bank, the organization of chit-chat. At a society tea. It serves to create order and clarity where there is none. It serves to create a state hierarchy. To set up classifications for rational work. To separate questions of a material order from those of a cerebral order, but to take the former very seriously. Intelligence is the triumph of sound education and pragmatism. Fortunately life is something else and its pleasures are innumerable. They are not paid for in the coin of liquid intelligence.

These observations of everyday conditions have led us to a realization which constitutes our minimum basis of agreement, aside from the sympathy which binds us and which is inexplicable. It would not have been possible for us to found our agreement on principles. For everything is relative. What are the Beautiful, the Good, Art, Freedom? Words that have a different meaning for every individual. Words with the pretension of creating agreement among all, and that is why they are written with capital letters. Words which have not the moral value and objective force that people have grown accustomed to finding in them. Their meaning changes from one individual, one epoch, one country to the next. Men are different. It is diversity that makes life interesting. There is no common basis in men's minds. The unconscious is inexhaustible and uncontrollable. Its force surpasses us. It is as mysterious as the last particle of a brain cell. Even if we knew it, we could not reconstruct it.

What good did the theories of the philosophers do us? Did they help us to take a single step forward or backward? What is forward, what is backward? Did they alter our forms of contentment? We are. We argue, we dispute, we get excited. The rest is sauce. Sometimes pleasant, sometimes mixed with a limitless boredom, a swamp dotted with tufts of dying shrubs.

We have had enough of the intelligent movements that have stretched beyond measure our credulity in the benefits of science. What we want now is spontaneity. Not because it is better or more beautiful than anything else. But because everything that issues freely from ourselves, without the intervention of speculative ideas, represents us. We must intensify this quantity of life that readily spends itself in every quarter. Art is not the most precious manifestation of life. Art has not the celestial and universal value that people like to attribute to it. Life is far more interesting. Dada knows the correct measure that should be given to art: with subtle, perfidious methods, Dada introduces it into daily life. And vice versa. In art, Dada reduces everything to an initial simplicity, growing always more relative. It mingles its caprices with the chaotic wind of creation and the barbaric dances of savage tribes. It wants logic reduced to a personal minimum, while literature in its view should be primarily intended for the individual who makes it. Words have a weight of their own and lend themselves to abstract construction. The absurd has no terrors for me, for from a more exalted point of view everything in life seems absurd to me. Only the elasticity of our conventions creates a bond between disparate acts. The Beautiful and the True in art do not exist; what interests me is the intensity of a personality transposed directly, clearly into the work; the man and his vitality; the angle from which he regards the elements and in what manner he knows how to gather sensation, emotion, into a lacework of words and sentiments.

Dada tries to find out what words mean before using them, from the point of view not of grammar but of representation. Objects and colors pass through the same filter. It is not the new technique that interests us, but the spirit. Why do you want us to be preoccupied with a pictorial, moral, poetic, literary, political or social renewal? We are well aware that these renewals of means are merely the successive cloaks of the various epochs of history, uninteresting questions of fashion and facade. We are well aware that people in the costumes of the Renaissance were pretty much the same as the people of today, and that Chouang-Dsi was just as Dada as we are. You are mistaken if you take Dada for a modern school, or even for a reaction against the schools of today. Several of my statements have struck you as old and natural, what better proof that you were Dadaists without knowing it, perhaps even before the birth of Dada.

You will often hear that Dada is a state of mind. You may be gay, sad, afflicted, joyous, melancholy or Dada. Without being literary, you can be romantic, you can be dreamy, weary, eccentric, a businessman, skinny, transfigured, vain, amiable or Dada. This will happen later on in the course of history when Dada has become a precise, habitual word, when popular repetition has given it the character of a word organic with its necessary content. Today no one thinks of the literature of the Romantic school in representing a lake, a landscape, a character. Slowly but surely, a Dada character is forming.

Dada is here, there and a little everywhere, such as it is, with its faults, with its personal differences and distinctions which it accepts and views with indifference.

We are often told that we are incoherent, but into this word people try to put an insult that it is rather hard for me to fathom. Everything is incoherent. The gentleman who decides to take a bath but goes to the movies instead. The one who wants to be quiet but says things that haven't even entered his head. Another who has a precise idea on some subject but succeeds only in expressing the opposite in words which for him are a poor translation. There is no logic. Only relative necessities discovered *a posteriori*, valid not in any exact sense but only as explanations.

The acts of life have no beginning or end. Everything happens in a completely idiotic way. That is why everything is alike. Simplicity is called Dada.

Any attempt to conciliate an inexplicable momentary state with logic strikes me as a boring kind of game. The convention of the spoken language is ample and adequate for us, but for our solitude, for our intimate games and our literature we no longer need it.

The beginnings of Dada were not the beginnings of an art, but of a disgust. Disgust with the magnificence of philosophers who for 3000 years have been explaining everything to us (what for?), disgust with the pretensions of these artists-God's-representatives-on-earth, disgust with passion and with real pathological wickedness where it was not worth the bother; disgust with a false form of domination and restriction *en masse*, that accentuates rather than appeases man's instinct of domination, disgust with all the catalogued categories, with the false prophets who are nothing but a front for the interests of money, pride, disease, disgust with the lieutenants of a mercantile art made to order according to a few infantile laws, disgust with the divorce of good and evil, the beautiful and the ugly (for why is it more estimable to be red rather than green, to the left rather than the right, to be large or small?). Disgust finally with the Jesuitical dialectic which can explain everything and fill people's minds with oblique and obtuse ideas without any physiological basis or ethnic roots, all this by means of blinding artifice and ignoble charlatan's promises.

As Dada marches it continuously destroys, not in extension but in itself. From all these disgusts, may I add, it draws no conclusion, no pride, no benefit. It has even stopped combating anything, in the realization that it's no use, that all this doesn't matter. What interests a Dadaist is his own mode of life. But here we approach the great secret.

Dada is a state of mind. That is why it transforms itself according to races and events. Dada applies itself to everything, and yet it is nothing, it is the point where the yes and the no and all the opposites meet, not solemnly in the castles of human philosophies, but very simply at street corners, like dogs and grasshoppers.

Like everything in life, Dada is useless.

Dada is without pretension, as life should be.

Perhaps you will understand me better when I tell you that Dada is a virgin microbe that penetrates with the insistence of air into all the spaces that reason has not been able to fill with words or conventions.

Constructive Realism

NAUM GABO

At the opposite pole from Tzara's Dadaism stands the constructivism of the émigré Russian artist Naum Gabo. Like cubism, vorticism, and several other schools of art in the early twentieth century, constructivism was an attempt to replace the academic naturalistic art of the nineteenth century with an art that captured the purity of abstract form. For a brief period after the 1917 Revolution, down to 1922, a pitched battle was fought in Russia by the academic painters, on the one hand, and Gabo's constructivists, on the other hand. The Communist Party, despite its revolutionary objectives in political and economic life, eventually came down on the side of the traditionalists, and Gabo had to accept exile abroad.

Since then, his work has fully matured, and he has become one of the most eloquent spokesmen among living artists for an art that expresses in poetic terms the order of the universe and the possibilities for order in human civilization. In the words of a letter he wrote to the British critic Herbert Read in 1944: "I am offering in my art what comfort I can to alleviate the pains and convulsions of our time. I try to keep our despair from assuming such proportions that nothing will remain in our devastated life to prompt us to live." His lecture at the Yale University Art Gallery in 1948, reprinted below, supplies insight into his theory of art and the place of art in a possible unified world civilization.

IT HAS always been my principle to let my work speak for itself, following the maxim that a work of art does not need to be explained by its author, that it is rather the other way around, it is the author who is explained by his work of art. However, I have often been called upon to use words to supplement the mute medium of my profession. I confess, that I was never happy about it. My only comfort, such as it may be, is the fact that I am not the only one who is encumbered by this overwhelming duty. All artists in all times had to do it in one way or another, and my contemporaries are certainly no exception. But it may be instruc-

SOURCE: "On Constructive Realism," by Naum Gabo, in *Three Lectures on Modern Art*, by Katherine S. Dreier *et al.* (Philosophical Library, New York, 1949), pp. 65–87. Reprinted by permission of Philosophical Library.

tive to notice the difference of methods used by the former and by the latter. When the artist of old times was challenged to justify his work, he had an easy and simple task. He lived in a stable society, tightly knitted in a pattern of a commonly accepted social, religious and moral codes; he and his society lived in accordance with a set of very well defined standards of what is good, what is bad, what is virtuous or vile, beautiful or ugly. All the artist had to do was to refer to these standards and argue that in his work he fulfilled their demands.

The artist of today, however, when called upon to justify his work finds himself confronted with a most difficult and complex problem. Here he stands in the midst of a world shattered to its very foundation, before a totally anonymous society, deprived of all measures, for evil, beauty, ugliness, etc. . . . . He has no norms to refer to. He is, in fact, an abnormal subject in an abnormal society. And there are only two ways left open to him; one is the reference to his personality.

Personality is one of those things which by some trick of our social disorder has been left as some sort of a little straw in the maelstrom of confused values, and many an artist is grasping that straw.

They, in justification of their work, appeal to their personality; their motto roughly amounts to this: "You are asking from me my personality—here I am;—this is how I see the world,—I, not you. You cannot judge my work, because you are not I—I paint what I see and how I see it. I paint what pleases me and you have to take it or leave it."

We have seen that more often than not this method has proved of some advantage and for a time was useful for many artists in so far as it gave them the opportunity to carry their revolt and their contempt to that very society which, having no personality of its own, yet demanded that the artist produce one.

Although I have the greatest esteem for the work these artists have done in their time, their method is not mine.

And although it would be a false humility on my part to deny to myself what is given to me by nature and what I have acquired through the experience of my life, namely, that I too have a personality, I do not hold, however, that personality alone, without its being integrated in the main body of the society in which it lives can constitute a strong enough basis for the justification of my

work or of any work of art, for that matter. I hold that personality
is an attribute of which any one and every one may boast. It is
there whether we want it or not. I hold that such a method of
justification may only result in that very baleful end from which
we are striving to escape; namely, it will end in the vanity fair of
personalities struggling to overpower each other. I see nothing but
confusion and social and mental disaster on this road.

But, there is something else at the artist's disposal to justify his
work; and this is when the artist in his art is led by an idea of which
he believes that it epitomises not only what he himself feels and
looks forward to as an individual, but what the collective human
mind of his time feels and aspires towards, but cannot yet express.

As such he is a fore-runner of some development in the mentality
of human society and though his idea may or may not eventually
prevail over other ideas of his time or of the future, it nevertheless
is performing a function without which no progress is possible.
This is my road and the purpose of this paper is to explain as
concisely as my time permits the fundamentals of the idea which I
profess and which I would call—The Idea of Constructive
Realism.

My art is commonly known as the art of Constructivism. Actually the word Constructivism is a misnomer. The word Constructivism has been appropriated by one group of constructive
artists in the 1920's who demanded that art should liquidate itself.
They denied any value to easel-painting, to sculpture, in fine, to
any work of art in which the artist's purpose was to convey ideas
or emotions for their own sake. They demanded from the artist,
and particularly from those who were commonly called constructivists that they should use their talents for construction of material
values, namely, in building useful objects, houses, chairs, tables,
stoves etc. Being materialist in their philosophy and Marxist in
their politics, they could not see in a work of art anything else but
a pleasurable occupation cherished in a decadent capitalistic society
and totally useless, even harmful in the new society of communism.
My friends and myself were strongly opposed to that peculiar
trend of thought. I did not and do not share the opinion that art is
just another game or another pleasure to the artist's heart. I believe
that art has a specific function to perform in the mental and social
structure of human life. I believe that art is the most immediate and
most effective means of communication between the members of

human society. I believe art has a supreme vitality equal only to the supremacy of life itself and that it, therefore, reigns over all man's creations.

It should be apparent from the foregoing that I thus ascribe to art a function of a much higher value and put it on a much broader plane than that somewhat loose and limited one we are used to when we say: painting, sculpture, music, etc. I denominate by the word art the specific and exclusive faculty of man's mind to conceive and represent the world without and within him in form and by means of artfully constructed images. Moreover, I maintain that this faculty predominates in all the processes of our mental and physical orientation in this world, it being impossible for our minds to perceive or arrange or act upon our world in any other way but through this construction of an ever-changing and yet coherent chain of images. Furthermore, I maintain that these mentally constructed images are the very essence of the reality of the world which we are searching for.

When I say images I do not mean images in the platonic sense,—not as reflections or shadows of some reality behind these constructed images of our minds and senses but the images themselves. Any talk and reference to a higher, to a purer, to a more exact reality which is supposed to be beyond these images, I take as a chase after illusions unless and until some image has been constructed by our mind about it to make it appear on the plane of our consciousness in some concrete and coherent form: tangible, visible, imageable, perceptible.

Obviously such a process as I visualize in our mental activity is manifestly a characteristic attribute of art. Consequently I go so far as to maintain that all the other constructions of our mind, be they scientific, philosophic or technical, are but arts disguised in the specific form peculiar to these particular disciplines. I see in human mind the only sovereign of this immeasurable and measurable universe of ours. It is the creator and the creation.

Since man started to think he has been persuading himself of the existence somewhere, somehow, in some form, of an external reality which we are supposed to search for, to approach, to approximate and to reproduce. Scientists as well as artists have obediently followed that persuasion. The scientists have made great strides in their search; the artists, however, stopped at the gates of our sensual world and by calling it naturalism they remain in the belief that they are reproducing the true reality. Little, it seems to me, do these artists know how shallow their image of reality must appear to the scientific mind of today; to the mind which conveys to us nowadays an image of a reality where there is no difference, no boundaries between a grain of sand and a drop of water; a flash of electricity and the fragrance of a tree. Both, however, claim reality and I shall be the last to deny them the truth of their assertions; both are artists and both are telling the truth. But neither of them have the right to claim exclusive truth for their image.

The external world, this higher and absolute reality, supposedly detached from us, may exist or may not—so long as our mind has not constructed a specific image about it, it may just as well be considered non-existent. I know only one indestructible fact, here and now, that I am alive and so are you. But what this mysterious process which is called life actually is, beyond that image which I and you are constructing about it, is unknown and unknowable.

It may easily be seen that it would have been indeed a source of unbearable suffering to us, a source of hopeless despair, should the human mind resign to this ignorance of its universe leaving its destiny to that something unknown, unknowable. The history of mankind, the history of its material and mental development, reassures us, however, on that point. It shows us that mankind never has and never will resign to that state of total ignorance and inexorable fatality. Mind knows that once born we are alive, and once alive we are in the midst of a stream of creation and once in it we are not only carried by it, but we are capable to influence its course. With indefatigable perseverance man is constructing his life giving a concrete and neatly shaped image to that which is supposed to be unknown and which he alone, through his constructions, does constantly let be known. He creates the images of his world, he corrects them and he changes them in the course of years, of centuries. To that end he utilizes great plants, intricate laboratories, given to him with life; the laboratory of his senses and the laboratory of his mind; and through them he invents, construes and constructs ways and means in the form of images for his orientation in this world of his. And what is known to us as acquisition of knowledge is therefore nothing else but the acquisition of skill in constructing and improving that grandiose artifice of images which in their entirety, represents to us the universe,

our universe. Whatever we discover with our knowledge is not
something lying outside us, not something which is a part of some
higher, constant, absolute reality which is only waiting for us to
discover it . . . but, we discover exactly that which we put into
the place where we make the discovery. We have not discovered
electricity, x-rays, the atom and thousands of other phenomena and
processes—we have made them. They are images of our own
construction. After all, it is not long ago that electricity to us was
the image of a sneezing and ferocious god—after that it became a
current, later on it became a wave, today it is a particle which
behaves like a wave which, in its turn, behaves like a particle—
tomorrow its image will shrink to the symbol of some concise
mathematical formula. What is it all if not an ever-changing chain
of images, ever true and ever real so long as they are in use—both
the old one which we discard and the new which we construe; and
when we discard them we do so not because they are untrue or
unreal, but because at a certain moment they lose their efficacy for
our new orientation in this world and do not fit with other images,
newly construed and newly created. The very question which we
often ask ourselves, whether these phenomena were there before
our knowing about them, or whether they are a part of some
constant reality independent of our mind—such questions are
themselves a product of our mind and they are characteristic for us
so long as we remain in the state of being alive—they lose all sense
and significance the moment we can face a state of nature where
mind is not.

These are the fundamental principles of the philosophy of Constructive Realism which I profess. This philosophy is not a guidance for my work, it is a justification for it. It helps me to reconcile
myself to the world around me in everyday activities and thoughts;
it helps me also to disentangle the complex snarl of contemporary
ideas, inimical to each other and, which is more important, it may
give you the reason as it does to me for what I am doing in my art
and why I am doing it in the way I do it.

But perhaps at this point I ought to be somewhat more explicit.

If you have followed me up till now you may perhaps grant me
that I am thinking consequently when I claim that I, as an artist,
have the right to discard images of the world which my predecessors have created before me and search for new images which
touch upon other sights of life and nature, other rhythm cor-

responding to new mental and sensual processes living in us today and that by representing these new images I have the right to claim that they are images of reality.

I say, indeed, with what right is the scientist allowed to discard views of the world which were so useful to mankind for so many thousands of years and replace them by new images entirely different from the old? With what right is the scientist allowed it and the artist not—and why? Take, for instance, our ancestors' anthropomorphic image of the world. For thousands of years it was serving them well in their everyday life and in their forward growth. That image of the world was populated by creatures who were replicas of ourselves. The sun and the earth and all the furniture of heaven were in the power of gods whose countenances were like our own. Accordingly their arts and their sciences (such as they were), their religions, their cosmologies, all were based on this anthropomorphic conception of the world without and within them. Yet it was taken for granted that when the mechanistic conception of the universe replaced the anthropomorphic one, it was quite all right; and when now our contemporary sciences are developing an image of the world so entirely different from both the previous ones as to appear to us almost absurd, incomprehensible to common sense, we are again willing to take it—we have already accepted it; we have gotten familiar with a world in which forces are permitted to become mass and matter is permitted to become light; a world which is pictured to us as a conglomeration of oscillating electrons, protons, neutrons, particles which behave like waves, which in their turn behave like particles—. If the scientist is permitted to picture to us an image of an electron which under certain conditions has less than zero energy (in common language, it means that it weighs less than nothing) and if he is permitted to see behind this simple common table, an image of the curvature of space—why, may I ask, is not the contemporary artist to be permitted to search for and bring forward an image of the world more in accordance with the achievements of our developed mind, even if it is different from the image presented in the paintings and sculptures of our predecessors?

I don't deny them their right to go on painting their images; I don't even deny that their images *are* real and true; the only thing I maintain is that the artists cannot go on forever painting the views from their window and pretending that this is all there is in the world, because it is not. There are many aspects in the world, unseen, unfelt and unexperienced, which have to be conveyed and we have the right to do it no less than they. It is, therefore, obvious that my question is purely rhetoric.

There is nothing whatsoever of any sense or validity to warrant the demand of some of those self-appointed public critics of ours, that unless we stick to the ancient, to the naive, anthropomorphic representation of our emotions, we are not doing serious art; we are escapists, decorators, abstractionists, murderers of art, dead men ourselves. Little do these critics know how preposterous, naive their demand is in a time and in a world entirely different from what they want us to represent, and which they themselves have already meekly accepted without realizing it.

There is, however, one argument which could be brought up by our adversaries had they known what they are talking about and it is this:

It may be argued that when the scientist is advancing a new conception or a new image as we call it, of the universe or of life, he takes it for granted that this new image he is presenting must needs first be verified; it has to be tested by our experience as unmistakable facts. Only then may he claim validity for his image in the scientific picture of the world he is constructing. Whereas you artists, the argument may go on, in your sort of constructions, are expecting us, the public, to take your image for granted, take it as valid without reference to any given fact except that it is a construction of your mind. This is a serious argument, at least on the surface, and my answer to it is this:

First of all, the so-authoritative word verification should not be taken too seriously—after all verification is nothing else but an appeal to that very tribunal which issued the verdict in the first place. In our ordinary processes of jurisprudence we would never dream of letting the defendant be his own prosecutor but in this case, we seem to do so without noticing the trap into which we are falling. But let us leave that for the moment; I shall come back to it presently.

The reference I so often make here to science and my claim for the artists' right should not be understood as meaning that I consider visual art and science exactly the same thing. I am not claiming my work to be a work of science; I am no scientist and I do not know more of science than anyone who has gone through the routine of the usual university education. I have learned to read the scientists' books and I presume that I understand their meaning, but I certainly cannot do their job. There is no more mathematics in my work than is anatomy in a figure of Michael Angelo and I have nothing but contempt for those artists who masquerade their works as scientific by titling them with algebraic formulas. This is plain profanation of both Art and Science. I may quote from an editorial statement of mine published in "Circle" in 1937, London: "Art and Science are two different streams which rise from the same creative source and flow into the same ocean of common human culture, but the currents of these streams flow in different beds. There is a difference between the art of science and the visual or poetic arts. Science teaches, explores, comprehends, reasons and proves. Art asserts, art acts, art makes believe. The force of art lies in its immediate influence on human psychology, in its impulsive contagiousness: art being a creation of man does recreate man." In closing the quotation I can, of course, add that Science too does recreate man, but I maintain that it cannot do it without the help of some visual sensual or poetic art.

Science in conveying a new image or conception can but state it; it can make it cogent by its own means but, it cannot, however, by its own means alone make this image an organic part of our consciousness, of our perceptions; it cannot bring that new image in the stream of our emotions and transfer it into a sensual experience. It is only through the means of our visual or poetic arts that this image can be experienced and incorporated in the frame of our attitude toward this world.

After all, the minds of our ancestors have in their time created a cosmology of their own, they have created an image of a single god in heaven to which even some of our scientists today still adhere, but it is not the mere proclamation and reasoning about the existence of such a god that made this image into a fact. It is the prayer of the poet who made the primitive man humiliate himself in an ecstasy of propitiation to that god; it is the music of the psalms, the edifice of the temple, the choir and the holy image painted on the icon and the liturgical performance at the holy services—all acts of pure visual and poetic art; it is this which incorporates the religious images of our forefathers into their life affecting their behavior and molding their mentality. Science has long ago told us that the image of the sun rising in the east is sheer nonsense, that it is the earth and ourselves who are turning towards the sun, making it appear to rise; yet this new conception does not seem to have left any trace at all in the rhythm of our everyday experience even now. Our poets are still chirping happily about the sun rising in the east; and why should they not? Theirs is still a valid image; it is real and it is poetic; but so is the new one no less real, no less poetic, no less worthy to serve as an image and be incorporated in our new vision.

In an age when the scientific eye of man is looking through matter into a fascinating all-embracing image of space-time as the very essence of our consciousness and of our universe, the old anthropomorphic image inherited by us from our primordial ancestry is still in full reign in the major part of our contemporary imagery. So long as our contemporary artists are incapable to see in a mountain anything but the image of some crouching naked figure, and so long as the sculptors are sweating in carving at various angles this very graven image, keeping themselves in the state of mind almost identical with that of a Papuan or a Hottentot, the sculptor cannot claim to have acquired a new vision of the world outside him or of the world in him and science with all its achievements in advanced creations cannot possibly claim to have incorporated its new image of the world into the mentality of mankind. It is only through the new plastic vision of the coming artist, advanced in his mind, that science can ever hope to achieve this. I think that the constructive artist of today is qualified for just that task. He has found the means and the methods to create new images and to convey them as emotional manifestations in our everyday experience. This means that shapes, lines, colors, forms are not illusory nor are they abstractions; they are a factual force and their impact on our senses is as real as the impact of light or of an electrical shock. This impact can be verified just as any other natural phenomenon. Shapes, colors and lines speak their own language. They are events in themselves and in an organized construction they become beings—their psychological force is immediate, irresistible and universal to all species of mankind; not being the result of a convention as words are, they are unambiguous and it is, therefore, that their impact can influence the human psyche; it can break or mold it, it exults, it depresses, elates or makes desperate; it can bring order where there was confusion and it can disturb and exasperate where there was an order. That is

why I use these elemental means for my expression, but far be it
from me to advocate that a constructive work of art should consist
merely of an arrangement of these elemental means for no other
purpose than to let them speak for themselves. I am constantly
demanding from myself and keep on calling to my friends, not to
be satisfied with that gratifying arrangement of elemental shapes,
colors and lines for the mere gratification of arrangement; I demand that they shall remain only means for conveying a well-
organized and clearly defined image—not just some image, any
image, but a new and constructive image by which I mean that
which by its very existence as a plastic vision should provoke in us
the forces and the desires to enhance life, assert it and assist its
further development.

I cannot help rejecting all repetitions of images already done,
already worn out and ineffective. I cannot help searching for new
images and this I do, not for the sake of their novelty but for the
sake of finding an expression of the new outlook on the world
around me and the new insight into the forces of life and nature
in me.

We are all living in a section of history of mankind when a new
civilization is being forged. Many of us know it and more of us are
talking about it, but few visualize what the image of that new
civilization is. The majority of our artists and poets of today stand
in a violent revolt against the new civilization. Many of them see in
it a curse and a nightmare. They prefer to look for shelter in the
civilization of the cave-man with all the consequences involved in a
cave mentality. None of them realizes the very fact that the so-
called new civilization is not here even in blue print. What we are
living in is not the civilization we are striving for, and it is not a
matter of our rejection or acceptance of this new civilization—it is
a matter of creating it and defining its image clearly. Civilizations
do not come to us from heaven in ready-made assortments to
choose from. Civilizations are constructions of man; they are the
result of a collective effort in which the artist has always played
and still has to play, no mean part. We have to face this inevitable
fact, that a new civilization must be built because the old one is
going to pieces. We shall be responsible for every trait in the
future structure of this new civilization—we, here and now, the
artist, the scientist as well as the common man, are the builders of
its edifice. How can we succeed in our task if we do not even try,

nay much more, if we are not even allowed to try, to clarify to ourselves what its image shall be, what order and structure should prevail in this new civilization we are having to build.

We shall be heading straight into disaster if we take it for granted that the main characteristic of the new civilization will consist alone in the material improvement of our surroundings; that the airplane and the refrigerator, the fluorescent light and the comfortable speed of our travels, the atomic clouds in our skies and the babel of our sky-scraping cities, that these are the traits of our coming civilization—we can be no further from the real image of it than by imagining it in this way. It is the man and his mentality, it is the trend of our aspirations, our ideals; it is our attitude toward mankind and the world which we have to acquire if we want to survive and to build something more propitious for the continuance of our life than what we have done up till now. It is the creation of new values, moral, social and aesthetic, which will constitute the main task in the construction of the new civilization. It is the establishment of new norms, by which I mean modes of thinking, feeling and behaving not in accordance with the wanton whim of an individual but corresponding to a constructed new image of man's relationship to mankind—it is all that, plus the reorganization of our external environment, the creation of the world we are living with in our homes and in our cities; it is all this which will make our civilization.

The new forces which the human mind is placing in our power are vast and destructive as any force always is and will be; but in the command of man these same forces can be harnessed for constructive ends as always was the case since the reign of man in this world of ours began, and as it always will be. It is my firm belief that our new civilization will be constructive or it will not be at all. And as a constructive artist I believe that the former will be the case. Being satisfied that we constructive artists are capable of facing the task of building this new civilization of ours, I claim the right to participate in the construction of it; both materially and spiritually.

I could just as well have finished with that, but I hold it appropriate at this moment to add something specific in order to be heard not only by this audience, but by all who are giving so much attention, wanted or unwanted, to the so-called modern arts, to which ours also belongs. It is perhaps the only thing in all of my exposition of which I am convinced that most of my comrades will agree with me.

I want to issue a warning to all those who hold the chains of power over the world today; to the self-appointed dictators as well as to the properly elected statesmen; to the ordained commissars as well as to the chosen heads of political departments; to the man in the street as well as to the self-appointed representatives of public opinion—I, the artist, the pushed and battered artist of today, warn them all that they will do better and will get more out of me if they leave me alone to do my work. They will never succeed, no matter how much they try, to enslave my mind without extinguishing it. I will never enlist in the suite of heralds and trumpeters of their petty glories and bestial quarrels. They may vilify my ideas, they may slander my work, they may chase me from one country to another, they may, perhaps, eventually succeed in starving me, but I shall never, never conform to their ignorance, to their prejudices.

We artists may dispute and argue amongst ourselves about ideologies and ideals—but nothing will more potently bind us together than the revolt against the blind forces trying to make us do what we do not believe is worth doing.

VI

Philosophies of History

The Decline of the West

OSWALD SPENGLER

Near the end of the First World War a young and unknown former
high school teacher published what is possibly the most characteristic
book of the early twentieth century, *Der Untergang des Abendlandes*.
A second volume appeared in 1922, and Charles Francis Atkinson
brought out his English translation between 1926 and 1928. With the
author's approval, Atkinson rendered *Untergang* as "decline," and the
book is known in English as *The Decline of the West*. But *Untergang*
means "going under"; Oswald Spengler was writing not of the decline
or decay of Western civilization, but of its approaching and certain
fall. War-shocked German readers in the autumn and winter of 1918
converted Spengler's book into the first intellectual best seller of the
postwar epoch. In all its editions, it has sold well over a hundred
thousand copies.

The Decline of the West appeals on many levels, as an essay in
comparative cultures, as an electrifying prophecy of doom, as a
defense of authoritarianism, and as a revival of the Greek cyclical
philosophy of history. Spengler maintained that each of the great
historic world cultures passes through a life-cycle similar to that of an
individual organism. He also sought to prove, by analogy with the fate
of past cultures, that the West had already entered old age. The
excerpts below are taken from the Introduction to the first volume,
and from the last page of the second volume, in which Spengler
proclaims (with some regret) the imminence of an era of Caesarism as
the final period in Western history before the inevitable collapse. The
Latin tag at the end may be rendered, "The willing man the Fates lead,
the unwilling man they drag."

SOURCE: *The Decline of the West*, by Oswald Spengler, trans. Charles
Francis Atkinson (Knopf, New York, 1926–28), Vol. I, pp. 15–26; and Vol.
II, p. 507. Reprinted by permission of Alfred A. Knopf, Inc., and George
Allen and Unwin, Ltd. Copyright 1926–28 by Alfred A. Knopf, Inc.

WHAT, THEN, *is* world-history? Certainly, an ordered presentation of the past, an inner postulate, the expression of a capacity for feeling form. But a feeling for form, however definite, is not the same as form itself. No doubt we feel world-history, experience it, and believe that it is to be read just as a map is read. But, even to-day, it is only forms of it that we know and not *the* form of it, which is the mirror-image of *our own* inner life.

Everyone of course, if asked, would say that he saw the inward form of History quite clearly and definitely. The illusion subsists because no one has seriously reflected on it, still less conceived doubts as to his own knowledge, for no one has the slightest notion how wide a field for doubt there is. In fact, the *lay-out* of world-history is an unproved and subjective notion that has been handed down from generation to generation (not only of laymen but of professional historians) and stands badly in need of a little of that scepticism which from Galileo onward has regulated and deepened our inborn ideas of nature.

Thanks to the subdivision of history into "Ancient," "Mediæval" and "Modern"—an incredibly jejune and *meaningless* scheme, which has, however, entirely dominated our historical thinking— we have failed to perceive the true position in the general history of higher mankind, of the little part-world which has developed on West-European[1] soil from the time of the German-Roman Em-

[1] Here the historian is gravely influenced by preconceptions derived from geography, which assumes a *Continent* of Europe, and feels himself compelled to draw an ideal frontier corresponding to the physical frontier between "Europe" and "Asia." The word "Europe" ought to be struck out of history. There is historically no "European" type, and it is sheer delusion to speak of the Hellenes as "European Antiquity" (were Homer and Heraclitus and Pythagoras, then, Asiatics?) and to enlarge upon their "mission" as such. These phrases express no realities but merely a sketchy interpretation of the map. It is thanks to this word "Europe" alone, and the complex of ideas resulting from it, that our historical consciousness has come to link Russia with the West in an utterly baseless unity—a mere abstraction derived from the reading of books—that has led to immense real consequences. In the shape of Peter the Great, this word has falsified the historical tendencies of a primitive human mass for two centuries, whereas the Russian *instinct* has very truly and fundamentally divided "Europe" from "Mother Russia" with the hostility that we can see embodied in Tolstoi, Aksakov or Dostoyevski. "East" and "West" are notions that contain real history, whereas "Europe" is an empty sound. Everything great that the Classical world created, it created in pure denial of the existence of any continental barrier between Rome and Cyprus, Byzantium and Alexandria. Everything that we imply by the term European Culture came into

pire, to judge of its relative importance and above all to estimate its direction. The Cultures that are to come will find it difficult to believe that the validity of such a scheme with its simple rectilinear progression and its meaningless proportions, becoming more and more preposterous with each century, incapable of bringing into itself the new fields of history as they successively come into the light of our knowledge, was, in spite of all, never whole-heartedly attacked. The criticisms that it has long been the fashion of historical researchers to level at the scheme mean nothing; they have only obliterated the one existing plan without substituting for it any other. To toy with phrases such as "the Greek Middle Ages" or "Germanic antiquity" does not in the least help us to form a clear and inwardly-convincing picture in which China and Mexico, the empire of Axum and that of the Sassanids have their proper places. And the expedient of shifting the initial point of "modern history" from the Crusades to the Renaissance, or from the Renaissance to the beginning of the 19th Century, only goes to show that the scheme *per se* is regarded as unshakably sound.

It is not only that the scheme circumscribes the area of history. What is worse, it rigs the stage. The ground of West Europe is treated as a steady pole, a unique patch chosen on the surface of the sphere for no better reason, it seems, than because we live on it—and great histories of millennial duration and mighty far-away Cultures are made to revolve around this pole in all modesty. It is a quaintly conceived system of sun and planets! We select a single bit of ground as the natural centre of the historical system, and make it the central sun. From it all the events of history receive their real light, from it their importance is judged in *perspective*. But it is in our own West-European conceit alone that this phantom "world-history," which a breath of scepticism would dissipate, is acted out.

We have to thank that conceit for the immense optical illusion (become natural from long habit) whereby distant histories of thousands of years, such as those of China and Egypt, are made to shrink to the dimensions of mere episodes while in the neighbourhood of our own position the decades since Luther, and particu-

---

existence between the Vistula and the Adriatic and the Guadalquivir and, even if we were to agree that Greece, the Greece of Pericles, lay in Europe, the Greece of to-day certainly does not.

larly since Napoleon, loom large as Brocken-spectres. We know quite well that the slowness with which a high cloud or a railway train in the distance seems to move is only apparent, yet we believe that the *tempo* of all early Indian, Babylonian or Egyptian history was really slower than that of our own recent past. And we think of them as less substantial, more damped-down, more diluted, because we have not learned to make the allowance for (inward and outward) distances.

It is self-evident that for the Cultures of the West the existence of Athens, Florence or Paris is more important than that of Lo-Yang or Pataliputra. But is it permissible to found a scheme of world-history on estimates of such a sort? If so, then the Chinese historian is quite entitled to frame a world-history in which the Crusades, the Renaissance, Cæsar and Frederick the Great are passed over in silence as insignificant. How, *from the morphological point of view*, should our 18th Century be more important than any other of the sixty centuries that preceded it? Is it not ridiculous to oppose a "modern" history of a few centuries, and that history to all intents localized in West Europe, to an "ancient" history which covers as many millennia—incidentally dumping into that "ancient history" the whole mass of the pre-Hellenic cultures, unprobed and unordered as mere appendix-matter? This is no exaggeration. Do we not, for the sake of keeping the hoary scheme, dispose of Egypt and Babylon—each as an individual and self-contained history quite equal in the balance to our so-called "world-history" from Charlemagne to the World-War and well beyond it—as a *prelude* to classical history? Do we not relegate the vast complexes of Indian and Chinese culture to foot-notes, with a gesture of embarrassment? As for the great American cultures, do we not, on the ground that they do not "fit in" (with what?), entirely ignore them?

The most appropriate designation for this current West-European scheme of history, in which the great Cultures are made to follow orbits round *us* as the presumed centre of all word-happenings, is the *Ptolemaic system* of history. The system that is put forward in this work in place of it I regard as the *Copernican discovery* in the historical sphere, in that it admits no sort of privileged position to the Classical or the Western Culture as against the Cultures of India, Babylon, China, Egypt, the Arabs, Mexico—separate worlds of dynamic being which in point of mass count for just as much in the general picture of history as the

Classical, while frequently surpassing it in point of spiritual greatness and soaring power.

The scheme "ancient-mediæval-modern" in its first form was a
creation of the Magian world-sense. It first appeared in the Persian
and Jewish religions after Cyrus,[2] received an apocalyptic sense in
the teaching of the Book of Daniel on the four world-eras, and was
developed into a world-history in the post-Christian religions of
the East, notably the Gnostic systems.[3]

This important conception, within the very narrow limits
which fixed its intellectual basis, was unimpeachable. Neither Indian nor even Egyptian history was included in the scope of the
proposition. For the Magian thinker the expression "world-
history" meant a unique and supremely dramatic act, having as its
theatre the lands between Hellas and Persia, in which the strictly
dualistic world-sense of the East expressed itself not by means of
polar conceptions like the "soul and spirit," "good and evil" of
contemporary metaphysics, but by the figure of a catastrophe, an
epochal change of phase between world-creation and world-decay.[4]

No elements beyond those which we find stabilized in the
Classical literature, on the one hand, and the Bible (or other sacred
book of the particular system), on the other, came into the picture,
which presents (as "The Old" and "The New," respectively) the
easily-grasped contrasts of Gentile and Jewish, Christian and
Heathen, Classical and Oriental, idol and dogma, nature and spirit
with a time connotation—that is, as a drama in which the one
prevails over the other. The historical change of period wears the
characteristic dress of the religious "Redemption." This "world-
history" in short was a conception narrow and provincial, but
within its limits logical and complete. Necessarily, therefore, it was
specific to this region and this humanity, and incapable of any
natural extension.

But to these two there has been added a third epoch, the epoch
that we call "modern," on Western soil, and it is this that for the
first time gives the picture of history the look of a progression. The
oriental picture was *at rest*. It presented a self-contained antithesis,
with equilibrium as its outcome and a unique divine act as its

[2] See Vol. II, pp. 31, 275.
[3] Windelband, *Gesch. d. Phil.* (1903), pp. 275 ff.
[4] In the New Testament the polar idea tends to appear in the dialectics of
the Apostle Paul, while the periodic is represented by the Apocalypse.

turning-point. But, adopted and assumed by a wholly new type of mankind, it was quickly transformed (without anyone's noticing the oddity of the change) into a conception of a *linear progress:* from Homer or Adam—the modern can substitute for these names the Indo-German, Old Stone Man, or the Pithecanthropus—through Jerusalem, Rome, Florence and Paris according to the taste of the individual historian, thinker or artist, who has unlimited freedom in the interpretation of the three-part scheme.

This third term, "modern times," which in form asserts that it is the last and conclusive term of the series, has in fact, ever since the Crusades, been stretched and stretched again to the elastic limit at which it will bear no more.[5] It was at least implied if not stated in so many words, that here, beyond the ancient and the mediæval, something definitive was beginning, a Third Kingdom in which, somewhere, there was to be fulfilment and culmination, and which had an objective point.

As to what this objective point is, each thinker, from Schoolman to present-day Socialist, backs his own peculiar discovery. Such a view into the course of things may be both easy and flattering to the patentee, but in fact he has simply taken the spirit of the West, as reflected in his own brain, for the meaning of the world. So it is that great thinkers, making a metaphysical virtue of intellectual necessity, have not only accepted without serious investigation the scheme of history agreed "by common consent" but have made of it the basis of their philosophies and dragged in God as author of this or that "world-plan." Evidently the mystic number three applied to the world-ages has something highly seductive for the metaphysician's taste. History was described by Herder as the education of the human race, by Kant as an evolution of the idea of freedom, by Hegel as a self-expansion of the world-spirit, by others in other terms, but as regards its ground-plan everyone was quite satisfied when he had thought out some abstract meaning for the conventional threefold order.

On the very threshold of the Western Culture we meet the great Joachim of Floris (c. 1145–1202),[6] the first thinker of the Hegelian stamp who shattered the dualistic world-form of Augustine,

[5] As we can see from the expression, at once desperate and ridiculous, "newest time" (*neueste Zeit*).

[6] K. Burdach, *Reformation, Renaissance, Humanismus*, 1918, pp. 48 et seq. (English readers may be referred to the article *Joachim of Floris* by Professor Alphandery in the Encyclopædia Britannica, XI ed., *Trans.*)

and with his essentially Gothic intellect stated the new Christianity of his time in the form of a third term to the religions of the Old and the New Testaments, expressing them respectively as the Age of the Father, the Age of the Son and the Age of the Holy Ghost. His teaching moved the best of the Franciscans and the Dominicans, Dante, Thomas Aquinas, in their inmost souls and awakened a world-outlook which slowly but surely took entire possession of the historical sense of our Culture. Lessing—who often designated his own period, with reference to the Classical as the "after-world"[7] (Nachwelt)—took his idea of the "education of the human race" with its three stages of child, youth and man, from the teaching of the Fourteenth Century mystics. Ibsen treats it with thoroughness in his *Emperor and Galilean* (1873), in which he directly presents the Gnostic world-conception through the figure of the wizard Maximus, and advances not a step beyond it in his famous Stockholm address of 1887. It would appear, then, that the Western consciousness feels itself urged to predicate a sort of finality inherent in its own appearance.

But the creation of the Abbot of Floris was a *mystical* glance into the secrets of the divine world-order. It was bound to lose all meaning as soon as it was used in the way of reasoning and made a hypothesis of *scientific* thinking, as it has been—ever more and more frequently—since the 17th Century.

It is a quite indefensible method of presenting world-history to begin by giving rein to one's own religious, political or social convictions and endowing the sacrosanct three-phase system with tendencies that will bring it exactly to one's own standpoint. This is, in effect, making of some formula—say, the "Age of Reason," Humanity, the greatest happiness of the greatest number, enlightenment, economic progress, national freedom, the conquest of nature, or world-peace—a criterion whereby to judge whole millennia of history. And so we judge that they were ignorant of the "true path," or that they failed to follow it, when the fact is simply that their will and purposes were not the same as ours. Goethe's saying, "What is important in life is life and not a result of life," is the answer to any and every senseless attempt to solve the riddle of historical form by means of a *programme*.

It is the same picture that we find when we turn to the historians

---

[7] The expression "antique"—meant of course in the dualistic sense—is found as early as the *Isagoge* of Porphyry (c. 300 A.D.).

of each special art or science (and those of national economics and philosophy as well). We find:

"Painting" from the Egyptians (or the cave-men) to the Impressionists, or
"Music" from Homer to Bayreuth and beyond, or
"Social Organization" from Lake Dwellings to Socialism, as the case may be,

presented as a linear graph which steadily rises in conformity with the values of the (selected) arguments. No one has seriously considered the possibility that arts may have an allotted span of life and may be attached as forms of self-expression to particular regions and particular types of mankind, and that therefore the total history of an art may be merely an additive compilation of separate developments, of special arts, with no bond of union save the name and some details of craft-technique.

We know it to be true of every organism that the rhythm, form and duration of its life, and all the expression-details of that life as well, are determined by the *properties of its species*. No one, looking at the oak, with its millennial life, dare say that it is at this moment, now, about to start on its true and proper course. No one as he sees a caterpillar grow day by day expects that it will go on doing so for two or three years. In these cases we feel, with an unqualified certainty, a *limit*, and this sense of the limit is identical with our sense of the inward form. In the case of higher human history, on the contrary, we take our ideas as to the course of the future from an unbridled optimism that sets at naught all historical, i.e., *organic*, experience, and everyone therefore sets himself to discover in the accidental present terms that he can expand into some striking progression-series, the existence of which rests not on scientific proof but on predilection. He works upon unlimited possibilities—never a natural end—and from the momentary top-course of his bricks plans artlessly the continuation of his structure.

"Mankind," however, has no aim, no idea, no plan, any more than the family of butterflies or orchids. "Mankind" is a zoological expression, or an empty word.[8] But conjure away the phantom, break the magic circle, and at once there emerges an astonishing

[8] "Mankind? It is an abstraction. There are, always have been, and always will be, men and only men." (Goethe to Luden.)

wealth of *actual* forms—the Living with all its immense fullness, depth and movement—hitherto veiled by a catchword, a dryasdust scheme, and a set of personal "ideals." I see, in place of that empty figment of *one* linear history which can only be kept up by shutting one's eyes to the overwhelming multitude of the facts, the drama of *a number* of mighty Cultures, each springing with primitive strength from the soil of a mother-region to which it remains firmly bound throughout its whole life-cycle; each stamping its material, its mankind, in *its own* image; each having *its own* idea, *its own* passions; *its own* life, will and feeling, *its own* death. Here indeed are colours, lights, movements, that no intellectual eye has yet discovered. Here the Cultures, peoples, languages, truths, gods, landscapes bloom and age as the oaks and the stone-pines, the blossoms, twigs and leaves—but there is no ageing "Mankind." Each Culture has its own new possibilities of self-expression which arise, ripen, decay, and never return. There is not *one* sculpture, *one* painting, *one* mathematics, *one* physics, but many, each in its deepest essence different from the others, each limited in duration and self-contained, just as each species of plant has its peculiar blossom or fruit, its special type of growth and decline. These cultures, sublimated life-essences, grow with the same superb aimlessness as the flowers of the field. They belong, like the plants and the animals, to the living Nature of Goethe, and not to the dead Nature of Newton. I see world-history as a picture of endless formations and transformations, of the marvellous waxing and waning of organic forms. The professional historian, on the contrary, sees it as a sort of tapeworm industriously adding on to itself one epoch after another.

But the series "ancient-mediæval-modern history" has at last exhausted its usefulness. Angular, narrow, shallow though it was as a scientific foundation, still we possessed no other form that was not wholly unphilosophical in which our data could be arranged, and world-history (as hitherto understood) has to thank it for filtering our classifiable solid residues. But the number of centuries that the scheme can by any stretch be made to cover has long since been exceeded, and with the rapid increase in the volume of our historical material—especially of material that cannot possibly be brought under the scheme—the picture is beginning to dissolve into a chaotic blur. Every historical student who is not quite blind knows and feels this, and it is as a drowning man that he clutches at the only scheme which he knows of. The word "Middle Age,"[9] invented in 1667 by Professor Horn of Leyden, has to-day to cover a formless and constantly extending mass which can only be defined, negatively, as every thing not classifiable under any pretext in one of the other two (tolerably well-ordered) groups. We have an excellent example of this in our feeble treatment and hesitant judgment of modern Persian, Arabian and Russian history. But, above all, it has become impossible to conceal the fact that this so-called history of the world is a limited history, first of the Eastern Mediterranean region and then,—with an abrupt change of scene at the Migrations (an event important only to us and therefore greatly exaggerated by us, an event of purely Western and not even Arabian significance),—of West-Central Europe. When Hegel declared so naïvely that he meant to ignore those peoples which did not fit into his scheme of history, he was only making an honest avowal of methodic premises that every historian finds necessary for his purpose and every historical work shows in its lay-out. In fact it has now become an affair of scientific tact to determine which of the historical developments shall be *seriously* taken into account and which not. Ranke is a good example.

To-day we think in continents, and it is only our philosophers and historians who have not realized that we do so. Of what significance to us, then, are conceptions and purviews that they put before us as universally valid, when in truth their furthest horizon does not extend beyond the intellectual atmosphere of Western Man?

Examine, from this point of view, our best books. When Plato speaks of humanity, he means the Hellenes in contrast to the barbarians, which is entirely consonant with the ahistoric mode of the Classical life and thought, and his premises take him to conclusions that *for Greeks* were complete and significant. When, however, Kant philosophizes, say on ethical ideas, he maintains the validity of his theses for men of all times and places. He does not say this in so many words, for, for himself and his readers, it is

---

[9] "Middle Ages" connotes the history of the space-time region in which *Latin was the language of the Church and the learned.* The mighty course of Eastern Christianity, which, long before Boniface, spread over Turkestan into China and through Sabæa into Abyssinia, was entirely excluded from this "world-history."

something that goes without saying. In his æsthetics he formulates the principles, not of Phidias's art, or Rembrandt's art, but of Art generally. But what he poses as necessary forms of thought are in reality only necessary forms of Western thought, though a glance at Aristotle and his essentially different conclusions should have sufficed to show that Aristotle's intellect, not less penetrating than his own, was of different structure from it. The categories of the Westerner are just as alien to Russian thought as those of the Chinaman or the ancient Greek are to him. For us, the effective and complete comprehension of Classical root-words is just as impossible as that of Russian[10] and Indian, and for the modern Chinese or Arab, with their utterly different intellectual constitutions, "philosophy from Bacon to Kant" has only a curiosity-value.

It is *this* that is lacking to the Western thinker, the very thinker in whom we might have expected to find it—insight into the *historically relative* character of his data, which are expressions of one *specific existence and one only;* knowledge of the necessary limits of their validity; the conviction that his "unshakable" truths and "eternal" views are simply true for him and eternal for his world-view; the duty of looking beyond them to find out what the men of other Cultures have with equal certainty evolved out of themselves. That and nothing else will impart completeness to the philosophy of the future, and only through an understanding of the living world shall we understand the symbolism of history. Here there is nothing constant, nothing universal. We must cease to speak of the forms of "Thought," the principles of "Tragedy," the mission of "The State." Universal validity involves always the fallacy of arguing from particular to particular.

But something much more disquieting than a logical fallacy begins to appear when the centre of gravity of philosophy shifts from the abstract-systematic to the practical-ethical and our Western thinkers from Schopenhauer onward turn from the problem of cognition to the problem of life (the will to life, to power, to action). Here it is not the ideal abstract "man" of Kant that is subjected to examination, but actual man as he has inhabited the earth during historical time, grouped, whether primitive or advanced, by peoples; and it is more than ever futile to define the

[10] See Vol. II, p. 362, foot-note. To the true Russian the basic proposition of Darwinism is as devoid of meaning as that of Copernicus is to a true Arab.

structure of his highest ideas in terms of the "ancient-mediæval-modern" scheme with its local limitations. But it is done, nevertheless.

Consider the historical horizon of Nietzsche. His conceptions of decadence, militarism, the transvaluation of all values, the will to power, lie deep in the essence of Western civilization and are for the analysis of that civilization of decisive importance. But what, do we find, was the foundation on which he built up his creation? Romans and Greeks, Renaissance and European present, with a fleeting and uncomprehending side-glance at Indian philosophy—in short "ancient, mediæval and modern" history. Strictly speaking, he never once moved outside the scheme, nor did any other thinker of his time.

What correlation, then, is there or can there be of his idea of the "Dionysian" with the inner life of a highly-civilized Chinese or an up-to-date American? What is the significance of his type of the "Superman"—for the world of Islam? Can image-forming antitheses of Nature and Intellect, Heathen and Christian, Classical and Modern, have any meaning for the soul of the Indian or the Russian? What can Tolstoi—who from the depths of his humanity rejected the whole Western world-idea as something alien and distant—*do* with the "Middle Ages," with Dante, with Luther? What can a Japanese do with Parzeval and "Zarathustra," or an Indian with Sophocles? And is the thought-range of Schopenhauer, Comte, Feuerbach, Hebbel or Strindberg any wider? Is not their whole psychology, for all its intention of world-wide validity, one of purely West-European significance?

How comic seem Ibsen's woman-problems—which also challenge the attention of all "humanity"—when, for his famous Nora, the lady of the North-west European city with the horizon that is implied by a house-rent of £100 to £300 a year and a Protestant upbringing, we substitute Cæsar's wife, Madame de Sévigné, a Japanese or a Turkish peasant woman! But, for that matter, Ibsen's own circle of vision is that of the middle class in a great city of yesterday and to-day. His conflicts, which start from spiritual premises that did not exist till about 1850 and can scarcely last beyond 1950, are neither those of the great world nor those of the lower masses, still less those of the cities inhabited by non-European populations.

All these are local and temporary values—most of them indeed limited to the momentary "intelligentsia" of cities of West-European type. World-historical or "eternal" values they emphatically are not. Whatever the substantial importance of Ibsen's and Nietzsche's generation may be, it infringes the very meaning of the word "world-history"—which denotes the totality and not a selected part—to subordinate, to undervalue, or to ignore the factors which lie outside "modern" interests. Yet in fact they are so undervalued or ignored to an amazing extent. What the West has said and thought, hitherto, on the problems of space, time, motion, number, will, marriage, property, tragedy, science, has remained narrow and dubious, because men were always looking for *the* solution of *the* question. It was never seen that many questioners implies many answers, that any philosophical question is really a veiled desire to get an explicit affirmation of what is implicit in the question itself, that the great questions of any period are fluid beyond all conception, and that therefore it is only by obtaining a *group of historically limited solutions* and measuring it by *utterly impersonal* criteria that the final secrets can be reached. The real student of mankind treats no standpoint as absolutely right or absolutely wrong. In the face of such grave problems as that of Time or that of Marriage, it is insufficient to appeal to personal experience, or an inner voice, or reason, or the opinion of ancestors or contemporaries. These may say what is true for the questioner himself and for his time, but that is not all. In other Cultures the phenomenon talks a different language, for other men there are different truths. The *thinker* must admit the validity of all, or of none.

How greatly, then, Western world-criticism can be widened and deepened! How immensely far beyond the innocent relativism of Nietzsche and his generation one must look—how fine one's sense for form and one's psychological insight must become—how completely one must free oneself from limitations of self, of practical interests, of horizon—before one dare assert the pretension to understand world-history, the *world-as-history*.

In opposition to all these arbitrary and narrow schemes, derived from tradition or personal choice, into which history is forced, I put forward the natural, the "Copernican," form of the historical process which lies deep in the essence of that process and reveals itself only to an eye perfectly free from prepossessions.

Such an eye was Goethe's. That which Goethe called *Living*

Nature is exactly that which we are calling here world-history, *world-as-history*. Goethe, who as artist portrayed the life and development, always the life and development, of his figures, the thing-becoming and not the thing-become ("Wilhelm Meister" and "Wahrheit und Dichtung") hated Mathematics. For him, the world-as-mechanism stood opposed to the world-as-organism, dead nature to living nature, law to form. As naturalist, every line he wrote was meant to display the image of a thing-becoming, the "impressed form" living and developing. Sympathy, observation, comparison, immediate and inward certainty, intellectual flair— these were the means whereby he was enabled to approach the secrets of the phenomenal world in motion. *Now these are the means of historical research*—precisely these and no others. It was this *godlike* insight that prompted him to say at the bivouac fire on the evening of the Battle of Valmy: "Here and now begins a new epoch of world history, and you, gentlemen, can say that you 'were there.' " No general, no diplomat, let alone the philosophers, ever so directly felt history "becoming." It is the deepest judgment that any man ever uttered about a great historical act in the moment of its accomplishment.

And just as he followed out the development of the plant-form from the leaf, the birth of the vertebrate type, the process of the geological strata—*the Destiny in nature and not the Causality*—so here we shall develop the form-language of human history, its periodic structure, its *organic logic* out of the profusion of all the challenging details.

In other aspects, mankind is habitually, and rightly, reckoned as one of the organisms of the earth's surface. Its physical structure, its natural functions, the whole phenomenal conception of it, all belong to a more comprehensive unity. Only in *this* aspect is it treated otherwise, despite that deeply-felt relationship of plant destiny and human destiny which is an eternal theme of all lyrical poetry, and despite that similarity of human history to that of any other of the higher life-groups which is the refrain of endless beast-legends, sagas and fables.

But only bring analogy to bear on this aspect as on the rest, letting the world of human Cultures intimately and unreservedly work upon the imagination instead of forcing it into a ready-made scheme. Let the words youth, growth, maturity, decay—hitherto, and to-day more than ever, used to express subjective valuations and entirely personal preferences in sociology, ethics and æsthetics —be taken at last as objective descriptions of organic states. Set forth the Classical Culture as a self-contained phenomenon embodying and expressing the Classical soul, put it beside the Egyptian, the Indian, the Babylonian, the Chinese and the Western, and determine for each of these higher individuals what is typical in their surgings and what is necessary in the riot of incident. And then at last will unfold itself the picture of world-history that is natural to us, men of the West, and to us alone.

* * *

Life is alpha and omega, the cosmic onflow in microcosmic form. It is *the* fact of facts within the world-as-history. Before the irresistible rhythm of the generation-sequence, everything built up by the waking-consciousness in its intellectual world vanishes at the last. Ever in History it is life and life only—race-quality, the triumph of the will-to-power—and not the victory of truths, discoveries, or money that signifies. *World-history is the world court*, and it has ever decided in favour of the stronger, fuller, and more self-assured life—decreed to it, namely, the right to exist, regardless of whether its right would hold before a tribunal of waking-consciousness. Always it has sacrificed truth and justice to might and race, and passed doom of death upon men and peoples in whom truth was more than deeds, and justice than power. And so the drama of a high Culture—that wondrous world of deities, arts, thoughts, battles, cities—closes with the return of the pristine facts of the blood eternal that is one and the same as the ever-circling cosmic flow. The bright imaginative Waking-Being submerges itself into the silent service of Being, as the Chinese and Roman empires tell us. Time triumphs over Space, and it is Time whose inexorable movement embeds the ephemeral incident of the Culture, on this planet, in the incident of Man—a form wherein the incident life flows on for a time, while behind it all the streaming horizons of geological and stellar histories pile up in the light-world of our eyes.

For us, however, whom a Destiny has placed in this Culture and at this moment of its development—the moment when money is celebrating its last victories, and the Cæsarism that is to succeed approaches with quiet, firm step—our direction, willed and obligatory at once, is set for us within narrow limits, and on any other

terms life is not worth the living. We have not the freedom to
reach to this or to that, but the freedom to do the necessary or to
do nothing. And a task that historic necessity has set *will* be
accomplished with the individual or against him.

Ducunt Fata volentem, nolentem trahunt.

The Historian's Point of View

ARNOLD J. TOYNBEE

That Spengler had not exhausted the curiosity of the general reader
with regard to cyclical theories of history became readily apparent in
the years immediately after the Second World War, when, in still
another postwar era, still another metahistorical prophet of *Untergang*
achieved immense popularity. Arnold J. Toynbee had begun his labors
many years earlier, under the direct influence of Spengler. The first
three volumes of his chief work, *A Study of History*, had appeared in
1934, the second three volumes in 1939. But it was only with the
publication of D. C. Somervell's authorized abridgment of all six in
1947 that Toynbee's thought succeeded in reaching the general public
and attracting universal scholarly interest. Toynbee was British, Christian, and a more thorough scholar than Spengler; but he came to many
of the same conclusions. Civilizations rose and fell, and the West was
doomed to go under like all the others, unless God himself chose to
reprieve it.

In recent years, Toynbee's world-view has broadened, especially
since the publication of the final six volumes of his *Study* (1954–61).
He now places his hope in the emergence of a world civilization to
which all the higher religions and cultural traditions of East and West
will contribute. The end of the West is seen as the possible beginning
of a radically new era in history that will enable mankind to transcend
the cyclical pattern of the past altogether.

The essay that follows is taken from a volume based on Toynbee's
1952–53 Gifford Lectures at the University of Edinburgh. He ex-
amines the contrast between the classical and the Judeo-Christian views
of history, and defends them against each other and against modern
"antinomianism." His support of the value of the Judeo-Christian view
of history springs not only from his own religious commitment but

SOURCE: *An Historian's Approach to Religion*, by Arnold J. Toynbee
(Oxford University Press, New York, 1956), pp. 3–17. Reprinted by per-
mission of Oxford University Press. Copyright 1956 by Oxford University
Press.

also from his thesis in the last six volumes of the *Study* that religious history, unlike political history, reveals a pattern of linear progress analogous to the Christian view of the progress of humanity from the Fall to the Second Coming. In at least one sphere, the sphere of religion, man has made definite advances since earliest times. Whether his progress in this direction will make posssible his eventual victory over the cyclical rhythm of political history remains to be seen. But Toynbee is clearly more optimistic now than he was in the 1930's.

WHEN A human being looks at the Universe, his view of the mystery cannot be more than a glimpse, and even this may be delusive. The human observer has to take his bearings from the point in Space and moment in Time at which he finds himself; and he is bound to be self-centred; for this is part of the price of being a living creature. So his view will inevitably be partial and subjective; and, if all human beings were exact replicas of one standard pattern, like the standardized parts of some mass-produced machine, Mankind's view of Reality would be rather narrowly limited. Fortunately, our human plight is not so bad as that, because the uniformity of Human Nature is relieved by the variety of human personalities. Each personality has something in it that is unique, and each walk of life has its peculiar experience, outlook, and approach. There is, for instance, the doctor's approach to the mystery of the Universe (*religio medici*); and there is the mathematician's, the sailor's, the farmer's, the miner's, the business man's, the shepherd's, the carpenter's, and a host of others, among which the historian's (*religio historici*) is one. By comparing notes and putting individual and professional experiences together, the Collective Human Intellect can widen Man's view a little, for the benefit of each and all. Any note of any point of view may be an aid to this collective endeavour, and the present book is an attempt to describe, not the personal religion of the author, but the glimpse of the Universe that his fellow-historians and he are able to catch from the point of view at which they arrive through following the historian's professional path. No doubt, every historian has his own personal angle of vision, and there are also different schools of historical thought which have their characteristically different sectarian outlooks. We must examine these differences between one school of historians and another; but it may be best to start by considering what it is that all historians, in virtue simply of being historians, will be found to have in common.

The historian's profession, whatever he makes of it, is an attempt
to correct a self-centredness that is one of the intrinsic limitations
and imperfections, not merely of human life, but of all life on the
face of the Earth. The historian arrives at his professional point of
view by consciously and deliberately trying to shift his angle of
vision away from the initial self-centred standpoint that is natural
to him as a living creature.

The role of self-centredness in Life on Earth is an ambivalent
one. On the one hand, self-centredness is evidently of the essence
of Terrestrial Life. A living creature might, indeed, be defined as a
minor and subordinate piece of the Universe which, by a *tour de
force*, has partially disengaged itself from the rest and has set itself
up as an autonomous power that strives, up to the limits of its
capacity, to make the rest of the Universe minister to its selfish
purposes. In other words, every living creature is striving to make
itself into a centre of the Universe, and, in the act, is entering into
rivalry with every other living creature, with the Universe itself,
and with the Power that creates and sustains the Universe and that
is the Reality underlying the fleeting phenomena. For every living
creature, this self-centredness is one of the necessities of life,
because it is indispensable for the creature's existence. A complete
renunciation of self-centredness would bring with it, for any living
creature, a complete extinction of that particular local and temporary vehicle of Life (even though this might not mean an extinction of Life itself); and an insight into this psychological truth is
the intellectual starting-point of Buddhism.

> With the ceasing of craving, grasping ceases; with the ceasing of
> grasping, coming into existence ceases.[1]

Self-centredness is thus a necessity of Life, but this necessity is
also a sin. Self-centredness is an intellectual error, because no living
creature is in truth the centre of the Universe; and it is also a moral
error, because no living creature has a right to act as if it were the
centre of the Universe. It has no right to treat its fellow-creatures,
the Universe, and God or Reality as if they existed simply in order
to minister to one self-centred living creature's demands. To hold
this mistaken belief and to act on it is the sin of *hybris* (as it is

---

[1] *Upādāna-Sutta*, ii, 84, quoted in Thomas, E. J., *The History of
Buddhist Thought* (London 1933, Kegan Paul), p. 62.

called in the language of Hellenic psychology); and this *hybris* is the inordinate, criminal, and suicidal pride which brings Lucifer to his fall (as the tragedy of Life is presented in the Christian myth).

Since self-centredness is thus both a necessity of life and at the same time a sin that entails a nemesis, every living creature finds itself in a life-long quandary. A living creature can keep itself alive only in so far, and for so long, as it can contrive to steer clear both of suicide through self-assertion and of euthanasia through self-renunciation. The middle path is as narrow as a razor's edge, and the traveller has to keep his balance under the perpetual high tension of two pulls towards two abysses between which he has to pick his way.

The problem set to a living creature by its self-centredness is thus a matter of life and death; it is a problem that continually besets every human being; and the historian's point of view is one of several mental tools with which human beings have equipped themselves for trying to respond to this formidable challenge.

The historian's point of view is one of Mankind's more recent acquisitions. It is inaccessible to Primitive Man, because it cannot be attained without the help of an instrument which Primitive Man does not possess. The historian's point of view presupposes the taking and keeping of records that can make the life of other people in other generations and at other places revive in the historian's imagination so vividly that he will be able to recognize that this alien life has had the same objective reality, and the same moral claims, as the life of the historian and his contemporaries has here and now. Primitive Man lacks this instrument, because the invention of techniques for the taking and keeping of records has been one of the accompaniments of the recent rise of the civilizations within the last 6,000 years out of the 600,000 or 1,000,000 years of Mankind's existence on Earth up to date. Primitive Man has no means of re-evoking the Past farther back in Time than the time-span of tradition. Before the invention of written records, it is true, the faculty of memory develops a potency that it does not maintain in the sequel; but its span, even in the primitive human psyche, is relatively short, except for the recollection of the bare names in a genealogy. Behind this close-drawn mental horizon, the whole past is confounded in an undifferentiated and nebulous 'Age of the Ancestors'. Within this short vista of unaided memory, Primitive Man has neither the mental room nor the intellectual means for jumping clear of Man's innate self-centredness. For Primitive Man, the Past—and therefore also the Future, which the human mind can imagine only by analogy with an already imagined Past—is simply the narrow, close-clipped penumbra of his Present.

By contrast, the art of taking and keeping records enables Man in Process of Civilization to see people who have lived in other times and places, not simply as a background to his own here and now, but as his counterparts and peers—his 'psychological contemporaries', so to speak. He is able to recognize that, for these other people in their different time and place, their own life seemed to be the centre of the Universe, as his generation's life seems to be to his generation here and now.

Moreover, when Man in Process of Civilization makes it his profession to be an historian, he not only understands intellectually an earlier generation's sense of its own importance in its own right; he also enters sympathetically into his predecessors' feelings. He can do this because the impulse that moves an historian to study the records of the Past is a disinterested curiosity—a curiosity that extends farther than the limits within which every living creature is constrained to feel some curiosity about its environment for the sake of its own self-preservation. In New York in A.D. 1956, for example, an historian will not live to do his work unless he shares his neighbours' self-regarding curiosity about the high-powered contemporary traffic on the roads; but the historian will be distinguished from his fellow-pedestrians in 1956 by being also interested in 'historic' horse-drawn vehicles, once plying in the same streets, in spite of these extinct conveyances' present impotence to take the historian unawares and run over him.

This margin of curiosity that is superfluous from a utilitarian point of view seems to be one of the characteristics that distinguish, not only historians, but all human beings from most other living creatures. It is this specifically human psychic faculty that inspires Man in Process of Civilization to take advantage of the opportunity, opened up for him by his accumulation of records, for partially extricating himself on the intellectual plane from the innate self-centredness of a living creature. Human Nature's surplus margin of curiosity, which the historian turns to professional account, is also perhaps an indication that this feat of breaking out of an inherited self-centredness is part of the birthright and the mission of Human

Nature itself. However that may be, it is evident that the Human Spirit is, in fact, in a position to break out of its self-centredness as soon as it interests itself in the lives of other people in other times and places for their own sake. For, when once a human being has recognized that these other human beings, in their time and place, had as *much* right as his own generation has, here and now, to behave as if they were the centre of the Universe, he must also recognize that his own generation has as *little* right as these other generations had to maintain this self-centred attitude. When a number of claimants, standing at different points in Time and Space, make the identical claim that each claimant's own particular point in Time-Space is the central one, common sense suggests that, if Time-Space does have any central point at all, this is not to be found in the local and temporary standpoint of any generation of any parochial human community.

Considering the inadequacy of human means of communication before the industrial revolution that broke out in the West less than two centuries ago, it would seem probable that the accumulation of records enabled historians to transcend self-centredness in the Time-dimension before they were able to transcend it in the Space-dimension. A Sumerian priest, studying records in the temple of a god personifying the priest's own parochial city-state, could become aware of previous generations of his own community as real people, on a psychological par with the living generation, some thousands of years before a Modern Western archaeologist, excavating a site at Tall-al-'Amārnah in Egypt, could become aware, in the same sense, of the reality of the Emperor Ikhnaton's generation in a society which had had a different geographical locus from the excavator's own, and which had been buried in oblivion for perhaps as long as 1,600 years before being disinterred by the curiosity of Modern Western Man. The disinterment of Ikhnaton is a classic feat of the historian's art of bringing the dead back to life, since this controversial figure has aroused in his re-discoverers some of the feeling that he evoked in his contemporaries. A twentieth-century Western historian who finds himself moved to take sides for or against this revolutionary Egyptian philosopher-king has undoubtedly broken out of the prison-house of self-centredness; but this feat of breaking out into the realm of spiritual freedom is hard and rare even on the intellectual plane, on which it is relatively easy to achieve; and, even when it is carried on to the plane of feeling, it is, at best, never more than very imperfect.

The Modern Western philosopher Croce has said that all history is contemporary history and that no history can be anything but this.[2] His meaning is that even a comparatively sophisticated Man in Process of Civilization is still, like Primitive Man, the prisoner of his own time and place. He is, indeed, their prisoner in two senses.

He is their prisoner in the objective sense that his only standing-ground for viewing the upper reaches of the river of History is the constantly moving locus of the mast-head of the little boat in which the observer himself is travelling all the time down a lower reach of the same ever-rolling stream. This is the reason why each successive generation of historians in the Modern Age of Western history has been impelled to write its own history of the Graeco-Roman Civilization. Each successive generation sees this identical episode of past history in a new perspective imposed by the transit to this generation's historical position from the position of its predecessors. This new perspective brings the familiar features of an old landscape into a new relation with one another; it changes their relative prominence; and it even brings previously invisible features to light and at the same time screens previous landmarks.

The historian is also the prisoner of his own time and place in a subjective sense. We have just observed that our Modern Western historians have been so successful in bringing the Egyptian emperor Ikhnaton back to life that they too, like his Egyptian contemporaries, are moved to feel strongly about him. Yet they do not feel about him in the same way as his Egyptian contemporaries felt. Their feelings about this reanimated Egyptian figure who was so controversial a character in his own lifetime find their fuel, not in the philosophical, religious, and political controversies that were rife in the New Empire of Egypt in the fourteenth century B.C., but in controversial current issues in the life of the historians' own society in their own day. They have written about Ikhnaton with something of the same animus, for him or against him, which they would have shown if they had been writing about Lenin or Hitler or Churchill or Franklin D. Roosevelt. In other words, they have

[2] Croce, Benedetto, *Teoria e Storia Storiografia*, 2nd edition (Bari 1920, Laterza), p. 4: 'Ogni vera storia è storia contemporanea'; p. 5: 'La contemporaneità non è carattere di una classe di storie . . . ma carattere intrinseco di ogni storia.'

ARNOLD J. TOYNBEE   229

imported into their feelings about Ikhnaton something of their
feelings about controversial contemporaries of their own; and, in so
far as they have done this, they have drawn Ikhnaton out of his
own social milieu into theirs.

Even the most highly gifted historians will be found, on examination, to have remained prisoners to some extent—as can be
seen in the case of Gibbon, who, in writing *The History of the
Decline and Fall of the Roman Empire*, might seem, at first sight,
to have chosen a subject that was sharply detached from the life of
the historian's own prosperous and confident generation in his own
Western Society. Yet Gibbon was a prisoner of his own time and
place in at least three ways. He was inspired to choose his subject
by a personal experience which linked the Roman Empire in the
Age of the Antonines with the Rome of A.D. 1764; he was able to
enter imaginatively into the life of the Roman Empire in the
Antonine Age because he felt an affinity between this and the life
of his own generation in a Modern Western Society; and he was
concerned to inquire whether his own society could ever be overtaken by the disaster that had actually overtaken another society
whose affinity with his own he had recognized.

Thus the historian's trancendence of self-centredness is never
more than partial and imperfect; and even contemporaries who
have been brought up in different cultural milieux find it difficult
to appreciate one another's mutually alien cultural heritages now
that a Modern Western technology has given them the means of
meeting one another. In the world of A.D. 1956 the greatest cultural
gulf was not the rift between a Judaic Western Liberalism and a
Judaic Western Communism; it was the chasm between the whole
Judaic group of ideologies and religions—Communism, Liberalism,
Christianity, Islam, and their parent Judaism itself—on the one
hand and the Buddhaic group of philosophies and religions—post-
Buddhaic Hinduism, the Mahāyāna, and the Hīnayāna—on the
other hand. In the bridging of this chasm the contemporary historian has a part to play which is as difficult as it is important. The
self-correction through self-transcendence, which is the essence of
his profession, no doubt always falls short of its objective; yet,
even so, it is something to the good; for to some extent it does
succeed in shifting the mental standpoint, and widening the mental
horizon, of an innately self-centred living creature.

This transcendence of self-centredness to some degree—though, no doubt, imperfectly, at best—is therefore an achievement that is common to all historians of all schools. But the slightly widened horizon which the historian's angle of vision opens up has displayed different pictures of the Universe to historians of different schools. So far, there have been two fundamental alternative views.

One of these two views sees the rhythm of the Universe as a cyclic movement governed by an Impersonal Law. On this view the apparent rhythm of the stellar cosmos—the day-and-night cycle and the annual cycle of the seasons—is assumed to be the fundamental rhythm of the Universe as a whole. This astronomical view of History provides a radical correction of the bias towards self-centredness that is innate in every living creature; but it corrects self-centredness at the price of taking the significance out of History—and, indeed, out of the Universe itself. From this astronomical standpoint it is impossible for an historian to believe that his own here and now has any special importance; but it is equally difficult for him to believe that any other human being's here and now has ever had, or will ever have, any special importance either. In the words of an Hellenic philosopher-king,

> The rational soul ranges over the whole cosmos and the surrounding void and explores the scheme of things. It reaches into the abyss of boundless Time and not only comprehends, but studies the significance of, the periodic new birth of the Universe. These studies bring the rational soul to a realization of the truth that there will be nothing new to be seen by those who come after us, and that, by the same token, those that have gone before us have not seen anything, either, that is beyond *our* ken. In this sense it would be true to say that any man of forty who is endowed with moderate intelligence has seen—in the light of the uniformity of Nature—the entire Past and Future.[3]

Hence, in the Graeco-Roman World and in the Indian World, in both of which this view was prevalent, History was rated at a low value. In the words of an Hellenic philosopher-scientist,

> The poet and the historian differ not by writing in verse or in prose. The work of Herodotus might be put into verse, and it would still be a species of History, *with* metre no less than without it. The true difference is that one relates what has happened, the other what *may* happen. Poetry, therefore, is a more philosophical and a higher (σπουδαιότερον) thing than History; for Poetry tends

---

[3] Marcus Aurelius Antoninus, *Meditations*, Book XI, chap. 1.

to express the universal, History the particular. By the universal I mean how a person of a certain type will on occasion speak or act, or according to the law of probability or necessity. . . . The particular is—for example—what Alcibiades did or suffered.[4]

The Indians, being more whole-hearted than the Greeks in living up to this Greek and Indian philosophy, disdained to write history. The Greeks, though their theoretical contempt for History was as great as the Indians' contempt for it was, were moved by their keen curiosity to study History, and by their fine aesthetic sense to embody the results in great works of literary art. Yet, in spite of the production of these monuments of Greek historical writing, Aristotle's low estimate of History was the considered verdict on History that would have been given by most Greeks in most ages of Hellenic history, as well as by almost all Indians at all times.

The other fundamental view sees the rhythm of the Universe as a non-recurrent movement governed by Intellect and Will. The play of Intellect and Will is the only movement known to Man that appears to be unquestionably non-recurrent; and on this view the fundamental rhythm of the Universe as a whole is assumed to be identical with the rhythm in the career of an individual human being. It is assumed to be a drama that has a beginning and an end, that is punctuated by crises and by decisive events, that is animated by challenges and responses, and that unfolds a plot like the plot of a play. This volitional view of History gives History the maximum of significance, in contrast to the cyclic impersonal view; but it does this at the risk of tempting the historian to relapse into the self-centredness—innate in every creature—which it is the historian's mission to transcend.

This is the view of History that was prevalent in Israel and that has been inherited from Israel, through Jewry and through Jewry's congener the Zoroastrian Church, by Christianity and Islam. In the Judaic societies, History has been rated at a high value at the cost of a relapse into a sense of self-importance which a sense of History ought to correct.

It is true that the intellect and will whose plan and purpose are deemed, on this view, to govern History are those, not of any human beings, acting either severally or collectively, but of a

[4] Aristotle, *Poetics*, chap. 9 (1451 B), translated by Butcher, S. H., in *Aristotle's Theory of Poetry and Fine Art* (London 1902, Macmillan).

transcendent and omnipotent One True God; and *a priori*, a sense
of the greatness of God might be expected to be as effective a cure
for the self-centredness of one of God's creatures as a sense of the
inexorability of laws of Nature. But the Judaic societies have re-
opened the door to self-centredness by casting themselves, in
rivalry with one another and ignoring the rest of Mankind, for the
privileged role of being God's 'Chosen People', who, in virtue of
God's choice of them, have a key-part to play in History—in
contrast to a heathen majority of Mankind who are worshippers of
false gods. A *soi-disant* 'Chosen People's' attitude towards the rest
of their fellow human beings is a corollary and counterpart of the
attitude towards other gods which they ascribe to the God by
whom they believe themselves to have been singled out. The One
True God is conceived of as being a jealous god. He is not merely
the One True God in fact; He is intolerant of the worship
wrongly paid to spurious divinities. The affirmation that 'there is
no god but God' is deemed, by the adherents of the Judaic
religions, to entail the commandment: 'Thou shalt have none other
gods but Me'; and what God is believed to feel about false gods sets
the standard for what God's 'Chosen People' believe themselves
entitled to feel about heathen human beings.

Thus, in the Judaic societies, Human Nature's innate self-
centredness is consecrated by being given the blessing of a God
who is held to be not only almighty but also all-wise and all-
righteous. This formidable enhancement of self-centredness is an
evil that is inherent in the belief that there is a 'Chosen People' and
that I and my fellow-tribesmen are It. And this evil is not exorcised
by rising, as the Prophets have risen, to a sublimely austere conception of the mission to which the 'Chosen People' have been
called. They may accept the hard doctrine that they have been
called, not to enjoy unique power, wealth, and glory, but to bear
unique burdens and to suffer unique tribulations for the fulfilment
of God's purposes;[5] but, even then, their abiding belief in their
own uniqueness still orients them towards a centre that lies in
themselves and not in the God from whose fiat their uniqueness
derives. This is the moral effect, *a fortiori*, of those latterday
Western ideologies, such as Communism and National Socialism, in

[5] See Wright, G. E., *The Old Testament against its Environment*
(London 1950, Student Christian Movement Press); Rowley, H. H., *The
Biblical Doctrine of Election* (London 1950, Lutterworth Press).

which the Judaic belief in being a 'Chosen People' has been retained while the complementary Judaic belief in the existence of an Almighty God has been discarded.

Thus the Judaeo-Zoroastrian view of History, like the Indo-Hellenic view, offers us an escape from one evil at the price of involving us in another. The picture of a cyclic Universe governed by impersonal laws of Nature promises to cure Human Nature of its self-centredness at the cost of robbing History of its significance; the picture of a non-repetitive Universe governed by a personal God promises to give History a maximum of significance at the cost of tempting holders of this view to relapse into self-centredness and to allow themselves to run to extremes of it with an untroubled conscience. Confronted with a choice between these two alternatives, we may find ourselves shrinking from choosing either of them when we have observed the sinister side of each. Yet these are the two fundamental alternative views that have been accessible to human souls so far; and today a majority of Mankind holds either one of these two views or the other. The dilemma presented by the choice between them will haunt us throughout our inquiry. At the same time there have been other views in the field; and two, at least, of these have been important enough in the history of Man in Process of Civilization to deserve some notice.

One of these two views sees in History a structure like that of a Modern Western piece of music—though, in origin, this view is not Western but is Chinese. In this Chinese view, History is a series of variations on a theme enunciated at the start; and this view cuts across both the Judaeo-Zoroastrian view and the Indo-Hellenic, which are complementary to each other besides being mutually exclusive.

The Chinese view is akin to the Hellenic both in seeing the rhythm of History as being repetitive and in not being self-centred. My generation, here and now, is felt to have no worth by comparison with a Classical Past whose example is believed to provide an absolute standard of conduct for all subsequent ages in all conceivable circumstances. The best that we, in our generation, can do to make ourselves less unworthy of our forebears is to model our conduct on theirs, as recorded in a classical literature, as faithfully as we can. On the other hand the Chinese view is akin to the Judaeo-Zoroastrian in seeing History in terms of personality and in seeing it as being full of significance. The repetition of classical precedents is not an automatic result of the operation of an Impersonal Law; it is a conscious and deliberate act which is inspired by admiration and is achieved by moral effort. There is a sense—self-evident, no doubt, to Chinese minds when they come across the Judaic and Indian views and compare these with their own view—in which this Chinese view gets the best of both the Indian and the Jewish World and so eludes our Indo-Jewish dilemma by a characteristically Chinese feat of deftness and tact. This Chinese view, like the Greek, has inspired notable works of historical literature, and, under a recent exotic top-dressing of Communism, it was perhaps still reigning, in A.D. 1956, in the psychic underworld of nearly a quarter of the human race. The weakness of the Chinese view is that, in contrast to both the Jewish and the Indian, it is archaistic, epimethean, and static.

The other of the two secondary views sees the movement of the Universe as a chaotic, disorderly, fortuitous flux, in which there is no rhythm or pattern of any kind to be discerned. This has been the prevalent view of one school of Western historians in a post-Christian age of Western history. It will not bear comparison with either the Indian view or the Jewish; for, when confronted with either of these, it stands convicted of failing to go to the root of the question—'What is the nature of the Universe?'—that all historians ought to be trying to answer.

This Late Modern Western answer to a fundamental question is a superficial answer because it is content to accept the concept of Chance uncritically as being a sufficient explanation of the nature of the Universe, without taking cognizance of the philosophers' analysis of it. Yet Bergson, among other contemporary Western philsophers, has pointed out[6] that the notion of Chance, Disorder, and Chaos is merely a relative and not an absolute one.

> If, at a venture, I select a volume in my library, I may replace it on the shelves, after taking a glance at it, with the remark 'This isn't verse'. But is this really what I perceived when I was turning the pages? Clearly not. I did not see, and I never shall see, an absence of verse. What I did see was prose. But, as it is poetry that I am wanting, I express what I find in terms of what I am looking for; and, instead of saying 'Here is some prose', I say 'This isn't verse'. Inversely, if it takes my fancy to read some prose and I stumble on a volume of verse, I shall exclaim 'This isn't prose'; and in using these

[6] In *L'Évolution Créatrice*, 24th edition (Paris 1921, Alcan), pp. 239–58.

words I shall be translating the data of my perception, which shows me verse, into the language of my expectation and my interest, which are set upon the idea of prose and therefore will not hear of anything else.

As Bergson lucidly explains, the appearance of Chance, Disorder, or Chaos is nothing but a negative finding disguised in an illusorily positive form of expression. The order that we fail to find in a particular situation is not Order in the absolute but merely one order, out of a number of alternative possible orders, for which we happen to have been looking. In finding a chaos, all that we have discovered is that we have stumbled upon some order which is not the particular order that we are seeking. Our investigation will not be complete till we have verified what this unsought and unexpected order is; and, when we have identified it, we shall have under our eyes an order and not a chaos.

On this showing, perhaps all that is meant by historians of this antinomian Late Modern Western school, when they declare that History is an unintelligible chaos, is that they do not find in it either of the two forms of order that are most familiar to them. They do not find in History either the Jewish rule of a living God or the Greek rule of an Impersonal Law. But they have still to elucidate for themselves the third alternative form of order that, in not finding either of those other two, they are bound to find in History *ex hypothesi*; and we may be sure that, in the meantime, they do see some order, pattern, and shape in History at some level of the Psyche; for, if they saw no shape in History, they could have no vision of it. When they protest that they see no shape, what they are really doing is to refuse to bring a latent picture of the Universe up and out into the light of consciousness; and, in making this refusal, they are allowing their historical thought to be governed by some pattern embedded in their minds at the subconscious level. This subconscious pattern will be holding their conscious thought at its mercy because they are deliberaely leaving it out of conscious control; and a mental pattern that is not consciously criticized is likely to be archaic, infantile, and crude.

The crudeness of the pattern that some Late Modern historians are subconsciously following is indicated by the crudeness of the fragments of it that rise to the level of their consciousness like the flotsam that rises to the surface of the sea from a hulk that has gone to the bottom. Samples of these uncritically accepted intellectual *clichés* are the conventional terms 'Europe'; 'the European heritage from Israel, Greece, and Rome'; 'a cycle of Cathay' (perhaps, after all, not worse than a recent 'fifty years of Europe' that Tennyson did not live to experience); and 'Oriental' as a standing epithet for the pejorative abstract nouns decadence, stagnation, corruption, despotism, fanaticism, superstition, and irrationality.

Such shreds and tatters of foundered and forgotten patterns are bound to govern the thinking of historians for whom it is a dogma that, in History, no pattern of any kind is to be found; for, in truth, every thought and every word is a pattern found by the Mind in Reality; and a complete renunciation of all patterns, if this could really be achieved, would reduce the Mind's picture of the Universe to the 'perfect and absolute blank' that was the beauty of the Bellman's marine chart.[7] An antinomian historian who still had the courage of his convictions when he had grasped their philo- sophical consequences would find himself having to renounce not only Marcus Aurelius's pattern and Saint Augustine's and Con- fucius's, and not only those scraps of patterns—'Europe', 'Oriental' and the rest—which professedly antinomian historians have usually allowed themselves without realizing that this was inconsistent with their own doctrine. The uncompromising antinomian would have also to renounce the patterns inherent in the proper nouns 'Nicaragua' and 'Napoleon' and in the common nouns 'country', 'king', and 'man'. He would have, in fact, to achieve that suspen- sion of all discursive thought which is part of a mystic's *yoga* for extricating himself from the world of phenomena; and, since this is, of course, just the opposite of the antinomian historian's intended objective, it is a consequence that would seem to reduce his doctrine *ad absurdum*.

Meanwhile, pending a settlement of accounts between the an- tinomian historians and the philosophers, we shall perhaps be justified in seeing in the chaotic view of the nature of the Universe, not a distinct positive view, on a par with the cyclic view and with the volitional view, but simply a useful reminder that neither of these two fundamental views is more than a hypothesis that is open to challenge.

[7] See Carroll, Lewis, *The Hunting of the Snark*.

The Phenomenon of Man

PIERRE TEILHARD DE CHARDIN

The recent fashionableness of the late Father Pierre Teilhard de Chardin's magnum opus, *The Phenomenon of Man*, may be due in part to the warmth of the man and in part to the deep current of Christian mysticism that runs through all his writing. It may also testify to the emergence of a certain hunger for hopefulness in the Western psyche after decades of pessimism. At any rate, not everyone is able to survive on the stoical diet of the existentialists, and Teilhard has become, posthumously and unexpectedly, a force in contemporary thought.

He combined throughout his life the careers of a member of the Society of Jesus and a professional paleontologist and geologist. Forbidden by his religious order from publishing his philosophical works during his lifetime, he left the manuscripts in the care of a friend. *The Phenomenon of Man*, published in Paris after his death in 1955, was an instant success. The equally successful English translation followed in 1959, with an introduction by a non-Christian colleague of Teilhard's later years, Sir Julian Huxley. But the book is actually a product of the 1930's, finished in 1938, when Teilhard was engaged in geological work in China. In many ways it recalls the evolutionary philosophies of Bergson, Alexander, Smuts, and Whitehead.

These excerpts from *The Phenomenon of Man* are offered more as a sample of Teilhard's style than as a serious effort to represent the essentials of his thought. A full understanding of his technical terms, in particular, is impossible to acquire without reading the whole book. These passages from the first two chapters of Book IV do, however, contain some of his most seminal ideas, above all his vision of the growing spiritual and intellectual unification of mankind.

UNANIMITY

WE HAVE used the term mega-synthesis. When based on a better understanding of the collective, it seems to me that the word should be understood without attenuation or metaphors when applied to the sum of all human beings. The universe is necessarily

SOURCE: *The Phenomenon of Man*, by Pierre Teilhard de Chardin, trans. Bernard Wall (Harper & Row, New York, 1959), pp. 250–62. Reprinted by permission of Harper & Row, Publishers, and William Collins Sons and Co. Copyright 1959 by William Collins Sons and Co. and Harper & Row, Publishers.

homogeneous in its nature and dimensions. Would it still be so if the loops of its spiral lost one jot or tittle of their degree of reality or consistence in ascending ever higher? The still unnamed Thing which the gradual combination of individuals, peoples and races will bring into existence, must needs be *supra-physical*, not *infra-physical*, if it is to be coherent with the rest. Deeper than the common act in which it expresses itself, more important than the common power of action from which it emerges by a sort of self-birth, lies reality itself, constituted by the living reunion of reflective particles.

And what does that amount to if not (and it is quite credible) that the stuff of the universe, by becoming thinking, has not yet completed its evolutionary cycle, and that we are therefore moving forward towards some new critical point that lies ahead. In spite of its organic links, whose existence has everywhere become apparent to us, the biosphere has so far been no more than a network of divergent lines, free at their extremities. By effect of reflection and the recoils it involves, the loose ends have been tied up, and the noosphere [the "envelope" of thought in which man has wrapped his planet—*ed*.] tends to constitute a single closed system in which each element sees, feels, desires and suffers for itself the same things as all the others at the same time.

We are faced with a harmonised collectivity of consciousnesses equivalent to a sort of super-consciousness. The idea is that of the earth not only becoming covered by myriads of grains of thought, but becoming enclosed in a single thinking envelope so as to form, functionally, no more than a single vast grain of thought on the sidereal scale, the plurality of individual reflections grouping themselves together and reinforcing one another in the act of a single unanimous reflection.

This is the general form in which, by analogy and in symmetry with the past, we are led scientifically to envisage the future of mankind, without whom no terrestrial issue is open to the terrestrial demands of our action.

To the common sense of the 'man in the street' and even to a certain philosophy of the world to which nothing is possible save what has always been, perspectives such as these will seem highly improbable. But to a mind become familiar with the fantastic dimensions of the universe they will, on the contrary, seem quite natural, because they are directly proportionate with astronomical immensities.

In the direction of thought, could the universe terminate with anything less than the measureless—any more than it could in the direction of time and space?

One thing at any rate is sure—from the moment we adopt a thoroughly realistic view of the noosphere and of the hyper-organic nature of social bonds, the present situation of the world becomes clearer; for we find a very simple meaning for the profound troubles which disturb the layer of mankind at this moment.

The two-fold crisis whose onset began in earnest as early as the Neolithic age and which rose to a climax in the modern world, derives in the first place from a *mass-formation* (we might call it a 'planetisation') of mankind. Peoples and civilisations reached such a degree either of physical communion or economic interdependence or frontier contact that they could no longer develop save by interpenetration of one another. But it also arises out of the fact that, under the combined influence of machinery and the super-heating of thought, we are witnessing *a formidable upsurge of unused powers*. Modern man no longer knows what to do with the time and the potentialities he has unleashed. We groan under the burden of this wealth. We are haunted by the fear of 'unemployment.' Sometimes we are tempted to trample this super-abundance back into the matter from which it sprang without stopping to think how impossible and monstrous such an act against nature would be.

When we consider the increasing compression of elements at the heart of a free energy which is also relentlessly increasing, how can we fail to see in this two-fold phenomenon the two perennial symptoms of a leap forward of the 'radial'—that is to say of a new step in the genesis of mind?

In order to avoid disturbing our habits we seek in vain to settle international disputes by adjustments of frontiers—or we treat as 'leisure' (to be whiled away) the activities at the disposal of mankind. As things are now going it will not be long before we run full tilt into one another. Something will explode if we persist in trying to squeeze into our old tumble-down huts the material and spiritual forces that are henceforward on the scale of a world.

A new domain of psychical expansion—that is what we lack.

And it is staring us in the face if we would only raise our heads to look at it.

Peace through conquest, work in joy. These are waiting for us beyond the line where empires are set up against other empires, in an interior totalisation of the world upon itself, in the unanimous construction of a *spirit of the earth*.

How is it then that our first efforts towards this great goal seem merely to take us farther from it?

A Feeling to be overcome: Discouragement

The reasons behind the scepticism regarding mankind which is fashionable among 'enlightened' people today are not merely of a representative order. Even when the intellectual difficulties of the mind in conceiving the collective and visualising space-time have been overcome, we are left with another and perhaps a still more serious form of hesitation which is bound up with the incoherent aspect presented by the world of men today. The nineteenth century had lived in sight of a promised land. It thought that we were on the threshold of a Golden Age, lit up and organised by science, warmed by fraternity. Instead of that, we find ourselves slipped back into a world of spreading and ever more tragic dissension. Though possible and even perhaps probable in theory, the idea of a spirit of the earth does not stand up to the test of experience. No, man will never succeed in going beyond man by uniting with himself. That Utopia must be abandoned as soon as possible and there is no more to be said.

To explain or efface the appearances of a setback which, if it were true, would not only dispel a beautiful dream but encourage us to weigh up a radical absurdity of the universe, I would like to point out in the first place that to speak of experience—of the results of experience—in such a connection is premature to say the least of it. After all half a million years, perhaps even a million, were required for life to pass from the pre-hominids to modern man. Should we now start wringing our hands because, less than two centuries after glimpsing a higher state, modern man is still at loggerheads with himself? Once again we have got things out of focus. To have understood the immensity around us, behind us, and in front of us is already a first step. But if to this perception of depth another perception, that of *slowness*, be not added, we must realise that the transposition of values remains incomplete and that it can beget for our gaze nothing but an impossible world. Lach dimension has its proper rhythm. Planetary movement involves planetary majesty. Would not humanity seem to us altogether static if, behind its history, there were not the endless stretch of its prehistory? Similarly, and despite an almost explosive acceleration of noogenesis at our level, we cannot expect to see the earth transform itself under our eyes in the space of a generation. Let us keep calm and take heart.

In spite of all evidence to the contrary, mankind may very well be advancing all round us at the moment—there are in fact many signs whereby we can reasonably suppose that it is advancing. But, if it is doing so, it must be—as is the way with very big things— doing so almost imperceptibly.

This point is of the utmost importance and must never be lost sight of. To have made it does not, however, allay the most acute of our fears. After all we need not mind very much if the light on the horizon appears stationary. What does matter is when it seems to be going out. If only we could believe that we were merely motionless! But does it not sometimes seem that we are actually being thrust backwards or even swallowed up from behind—as though we were in the grip of some ineluctable forces of mutual repulsion and materialisation.

Repulsion. I have spoken of the formidable pressures which hem in the human particles in the present-day world, both individuals and peoples being forced in an extreme way, geographically and psychologically, up against one another. Now the strange fact is that, in spite of the strength of these energies bringing men to-gether, thinking units do not seem capable of falling within their radius of internal attraction. Leaving aside individual cases, where sexual forces or some extraordinary and transitory common passion come into play, men are hostile or at least closed to one another. Like a powder whose particles, however compressed, refuse to enter into molecular contact, deep down men exclude and repel one another with all their might: unless (and this is worse still) their mass forms in such a way that, instead of the expected *mind*, a new wave of determinism surges up—that is to say, of materiality.

Materialisation. Here I am not thinking of the laws of large numbers which, irrespective of their secret ends, enslave by struc-ture each newly-formed multitude. As with every other form of life, man, to become fully man, had to become legion. And, before becoming organised, a legion is necessarily prey to the play, however directed it be, of chance and probability. There are inponderable currents which, from fashion and rates of exchange to political and social revolutions, make us all the slaves of the obscure seethings of the human mass. However spiritualised we suppose its elements to be, every aggregate of consciousness, so long as it is not harmonised, envelops itself automatically (at its own level) with a veil of 'neo-matter,' superimposed upon all other forms of matter— matter, the 'tangential' aspect of every living mass in course of unification. Of course we must react to such conditions; but with the satisfaction of knowing that they are only the sign of and price paid for progress. But what are we to say of the other slavery, the one which gains ground in the world in very proportion to the efforts we make to organise ourselves?

At no previous period of history has mankind been so well equipped nor made such efforts to reduce its multitudes to order. We have 'mass movements'—no longer the hordes streaming down from the forests of the north or the steppes of Asia, but 'the Million' scientifically assembled. The Million in rank and file on the parade ground; the Million standardised in the factory; the Million motorised—and all this only ending up with Communism and National-Socialism and the most ghastly fetters. So we get the crystal instead of the cell; the ant-hill instead of brotherhood. Instead of the upsurge of consciousness which we expected, it is mechanisation that seems to emerge inevitably from totalisation.

'*Eppur si muove!*'

In the presence of such a profound perversion of the rules of noogenesis, I hold that our reaction should not be one of despair but of a determination to re-examine ourselves. When an energy runs amok, the engineer, far from questioning the power itself, simply works out his calculations afresh to see how it can be brought better under control. Monstrous as it is, is not modern totalitarianism really the distortion of something magnificent, and thus quite near to the truth? There can be no doubt of it: the great human machine is designed to work and *must* work—by producing a super-abundance of mind. If it does not work, or rather if it produces only matter, this means that it has gone into reverse.

Is it not possible that in our theories and in our acts we have neglected to give due place to the person, and the forces of *personalisation?*

THE PERSONAL UNIVERSE

UNLIKE the primitives who gave a face to every moving thing, or the early Greeks who defied all the aspects and forces of nature, modern man is obsessed by the need to depersonalise (or impersonalise) all that he most admires. There are two reasons for this tendency. The first is *analysis*, that marvellous instrument of scientific research to which we owe all our advances but which, breaking down synthesis after synthesis, allows one soul after another to escape, leaving us confronted with a pile of dismantled machinery, and evanescent particles. The second reason lies in the discovery of the sidereal world, so vast that it seems to do away with all proportion between our own being and the dimensions of the cosmos around us. Only one reality seems to survive and be capable of succeeding and spanning the infinitesimal and the immense: energy—that floating, universal entity from which all emerges and into which all falls back as into an ocean; energy, the new spirit; the new god. So, at the world's Omega, as at its Alpha, lies the Impersonal.

Under the influence of such impressions as these, it looks as though we have lost both respect for the person and understanding of his true nature. We end up by admitting that to be pivoted on oneself, to be able to say 'I', is the privilege (or rather the blemish) of the element in the measure to which the latter closes the door on all the rest and succeeds in setting himself up at the antipodes of the All. In the opposite direction we conceive the 'ego' to be diminishing and eliminating itself, with the trend to what is most real and most lasting in the world, namely the Collective and the Universal. Personality is seen as a specifically corpusucular and ephemeral property; a prison from which we must try to escape.

Intellectually, that is more or less where we stand today.

Yet if we try, as I have done in this essay, to pursue the logic and coherence of facts to the very end, we seem to be led to the precisely opposite view by the notions of space-time and evolution.

We have seen and admitted that evolution is an ascent towards consciousness. That is no longer contested even by the most materialistic, or at all events by the most agnostic of humanitarians. Therefore it should culminate forwards in some sort of supreme consciousness. But must not that consciousness, if it is to be

supreme, contain in the highest degree what is the perfection of
our consciousness—the illuminating involution of the being upon
itself? It would manifestly be an error to extend the curve of
hominisation in the direction of a state of diffusion. It is only
by hyper-reflection—that is to say hyper-personalisation—that
thought can extrapolate itself. Otherwise how could it garner our
conquests which are all made in the field of what is reflected? At
first sight we are disconcerted by the association of an Ego with
what is the All. The utter disproportion of the two terms seems
flagrant, almost laughable. That is because we have not sufficiently
meditated upon the three-fold property possessed by every consciousness: (i) of centring *everything* partially upon itself; (ii) of
being able to centre itself upon itself *constantly and increasingly;*
and (iii) of being brought by this very super-centration *into
association with all the other centres* surrounding it. Are we not at
every instant living the experience of a universe whose immensity,
by the play of our senses and our reason, is gathered up more and
more simply in each one of us? And in the establishment now
proceeding through science and the philosophies of a collective
human *Weltanschauung* in which every one of us co-operates and
participates, are we not experiencing the first symptoms of an
aggregation of a still higher order, the birth of some single centre
from the convergent beams of millions of elementary centres
dispersed over the surface of the thinking earth?

All our difficulties and repulsions as regards the opposition
between the All and the Person would be dissipated if only we
understood that, by structure, the noosphere (and more generally
the world) represent a whole that is not only closed but also
centred. Because it contains and engenders consciousness, space-
time is necessarily *of a convergent nature.* Accordingly its enormous layers followed in the right direction, must somewhere ahead
become involuted to a point which we might call *Omega,* which
fuses and consumes them integrally in itself. However immense the
sphere of the world may be, it only exists and is finally perceptible
in the directions in which its radii meet—even if this were beyond
time and space altogether. Better still: the more immense this
sphere, the richer and deeper and hence the more conscious is the
point at which the 'volume of being' that it embraces is concen-
trated; because the mind, seen from our side, is essentially the
power of synthesis and organisation.

Seen from this point of view, the universe, without losing any of its immensity and thus without suffering any anthropomorphism, begins to take shape: henceforward to think it, undergo it and make it act, it is *beyond* our souls that we must look, *not the other way round*. In the perspective of a noogenesis, time and space become truly humanised—or rather super-humanised. Far from being mutually exclusive, the Universal and Personal (that is to say the 'centred') grow in the same direction and culminate simultaneously in each other.

It is therefore a mistake to look for the extension of our being or of the noosphere in the Impersonal. The Future-Universal could not be anything else but the Hyper-Personal—at the Omega Point.

THE PERSONALISING UNIVERSE

Personalisation. It is by this eternal deepening of consciousness upon itself that we have characterised (Book III, Chapter I, Section I) the particular destiny of the element that has become fully itself by crossing the threshold of reflection—and there, as regards the fate of individual human beings—we brought our inquiry to a provisional halt. *Personalisation:* the same type of progress reappears here, but this time it defines the collective future of totalised grains of thought. There is an identical function for the element as for the sum of the elements brought together in a synthesis. How can we conceive and foresee that the two movements harmonise? How, without being impeded or deformed, can the innumerable particular curves can be inscribed or even prolonged in their common envelope?

The time has come to tackle this problem, and, for that purpose, to analyse still further the nature of the personal centre of convergence upon whose existence hangs the evolutionary equilibrium of the noosphere. What should this higher pole of evolution be, in order to fulfil its role?

It is by definition in Omega that—in its flower and its integrity —the hoard of consciousness liberated little by little on earth by noogenesis adds itself together and accumulates. So much has already been accepted. But what exactly do we mean, what is implied, when we use the apparently simple phrase 'addition of consciousness'?

When we listen to the disciples of Marx, we might think it was enough for mankind (for its growth and to justify the sacrifices imposed on us) to gather together the successive acquisitions we bequeath to it in dying—our ideas, our discoveries, our works of art, our example. Surely this imperishable treasure is the best part of our being.

Let us reflect a moment, and we shall soon see that for a universe which, by hypothesis, we admitted to be a 'collector and custodian of consciousness,' the mere hoarding of these remains would be nothing but a colossal wastage. What passes from each of us into the mass of humanity by means of invention, education and diffusion of all sorts is admittedly of vital importance. I have sufficiently tried to stress its phyletic value and no one can accuse me of belittling it. But, with that accepted, I am bound to admit that, in these contributions to the collectivity, far from transmitting the most precious, we are bequeathing, at the utmost, only the shadow of ourselves. Our works? But even in the interest of life in general, what is the work of human works if not to establish, in and by means of each one of us, an absolutely original centre in which the universe reflects itself in a unique and inimitable way? And those centres are our very selves and personalities. The very centre of our consciousness, deeper than all its radii; that is the essence which Omega, if it is to be truly Omega, must reclaim. And this essence is obviously not something of which we can dispossess ourselves for the benefit of others as we might give away a coat or pass on a torch. For we are the very flame of that torch. To communicate itself, my ego must subsist through abandoning itself or the gift will fade away. The conclusion is inevitable that the concentration of a conscious universe would be unthinkable if it did not re-assemble in itself *all consciousnesses* as well as all *the conscious;* each particular consciousness remaining conscious of itself at the end of the operation, and even (this must absolutely be understood) each particular consciousness becoming still more itself and thus more clearly distinct from others the closer it gets to them in Omega.

The exaltation, not merely the conversation, of elements by convergence: what, after all, could be more simple, and more thoroughly in keeping with all we know?

In any domain—whether it be the cells of a body, the members of a society or the elements of a spiritual synthesis—*union differentiates*. In every organised whole, the parts perfect themselves and fulfil themselves. Through neglect of this universal rule many a system of pantheism has led us astray to the cult of a great All in which individuals were supposed to be merged like a drop in the ocean or like a dissolving grain of salt. Applied to the case of the summation of consciousnesses, the law of union rids us of this perilous and recurrent illusion. No, following the confluent orbits of their centres, the grains of consciousness do not tend to lose their outlines and blend, but, on the contrary, to accentuate the depth and incommunicability of their *egos*. The more 'other' they become in conjunction, the more they find themselves as 'self.' How could it be otherwise since they are steeped in Omega? Could a centre dissolve? Or rather, would not its particular way of dissolving be to supercentralise itself?

Thus, under the influence of these two factors—the essential immiscibility of consciousnesses, and the natural mechanism of all unification—the only fashion in which we could correctly express the final state of a world undergoing physical concentration would be as a system whose unity coincides with a paroxysm of harmonised complexity. Thus it would be mistaken to represent Omega to ourselves simply as a centre born of the fusion of elements which it collects, or annihilating them in itself. By its structure Omega, in its ultimate principle, can only be a *distinct Centre radiating at the core of a system of centres;* a grouping in which personalisation of the All and personalisations of the elements reach their maximum, simultaneously and without merging, under the influence of a supremely autonomous focus of union.

Has History Any Meaning?

Karl Popper

As the readings from Spengler, Toynbee, and Teilhard de Chardin amply demonstrate, the search for meaning in history has not been neglected by twentieth-century writers. Each new metahistorical revelation has been greeted with enthusiasm by large numbers of thinking

SOURCE: *The Open Society and Its Enemies,* by Karl Popper (fourth edition, revised, Princeton University Press, Princeton, N.J., 1963), Vol. II, pp. 269–80. Reprinted by permission of Princeton University Press and Routledge and Kegan Paul, Ltd.

people. But most historians and philosophers of history in our time have found these revelations unacceptable as explanations of the historical process; they see them, rather, as explanations of the world-outlooks of the individual apocalyptists, valuable more for their ethical or religious content than for their insight into history as such.

Thinkers influenced by logical positivism and analytical philosophy, for example, incline to the view that history cannot have any absolute or comprehensive meaning; the attempt to work out historical "laws" with predictive power is seen as futile and perhaps even dangerous. The critical school of historicism founded by Wilhelm Dilthey and the existentialist movement have also thrown their weight against monolithic, absolutist interpretations of history. To believe that history has any single determinate structure or meaning is, for them, to deny human freedom.

Representing modern analytical philosophy in this controversy is the British logician Karl Popper. Viennese by birth and education, Popper has held academic posts since 1937 at Canterbury College in New Zealand and at the London School of Economics. His most systematic attacks on historical determinism, which he refers to idiosyncratically as "historicism," can be found in *The Open Society and Its Enemies* (1945), from which this excerpt is taken, and in *The Poverty of Historicism* (1957).

Is there a meaning in history?

I do not wish to enter here into the problem of the meaning of 'meaning'; I take it for granted that most people know with sufficient clarity what they mean when they speak of the 'meaning of history' or of the 'meaning or purpose of life'.[1] And in this sense, in the sense in which the question of the meaning of history is asked, I answer: *History has no meaning.*

In order to give reasons for this opinion, I must first say something about that 'history' which people have in mind when they ask whether it has meaning. So far, I have myself spoken about 'history' as if it did not need any explanation. That is no longer possible; for I wish to make it clear that *'history' in the sense in which most people speak of it simply does not exist;* and this is at least one reason why I say that it has no meaning.

How do most people come to use the term 'history'? (I mean

[1] For this refusal to discuss the problem of the 'meaning of meaning' (Ogden and Richards) or rather of the 'meanings of meaning' (H. Gomperz), cp. chapter 11 [of Popper's *The Open Society and Its Enemies* —Ed.], especially notes 26, 47, 50, and 51. See also note 16 below.

'history' in the sense in which we say of a book that it is *about* the history of Europe—not in the sense in which we say that it *is* a history of Europe.) They learn about it in school and at the University. They read books about it. They see what is treated in the books under the name 'history of the world' or 'the history of mankind', and they get used to looking upon it as a more or less definite series of facts. And these facts constitute, they believe, the history of mankind.

But we have already seen that the realm of facts is infinitely rich, and that there must be selection. According to our interests, we could, for instance, write about the history of art; or of language; or of feeding habits; or of typhus fever (see Zinsser's *Rats, Lice, and History*). Certainly, none of these is the history of mankind (nor all of them taken together). What people have in mind when they speak of the history of mankind is, rather, the history of the Egyptian, Babylonian, Persian, Macedonian, and Roman empires, and so on, down to our own day. In other words: They speak about the *history of mankind*, but what they mean, and what they have learned about in school, is the *history of political power*.

There is no history of mankind, there is only an indefinite number of histories of all kinds of aspects of human life. And one of these is the history of political power. This is elevated into the history of the world. But this, I hold, is an offence against every decent conception of mankind. It is hardly better than to treat the history of embezzlement or of robbery or of poisoning as the history of mankind. For *the history of power politics is nothing but the history of international crime and mass murder* (including, it is true, some of the attempts to suppress them). This history is taught in schools, and some of the greatest criminals are extolled as its heroes.

But is there really no such thing as a universal history in the sense of a concrete history of mankind? There can be none. This must be the reply of every humanitarian, I believe, and especially that of every Christian. A concrete history of mankind, if there were any, would have to be the history of all men. It would have to be the history of all human hopes, struggles, and sufferings. For there is no one man more important than any other. Clearly, this concrete history cannot be written. We must make abstractions, we must neglect, select. But with this we arrive at the many histories; and among them, at that history of international crime and mass murder which has been advertised as the history of mankind.

But why has just the history of power been selected, and not, for example, that of religion, or of poetry? There are several reasons. One is that power affects us all, and poetry only a few. Another is that men are inclined to worship power. But there can be no doubt that the worship of power is one of the worst kinds of human idolatries, a relic of the time of the cage, of human servitude. The worship of power is born of fear, an emotion which is rightly despised. A third reason why power politics has been made the core of 'history' is that those in power wanted to be worshipped and could enforce their wishes. Many historians wrote under the supervision of the emperors, the generals and the dictators.

I know that these views will meet with the strongest opposition from many sides, including some apologists for Christianity; for although there is hardly anything in the New Testament to support this doctrine, it is often considered a part of the Christian dogma that God reveals Himself in history; that history has meaning; and that its meaning is the purpose of God. Historicism is thus held to be a necessary element of religion. But I do not admit this. I contend that this view is pure idolatry and superstition, not only from the point of view of a rationalist or humanist but from the Christian point of view itself.

What is behind this theistic historicism? With Hegel, it looks upon history—political history—as a stage, or rather, as a kind of lengthy Shakespearian play; and the audience conceive either the 'great historical personalities', or mankind in the abstract, as the heroes of the play. Then they ask, 'Who has written this play?' And they think that they give a pious answer when they reply, 'God'. But they are mistaken. Their answer is pure blasphemy, for the play was (and they know it) written not by God, but, under the supervision of generals and dictators, by the professors of history.

I do not deny that it is as justifiable to interpret history from a Christian point of view as it is to interpret it from any other point of view; and it should certainly be emphasized, for example, how much of our Western aims and ends, humanitarianism, freedom, equality, we owe to the influence of Christianity. But at the same time, the only rational as well as the only Christian attitude even

towards the history of freedom is that we are ourselves responsible
for it, in the same sense in which we are responsible for what we
make of our lives, and that only our conscience can judge us and
not our worldly success. The theory that God reveals Himself and
His judgement in history is indistinguishable from the theory that
worldly success is the ultimate judge and justification of our
actions; it comes to the same thing as the doctrine that history will
judge, that is to say, that future might is right; it is the same as
what I have called 'moral futurism'.[2] To maintain that God reveals
Himself in what is usually called 'history', in the history of international crime and of mass murder, is indeed blasphemy; for what
really happens within the realm of human lives is hardly ever
touched upon by this cruel and at the same time childish affair. The
life of the forgotten, of the unknown individual man; his sorrows
and his joys, his suffering and death, this is the real content of
human experience down the ages. If that could be told by history,
then I should certainly not say that it is blasphemy to see the finger
of God in it. But such a history does not and cannot exist; and all
the history which exists, our history of the Great and the Powerful, is at best a shallow comedy; it is the opera buffa played by the
powers behind reality (comparable to Homer's opera buffa of the
Olympian powers behind the scene of human struggles). It is what
one of our worst instincts, the idolatrous worship of power, of
success, has led us to believe to be real. And in this not even man-
made, but man-faked 'history', some Christians dare to see the hand
of God! They dare to understand and to know what He wills when
they impute to Him their petty historical interpretations! 'On the
contrary', says K. Barth, the theologian, in his *Credo*, 'we have to
begin with the admission . . . that all that we think we know
when we say "God" does not reach or comprehend Him . . . but
always one of our self-conceived and self-made idols, whether it is
"spirit" or "nature", "fate" or "idea" . . .'[3] (It is in keeping with

[2] For moral futurism, cp. chapter 22.
[3] Cp. K. Barth, *Credo* (1936), p. 12. For Barth's remark against 'the Neo-
Protestant doctrine of the revelation of God in history', cp. *op. cit.*, 142. See
also the Hegelian source of this doctrine, quoted in text to note 49, chapter
12. Cp. also note 51 to chapter 24. For the next quotation cp. Barth, *op. cit.*,
79. Concerning my remark that the story of Christ was *not* 'the story of an
unsuccessful . . . nationalist revolution', I am now inclined to believe that it
may have been precisely this; see R. Eisler's book *Jesus Basileus*. But in any
case, it is not a story of worldly success.

this attitude that Barth characterizes the 'Neo-Protestant doctrine of the revelation of God in history' as 'inadmissible' and as an encroachment upon 'the kingly office of Christ'.) But it is, from the Christian point of view, not only arrogance that underlies such attempts; it is, more specifically, an anti-Christian attitude. For Christianity teaches, if anything, that worldly success is not decisive. Christ 'suffered under Pontius Pilate'. I am quoting Barth again: 'How does Pontius Pilate get into the Credo? The simple answer can at once be given: it is a matter of date.' Thus the man who was successful, who represented the historical power of that time, plays here the purely technical role of indicating when these events happened. And what were these events? They had nothing to do with power-political success, with 'history'. They were not even the story of an unsuccessful non-violent nationalist revolution (à la Gandhi) of the Jewish people against the Roman conquerors. The events were nothing but the sufferings of a man. Barth insists that the word 'suffers' refers to the whole of the life of Christ and not only to His death; he says:[4] 'Jesus *suffers*. Therefore He does not conquer. He does not triumph. He has no success. . . . He achieved nothing except . . . His crucifixion. The same could be said of His relationship to His people and to His disciples.' My intention in quoting Barth is to show that it is not only my 'rationalist' or 'humanist' point of view from which the worship of historical success appears as incompatible with the spirit of Christianity. What matters to Christianity is not the historical deeds of the powerful Roman conquerors but (to use a phrase of Kierkegaard's[5]) 'what a few fishermen have given the world'. And yet all theistic interpretation of history attempts to see in history as it is recorded, i.e. in the history of power, and in historical success, the manifestation of God's will.

To this attack upon the 'doctrine of the revelation of God in history', it will probably be replied that it *is* success, His success after His death, by which Christ's unsuccessful life on earth was finally revealed to mankind as the greatest spiritual victory; that it was the success, the fruits of His teaching which proved it and justified it, and by which the prophecy 'The last shall be first and the first last' has been verified. In other words, that it was the historical success of the Christian Church through which the will

[4] Cp. Barth, *op. cit.*, 76.
[5] Cp. Kierkegaard's Journal of 1854; see the German edition (1905) of his *Book of the Judge*, p. 135.

of God manifested itself. But this is a most dangerous line of defence. Its implication that the worldly success of the Church is an argument in favour of Christianity clearly reveals lack of faith. The early Christians had no worldly encouragement of this kind. (They believed that conscience must judge power,[6] and not the other way round.) Those who hold that the history of the success of Christian teaching reveals the will of God should ask themselves whether this success was really a success of the spirit of Christianity; and whether this spirit did not triumph at the time when the Church was persecuted, rather than at the time when the Church was triumphant. Which Church incorporated this spirit more purely, that of the martyrs, or the victorious Church of the Inquisition?

There seem to be many who would admit much of this, insisting as they do that the message of Christianity is to the meek, but who still believe that this message is one of historicism. An outstanding representative of this view is J. Macmurray, who, in *The Clue to History*, finds the essence of Christian teaching in historical prophecy, and who sees in its founder the discoverer of a dialectical law of 'human nature'. Macmurray holds[7] that, according to this law, political history must inevitably bring forth 'the socialist commonwealth of the world. The fundamental law of human nature cannot be broken. . . . It is the meek who will inherit the earth.' But this historicism, with its substitution of certainty for hope, must lead to a moral futurism. 'The law *cannot* be broken.' So we can be sure, on psychological grounds, that whatever we do will lead to the same result; that even fascism must, in the end, lead to that commonwealth; so that the final outcome does not depend upon our moral decision, and that there is no need to worry over our responsibilities. If we are told that we can be *certain*, on scientific grounds, that 'the last will be first and the first last', what else is this but the substitution of historical prophecy for conscience? Does not this theory come dangerously close (certainly against the intentions of its author) to the admonition: 'Be wise, and take to heart what the founder of Christianity tells you, for he was a great psychologist of human nature and a great prophet of history. Climb in time upon the band-waggon of the meek; for according to the inexorable scientific laws of human nature, this is

[6] Cp. note 57 to chapter 11, and text.
[7] Cp. the concluding sentences of Macmurray's *The Clue to History* (1938; p. 237).

the surest way to come out on top!' Such a clue to history implies the worship of success; it implies that the meek will be justified because they will be on the winning side. It translates Marxism, and especially what I have described as Marx's historicist moral theory, into the language of a psychology of human nature, and of religious prophecy. It is an interpretation which, by implication, sees the greatest achievement of Christianity in the fact that its founder was a forerunner of Hegel—a superior one, admittedly.

My insistence that success should not be worshipped, that it cannot be our judge, and that we should not be dazzled by it, and in particular, my attempts to show that in this attitude I concur with what I believe to be the true teaching of Christianity, should not be misunderstood. They are not intended to support the attitude of 'other-worldliness' which I have criticized in the last chapter.[8] Whether Christianity is other-worldly, I do not know, but it certainly teaches that the only way to prove one's faith is by rendering practical (and worldly) help to those who need it. And it is certainly possible to combine an attitude of the utmost reserve and even of contempt towards worldly success in the sense of power, glory, and wealth, with the attempt to do one's best in this world, and to further the ends one has decided to adopt with the clear purpose of making them succeed; not for the sake of success or of one's justification by history, but for their own sake.

A forceful support of some of these views, and especially of the incompatibility of historicism and Christianity, can be found in Kierkegaard's criticism of Hegel. Although Kierkegaard never freed himself entirely from the Hegelian tradition in which he was educated,[9] there was hardly anybody who recognized more clearly what Hegelian historicism meant. 'There were', Kierkegaard wrote,[10] 'philosophers who tried, before Hegel, to explain . . .

[8] Cp. especially note 55 to chapter 24, and text.

[9] Kierkegaard was educated at the University of Copenhagen in a period of intense and even somewhat aggressive Hegelianism. The theologian Martensen was especially influential. (For this aggressive attitude, cp. the judgement of the Copenhagen Academy against Schopenhauer's prize essay on the *Foundations of Morals*, of 1840. It is very likely that this affair was instrumental in making Kierkegaard acquainted with Schopenhauer, at a time when the latter was still unknown in Germany.)

[10] Cp. Kierkegaard's *Journal* of 1853; see the German edition of his *Book of the Judge*, p. 129, from which the passage in the text is freely translated.

Kierkegaard is not the only Christian thinker protesting against Hegel's historicism; we have seen (cp. note 3 above) that Barth also protests against history. And providence could only smile when it saw these attempts. But providence did not laugh outright, for there was a human, honest sincerity about them. But Hegel—! Here I need Homer's language. How did the gods roar with laughter! Such a horrid little professor who has simply seen through the necessity of anything and everything there is, and who now plays the whole affair on his barrel-organ: listen, ye gods of Olympus!' And Kierkegaard continues, referring to the attack[11] by the atheist Schopenhauer upon the Christian apologist Hegel: 'Reading Scho-

---

it. A remarkably interesting criticism of Hegel's teleological interpretation of history was given by the Christian philosopher, M. B. Foster, a great admirer (if not a follower) of Hegel, at the end of his book *The Political Philosophies of Plato and Hegel*. The main point of his criticism, if I understand him rightly, is this. By interpreting history teleologically, Hegel does not see, in its various stages, ends in themselves, but merely means for bringing about the final end. But Hegel is wrong in assuming that historical phenomena or periods are means to an end which can be conceived and stated as something distinguishable from the phenomena themselves, in a way in which a purpose can be distinguished from the action which seeks to realize it, or a moral from a play (if we wrongly assume that the sole purpose of the play was to convey this moral). For this assumption, Foster contends, shows a failure to recognize the difference between the work of a *creator* and that of an instrument maker, a technician or '*Demiurge*'. '. . . a series of works of creation may be understood as a development', Foster writes (*op. cit.*, pp. 201–3), '. . . without a distinct conception of the end to which they progress . . . the painting, say, of one era may be understood to have developed out of the era preceding it, without being understood as a nearer approximation to a perfection or end. . . . Political history, similarly . . . may be understood as development, without being interpreted as a teleological process.—But Hegel, here and elsewhere, lacks insight in the significance of creation.' And later, Foster writes (*op. cit.*, p. 204; italics partly mine): 'Hegel regards it as a sign of inadequacy of the religious imagery that those who hold it, while they assert that there is a plan of Providence, deny that the plan is knowable. . . . To say that the plan of Providence is inscrutable is, no doubt, an inadequate expression, but the truth which it expresses inadequately is not that God's plan is knowable, but that, as Creator and not as a Demiurge, *God does not work according to plan at all.*'

I think that this criticism is excellent, even though the creation of a work of art may, in a very different sense, proceed according to a '*plan*' (although not an end or purpose); for it may be an attempt to realize something like the Platonic idea of that work—that perfect model before his mental eyes or ears which the painter or musician strives to copy. (Cp. note 9 to chapter 9 and notes 25–26 to chapter 8.)

[11] For Schopenhauer's attacks upon Hegel, to which Kierkegaard refers, cp. chapter 12, for example, text to note 13, and the concluding sentences. The partly quoted continuation of Kierkegaard's passage is *op. cit.*, 130. (In a note, Kierkegaard later inserted 'pantheist' before 'putridity'.)

penhauer has given me more pleasure than I can express. What he says is perfectly true; and then—it serves the Germans right—he is as rude as only a German can be.' But Kierkegaard's own expressions are nearly as blunt as Schopenhauer's; for Kierkegaard goes on to say that Hegelianism, which he calls 'this brilliant spirit of putridity', is the 'most repugnant of all forms of looseness'; and he speaks of its 'mildew of pomposity', its 'intellectual voluptuousness', and its 'infamous splendour of corruption'.

And, indeed, our intellectual as well as our ethical education is corrupt. It is perverted by the admiration of brilliance, of the way things are said, which takes the place of a critical appreciation of the things that are said (and the things that are done). It is perverted by the romantic idea of the splendour of the stage of History on which we are the actors. We are educated to act with an eye to the gallery.

The whole problem of educating man to a sane appreciation of his own importance relative to that of other individuals is thoroughly muddled by these ethics of fame and fate, by a morality which perpetuates an educational system that is still based upon the classics with their romantic view of the history of power and their romantic tribal morality which goes back to Heraclitus; a system whose ultimate basis is the worship of power. Instead of a sober combination of individualism and altruism (to use these labels again[12])—that is to say, instead of a position like 'What really matters are human individuals, but I do not take this to mean that it is I who matter very much'—a romantic combination of egoism and collectivism is taken for granted. That is to say, the importance of the self, of its emotional life and its 'self-expression', is romantically exaggerated; and with it, the tension between the 'personality' and the group, the collective. This takes the place of the other individuals, the other men, but does not admit of reasonable personal relations. 'Dominate or submit' is, by implication, the device of this attitude; either be a Great Man, a Hero wrestling with fate and earning fame ('the greater the fall, the greater the fame', says Heraclitus), or belong to 'the masses' and submit yourself to leadership and sacrifice yourself to the higher cause of your collective. There is a neurotic, an hysterical element in this exaggerated stress on the importance of the tension between the self and the

[12] Cp. chapter 6, especially text to note 26.

collective, and I do not doubt that this hysteria, this reaction to the strain of civilization, is the secret of the strong emotional appeal of the ethics of hero-worship, of the ethics of domination and submission.[13]

At the bottom of all this there is a real difficulty. While it is fairly clear . . . that the politician should limit himself to fighting against evils, instead of fighting for 'positive' or 'higher' values, such as happiness, etc., the teacher, in principle, is in a different position. Although he should not *impose* his scale of 'higher' values upon his pupils, he certainly should try to *stimulate* their interest in these values. He should care for the souls of his pupils. (When Socrates told his friends to care for their souls, *he* cared for them.) Thus there is certainly something like a romantic or æsthetic element in education, such as should not enter politics. But though this is true in principle, it is hardly applicable to our educational system. For it presupposes a relation of friendship between teacher and pupil, a relation which . . . each party must be free to end. (Socrates chose his companions, and they him.) The very number of pupils makes all this impossible in our schools. Accordingly, attempts to impose higher values not only become unsuccessful, but it must be insisted that they lead to *harm*—to something much more concrete and public than the ideals aimed at. And the principle that those who are entrusted to us must, before anything else, not be harmed, should be recognized to be just as fundamental for education as it is for medicine. 'Do no harm' (and, therefore, 'give the young what they most urgently need, in order to become independent of us, and be able to choose for themselves') would be a very worthy aim for our educational system, and one whose realization is somewhat remote, even though it sounds modest. Instead, 'higher' aims are the fashion, aims which are typically romantic and indeed nonsensical, such as 'the full development of the personality'.

It is under the influence of such romantic ideas that individualism is still identified with egoism, as it was by Plato, and altruism with collectivism (i.e. with the substitution of group egoism for the individualist egoism). But this bars the way even to a clear formulation of the main problem, the problem of how to obtain a sane

[13] For the Hegelian ethics of domination and submission, cp. note 25 to chapter 11. For the ethics of hero-worship, cp. chapter 12, especially text to notes 75 ff.

appreciation of one's own importance in relation to other individuals. Since it is felt, and rightly so, that we have to aim at
something beyond our own selves, something to which we can
devote ourselves, and for which we may make sacrifices, it is
concluded that this must be the collective, with its 'historical
mission'. Thus we are told to make sacrifices, and, at the same time,
assured that we shall make an excellent bargain by doing so. We
shall make sacrifices, it is said, but we shall thereby obtain honour
and fame. We shall become 'leading actors', heroes on the Stage of
History; for a small risk we shall gain great rewards. This is the
dubious morality of a period in which only a tiny minority
counted, and in which nobody cared for the common people. It is
the morality of those who, being political or intellectual aristocrats,
have a chance of getting into the textbooks of history. It cannot
possibly be the morality of those who favour justice and equali-
tarianism; for historical fame cannot be just, and it can be attained
only by a very few. The countless number of men who are just as
worthy, or worthier, will always be forgotten.

It should perhaps be admitted that the Heraclitean ethics, the
doctrine that the higher reward is that which only posterity can
offer, may in some way perhaps be slightly superior to an ethical
doctrine which teaches us to look out for reward now. But it is not
what we need. We need an ethics which defies success and reward.
And such an ethics need not be invented. It is not new. It has been
taught by Christianity, at least in its beginnings. It is, again, taught
by the industrial as well as by the scientific co-operation of our
own day. The romantic historicist morality of fame, fortunately,
seems to be on the decline. The Unknown Soldier shows it. We are
beginning to realize that sacrifice may mean just as much, or even
more, when it is made anonymously. Our ethical education must
follow suit. We must be taught to do our work; to make our
sacrifice for the sake of this work, and not for praise or the
avoidance of blame. (The fact that we all need some encouragement, hope, praise, and even blame, is another matter altogether.)
We must find our justification in our work, in what we are doing
ourselves, and not in a fictitious 'meaning of history'.

History has no meaning, I contend. But this contention does not
imply that all we can do about it is to look aghast at the history of
political power, or that we must look on it as a cruel joke. For we

can interpret it, with an eye to those problems of power politics whose solution we choose to attempt in our time. We can interpret the history of power politics from the point of view of our fight for the open society, for a rule of reason, for justice, freedom, equality, and for the control of international crime. Although history has no ends, we can impose these ends of ours upon it; and *although history has no meaning, we can give it a meaning.*

It is the problem of nature and convention which we meet here again.[14] Neither nature nor history can tell us what we ought to do. Facts, whether those of nature or those of history, cannot make the decision for us, they cannot determine the ends we are going to choose. It is we who introduce purpose and meaning into nature and into history. Men are not equal; but we can decide to fight for equal rights. Human institutions such as the state are not rational, but we can decide to fight to make them more rational. We ourselves and our ordinary language are, on the whole, emotional rather than rational; but we can try to become a little more rational, and we can train ourselves to use our language as an instrument not of self-expression (as our romantic educationists would say) but of rational communication.[15] History itself—I mean the history of power politics, of course, not the non-existent story of the development of mankind—has no end nor meaning, but we can decide to give it both. We can make it our fight for the open society and against its enemies (who, when in a corner, always protest their humanitarian sentiments, in accordance with Pareto's advice); and we can interpret it accordingly. Ultimately, we may say the same about the 'meaning of life'. It is up to us to decide what shall be our purpose in life, to determine our ends.[16]

[14] Cp. chapter 5 (especially text to note 5).

[15] We can 'express ourselves' in many ways without communicating anything. For our task of using language for the purpose of rational communication, and for the need of keeping up the standards of clarity of the language, cp. notes 19 and 20 to chapter 24 and note 30 to chapter 12.

[16] This view of the problem of the 'meaning of life' may be contrasted with Wittgenstein's view of the problems of the 'sense of life' in the *Tractatus* (p. 187): 'The solution of the problem of life is seen in the vanishing of this problem.—(Is not this the reason why men to whom after long doubting the sense of life became clear, could not then say wherein this sense consisted?)' For Wittgenstein's mysticism, see also note 32 to chapter 24. For the interpretation of history here suggested, cp. notes 61 (1) to chapter 11, and 18 below.

This dualism of facts and decisions[17] is, I believe, fundamental. Facts as such have no meaning; they can gain it only through our decisions. Historicism is only one of many attempts to get over this dualism; it is born of fear, for it shrinks from realizing that we bear the ultimate responsibility even for the standards we choose. But such an attempt seems to me to represent precisely what is usually described as superstition. For it assumes that we can reap where we have not sown; it tries to persuade us that if we merely fall into step with history everything will and must go right, and that no fundamental decision on our part is required; it tries to shift our responsibility on to history, and thereby on to the play of demoniac powers beyond ourselves; it tries to base our actions upon the hidden intentions of these powers, which can be revealed to us only in mystical inspirations and intuitions; and it thus puts our actions and ourselves on the moral level of a man who, inspired by horoscopes and dreams, chooses his lucky number in a lottery.[18]

[17] Cp., for example, note 5 to chapter 5 and note 19 to chapter 24.
It may be remarked that the world of facts is in itself complete (since every decision can be interpreted as a fact). It is therefore for ever impossible to *refute* a monism which insists that there are only facts. But irrefutability is not a virtue. Idealism, for example, cannot be refuted either.

[18] It appears that one of the motives of historicism is that the historicist does not see that there is a third alternative, besides the two which he allows: either that the world is ruled by superior *powers*, by an 'essential destiny' or Hegelian 'Reason', or that it is a mere wheel of chance, irrational, on the level of a gamble. *But there is a third possibility:* that *we* may introduce reason into it (cp. note 19 to chapter 24); that although the world does not progress, *we* may progress, individually as well as in co-operation.
This third possibility is clearly expressed by H. A. L. Fisher in his *History of Europe* (vol. I, p. vii, italics mine; partly quoted in text to note 8 to chapter 21): 'One intellectual excitement has . . . been denied me. Men wiser and more learned than I have discerned in history a plot, a rhythm, a predetermined pattern. These harmonies are concealed from me. I can see only one emergency following upon another as wave follows wave, only one great fact with respect to which, *since it is unique, there can be no generalizations*, only one safe rule for the historian: that he should recognize . . . the play of the contingent and the unforeseen.' And immediately after this excellent attack upon historicism (with the passage in italics, cp. note 13 to chapter 13), Fisher continues: 'This is not a doctrine of cynicism and despair. *The fact of progress is written plain and large on the page of history; but progress is not a law of nature.* The ground gained by one generation may be lost by the next.'
These last three sentences represent very clearly what I have called the 'third possibility', the belief in our responsibility, the belief that everything rests with us. And it is interesting to see that Fisher's statement is interpreted by Toynbee (*A Study of History*, vol. V, 414) as representing 'the

Like gambling, historicism is born of our despair in the rationality and responsibility of our actions. It is a debased hope and a debased faith, an attempt to replace the hope and the faith that springs from our moral enthusiasm and the contempt for success by a certainty that springs from a pseudo-science; a pseudo-science of the stars, or of 'human nature', or of historical destiny.

Historicism, I assert, is not only rationally untenable, it is also in conflict with any religion that teaches the importance of conscience. For such a religion must agree with the rationalist attitude towards history in its emphasis on our supreme responsibility for our actions, and for their repercussions upon the course of history. True, we need hope; to act, to live without hope goes beyond our strength. But we do *not* need more, and we must not be given more. We do not need certainty. Religion, in particular, should not be a substitute for dreams and wish-fulfillment; it should resemble neither the holding of a ticket in a lottery, nor the holding of a policy in an insurance company. The historicist element in religion is an element of idolatry, of superstition.

This emphasis upon the dualism of facts and decisions determines also our attitude towards such ideas as 'progress'. If we think that history progresses, or that we are bound to progress, then we commit the same mistake as those who believe that history has a meaning that can be discovered in it and need not be given to it. For to progress is to move towards some kind of end, towards an end which exists for us as human beings. 'History' cannot do that; only we, the human individuals, can do it; we can do it by

---

modern Western belief in the omnipotence of Chance'. Nothing could show more clearly the attitude of the historicist, his inability to see the third possibility. And it explains perhaps why he tries to escape from this alleged 'omnipotence of chance' into a belief in the omnipotence of the *power* behind the historical scene—that is, into historicism. (Cp. also note 61 to chapter 11.)

I may perhaps quote more fully Toynbee's comments on Fisher's passage (which Toynbee quotes down to the words 'the unforeseen'): 'This brilliantly phrased passage', Toynbee writes, 'cannot be dismissed as a scholar's conceit; for the writer is a Liberal who is formulating a creed which Liberalism has translated from theory into action. . . . This modern Western belief in the omnipotence of Chance gave birth in the nineteenth century of the Christian Era, when things still seemed to be going well with Western Man, to the policy of *laissez faire* . . .' (Why the belief in a progress for which we ourselves are responsible should imply a belief in the omnipotence of Chance, or why it should produce the policy of *laissez faire*, Toynbee leaves unexplained.)

defending and strengthening those democratic institutions upon which freedom, and with it progress, depends. And we shall do it much better as we become more fully aware of the fact that progress rests with us, with our watchfulness, with our efforts, with the clarity of our conception of our ends, and with the realism[19] of their choice.

Instead of posing as prophets we must become the makers of our fate. We must learn to do things as well as we can, and to look out for our mistakes. And when we have dropped the idea that the history of power will be our judge, when we have given up worrying whether or not history will justify us, then one day perhaps we may succeed in getting power under control. In this way we may even justify history, in our turn. It badly needs a justification.

[19] By the 'realism' of the choice of our ends I mean that we should choose ends which can be realized within a reasonable span of time, and that we should avoid distant and vague Utopian ideals, unless they determine more immediate aims which are worthy in themselves. Cp. especially the principles of piecemeal social engineering, discussed in chapter 9.

VII

Capitalism, Socialism, and Democracy

The Case for Human Happiness

G. D. H. COLE

Of all the ideologies competing for followers in the early twentieth century, socialism appeared to have the greatest chance of achieving its objectives. Politically oriented intellectuals turned to it by the thousands. In each of the industrialized countries of Western Europe socialist parties grew rapidly. After 1917 the international socialist movement split in two, but socialism continued to prosper in the 1920's. Socialist prime ministers led coalition cabinets in several Western countries, while Bolsheviks ruled the empire of the Romanovs. The various socialist parties could expect to poll as much as 40 per cent of the popular vote in such countries as Germany and Great Britain. During the Depression of the 1930's many intellectuals arrived at the conclusion that capitalism had demonstrated its bankruptcy as a socioeconomic system once and for all.

But since the Second World War, with the introduction of Keynesian planning and the progress of the Welfare State, Western European socialism has lost its messianic fervor. The objectives of socialism, in large measure, have been realized without resort to socialist policies. Even where democratic socialist parties have managed to reach power through free elections, as in Britain and Scandinavia, so many compromises have been made with private enterprise that the traditional program of the socialist movement has all but disintegrated.

The contrast between the lukewarm, pragmatic movement of the 1960's and the evangelical visions of the 1930's, the last great decade of socialist purism, stands out clearly in this first chapter of the late G. D. H. Cole's book *The Simple Case for Socialism*, published in 1935. Although never the most subtle or profound of socialist thinkers, Cole

SOURCE: *The Simple Case for Socialism*, by G. D. H. Cole (Gollancz, London, 1935), pp. 7–18. Reprinted by permission of Mrs. M. I. Cole and Victor Gollancz, Ltd.

had phenomenal energy, and his idealism was beyond question. In 1908, while still a student at Oxford, he joined the Fabian Society. He became one of its outstanding leaders in the Depression years and thereafter, serving as chairman for all but two years between 1939 and 1950. He was the author of dozens of books and pamphlets, including a definitive *History of Socialist Thought* in five volumes (1953–60).

I AM SETTING out in this book to put down the case for Socialism in the simplest possible terms. By Socialism I mean a form of society in which men and women are not divided into opposing economic classes, but live together under conditions of approximate social and economic equality, using in common the means that lie to their hands of promoting social welfare. Socialism, as I understand it, means four closely connected things—a human fellowship which denies and expels distinctions of class, a social system in which no one is so much richer or poorer than his neighbours as to be unable to mix with them on equal terms, the common ownership and use of all the vital instruments of production, and an obligation upon all citizens to serve one another according to their capacities in promoting the common well-being. Nothing is Socialism that does not embrace all these four things; and, given the means of realising these four, nothing further is needed to make a Socialist society.

Or rather, only this is needed: that the Socialist society shall be able to live on terms of peace and amity with its neighbours, sharing with them in the promotion of the welfare and happiness of the whole world. It follows from this that Socialism is a gospel not for one people but for all. Socialist institutions may take many different forms in different countries according to the various cultures and ways of living which the peoples of these countries have inherited from the past, and the variety of problems with which they are confronted here and now. These national differences are not evil but positively good; and in each country Socialist institutions will have to be shaped in accordance with the national traditions of the people. But Socialism, in the broad sense which I am giving to the word, is a gospel and a necessity for all countries if they are to escape from the confusions of the present time into a saner and happier world. Socialism has its message for India and China and Africa no less than for Great Britain and Germany and the United States. Already in distant Russia the Socialist gospel is showing its adaptability to the needs and cultures of an immense variety of peoples at every stage of civilisation, from the nomadic horsemen of Mongolia to the advanced industrial populations of Leiningrad and Moscow. Not that Russia is yet fully a Socialist country; but admittedly the driving force behind the Russian experiment is the driving force of Socialism, and the new civilisation which is emerging out of Russia's barbarism and anarchy is clearly Socialist in its conception and attitude to the art of living.

Socialism established in one country and not in others is bound to be fragmentary and incomplete. It can, indeed, work miracles even within a single country, doing away with the extremes of poverty and riches, organising production for the common service of all the citizens, and creating an oasis of comradeship and collective endeavour in a desert of riot and confusion. But a Socialist country set in a ring of capitalist and imperialist States cannot hope to harvest the full fruits of Socialism. It must remain under the menace of war, compelled to waste its substance on armaments, to build up senseless barriers in the way of the open exchange of goods and services between country and country, suspect by its capitalist neighbours as a breeding ground of revolution, and unable to join with them in building up a common culture based on a fundamental community of moral and social ideas. It is well worth while to endeavour to establish Socialism in a single country —for where shall a man seek first to achieve happiness if not at home?—but each national victory for Socialism can be regarded only as a step towards its establishment as a world-wide system of international fellowship.

For short, let us say that Socialism aims at a classless society in which the means to wealth will be communally controlled. It follows that Socialism must aim at democracy—that is, at assuring to every citizen a real and effective share in the government of his own country and of the world. Class equality and communal control mean nothing unless they mean democracy. Class equality is inconsistent with any sort of monopoly or dictatorship in the sphere of government; and communal control means control by all. No system can ensure that all men and all women will actually take an equal share in the work of government or exert an equal influence on public affairs. But this is not required. Democracy means not that all can be equal in this sense but that all men and women ought to have an equal chance of making their voices effectively heard according to their several capacities and interests. Under no system will every citizen ever wish to play an active part in the work of government; but under Socialism the aim will be to give every citizen the fullest possible chance of doing this and to encourage all who will to give their citizenship an active character.

The forms of government are many, and no one of them is adapted to all peoples. We in Great Britain, with our long parliamentary tradition behind us, may choose to give the government of our Socialist Republic a parliamentary form, though assuredly the British Parliament will have to undergo vast changes if it is to become a truly democratic instrument of government in a Socialist society. The Russians may continue to prefer the Soviet to the Parliament, which has no roots in their national tradition. India, China, Africa, may strike out on yet other lines, devising new constitutional forms to suit their varying needs and traditions. It is indeed all to the good that they should do this; for least of all people do Socialists, who set the highest value on human freedom and initiative, desire to impose a common pattern of government or organisation upon all the world.

We Socialists have in mind no rigid and inflexible Utopia in which, when it is once established, nothing will ever change. Far from it. Most of all social doctrines, Socialism rests on the belief that change is rooted in the nature of human living. Nature herself changes, and is changed faster and faster as men work upon natural forces with growing knowledge and with ripening skill. Institutions that were once useful and progressive reach the point at which they have served their turn. They cease to be aids to human advancement and become fetters upon the wrists of developing humanity. It is so with capitalism to-day; and if we get Socialism, a day will come when the institutions which we establish for the administration of our Socialist society will themselves become obsolete. The coming of Socialism is not the end of human history, but the entry of humanity upon a new phase of social and cultural development. As long as humanity endures, new needs will continue to arise, calling for new responses from man's inventive talent and genius for the art of living. There is no "Utopia"—all that we can envisage is a next stage in human civilisation that will lift us up beyond the confusions of the present time.

Nor have Socialists a belief that Socialism, even to the extent to which its institutions can be foreseen, can spring suddenly into being full and complete. Whether the advance towards it be rapid or slow, it is bound on all accounts to be by stages. Even where, as in Russia, Socialist control has been ushered in by revolution and preceded by an almost entire dissolution of the old order, Socialist institutions and ways of living cannot be built in a day. They have to be developed by stages, as enough people become ready to accept them and have strength and skill to build them up. Still more, if Socialism comes in, not through war and revolution as it did in Russia, but by peaceful conquest of power, as we hope it may in Great Britain, must its coming be by steps and stages so contrived as to keep the old order still working until the new institutions can be got ready to take its place. That conservation of the old order during the process of transition to the new is the hardest part of the task for those who seek to bring in Socialism by evolutionary means; for it cannot be easy to keep the two systems working smoothly side by side. Indeed it cannot be done at all without strong government animating the whole system with a single conscious driving force in the direction of Socialism.

In the ranks of the Socialist movement there has been much controversy over the question of "gradualism" in Socialist policy; and a good deal of this controversy has been beside the mark. If "gradualism" means only that Socialism cannot be brought in at a blow, then every sensible Socialist is a gradualist. If, however, it means that a society can slide by imperceptible gradations from a capitalist to a Socialist system, then "gradualism" is at fault; for such a view misses out the vital importance of conscious human purpose, of the striving of millions of ordinary people towards the realisation of a new way of life, as the indispensable driving force towards a Socialist society. The coming of Socialism means for the whole people a change of mind and heart and not merely a change of machinery. It means a conscious will towards equality and good fellowship that will stir the imaginations of the young and make men and women ready and eager to work and sacrifice for their ideal. Without this impulsion behind it, Socialism cannot be brought into existence; and if, without this, we get "socialistic" changes in the machinery of society, we shall not therewith be getting Socialism. For Socialism is in its essence not mainly a new gospel of mechanical efficiency, but a way of life.

The danger of "gradualism" is that its exponents, conceiving the change as one of machinery and administration, that can be made by barely noticeable stages, without shock to the minds and habits of the people, will fail to arouse the enthusiasm and the strength that are needed for every great adventure. The force of habit and of tradition is very great: most of us live mainly under it for most of our lives. Now the habits and traditions of today are built on the requirements and adaptations of the past. So far from showing that human nature never changes, they are the crystallisation of past changes that were revolutionary in their day. Of these existing habits and traditions very many must be taken up almost without outward change into the way of living of the new social order; for no social order can be made at all except on the foundations laid by the past. But habits once rooted in men outlive their use: traditions that were once fountains of lively development turn into frozen monuments to the past. Men cannot live without habits and traditions; but they must be always making new ones if they are to live well.

Enthusiasm based on glowing belief that is a blend of intellect and emotion is the active force that brings new habits and traditions to birth. Intellect by itself makes no movements; for intellect alone can never tell us what we *ought* to do. *Ought* is a matter of emotion and sentiment—not of sheer intellect alone. But men's emotions are stirred to great deeds not by little things but only by great hopes and high beliefs. Unless men passionately want and value freedom, fellowship, class equality, comradeship in using and enjoying the great resources that lie ready to their hands, they will not succeed in achieving Socialism in any real sense. Collectivism of a sort they may achieve. For the technical forces of modern industrialism are driving them incessantly towards collective forms of administration. But collectivism is as compatible with the Slave State as with Socialism; and if we seek Socialism without assiduously preaching to mankind a new way of living together we are in grievous danger of making only the Slave State where bureaucrats will rule and the quality of life decay.

Our Socialism is, then, ardent, passionate, an affair of the heart as well as of the mind. We are in love with Socialism—with the vast new opportunities it offers for living together on terms of which no one of us will need to feel ashamed, of assuring to one and all, as far as in our knowledge lies, the means to health and strength and balanced growth of body and of mind, of doing away with all those twists and miseries of living that come of undernourishment, starvation of mental strength and hope, uneasiness at the sense of the crookedness of human dealing, thwarted personality and sheer disillusionment and loss of faith in life. That these ills can be conquered must be our faith, which is at bottom the simple belief that, given opportunity, most men will respond to an appeal to decent feeling and be ready to give as good as they get and often more.

That is what our "gradualists" are apt to miss, where our "extremists" get at least a glimpse of it. It is our tragedy that so often this fitful vision of the "extremists" runs to waste in hate. It is abundantly right to hate those things which are clear causes of needless human suffering—to hate them and to fight against them ceaselessly and with all our strength. It is right, even, to hate those who, with conscious malignancy, uphold these things and treat most human beings as mere tools to serve their ends. But we must love as well as hate if we are to build as well as destroy; for hate, not love, is the blind God who strikes amiss and slays his worshippers.

Put the case another way. If we are to build Socialism without an infinity of lost labour and needless setback and suffering, we shall need every ally who will work with us, even if many of these allies seem to us faint-hearted, half-hearted, or purblind. If we can persuade them to help us at all, maybe the task will grip them and give them greater faith, greater courage, and more vision. Whether or no, we cannot afford to do without their help; for we shall need to call all hands to the work—all, that is, who are ready to help at all. And let us not be unmindful that from those we deem faint-hearted or half-hearted or purblind we too may have something to learn; for though we Socialists are sure of our rightness in wanting Socialism, let us not delude ourselves that we are a hundred per cent right.

To my fellow-Socialists, then, I say, Be passionate, and yet be tolerant. Fight hard; but hunt heresies as little as you may. Spare no effort of mind in working out the intellectual case for Socialism; for clear thinking is assuredly a prime need for us who are set on creating a new order. But act also as men and women who have faith in human fellowship, who love their neighbours and extend their notion of neighbourhood to the whole interrelated, interdependent world. Our neighbour in China cannot and need not mean to us so much as our neighbour in the next street. But he is still our neighbour. In that sense Socialism knows no frontiers save the world's. But in another sense the Socialist no more wants to pull down the frontiers between Germany and France than between England and Scotland. Every Socialist feels the call to work for Socialism with special intensity within the narrower national group to which he is particularly attached and whose traditions and habits of living he shares and understands. There is no inconsistency between cultural nationalism and international Socialism.

In the nation and in the world, the will to Socialism is based on a lively sense of wrongs crying for redress. Socialism is an ethical as well as an economic movement, or it has no meaning. If human suffering does not matter, whether it be our own or another's, if starvation of health or opportunity or happiness does not matter, the case for Socialism collapses. For then indeed it is a question of each man for himself and for the few he reckons his friends, and devil take the rest of mankind. Demonstrate as we may that Socialism offers the prospect of far higher efficiency than capitalism in the production and distribution of wealth, what of it unless we care that the social production of wealth should be maximised and its distribution be made to serve the greatest happiness of the greatest number? A smaller sum-total of wealth so distributed as to create a smaller total of human happiness may better serve our turn if we can grab more out of it for ourselves and our friends. Only when we have made the promotion of human welfare and happiness our end, recognising other men's claims as standing on an equality with our own and positively wanting these claims of others to be made into rights on a par with ours, have we the impulsion within us to create a Socialist society. No Materialist Conception of History, however true, and no scientific version of the Socialist gospel, can get us away from that universal "ought." Even if the forces of history are fighting for Socialism, why should we trouble to fight on their side unless we believe that Socialism is right?

I ask no one to call himself a Socialist unless he wants society to recognize other men's claims as no less valid than his own. Socialism is an imaginative belief that all men, however unequal they may be in powers of mind and body or in capacity for service, are in a really significant sense *equal*, not merely before the law but one with another. They are equal as brothers and sisters are equal, the strong with the weak, the foolish with the wise—and the bad with the good, as far as men are good or bad in any final sense. Luck no social system can ever eliminate: there will be lucky ones and unlucky ones under Socialism as there are to-day. Differences of quality and attainment, too, will exist, however society is orga-nised. There will be waste of genius, square pegs in round holes, backslidings and misfortunes due to passion and evil impulses under any social system. But we can at least greatly improve the chances of well-being and bring them nearer to equality between man and man. We can give everyone a much fairer start, a far more even chance of making the best of body and mind, and therewith a far better hope of escaping the doom of body or mind twisted awry by forces of nurture and environment. There is immense scope for increasing the sum of human happiness, even though, whatever we do, much unhappiness is bound to remain. The reason—the only valid reason—for being a Socialist is the desire, the impassioned will, to seek the greatest happiness and well-being of the greatest number.

At this point, both metaphysicians and politicians will begin to split hairs. The metaphysician will ask us for a definition of happiness, and the politician accuse us of seeking a "well-being" that is not what people do want but only what we Socialists think they ought to want. To the latter the answer is that, though it be true that the foundations of a man's happiness lie within himself, it is beyond all manner of doubt that physical health, security of mind and body, and reasonable comfort in the supply of material needs do make for happiness. Now is it doubtful that if, in politics, we aim chiefly at these we can be sure of helping men towards making themselves happier in their several individual ways? We can add further that, if we can assure to all men these prerequisites of happiness, we can also feel confident that men, in their indi-vidual ways of living, will do far more than at present to promote the happiness one of another. There is no political antithesis be-tween happiness and well-being; and material well-being, though it is not happiness, assuredly ranks high among means to happiness.

To the metaphysicians our answer is that for our practical and political purpose we need no definition of happiness beyond what common sense supplies. Happiness is a state of being to be defined by each man in his own way, to which the art of politics is to minister. If we are in no doubt that certain means do minister to happiness, and that happiness is a good, we can leave further definition to the philosophers and get on with the job that is ours.

Our job is to promote happiness by promoting, not for a few but for all, those means to happiness which are most capable of being maximised by collective action. The only arguments against Socialism that are worth considering are those in which it is alleged that Socialists are mistaken in believing that the collective control of social forces can increase the sum of human well-being. All other arguments turn out on analysis to be mere defences of vested "rights" and claims to superiority over other men. One cannot argue with a man who really holds that the rights of property are sacred irrespective of their social expediency, any more than it was possible to argue with the upholders of the Divine Right of Kings. It is possible only to demonstrate whither such principles lead by referring them to some standard which their upholders *ex hypothesi* reject. Men can and do believe disinterestedly in the Divine Right of Property, just as some men used to believe disinterestedly in the Divine Right of Kings. But, ninety-nine times out of a hundred, behind the assertion of absolute right lies vested interest; and vested interest has not seldom an uneasy conscience that may weaken or even paralyse its resistance when we expose it for what it is. If the upholders of absolute right stick to their guns, they cannot be driven out by argument. But as soon as they invoke expediency to buttress absolutism, we Socialists can have them on the hip. That is, we can do so if, on our chosen ground of human happiness, our case is sound. If Socialism will, as we believe, make the race of men stronger in mind and body, teach them not to abuse their strength, but to employ it as brothers in the common service, teach them to practise better the living arts of production and creation in every sphere, and enable them to dwell together on terms of amity and fellowship which class distinctions and gross disparities of wealth and breeding make impossible to-day, then truly our case is unanswerable.

We believe that Socialism can work these miracles—for miracles they are bound to seem amid the tangles and disillusionments of the present. But if we wish others to share our faith we must give good reasons for it. The reasons will not convert men to Socialism unless they share our ideals. But neither will our ideals gain converts unless we can adduce good reasons for our confidence. The Socialist case needs reasoned statement; but in stating our reasons we must never lose sight of the ideal, the passion for human fellowship which alone can give them any cogency. Reasons are always reasons for something; and that something involves an ideal. We

are Socialists not *because* we think Socialism an historic necessity
or a more efficient way than capitalism of organising mass production, but because we believe that Socialism will make for the
greatest happiness and well-being of the greatest number, and
because that above all else is what we want.

The Historical Significance of Modern Socialism

LUDWIG VON MISES

The wide publicity given to both socialism and fascism in the
twentieth century obscures the fact that in Western Europe until at
least the 1930's, and in a modified form down to the present day, free-
enterprise capitalism has been the dominant mode of economic life.
The classical economic liberalism of the nineteenth century still finds
distinguished exponents in Western Europe. Friedrich Hayek's polemi-
cal masterpiece, *The Road to Serfdom* (1944), warned of the perils of
economic planning and suggested a necessary causal relationship between planning, on the one hand, and the rise of totalitarianism, on the
other. Bertrand de Jouvenel and Wilhelm Röpke have written in much
the same vein.

The senior statesman of their school is Ludwig von Mises, born in
Vienna in 1881, a professor of economics at the universities of Vienna
and Geneva, and now living in retirement in New York. For von
Mises, socialism, Bolshevism, fascism, the New Deal, and the contemporary Welfare State are all different facets of the same pernicious
and wrong-headed doctrine. They all demand that the free-market
economy (which he calls "economic democracy") must be replaced
by government planning, and government planning in turn inevitably
leads to "totalitarian barbarism." The selection here is from the
conclusion of a long theoretical work refuting both the political and
the economic arguments for socialism; it was first published in 1922
and substantially revised in 1932.

1. Socialism in History

NOTHING IS more difficult than to get a clear, historical perspective
of a contemporary movement. The proximity of the phenomenon

SOURCE: *Socialism: An Economic and Sociological Analysis*, by Ludwig von
Mises, trans. J. Kahane (Yale University Press, New Haven, Conn., 1951),
pp. 511–15. Reprinted by permission of Professor Ludwig von Mises.

makes it difficult to recognize the whole in true proportion. Historical judgment above all demands distance.

Wherever Europeans or the descendants of European emigrants live, we see Socialism at work today; and in Asia it is the banner round which the antagonists of European civilization gather. If the intellectual dominance of Socialism remains unshaken, then in a short time the whole co-operative system of culture which Europe has built up during thousands of years will be shattered. For a socialist order of society is unrealizable. All efforts to realize Socialism lead only to the destruction of society. Factories, mines, and railways will come to a standstill, towns will be deserted. The population of the industrial territories will die out or migrate elsewhere. The farmer will reutrn to the self-sufficiency of the closed, domestic economy. Without private ownership in the means of production there is, in the long run, no production other than a hand-to-mouth production for one's own needs.

We need not describe in detail the cultural and political consequences of such a transformation. Nomad tribes from the Eastern steppes would again raid and pillage Europe, sweeping across it with swift cavalry. Who could resist them in the thinly populated land left defenceless after the weapons inherited from the higher technique of Capitalism had worn out?

This is one possibility. But there are others. It might so happen that some nations would remain socialistic while others returned to Capitalism. Then the socialist countries alone would proceed towards social decline. The capitalist countries would progress to a higher development of the division of labour until at last, driven by the fundamental social law to draw the greatest number of human beings into the personal division of labour, and the whole earth's surface into the geographical division of labour, they would impose culture upon the backward nations or destroy them if they resisted. This has always been the historical fate of nations who have eschewed the road of capitalist development or who have halted prematurely upon it.

It may be that we exaggerate enormously the importance of the present-day socialist movement. Perhaps it has no more significance than the outbreaks against private property in the medieval persecution of the Jews, in the Franciscan movement, or in the Reformation period. And the Bolshevism of Lenin and Trotsky is possibly no more important than Knipperdolling's and Bockelson's anabaptist rule in Münster; it is no greater in proportion to the latter than is modern Capitalism in proportion to the Capitalism of the sixteenth century. Just as civilization overcame those attacks so it may emerge stronger and purer from the upheavals of our time.

2. The Crisis of Civilization

Society is a product of will and action. Only human beings are able to will and act. All the mysticism and symbolism of collectivist philosophy cannot help us over the fact that we can speak only figuratively of the thinking, willing, and acting of communities, and that the conception of sentient thinking, willing, and acting communities is merely anthropomorphism. Society and the individual postulate each other; those collective bodies, which collectivism assumes to have existed logically and historically before individuals, may have been herds and hordes, but they were in no way societies—that is, associations created and existing by means of the collaboration of thinking creatures. Human beings construct society by making their actions a mutually conditioned co-operation.

The basis and starting point of social co-operation lie in peace-making, which consists in the mutual recognition of the 'state of property'. Out of a *de facto having*, maintained by force, arises the legal concept of ownership, and simultaneously, the legal order and the coercive apparatus to maintain it. All this is the result of conscious willing and awareness of the aims willed. But this willing sees and wills only the most immediate and direct result: of the remoter consequences it knows nothing and can know nothing. Men who create peace and standards of conduct are only concerned to provide for the needs of the coming hours, days, years; that they are, at the same time, working to build a great structure like human society, escapes their notice. Therefore the individual institutions, which collectively support the social organism, are created with no other view in mind than the utility of the moment. They seem individually necessary and useful to their creators; their social function remains unknown to them.

The human mind ripens slowly to the recognition of social interdependence. At first, society is so mysterious and incomprehensible a formation to man that, to grasp its origin and nature, he continues to assume a divine will guiding human destinies from outside long after he has renounced this concept in the natural sciences. Kant's *Nature*, which leads humanity towards a special aim, Hegel's *World Spirit*, and the Darwinian *Natural Selection* are the last great expressions of this method. It remained for the liberal social philosophy to explain society through the actions of mankind without having to draw on metaphysics. It alone succeeds in interpreting the social function of private property. It is not content to accept the Just as a given category which cannot be analysed, or to account for it by an inexplicable predilection for just conduct. It bases its conclusions on the considerations of the consequences of acts and from a valuation of these consequences.

Judged from the old standpoint, property was sacred. Liberalism destroyed this nimbus, as it destroys all others. It 'debased' property into a utilitarian, wordly matter. Property no longer has absolute value; it is valued as a means, that is, for its utility. In philosophy such a change of views involves no special difficulties; an inadequate doctrine is replaced by one more adequate. But a fundamental revolution of the mind cannot be carried out in life and in the consciousness of the masses with the same lack of friction. It is no trifle when an idol before which humanity has trembled and feared for thousands of years is destroyed and the frightened slave gets his freedom. That which was law because God and conscience so ordained, is now to be law because one can oneself make it so at will. What was certain becomes uncertain; right and wrong, good and evil, all these conceptions begin to totter. The old tables of the law are shattered and man is left to make new commandments for himself. This cannot be achieved by means of parliamentary debate or in peaceful voting. A revision of the moral code can only be carried through when minds are deeply stirred and passions unloosed. To recognize the social utility of private property one must first be convinced of the perniciousness of every other system.

That this is the substance of the great fight between Capitalism and Socialism becomes evident when we realize that the same process is taking place in other spheres of moral life. The problem of property is not the only one which is being discussed to-day. It is the same with the problem of bloodshed which, in its many aspects—and particularly in connection with war and peace—agitates the whole world. In sexual morality, too, age-old moral precepts are undergoing transformation. Things which were held to be taboo, rules which have been obeyed for moral and almost sacred reasons, are now prescribed or prohibited according to the importance attached to them in respect of the promotion of public welfare. This revaluation of the grounds on which precepts of conduct have been based has inevitably caused a general revision of standards which have been in force up till now. Men ask: are they really useful or might they not really be abolished?

In the inner life of the individual the fact that the moral equilibrium has not yet been reached causes grave psychological shocks, well known to medicine as neuroses.[1] This is the characteristic malady of our time of moral transition, of the *spiritual adolescence of the nations*. In social life the discord works itself out in conflicts and errors which we witness with horror. Just as it is decisively important in the life of the individual man whether he emerges safe and sound from the troubles and fears of adolescence or whether he carries away scars which hinder him permanently from developing his abilities, so is it important in what manner human society will struggle through the vexed problems of organization. A rise to a closer interdependence of individuals and hence to a higher well-being, on the one hand; a decay of cooperation and hence of wealth, on the other: these are the choice before us. There is no third alternative.

The great social discussion cannot proceed otherwise than by means of the thought, will, and action of individuals. Society lives and acts only in individuals; it is nothing more than a certain attitude on their part. Everyone carries a part of society on his shoulders; no one is relieved of his share of responsibility by others. And no one can find a safe way out for himself if society is sweeping towards destruction. Therefore everyone, in his own interests, must thrust himself vigorously into the intellectual battle. None can stand aside with unconcern; the interests of everyone hang on the result. Whether he chooses or not, every man is drawn into the great historical struggle, the decisive battle into which our epoch has plunged us.

Neither God nor a mystical 'Natural Force' created society; it was created by mankind. Whether society shall continue to evolve or whether it shall decay lies—in the sense in which causal determination of all events permits us to speak of freewill—in the

[1] Freud, *Totem und Tabu*, Vienna 1913, p. 62 *et seq.*

hand of man. Whether Society is good or bad may be a matter of individual judgment; but whoever prefers life to death, happiness to suffering, well-being to misery, must accept society. And whoever desires that society should exist and develop must also accept, without limitation or reserve, private ownership in the means of production.

The General Theory

JOHN MAYNARD KEYNES

If any single man deserves the credit (or blame) for rescuing capitalist economics from the *débâcle* of 1929, setting it on new foundations, and undermining the case for doctrinaire socialism, it is John Maynard Keynes. Born in 1883 in Cambridge, where his father was a university lecturer, Keynes joined the staff of the British Treasury in 1915 and first attracted international attention by his scorching indictment of the economic and political wisdom of the Treaty of Versailles in *The Economic Consequences of the Peace*, published in 1919. In the 1920's, he won further fame as a skillful investor and businessman, journalist, Cambridge lecturer in economics, and author of several important technical books, including the two-volume *Treatise on Money*, in which he examined the business cycle in detail.

But Keynes quickly perceived, as the world Depression of 1929 worsened in the early thirties, that his theories were not adequate to explain the way in which slumps could last beyond their "natural" limits and, in a sense, feed on themselves. The automatic mechanisms by which a depressed economy normally extricated itself from its difficulties were only figments of the classical economist's imagination. When private investors failed to get the wheels turning again, a depression could last indefinitely, unless governments renounced their devotion to laissez-faire doctrine and undertook large-scale investment on their own initiative. Government spending was not socialism but pump-priming: action taken by public authorities to reinvigorate the private sector of the economy.

Keynes systematically expounded his case in his most important theoretical work, *The General Theory of Employment, Interest, and Money*, in 1936. The book was recognized almost at once as a masterpiece, comparable to Adam Smith's *Wealth of Nations* or Karl Marx's

SOURCE: *The General Theory of Employment, Interest, and Money*, by John Maynard Keynes (Harcourt, Brace, New York, 1936), pp. 372–84. Reprinted by permission of Harcourt, Brace and World, Inc.; Macmillan and Co., Ltd.; and the Trustees of the Estate of Lord Keynes.

Das Kapital, and it has provided many of the guidelines for government economic policy in the Western democracies ever since. *The General Theory* is a professional economist's book, beyond the reach of the uninitiated layman. But Keynes was a brilliant stylist, and, at the end of the book, he recapitulates part of its thesis in nontechnical terms and goes on to examine some of its implications for future policy.

I

THE OUTSTANDING faults of the economic society in which we live are its failure to provide for full employment and its arbitrary and inequitable distribution of wealth and incomes. The bearing of the foregoing theory on the first of these is obvious. But there are also two important respects in which it is relevant to the second.

Since the end of the nineteenth century significant progress towards the removal of very great disparities of wealth and income has been achieved through the instrument of direct taxation—income tax and surtax and death duties—especially in Great Britain. Many people would wish to see this process carried much further, but they are deterred by two considerations; partly by the fear of making skilful evasions too much worth while and also of diminishing unduly the motive towards risk-taking, but mainly, I think, by the belief that the growth of capital depends upon the strength of the motive towards individual saving and that for a large proportion of this growth we are dependent on the savings of the rich out of their superfluity. Our argument does not affect the first of these considerations. But it may considerably modify our attitude towards the second. For we have seen that, up to the point where full employment prevails, the growth of capital depends not at all on a low propensity to consume but is, on the contrary, held back by it; and only in conditions of full employment is a low propensity to consume conducive to the growth of capital. Moreover, experience suggests that in existing conditions saving by institutions and through sinking funds is more than adequate, and that measures for the redistribution of incomes in a way likely to raise the propensity to consume may prove positively favourable to the growth of capital.

The existing confusion of the public mind on the matter is well illustrated by the very common belief that the death duties are responsible for a reduction in the capital wealth of the country. Assuming that the State applies the proceeds of these duties to its ordinary outgoings so that taxes on incomes and consumption are correspondingly reduced or avoided, it is, of course, true that a fiscal policy of heavy death duties has the effect of increasing the community's propensity to consume. But inasmuch as an increase in the habitual propensity to consume will in general (*i.e.* except in conditions of full employment) serve to increase at the same time the inducement to invest, the inference commonly drawn is the exact opposite of the truth.

Thus our argument leads towards the conclusion that in contemporary conditions the growth of wealth, so far from being dependent on the abstinence of the rich, as is commonly supposed, is more likely to be impeded by it. One of the chief social justifications of great inequality of wealth is, therefore, removed. I am not saying that there are no other reasons, unaffected by our theory, capable of justifying some measure of inequality in some circumstances. But it does dispose of the most important of the reasons why hitherto we have thought it prudent to move carefully. This particularly affects our attitude towards death duties: for there are certain justifications for inequality of incomes which do not apply equally to inequality of inheritances.

For my own part, I believe that there is social and psychological justification for significant inequalities of incomes and wealth, but not for such large disparities as exist to-day. There are valuable human activities which require the motive of money-making and the environment of private wealth-ownership for their full fruition. Moreover, dangerous human proclivities can be canalised into comparatively harmless channels by the existence of opportunities for money-making and private wealth, which, if they cannot be satisfied in this way, may find their outlet in cruelty, the reckless pursuit of personal power and authority, and other forms of self-aggrandisement. It is better that a man should tyrannise over his bank balance than over his fellow-citizens; and whilst the former is sometimes denounced as being but a means to the latter, sometimes at least it is an alternative. But it is not necessary for the stimulation of these activities and the satisfaction of these proclivities that the game should be played for such high stakes as at present. Much lower stakes will serve the purpose equally well, as soon as the players are accustomed to them. The task of transmuting human nature must not be confused with the task of managing it. Though in the ideal commonwealth men may have been taught or inspired or bred to take no interest in the stakes, it may still be wise and prudent statesmanship to allow the game to be played, subject to rules and limitations, so long as the average man, or even a significant section of the community, is in fact strongly addicted to the money-making passion.

II

There is, however, a second, much more fundamental inference from our argument which has a bearing on the future of inequalities of wealth; namely, our theory of the rate of interest. The justification for a moderately high rate of interest has been found hitherto in the necessity of providing a sufficient inducement to save. But we have shown that the extent of effective saving is necessarily determined by the scale of investment and that the scale of investment is promoted by a *low* rate of interest, provided that we do not attempt to stimulate it in this way beyond the point which corresponds to full employment. Thus it is to our best advantage to reduce the rate of interest to that point relatively to the schedule of the marginal efficiency of capital at which there is full employment.

There can be no doubt that this criterion will lead to a much lower rate of interest than his ruled hitherto; and, so far as one can guess at the schedules of the marginal efficiency of capital corresponding to increasing amounts of capital, the rate of interest is likely to fall steadily, if it should be practicable to maintan conditions of more or less continuous full employment—unless, indeed, there is an excessive change in the aggregate propensity to consume (including the State).

I feel sure that the demand for capital is strictly limited in the sense that it would not be difficult to increase the stock of capital up to a point where its marginal efficiency had fallen to a very low figure. This would not mean that the use of capital instruments would cost almost nothing, but only that the return from them would have to cover little more than their exhaustion by wastage and obsolescence together with some margin to cover risk and the exercise of skill and judgment. In short, the aggregate return from durable goods in the course of their life would, as in the case of short-lived goods, just cover their labour-costs of production *plus* an allowance for risk and the costs of skill and supervision.

Now, though this state of affairs would be quite compatible with some measure of individualism, yet it would mean the euthanasia of the rentier, and, consequently, the euthanasia of the cumulative oppressive power of the capitalist to exploit the scarcity-value of capital. Interest to-day rewards no genuine sacrifice, any more than does the rent of land. The owner of capital can obtain interest because capital is scarce, just as the owner of land can obtain rent because land is scarce. But whilst there may be intrinsic reasons for the scarcity of land, there are no intrinsic reasons for the scarcity of capital. An intrinsic reason for such scarcity, in the sense of a genuine sacrifice which could only be called forth by the offer of a reward in the shape of interest, would not exist, in the long run, except in the event of the individual propensity to consume proving to be of such a character that net saving in conditions of full employment comes to an end before capital has become sufficiently abundant. But even so, it will still be possible for communal saving through the agency of the State to be maintained at a level which will allow the growth of capital up to the point where it ceases to be scarce.

I see, therefore, the rentier aspect of capitalism as a transitional phase which will disappear when it has done its work. And with the disappearance of its rentier aspect much else in it besides will suffer a sea-change. It will be, moreover, a great advantage of the order of events which I am advocating, that the euthanasia of the rentier, of the functionless investor, will be nothing sudden, merely a gradual but prolonged continuance of what we have seen recently in Great Britain, and will need no revolution.

Thus we might aim in practice (there being nothing in this which is unattainable) at an increase in the volume of capital until it ceases to be scarce, so that the functionless investor will no longer receive a bonus; and at a scheme of direct taxation which allows the intelligence and determination and executive skill of the financier, the entrepreneur *et hoc genus omne* (who are certainly so fond of their craft that their labour could be obtained much cheaper than at present), to be harnessed to the service of the community on reasonable terms of reward.

At the same time we must recognise that only experience can show how far the common will, embodied in the policy of the State, ought to be directed to increasing and supplementing the inducement to invest; and how far it is safe to stimulate the average propensity to consume, without foregoing our aim of depriving capital of its scarcity-value within one or two generations. It may turn out that the propensity to consume will be so easily strengthened by the effects of a falling rate of interest, that full employment can be reached with a rate of accumulation little greater than at present. In this event a scheme for the higher taxation of large incomes and inheritances might be open to the objection that it would lead to full employment with a rate of accumulation which was reduced considerably below the current level. I must not be supposed to deny the possibility, or even the probability, of this outcome. For in such matters it is rash to predict how the average man will react to a changed environment. If, however, it should prove easy to secure an approximation to full employment with a rate of accumulation not much greater than at present, an outstanding problem will at least have been solved. And it would remain for separate decision on what scale and by what means it is right and reasonable to call on the living generation to restrict their consumption, so as to establish, in course of time, a state of full investment for their successors.

III

In some other respects the foregoing theory is moderately conservative in its implications. For whilst it indicates the vital importance of establishing certain central controls in matters which are now left in the main to individual initiative, there are wide fields of activity which are unaffected. The State will have to exercise a guiding influence on the propensity to consume partly through its scheme of taxation, partly by fixing the rate of interest, and partly, perhaps, in other ways. Furthermore, it seems unlikely that the influence of banking policy on the rate of interest will be sufficient by itself to determine an optimum rate of investment. I conceive, therefore, that a somewhat comprehensive socialisation of investment will prove the only means of securing an approximation to full employment; though this need not exclude all manner of compromises and of devices by which public authority will co-operate with private initiative. But beyond this no obvious case is made out for a system of State Socialism which would embrace most of the economic life of the community. It is not the ownership of the instruments of production which it is important for the

State to assume. If the State is able to determine the aggregate amount of resources devoted to augmenting the instruments and the basic rate of reward to those who own them, it will have accomplished all that is necessary. Moreover, the necessary measures of socialisation can be introduced gradually and without a break in the general traditions of society.

Our criticism of the accepted classical theory of economics has consisted not so much in finding logical flaws in its analysis as in pointing out that its tacit assumptions are seldom or never satisfied, with the result that it cannot solve the economic problems of the actual world. But if our central controls succeed in establishing an aggregate volume of output corresponding to full employment as nearly as is practicable, the classical theory comes into its own again from this point onwards. If we suppose the volume of output to be given, *i.e.* to be determined by forces outside the classical scheme of thought, then there is no objection to be raised against the classical analysis of the manner in which private self-interest will determine what in particular is produced, in what proportions the factors of production will be combined to produce it, and how the value of the final product will be distributed between them. Again, if we have dealt otherwise with the problem of thrift, there is no objection to be raised against the modern classical theory as to the degree of consilience between private and public advantage in conditions of perfect and imperfect competition respectively. Thus, apart from the necessity of central controls to bring about an adjustment between the propensity to consume and the inducement to invest, there is no more reason to socialise economic life than there was before.

To put the point concretely, I see no reason to suppose that the existing system seriously misemploys the factors of production which are in use. There are, of course, errors of foresight; but these would not be avoided by centralising decisions. When 9,000,-000 men are employed out of 10,000,000 willing and able to work, there is no evidence that the labour of these 9,000,000 men is misdirected. The complaint against the present system is not that these 9,000,000 men ought to be employed on different tasks, but that tasks should be available for the remaining 1,000,000 men. It is in determining the volume, not the direction, of actual employment that the existing system has broken down.

Thus I agree with Gesell that the result of filling in the gaps in the classical theory is not to dispose of the "Manchester System", but to indicate the nature of the environment which the free play of economic forces requires if it is to realise the full potentialities of production. The central controls necessary to ensure full employment will, of course, involve a large extension of the traditional functions of government. Furthermore, the modern classical theory has itself called attention to various conditions in which the free play of economic forces may need to be curbed or guided. But there will still remain a wide field for the exercise of private initiative and responsibility. Within this field the traditional advantages of individualism will still hold good.

Let us stop for a moment to remind ourselves what these advantages are. They are partly advantages of efficiency—the advantages of decentralisation and of the play of self-interest. The advantage to efficiency of the decentralisation of decisions and of individual responsibility is even greater, perhaps, than the nineteenth century supposed; and the reaction against the appeal to self-interest may have gone too far. But, above all, individualism, if it can be purged of its defects and its abuses, is the best safeguard of personal liberty in the sense that, compared with any other system, it greatly widens the field for the exercise of personal choice. It is also the best safeguard of the variety of life, which emerges precisely from this extended field of personal choice, and the loss of which is the greatest of all the losses of the homogeneous or totalitarian state. For this variety preserves the traditions which embody the most secure and successful choices of former generations; it colours the present with the diversification of its fancy; and, being the handmaid of experiment as well as of tradition and of fancy, it is the most powerful instrument to better the future.

Whilst, therefore, the enlargement of the functions of government, involved in the task of adjusting to one another the propensity to consume and the inducement to invest, would seem to a nineteenth-century publicist or to a contemporary American financier to be a terrific encroachment on individualism, I defend it, on the contrary, both as the only practicable means of avoiding the destruction of existing economic forms in their entirety and as the condition of the successful functioning of individual initiative.

For if effective demand is deficient, not only is the public scandal of wasted resources intolerable, but the individual enterpriser who seeks to bring these resources into action is operating with the odds loaded against him. The game of hazard which he plays is furnished with many zeros, so that the players *as a whole* will lose if they have the energy and hope to deal all the cards. Hitherto the increment of the world's wealth has fallen short of the aggregate of positive individual savings; and the difference has been made up by the losses of those whose courage and initiative have not been supplemented by exceptional skill or unusual good fortune. But if effective demand is adequate, average skill and average good fortune will be enough.

The authoritarian state systems of to-day seem to solve the problem of unemployment at the expense of efficiency and of freedom. It is certain that the world will not much longer tolerate the unemployment which, apart from brief intervals of excitement, is associated—and, in my opinion, inevitably associated—with present-day capitalistic individualism. But it may be possible by a right analysis of the problem to cure the disease whilst preserving efficiency and freedom.

IV

I have mentioned in passing that the new system might be more favourable to peace than the old has been. It is worth while to repeat and emphasise that aspect.

War has several causes. Dictators and others such, to whom war offers, in expectation at least, a pleasurable excitement, find it easy to work on the natural bellicosity of their peoples. But, over and above this, facilitating their task of fanning the popular flame, are the economic causes of war, namely, the pressure of population and the competitive struggle for markets. It is the second factor, which probably played a predominant part in the nineteenth century, and might again, that is germane to this discussion.

I have pointed out . . . that, under the system of domestic *laissez-faire* and an international gold standard such as was orthodox in the latter half of the nineteenth century, there was no means open to a government whereby to mitigate economic distress at home except through the competitive struggle for markets. For all measures helpful to a state of chronic or intermittent underemployment were ruled out, except measures to improve the balance of trade on income account.

Thus, whilst economists were accustomed to applaud the pre-

vailing international system as furnishing the fruits of the international division of labour and harmonising at the same time the
interests of different nations, there lay concealed a less benign
influence; and those statesmen were moved by common sense and a
correct apprehension of the true course of events, who believed
that if a rich, old country were to neglect the struggle for markets
its prosperity would droop and fail. But if nations can learn to
provide themselves with full employment by their domestic policy
(and, we must add, if they can also attain equilibrium in the trend
of their population), there need be no important economic forces
calculated to set the interest of one country against that of its
neighbours. There would still be room for the international division of labour and for international lending in appropriate conditions. But there would no longer be a pressing motive why one
country need force its wares on another or repulse the offerings of
its neighbour, not because this was necessary to enable it to pay for
what it wished to purchase, but with the express object of up-
setting the equilibrium of payments so as to develop a balance of
trade in its own favour. International trade would cease to be what
it is, namely, a desperate expedient to maintain employment at
home by forcing sales on foreign markets and restricting purchases,
which, if successful, will merely shift the problem of unemployment to the neighbour which is worsted in the struggle, but a
willing and unimpeded exchange of goods and services in conditions of mutual advantage.

V

Is the fulfilment of these ideas a visionary hope? Have they
insufficient roots in the motives which govern the evolution of
political society? Are the interests which they will thwart stronger
and more obvious than those which they will serve?

I do not attempt an answer in this place. It would need a volume
of a different character from this one to indicate even in outline the
practical measures in which they might be gradually clothed. But if
the ideas are correct—an hypothesis on which the author himself
must necessarily base what he writes—it would be a mistake, I
predict, to dispute their potency over a period of time. At the
present moment people are unusually expectant of a more fundamental diagnosis; more particularly ready to receive it; eager to try

it out, if it should be even plausible. But apart from this contemporary mood, the ideas of economists and political philosophers, both when they are right and when they are wrong, are more powerful than is commonly understood. Indeed the world is ruled by little else. Practical men, who believe themselves to be quite exempt from any intellectual influences, are usually the slaves of some defunct economist. Madmen in authority, who hear voices in the air, are distilling their frenzy from some academic scribbler of a few years back. I am sure that the power of vested interests is vastly exaggerated compared with the gradual encroachment of ideas. Not, indeed, immediately, but after a certain interval; for in the field of economic and political philosophy there are not many who are influenced by new theories after they are twenty-five or thirty years of age, so that the ideas which civil servants and politicians and even agitators apply to current events are not likely to be the newest. But, soon or late, it is ideas, not vested interests, which are dangerous for good or evil.

An Age of Disintegration

KARL MANNHEIM

Sociologists traditionally regard Auguste Comte, who died in 1857, as the founding father of their discipline. In the period between Comte's death and the First World War, Western Europe produced many brilliant theorists in the field. Lilienfeld, Schäffle, Tönnies, Gumplowicz, Ratzenhofer, Simmel, and Max Weber in the German-speaking world and Durkheim, Tarde, Le Bon, Bouglé, and Pareto in France and Italy brought sociology to the rank of a major science. Since 1918 the leadership in sociological theory and research has shifted to the United States. Although the influence of such thinkers as Weber and Durkheim would be difficult to exaggerate, most of the best work is now being done in American universities, even if some of the sociologists involved are not native-born Americans.

One exception to this rule is Karl Mannheim, who established

SOURCE: *Freedom, Power, and Democratic Planning*, by Karl Mannheim (Oxford University Press, New York, 1950), pp. 3–21 and 315–17. Reprinted by permission of Oxford University Press and Routledge and Kegan Paul, Ltd. Copyright 1950 by Oxford University Press.

himself after Weber's death in 1920 as the chief representative of the Weber tradition in German sociological thought. Born in Budapest in 1893, Mannheim came under a rich variety of influences, including Marxism, the phenomenological school of philosophy founded by Scheler and Husserl, and the neo-Kantianism of Rickert. His first major work, *Ideology and Utopia* (1929), is still more or less the textbook of *Wissensoziologie*, that branch of sociology which deals with the impact of class interests on cognition and belief. In the second half of his career, he became interested in the problem of social disintegration, a theme suggested to him by the Nazi catastrophe. Leaving his chair at the University of Frankfurt after Hitler's rise to power in 1933, he accepted a post at the London School of Economics, where until his death in 1947 he published a series of luminous studies on social breakdown and reconstruction, including *Man and Society in an Age of Reconstruction* and *Diagnosis of Our Time*. His last book, *Freedom, Power, and Democratic Planning*, from which this selection is drawn, was published posthumously in 1950.

After the diagnosis of the crisis in Western civilization presented here, Mannheim goes on in the rest of the book to state the case for what he calls "democratic planning." He advocates extensive economic planning and also a system of democratic controls over press and radio, education, and the social structure generally, to encourage the production of well-integrated "democratic personalities" and to counteract the disintegrative tendencies at work in modern society.

FOR CENTURIES it has been the Anglo-Saxon procedure to amend and remodel institutions whenever a new course becomes unavoidable. Like the ancient cathedrals that man has built, enlarged, and reconstructed down the centuries, adding new aisles in the new style of the age but never tearing up the old, the social structure has been overhauled and renewed by a process of additions, emendations, and alterations of institutions. Without compunction, Gothic builders added their lofty arches to the sterner Norman vaults, and later periods added decorations and features to their taste, yet the cathedral still remains one whole and the various styles fit together. The break was visible only to the historian who began dividing the centuries into stylistic periods; he undertook, as it were, to analyze the principles upon which the various parts were built. Following the pattern of organic growth, the British, unconscious of changed principles and methods, have modified the social structure by remaking institutions inherited from the past. This method of reform without fanfare has been the strength of Britain's policy—but there are junctures in history when the mere conversion of a structure is not enough. The change has come either so rapidly or so profoundly that the builder must stop to analyze the principle of what he finds and visualize what he wants to achieve.

The present trust in the British tradition of 'muddling through,' just because former generations have been fortunate enough to switch over at the right moment, is a liability. Diagnosis of the situation will show that basic social change can no longer be met by mere repairs and institutional patchwork. We must consciously assess our objectives to get us out of the rut: this requires thoroughgoing comprehension of the new trend, of social change.

At times the wagon of history moves along a straight and open road, at others it has to turn a sharp corner. On the smooth highway little or no steering is necessary, nor need the map be consulted. But at the sharp corner, careful and alert driving is necessary, lest the precious load of tradition, culture, and worldly goods be upset. At the crossroads of history we must look for reorientation, consult the map, and ask ourselves: Where do the roads lead, where do we want to go?

It is at such crucial crossroads of history that we find ourselves. No lament for the age is needed, no nostalgic moan about deterioration, but a critical analysis of what has engendered it.

If one wishes to build a social system, one must have a guiding idea of the new system, an awareness of shortcomings in the existing one and of what causes current maladjustments. Eventually one may ask for ways and means to change the social mechanism. A diagnosis of the situation must precede any statement of new aims and proposed means.

Most symptoms of maladjustment in modern society can be traced to the fact that a parochial world of small groups expanded into a Great Society in a comparatively short time. This unguided transformation caused manifold disturbances and unsolved problems throughout social life. They can be set right only with due attention to the circumstances surrounding the calamities.

Unguided, unplanned transition does not cause major disturbances where the social units are small and when sufficient time is allowed for adjustment by trial and error. Even then maladjustments occur through the occasional inexpediency of a prevailing pattern of action or thought in an unforeseen situation. Usually, however, a new adjustment is made with no hiatus in the process of socially co-ordinated living. The case is quite different when society develops on a large scale unguided. Here, too, innumerable efforts are made to replace obsolete patterns of behavior and organization by new ones; but either no new pattern can be found on the level of blind experimentation, or, if such a new solution emerges at last, there is a hiatus in which no satisfactory reaction is forthcoming. In such cases we shall speak of social disintegration.

While there is much talk of disintegration, the term is often used too vaguely to convey any meaning. Surely we should not speak of disintegration if a social order cherished by the observer were to vanish and be replaced by another. This is social change indeed, but not social disintegration. The cardinal point is a gradual weakening of the prevailing social structure and of the forces that sustain it, without the simultaneous growth of a new order. It is true, there are borderline cases where we are uncertain whether the lack of a new solution is a symptom of transition only or whether a serious void threatens. But by and large we know the difference. Everyone knows that occasional unemployment of a few people is just a gap in adjustment, whereas recurrent unemployment, which in its cumulative effects upsets the working of a whole social order, should be considered a symptom of disintegration. The same applies to the moral sphere. People may occasionally be uncertain about what is right or wrong and this may be taken as a matter of course. But when mass anxieties prevail, because the general ideological upheaval leaves no sound basis for common action, and when people do not know where they stand or what they ought to think about the most elementary problems of life, then again we may rightly speak of the spiritual disintegration of society.

While we attempt to show in the following pages that we are living in such an age of disintegration, we of course do not mean that disintegration is ever total. Were this the case, we could no longer go on living. Even in a disintegrating society there are self-healing processes and spontaneous adjustments that make life somehow bearable. Still, even under conditions of comparative tranquillity, the sociologically trained eye can see the gaps in the social fabric, the void in the individual intellectual, moral, and emotional make-up. In a given situation, once the cumulative effects of disintegration get out of hand, implicit chaos becomes apparent to all. There are a number of traditional answers to the threat of modern social disintegration.

The alternatives of capitalism *versus* socialism, dictatorship *versus* democracy, secular *versus* Christian society are such traditions in group thinking. Yet, however representative of important group forces these alternatives may be, they are less diagnosis than therapeusis, and our therapeutic choice may depend on our preference for different values. But before we choose on the basis of such preference, we must ascertain whether in fact the disturbances in our social body may be thus treated. Our diagnosis must detect the symptoms and causes of social disintegration; only then can we consider the pros and cons of different treatments.

I. New Social Techniques Making for Minority Rule

In our present analysis we take it for granted that the mere numerical increase of modern societies is a fundamental cause of our difficulties. This growth is primarily due to the astounding increase in population since the Industrial Revolution—itself the product of the machine technique.[1] For a long time we have been

Population (in millions)

	1650	1800	1850	1900	1940
Great Britain	6	10	21	37	46
France	16	27	35	41	42
Germany	14	20	35	54	70
Italy	13	17	24	32	44
U.S.A.	..	5	23	75	131
Ireland	1	5	6½	4½	4¼

aware that the widespread use of machinery carries its own social implications. Thus it is well known that the transition from the handloom to the mechanical loom revolutionized the division of labor and created factory life with its mechanized and rationalized work. But this is only one aspect of technological change following population growth. The economic inventions that provided the masses with food, clothing, and shelter have often received due

[1] This development can be traced from the following table, taken from J. R. Hicks and A. R. Hart, *The Social Framework of the American Economy* (New York, 1945), p. 39.

attention, whereas the development of other techniques, likewise in consequence of population growth, have almost been overlooked. We have in mind 'social techniques' in the sphere of politics, education, warfare, communication, propaganda, and so on. Their true nature has come to light only during the last few decades.[2]

By social techniques[3] I refer to all methods of influencing human behavior so that it fits into the prevailing patterns of social interaction and organization. The existence of social techniques is especially evident in the Army, where efficiency rests mainly upon stringent organization, training, and discipline, specific forms of self-control and obedience. Not only in the Army, but also in so-called civilian life people have to be conditioned and educated to fit into prevailing patterns of social life. Factory work requires specialized training of skill, behavior, and habits, a specific form of discipline and rank, a well-defined division of labor and controlled interrelations between people and their jobs. The dominant pattern may be democratic or authoritarian; education serves both systems. At the same time it is only one of the social techniques aimed at the creation of the desired type of citizen.

In order to solve the problem of mass organization, modern society had to improve and extend these social techniques as well as those of the machine. Social inventions are made daily, and though little is heard of them they are nonetheless important sociologically. But the main thing about such improved social techniques today is not only their greater efficiency, but that such efficiency favors minority rule. Modern military technique, for instance, allows a much greater concentration of power in a few hands than did the techniques of any previous period. A man with a rifle could threaten a handful of people, a man with a Tommy gun or the dive bomber can intimidate a hundred, and the atom bomb, millions. Centralized control in the field of government and administration is made equally easy by such inventions as the telephone, radio, and air communications. Vast industrial empires could not be held

[2] Cf. Gilfillan, S. C., *The Sociology of Invention* (Chicago, 1935). Ogburn, W. F., *Social Change* (New York, 1929).
[3] In all my writings on modern society I have emphasized the significance of social techniques as well as other points to be mentioned in the present diagnosis. In order to weight them properly, I cannot avoid referring to them again. Here, however, they are not dealt with merely casually but form part of a more comprehensive and systematic survey of the factors making for disintegration.

together without these modern means of rapid communication. Yet these very same techniques also make for dictatorship.

As long as society was regulated by a natural interplay between small self-contained units, mutual controls could work. One individual could control the other, or one group the other, or the group the individual. Just as in economic life where huge combines with their monopolies replace free competition between small enterprises, so in other spheres complex social units arise that are too arbitrary to reorganize themselves, and must be governed from a center. News service, for instance, is handled by a few agencies, and scientific research is also increasingly controlled either by the State or by big industry. Large bureaucracies appear everywhere, and where formerly individuals made independent decisions according to their own best knowledge and experience, the majority now must follow instructions, and only a few departmental heads are in a position to form comprehensive judgments and a policy of their own.

Similar concentration can be observed in the methods of education and of molding public opinion. Mechanized mass production of ideas through press and radio propaganda works in the same direction. Education tends to become part of the new art of manipulating human behavior and can develop into an instrument for suppression of the many by the few. Even social work, which was formerly the sphere of private charity or the individual reformer, has been handed over to trained professionals. Its misuse can only end in constant meddling with private affairs, with little freedom from central interference or scope for living a life of one's own.

The feature common to all these examples is a tendency to establish key positions from which central decisions are made. The very existence of key positions automatically makes for minority rule.

The end of *laissez-faire* and the necessity for planning are unavoidable consequences of the present situation and the nature of modern techniques. All of us might have preferred living as cultured gentlemen of leisure in ancient Athens or as daring pioneers in the eighteenth and nineteenth centuries. But it is not given to us to choose the epoch in which we live or the problems we are called upon to solve. The concentration of all kinds of controls—economic, political, psychological, and mechanical—has gone so far (and the last war has so enormously accelerated this trend) that the question is only who shall use these means of control for what end. For used they will certainly be.

The alternatives are no longer 'planning or *laissez-faire*' but 'planning for what?' and 'what kind of planning?'

II. The New Techniques and the Power Complex

From the very beginning modern techniques were associated with the power complex. Much knowledge was acquired to increase power. Technology, both economic and social, has been developed as an instrument for seeking and increasing personal power. The capitalist pioneer, the industrialist, the financier, and the inventor are children of the same spirit. They sought knowledge or financed it in the interest of expansion and exploitation. They were interested in nature or in man only in so far as these promised profits and power; and they were interested in other countries only as markets, colonies, and military bases.[4] As Lewis Mumford[5] puts it, they stepped from the walled horizon of the medieval city into the limitless world only to bring home quick profits, and cared nothing for the wasted landscape they left on their trail. The fruits of their spoils included the destruction of tribal customs, semistarvation, tuberculosis, and soil erosion. The exclusive emphasis on power, the neurotic complex of an age rather than a character trait, destroys the world's equilibrium just as it upsets our whole mental balance. The disgraceful slums on the outskirts of our cities, built speculatively without regard to human needs, the skyscrapers erected centrally in towns not in answer to economic need but as

[4] Sir George Cornewall Lewis, in 1841, summed up "the advantages derived by the dominant country from its supremacy over a dependency under the following heads:

1. Tribute or revenue paid by the dependency.
2. Assistance for military or naval purposes furnished by the dependency.
3. Advantages to the dominant country from its trade with a dependency.
4. Facilities afforded by dependencies to the dominant country for the emigration of its surplus population, and for an advantageous employment of its capital.
5. Transportation of convicts to a dependency.
6. Glory of possessing dependencies."
From *An Essay on the Government of Dependencies*, ed. with an Introduction by C. P. Lucas (Oxford, 1891), p. xlv.

[5] Mumford, Lewis, *Faith for Living* (New York, 1940), p. 149.

beacons of prestige and power-display—both are expressions of the
same malignant growth.

So long as modern capitalist society was an expanding system
with undeveloped countries to absorb men, capital, and energies,
there was always an outlet for the misuse of power and extreme
forms of exploitation.[6] The liberal revolutionaries of 1848 were
defeated by the reactionary powers of their countries, but there
were still other worlds for them and they found a new existence
and new scope for action elsewhere. Men like Mazzini, Kossuth,
and Marx continued their work in England, and Karl Schurz[7]
made a distinguished career in the United States. By now, however,
Imperialism, the cause of recurrent international friction and economic upheaval, seems to have reached a point of saturation. The
world is divided; there are no more open spaces with free home-
steads for immigrants, and the backward peoples have been awakened through communication with, and education by, their rulers
or trading partners. A new distribution of wealth is taking place
and for European powers this will be, in contrast to the past three
or four centuries, a process of contraction rather than of expansion. At least such are the prospects, so long as power is the main
driving force, and expansion for the sake of exploitation is the
organizing principle.

In the domestic pageant the social groups and classes tend to
become more rigid and sharply stratified. No longer is social ascent
easy for the enterprising nor are the chances of rapid success the

---

[6] 'It is argued that the economic opportunities for investment available in
the 19th century were the consequence of there being vast uncultivated or
semi-cultivated areas and great demand for goods by an increasing population. More recently, it is argued, the basic capital installations—mines,
railways, factories, tele-communications, etc.—have been provided and required, not total replacement, but only maintenance, repair and improvement. Even such improvement, it is argued, gives more productive results
with less capital outlay than before. Hence, economic expansion is to be
sought by more intensive cultivation, industrial or otherwise, of the opportunities still remaining. Even then it is thought difficult to discover ways of
using all the natural savings and feared that in default of a comprehensive
fiscal policy some of the savings may be simply sterilised by hoarding.'
H. Finer, *The T.V.A.* (*Montreal*, 1944), p. 218, note 2.
     Hansen, A. H., *Fiscal Policy and Business Cycles* (New York, 1941),
ch. VI.
     Temporary National Economic Committee Hearings, Part 9.
     Ibid. Currie, pp. 3520 ff.
[7] Easum, Chester V., *Karl Schurz* (Weimar, 1937).

same for the small owner. The more refined the techniques and division of labor, the less flexible the social pattern seems.

Striving for power in society is not a constant factor but grows with the opportunities. In earlier stages, this urge was still more or less controlled; the inventions and techniques it set in motion even promoted public welfare. In the final stage nothing remains but megalomanic passion, terror, and extermination,[8] a drama no one of us can watch any longer dispassionately.

III. From Communal Economy Through Free Competition to Monopolies

Just as technology in its aspects of expansion and profiteering corresponds to the old spirit of conquest and exploitation, so the whole economic system of free competition and private ownership of the means of production corresponds to one historical phase—an intermediary phase between two planned economies. At the one end was the local, self-sufficient, nonprofit economy of agrarian and handicraft communities[9]—at the other we envisage a planned economy over vast areas with international exchange and integration based upon highly developed techniques.

If we look at early capitalism and liberalism from this point of view it becomes obvious that their 'sacrosanct' institutions—the free market and free competition, based on the absolute concept of

[8] Arendt, Hannah, 'The Concentration Camps,' *Partisan Review*, vol. xv, no. 7, pp. 762 f.

(Balticus), 'The Two "G"s: Gestapo and GPU, Phenomena of Modern Revolution,' *Foreign Affairs* (1939), vol. 17, pp. 489–507.

Baron, Salo W., *A Social and Religious History of the Jews* (New York, 1937).

Bettelheim, Bruno, 'Concentration Camps, German,' *Ten Eventful Years* (Chicago, 1947), vol. 2.

—— 'Individual and Mass Behavior in Extreme Situations,' *Journal of Abnormal and Social Psychology*, vol. 38, no. 4.

Bloch, Herbert A., 'The Personality of Inmates of Concentration Camps,' *American Journal of Sociology* (Jan. 1947), vol. 52.

Bondy, Curt, 'Problems of Internment Camps,' *Journal of Abnormal and Social Psychology*, vol. 38, no. 4.

Bramsted, Ernest K., *Dictatorship and Political Police* (London, 1945).

Kautsky, Benedict, *Teufel und Verdammte* (Zurich, 1946).

Kogon, Eugen, *Der SS-Staat* (Berlin, 1947).

Rousset, David, *The Other Kingdom* (New York, 1947).

[9] Coulton, G. G., *The Medieval Village* (Cambridge, 1925).

private property[10] with no external intervention—were the products of a unique and transient situation. They exactly correspond to the stage in economic development when expansion could no longer be carried out by tribal or local units, which were too small and too parochial in outlook. Later economic expansion took the form of individual penetration on the part of 'pioneers,' men with an intrepid spirit of enterprise and venture. The right to absolute disposal of individual property, as upheld against the older notion of family and corporate property and as a defense against state interference, can be fully understood as the only adequate stimulus for these individual entrepreneurs. The concept of private property operated as a dynamic force in the individual's mind, continually spurring him to risk his capital, to save the profits for further accumulation and investment, to give up leisure and pleasure for power and profits.

The picture changed when the scale of these independent economic enterprises increased more and more, while their numbers declined. Then free competition in its true sense disappeared, the scope of individual initiative began to shrink, and a new business bureaucracy[11] took the place of the independent owner. This new managerial class develops its own administrative technique, as well as new key positions. It almost invisibly creates new dependencies. With this the concept of absolute private ownership and unrestricted *laissez-faire* loses its functional justification, since it is no longer indispensable for the development and maintenance of the economic system. Not only are the newly created power positions abused in monopolistic practices, but the growing immobility of the system turns competition into a positive danger to stability. What once claimed to promote the best interests of all now abandons the employment and income of the masses to the vagaries of the business cycle.[12]

[10] For sociological definitions see Max Weber, *The Theory of Social and Economic Organization,* trans. A. M. Henderson and Talcott Parsons, ed. with an Introduction by Talcott Parsons (New York, 1947), pp. 140, 238–45.

Cahn, Edmond N. (ed.), *Social Meaning of Legal Concepts* (New York, 1948), no. 1, 'Inheritance of Property and the Power of Testamentary Disposition.' (An annual conference conducted by the New York University School of Law.)

[11] See note 53, ch. 5 [of Mannheim's *Freedom, Power, and Democratic Planning*—Ed.]

[12] Cf. Brady, R. A., *Business as a System of Power* (New York, 1943). Schumpeter, Joseph A., *Business Cycles* (New York, 1939).

This utterly chaotic state of affairs is well known to all of us from the cruel experience of many years. For most people the crisis of the age is more evident in its economic symptoms than in other terms. But economic patterns only repeat the very same tendencies of disintegration leading to chaos in all spheres of society, though no other symptom except war spreads so widely and deeply as mass unemployment.

IV. Displacement of Self-Regulating Small Groups

Uncontrolled growth in the economic system is, as we have said, just one aspect of uncontrolled growth in modern society at large. Society is gradually becoming a conglomeration of smaller and larger groups, very often held together only by administrative agencies replacing the older small organic groups.[13] By organic we mean that self-regulating power which is characteristic of small groups but gradually vanishes in large ones. There is nothing mysterious about this self-regulating power which guarantees a certain evenness, balance, and continuity in development so long as the size of the community is limited and everybody can see approximately how things will work out. There is no mystery about correlating supply and demand in a household economy where the decision about the goods to be produced and consumed is in the same hands. Nor is there mystery in correlating supply and demand when the craftsman works for a certain number of customers whom he knows personally and whose wishes he can foresee. There is even no special mystery about the self-regulating powers of the market as long as small units compete.

The phenomenon of self-regulation in small groups has been studied more extensively in the economic sphere, but the same self-regulation takes place in other spheres. Limited size allows everyone to understand what is required of him and what to expect from the group. In direct everyday contacts with other group members, each can discover for himself the causes of success or failure and seek collective remedies when things go wrong. The *Agora* of the Greek city, the market place of the medieval town, where the church, the guildhall, and the market stalls were close to one

[13] See, for instance, the observations made in the recent social development in Central Asia by G. and M. Wilson, *The Analysis of Social Change* (Cambridge, 1945).

another, enabled the citizen to take in the whole orbit of his world
at a glance. Differentiation of human activities and growth of the
corresponding social types happened along the lines of gradually
expanding co-operation. Everybody knew his function since he
could clearly see how the village supplied the town and the town,
the village; how the different occupations served and balanced each
other and regulated their mutual relationships. Yet among the
members not only were the formal relations of social hierarchy and
function clearly defined but the whole edifice of growing society
was still supported by the basic institutions of family, neighborhood, and community.

All this is not said in the spirit of eulogy. The narrow outlook,
the inescapable limitations, would probably have made life in such
a world unbearable for us. All we want to emphasize is the nature
of an integrated social pattern which is now vanishing. The most
adequate expression of this evanescence is the mushroom growth of
the metropolis where the last traces of organic cohesion are fading
away and the principle of common living, functional interdependence, and clarity of common purpose are completely destroyed.

V. Disintegration of Traditional Group Controls

Another important aspect of the same process is the disintegration
of ancient forms of social control.

As long as the self-regulating powers of small groups remain
undisturbed, action and thought are controlled by common sense
and the rules fixed by custom and precedent. Traditions are ultimately the accumulated experience of successful adjustment.
Acting on the basis of tradition has the advantage of saving the
individual the trouble of making a choice, or of inventing new
ways where the old are capable of solving the difficulty. But tradition and custom maintain their power to control events only so
long as certain conditions prevail, and it is important to enumerate
at least some of these. The tasks must be simple and recurrent,
needing only limited organization for their performance. Only in
these circumstances does the established pattern apply; as variety
increases, tasks grow too complex. Rational analysis is necessary to
divide the whole into its component parts, creating new combinations and transgressing precedents.

Tradition works only so long as transformation is slow and gradual and the home, the market, the church, and the city do not represent entirely different and even antagonistic influences; or if they do, there is time to reconcile these differences and to assimilate discordant habits. Thus, as long as growth is gradual, traditions will act as controls safeguarding the amount of conformity without which co-operation is impossible. You can act only if you can base your conduct upon reasonable expectation of how people will react. People can be united in war and peace only if certain basic values are tacitly accepted by the community. So long as the group is more or less homogeneous and people live in roughly the same sort of social and cultural surroundings, and so long as there is not too much rise and fall in the social scale, customary habits will remain stable.

Historically, not only have we passed from the stage of neighborhood community to the Great Society in a relatively short time, but this growth has frequently been by fits and starts. Technical development in itself undermined those conditions that were the mainstay of tradition. Whole groups were eradicated at times, as were the old English aristocracy in the Wars of the Roses or the rural workers during the Industrial Revolution; others were driven to emigrate by economic, political, or ecclesiastic forces.

This rapid, spasmodic transformation contributed to the disintegration of ancient group controls. We can scarcely maintain that we have been able to substitute adequately for them. Undoubtedly we have succeeded in inventing a few patterns of large-scale organization, like that of the Army, the Factory, the Civil Service. But none of these has developed the elasticity and responsiveness to human needs of the small group. We still take it for granted that large-scale organizations should be abstract, arbitrary, and dehumanizing, in emulation of the first great pattern of large-scale organization, the Army.[14] Today, after shattering experiences, we can see that the controls which prevail in the Army and the Factory have, in themselves, a demoralizing effect. In the long run treating men like the cogs and wheels of a machine can only lead to deliberate inefficiency or sabotage. The equation—natural

[14] It is characteristic that in England after the war Field Marshal Montgomery laid down the rule that the patterns and standards of life in the Army should be similar to those of civil society.

controls in small groups, mechanical devices in large-scale organizations—no longer holds. For we know that the greatest demoralization of the individual arises from overformalization.[15] The raw material for chaos is not the undisciplined barbarian but the over-disciplined factory worker or soldier who in consequence loses vitality whenever the plant closes down or when there is no one to give commands.

VI. Failure of Large-Scale Co-ordination

As for special controls, an added irritant in modern society is the lack of successful co-ordination between different large-scale organizations. Developed as business enterprises, as state bureaucracies, or as voluntary associations, they frequently overlap in function. Unco-ordinated institutions cancel each other's effectiveness. It was quite different in medieval society where, for example, the medieval guild was an elaborate system of well-defined functions, privileges, and prohibitions. Not only were the formal relationships between the members, their social hierarchy, and their functions within the community clearly established, not only were all aspects of their life, work, leisure, culture, and worship clearly shaped and determined by the purposes of the community, but the corporations themselves were co-ordinated. They constituted the medieval city and thus differed essentially from modern employers' associations or trade unions which have only segmental functions and are hardly controlled by the community. Admitting that a large-scale society cannot continue without a certain co-ordination of its institutions does not mean a plea for corporations either in the medieval or the fascist sense. But it is equally impossible to go on conceiving of individuals as millions of abstract atoms without considering the educational and moral significance of their associations.

As long as the various social functions represented by the associations remain unco-ordinated and the associations are not considered as an organic part of the community, it is too easy to manipulate the individual by these means. In a hundred ways the modern shrewd technician of influence can reach the individual, as employer or employee, as consumer, student, radio listener, sports-

---

[15] Cf. Cooley's idea of over-formalization, 'Formalism and Disorganization,' *Social Organization* (New York, 1924), ch. XVI.

man, or holiday-maker, in days of health or sickness. The result is general disorientation.[16]

The weakening and passing of controls also implies the weakening and passing of liberty. There is no real freedom in the abstract. There are only liberties. Certain types of freedom and restriction belong with each control. The soldier's freedom is different from that of the monk; the teacher's freedom is different from that of the pupil; the father's freedom within his family is different from that in his business relations; and the civil servant's freedom different from that of a free-lance artist or journalist. As long as society functions properly, all are bound by different rules and commitments, but they are also free within the framework of these commitments. What appears as unbridled behavior or license from the point of view of one control may reveal itself as bondage from some other. Where freedom begins for one person, a new type of responsibility exists for another. At first glance, the artist and free-lance journalist seem freer than the soldier or civil servant. But more thorough investigation may reveal that once the soldier and civil servant leave their strictly regulated work they are free of further responsibility and can relax. On the other hand, the artist who seems outwardly free may be bound by the higher responsibilities of his art, and the journalist by his professional code.[17] Qualitative freedom exists only in relation to qualitatively defined commitments. Absolute freedom exists only in anarchy; but this indeed proves that when the laws regulating behavior lose their power of control, freedom, too, is disappearing.

[16] For a case study of a radio-manipulated public scare and the confusion of the public, cf. Cantril, Hadley, *The Invasion from Mars* (Princeton, 1940).

[17] 'Freedom of Inquiry and Expression, a Collection of Facts and Judgments concerning Freedom and Suppression of Freedom of All Forms of Intellectual Life,' *The Annals of the American Academy of Political and Social Science* (November, 1938), vol. 200.

Lippmann, Walter, *Public Opinion* (New York, 1922; Pelican, 1946).

Lovejoy, A. D., 'Professional Ethics and Social Progress,' *The North American Review*, vol. 219, pp. 398–407.

MacIver, Robert, 'The Social Significance of Professional Ethics,' *The Annals* (Amer. Acad. Soc. Pol. Science), vol. 101, pp. 5–11.

Parsons, Talcott, 'The Professions and Social Structure,' *Social Forces* (May, 1939), vol. 17, pp. 457–87.

Steed, Wickham, *The Press* (London, 1938, Penguin ed.).

Whitehead, Alfred North, 'Aspects of Freedom,' *Freedom: Its Meaning*, planned and edited by Ruth Nanda Anshen (New York, 1940).

VII. Disintegration of Co-operative Controls

The waning power of small communities also results in the vanishing of techniques once so characteristic of them, those of co-operative control.

In any social situation there are two forms of group control. One is the authoritative pattern of command and obedience, the other the pattern of development and guidance of action through co-operation. All the complicated forms of political and social organization on a higher level are derivations of these two original patterns. They are alternative methods for achieving division of labor and differentiation of social functions. The first method, that of command and obedience, very often attains great efficiency but is in most cases detrimental to the individuals concerned. The alternative of co-operation represents a creative principle. This method of shared control is one of the most significant inventions in the field of social techniques. In its conception of a common purpose which can be realized under conditions of shared responsibility, it represents, ancient as it may be, a great advance over the method that forces everyone blindly to follow the commands of one man. Allocation of different tasks in a way that enables everybody to contribute his best should be a comparatively easy division of labor; it is somewhat more difficult to develop co-operative forms of thinking, as in a debate. But in a large-scale society it is extremely difficult to find a co-operative method of creating consensus and sharing common power. Indeed, one of the greatest problems of modern Democracy is to project patterns for establishing consensus and sharing common power in large communities.

In a small sect or community of limited size one can expect all members to sense the spirit of the meeting and find through discussion how much unconscious agreement exists in their minds. However, when the growth of society produces surroundings indicative of class as well as spatial distinctions, with conflicting mental climates, and when the structure of society produces vested interests with organized pressure groups, it becomes increasingly difficult to adhere to the same methods of creating consensus. Those that worked fairly well in the simpler stages of democratic organization scarcely seem adequate now.

The democratic technique of voting tried to replace consensus and the shared responsibility of simpler groups. The institution of voting originated in primitive forms of acclamation, which later became counting of heads and finally led to various schemes of representation, developed with particular skill during the nineteenth century. But those who consider voting and the present system of suffrage the fundamental weapon of democratic control overlook the fact that democratic procedure is vitiated in many ways by manipulated opinion, organized parties, and pressure groups. Moreover, they fail to see that sharing of control is essential not only in the sphere of voting but in all functions and all sections of the community; and we have not yet succeeded in finding methods of sharing controls adequate to the demands of a Great Society.

VIII. Disruptive Effects of Class Antagonism

Left to itself modern society develops a specific kind of disruptive effect from class distinctions and the psychological factors intensifying class antagonisms.

This aspect of modern society has often been discussed and tends to overshadow other causes of disorganization in our social system. It is, indeed, a very significant disruptive force and surely if allowed to develop uncontrolled will lead to class wars and destroy the preconditions of freedom and democratic agreement.

Contrary to the fatalistic belief in the 'class struggle,' we must emphasize that having developed methods of control that could check growing class differences, we could use them if only we wanted to do so. The obstacles to their application are considerable but essentially no more so than the other disruptive factors discussed. The first step toward mastering this sort of disintegration is to forego the negativist attitude of fatalism and to weigh the pros and cons of a reformist and a revolutionary solution. We shall return to this problem presently.

IX. Disintegration of Personalities

Today we know that we cannot consider separately the disintegration of the primary patterns of co-operation and common life, the deterioration of social controls, the failure to co-ordinate large-scale organizations, and so on. These are not just institutions gone

astray, which some objective procedure of 'institutional reconstruction' will set right. Today we know that human conduct and
personality formation depend to a large extent on these same
institutions. Their disintegration means the disintegration of personality. We expect disorganization of personality where institutions disintegrate because today we know that behavior and
character are not abstract entities in themselves but develop primarily out of the context of activities and, to a large extent, out of
the institutionalized patterns of co-operative action. That is, if the
pattern of co-operation loses its regulative powers, controls are no
longer acceptable. They lose their vitality and prestige: accordingly, behavior is bound to disintegrate.

A man who follows traditional patterns unquestioningly is at a
complete loss if his belief in tradition is shattered and no new
pattern of conduct is at hand to adopt. The same applies when
there is a hiatus in the co-ordination of institutions immediately
affecting human behavior.

Most of the commands we obey are supported and sanctioned by
groups. There are the army code, professional codes, business
codes, and moral codes governing neighborly relations. In modern
society, if large organizations fail to develop their own standards, if
there are no adequate ethics of industrial relations, no thorough
education for citizenship bringing home the virtues of communal
responsibility and, finally, if in international relations the law of the
jungle prevails, then these lapses will be reflected in the conduct
and character of the individuals concerned. People will still behave
decently where some remnants of the family code or of the
professional code are valid, but will feel lost where the old prescriptions vanish without being replaced by new ones, or where
new spheres of life develop that are not yet subject to the moral
consciousness of the community. The broader these spheres of
lawlessness the more they disintegrate personality, until we reach a
stage that Durkheim called *anomie* (*nomos*, law; *a-nomos*, lawlessness).[18] And this is the real state in which people live in a mass
society that took the idea of *laissez-faire* literally, not realizing that
with the disappearance of older controls, man would be left without orientation. Such a society is morally 'undermined.'

[18] Durkheim, Emile, *Le Suicide, étude de sociologie* (Paris, 1897), pp.
272–88. (Trans. William C. Bradbury, Jr., with an Introduction by Sebastian
de Grazia, *University Observer*, Chicago, Winter 1947.)

If we have not yet reached the *anomic* state, it is because the existing undercurrent of tradition and still working and expanding techniques allow agreement on day-to-day issues. But it could be seen how flabby both social conduct and moral character had become, when the first shocks of upheaval came in the shape of war, economic crises, and inflation. Then the latent perplexity and moral insecurity of the little man came to the fore, and whole nations answered with the desperate cry for 'security,' the demand for something to hold on to. People considered anybody who promised anything resembling security a prophet, a savior, and a leader whom they would follow blindly rather than remain in a state of utter instability and lawlessness.

X. Disintegration of Consensus and of Religious Bonds

If our observation is limited to how conduct deteriorates in the context of action, we have not yet fully perceived the disintegration of behavior and personality. By analyzing the causes of social disintegration, we realize that in properly integrated societies there is an additional process at work over and above the formation of conduct and character in action. It is the integrating function of ideological or spiritual inspiration chiefly represented by religion.

When speaking of Religion, the sociologist does not mean this or that creed or denomination, but a basic institution which is fairly well expressed in the word 'religion' itself. By derivation *re-ligere* means to 'bind closely' whatever you do to a supreme cause. Human activity in the context of living is first woven into a pattern through habits and conventions. But this primary integration is not enough. Man craves a more fundamental oneness relating all his scattered activities to a common purpose. If this commonly accepted purpose disappears, the social machine continues for a while to work as usual since the mutual dependencies and obligations arising from the division of labor do not allow people just to run away. But, whenever a major crisis occurs, it becomes apparent that mutual obligations are only valid if they are rooted in conscience; and conscience, although the most personal experience in man, is a guide to common life only if a moral and religious interpretation of commonly experienced events is accepted and assimilated by the members of that community.

Religion in this sense means linking individual actions and responsibilities to a broader stream of common experience. Religion, therefore, integrates once more on a deeper plane what has already been integrated for limited utilitarian purposes on the more pragmatic level of daily activity.

When religion ceases to be the deeper integrating force in human affairs, the change becomes socially apparent. Until the dissolution of medieval society, religion was alive because it was not only a creed but also a social control inspiring patterns of behavior and ideals of the good life. When this influence was first withdrawn, allowing the state, industry, and other sections of life to take care of themselves, religion lost vigor, and social life found no substitute. First Nationalism, then Socialism tried to fill this gap. In an age awaiting for world integration the self-defeating tendency and harmful influence of Nationalism, especially when it becomes an instrument of aggression, are beyond question. Certainly for a time Socialism and Communism had the power to bind human activities to a higher purpose—that of building a society based upon social justice. But this much is clear: they cannot mean religion for a great part of mankind and thus split instead of uniting men for the next great venture of building a co-operative world society.

The great paradox of any fundamental integration on the plane of *re-ligere* at the present historical juncture is that the so much needed unification of larger communities is too often achieved by antagonism against other religious creeds. These seem to create the kind of zeal and intolerance that with the help of the present perfected tools of warfare can only lead to the extinction of nations.

As long as the world consisted of several units which could develop side by side, religious zeal, time and again, resulted in wars. But those struggles of bygone days seem relatively innocent maneuvers compared with the two world wars, and even more so, in contemplation of the destructive potentialities of wars to come. The criterion of any future spiritual revival as a creative force will be its ability to integrate men without antagonizing them. The fact that this has hardly happened yet cannot be accepted as conclusive by those who believe in the creative powers in man. For in the past man has often shown that he could meet the challenge of an entirely changed environment through the emergence of a completely new mental attitude.

As we contemplate the chaotic state of unregulated capitalist society, one thing becomes quite clear: the present state of society cannot last long. We have seen that social chaos may remain latent so long as no major crisis occurs. But whenever mass unemployment or war brings the tension to a climax, new solutions must be found. By this time the world has learned that such crises are not chance, but that both mass unemployment and wars are inherent in the system. Thus the two basic evils will not disappear without a conscious and systematic attack on them. This of itself indicates that the age of *laissez-faire* is over and that only through planning can catastrophe be avoided.

The Problem of Power in Socialist Regimes

PAUL RICOEUR

With the disappearance of fascism and the gradual erosion of socialism and communism as European society becomes more and more bourgeois in ways of life and thought, one of the prominent tendencies in recent Western European political theory has been a revival of interest in the relevance of Christian teaching to politics. Parties subscribing to one form or another of "Christian democracy" have captured most of the nonleftist vote and dominated most of the governments of France, Germany, and Italy since the Second World War.

At the level of ideas, the situation in France is especially interesting. The Christian existentialism of Gabriel Marcel, the Christian personalism of Emmanuel Mounier, and the neo-Thomism of Jacques Maritain have been the chief influences from the older generation, each tending in much the same general direction, stressing the need for organic social relationships, personal freedom, and a democratic rather than totalitarian politics. The claims of individualism and collectivism are mediated by a liberal and humanistic interpretation of the Christian message. At the same time, independent philosophical inquiry is alleged to bring the thinker to conclusions that parallel Christian teaching.

Paul Ricoeur, a professor of philosophy at the Sorbonne, has long been associated with this movement in French thought. He is at once a phenomenologist in the tradition of Husserl, an existentialist in the tradition of Jaspers and Marcel, and a leading force in the personalist

SOURCE: *History and Truth*, by Paul Ricoeur, trans. Charles A. Kelbley (Northwestern University Press, Evanston, Ill., 1965), pp. 261–70. Reprinted by permission of Northwestern University Press. Copyright 1965 by Northwestern University Press.

movement launched by Mounier. He opposes to the negative existentialism of Sartre an existentialism of affirmation and hope, in which all true negation, he believes, is founded. What follows is the concluding section of an article entitled "The Political Paradox," first published in Mounier's journal, *Esprit*, in 1957. Ricoeur disputes Marx's contention that the state is dispensable: "man cannot evade politics under penalty of evading his humanity." Yet "power is one of the splendors of man that is eminently prone to evil."

IF OUR analysis of the paradox of power is correct, if the State is at once more rational and more passional than the individual, the great problem of democracy concerns the *control* of the State by the people. The problem of the control of the State, like that of its rationality, is equally irreducible to socio-economic history, as is its evilness irreducible to class contradictions. The problem of the control of the State consists in this: to devise institutional techniques especially designed to render possible the exercise of power and render its abuse impossible. The notion of "control" derives directly from the central paradox of man's political existence; it is the *practical* resolution of this paradox. To be sure, it is, of course, necessary that the State *be* but that it not be too much. It must direct, organize, and make decisions so that the political animal himself might be; but it must not lead to the tyrant.

Only a political philosophy which has perceived the specific nature of polity—the specific nature of its function and the specific nature of its evil—is in a position to pose correctly the problem of political control.

Thus the reduction of political alienation to economic alienation would seem to be the weak point in the political thought of Marxism. This reduction of political alienation has, in effect, led Marxism-Leninism to substitute another problem for the problem of State control, that of the *withering away* of the State. This substitution seems disastrous to me; it grounds the end of the iniquity of the State upon an indefinite future, whereas the true, practical political problem pertains to the limitation of this evil in the present. An eschatology of innocence takes the place of an ethic of limited violence. At one and the same time, the thesis of the withering away of the State, by promising too much for the future, equally tolerates too much in the present. The thesis of the future withering away of the State serves as a cloak and an alibi for the perpetuation of terrorism. By means of a sinister paradox, the thesis of the provisory character of the State turns into the best justification for the endless prolongation of the dictatorship of the proletariat and forms the essence of totalitarianism.

It is quite necessary to realize that the theory of the withering away of the State is a logical consequence of the reduction of political alienation to economic alienation. If the State is merely an organ of *repression*, which springs from class antagonisms and expresses the domination of one class, then the State will disappear along with all the aftereffects of the division of society into classes.

But the question is whether the end of the private appropriation of the means of production can bring about the end of *all* alienations. Perhaps appropriation itself is but one privileged form of the power of man over man; perhaps money itself is but one means of domination among others; perhaps the same spirit of domination is given expression in various forms: in economic exploitation, in bureaucratic tyranny, in intellectual dictatorship, and in clericalism.

Our concern here is not the hidden unity of all alienations. In any case, the reduction of the political form to the economic form is indirectly responsible for the myth of the withering away of the State.

It is true that Marx, Engels, and Lenin have attempted to elaborate this theory on the basis of experience. They interpreted the Paris Commune as the guarantee and the commencement of the experimental verification of the thesis of the withering away of the State; for them it demonstrated that the dictatorship of the proletariat may be something quite different from the mere transfer of the State's power into other hands, but indeed the overthrow of the State machine as the *"special force"* of repression. If the armed populace is substituted for the permanent army, if the police force is subject to dismissal at any moment, if bureaucracy is dismantled as an organized body and reduced to the lowest paid condition, then the general force of the majority of the people replaces the special force of repression found in the bourgeois State, and the beginning of the withering away of the State coincides with the dictatorship of the proletariat. As Lenin says, "it is impossible to pass from capitalism to socialism without a certain return to a primitive form of democracy." The withering away of the State is therefore contemporaneous to the dictatorship of the proletariat, in the measure that the latter is a truly popular revolution which smashes the repressive organs of the bourgeois State. Marx could even say: "The Commune was no longer a State in the literal sense of the word."

In the thought of Marx and Lenin, the thesis of the withering away of the State was therefore not a hypocritical thesis but a sincere one. To be sure, few men have demanded so little of the State as the great Marxists: "So long as the proletariat still has need of a State," reads the *Letter to Bebel*, "it is not in order to secure freedom but to put down its adversaries; and the day when it becomes possible to speak of freedom, the State will cease to exist as such."

But if the withering away of the State is the critical test for the dictatorship of the proletariat, then the crucial question is posed: why has the withering away of the State not *in fact* coincided with the dictatorship of the proletariat? Why, in fact, has the socialist State reinforced the power of the State to the point of confirming the axiom which Marx believed to be applicable only to bourgeois revolutions: "All revolutions have only served to perfect this machine instead of smashing it."[1] The attempt to reply to this question is at the same time to provide the missing link to the Khrushchev report, for it is to explain how the phenomenon of Stalin was possible in the midst of a socialist regime.

My working hypothesis, such as is suggested by the preceding reflection, is that Stalin was possible *because* there was no recognition of the permanence of the problematic of power in the transition from the old to the new society, because it was believed that the end of economic exploitation necessarily implied the end of political repression, because it was believed that the State is provisory, because one had substituted the problem of the withering away of the State for that of its control. In short, my working hypothesis is that the State cannot wither away and that, not being able to wither away, it must be controlled by a special institutional form of government.

Furthermore, it would seem that the socialist State, more than the bourgeois State, requires a vigilant, popular control precisely because its rationality is greater, because it enlarges its sphere of analyses and forecasts so as to encompass sectors of human exist-

[1] Marx, *The Eighteenth Brumaire of Louis Bonaparte*.

ence which elsewhere and in former times were given over to chance and improvisation. The rationality of a socialist State, striving as it does to suppress class antagonisms and even aspiring to put an end to the division of society into classes, is certainly greater. But you see at once that its scope of power is also greater as well as the possibilities for tyranny.

It would seem that the task of a critique of socialist power should be to articulate lucidly and faithfully the new possibilities of political alienation, that is to say those which are opened up by the very battle against economic alienation as well as by the reinforcement of State power which this battle entails.

Here are some avenues of approach which might be pursued by an investigation of power in socialist regimes:

1. We should first have to determine in what measure "the administration of things" necessarily involves a "governing of persons" and in what measure the progress in the administration of things gives rise to an augmentation of political power of man over man.

For example: planning implies a choice of an economic character concerning the order of priority in the satisfaction of needs and the employment of means of production; but this choice is from the very outset *more* than a matter of economics. It is the function of a general politics, that is to say of a long-term project concerning the orientation of the human community engaged in the experience of planning. The proportion of the part reinvested and the part consumed, the proportion of cultural and material goods in the general equilibrium of the plan, spring from a "global strategic vision" in which economics is woven into politics. A plan is a technique serving a global project, a civilizing project animated by implicit values, in short, a project which in the last analysis pertains to man's very nature. Hence, insofar as it gives expression to *will* and power, polity is the soul of economics.

Thus the administration of things may not be substituted for the governing of persons, since the rational technique of ordering man's needs and activities on the macroscopic scale of the State cannot extricate itself from all ethico-cultural contexts. Consequently, in the last analysis, political power unites scales of value and technological possibilities, the latent aspirations of the human community, and the means unleashed by knowledge of economic laws. The connection between ethics and technics in the "task" of planning is the fundamental reason why the administration of things *implies* the governing of persons.

2. Next, we should have to determine how the reinforcement of State power, which is intimately linked to the expansion of the jurisdiction of the socialist State in comparison with the bourgeois State, fosters *abuses which are inherent to it in virtue of its nature as a socialist State*. This would constitute the elucidation of the idea mentioned earlier, that the most rational State possesses the most opportunities for being passional.

Engels pointed out in *Anti-Dühring* that the organization of production will remain authoritarian and repressive, even after the expropriation of expropriators, so long as there is a perpetuation of the old division of work and the other alienations which make working a burden and not a joy. When it is not spontaneous, the division of work still arises from constraint, and this constraint is precisely connected to the passage from hazard to rationality.

The temptation toward forced labor therefore becomes one of the major temptations of the socialist State. But it can easily be seen that the socialist State is the least protected against this temptation, since its method of global planning also endows it with the *economic* monopoly over psychological constraint (culture, the press, and propaganda are encompassed within the plan and are therefore *economically* determined by the State). Hence, the socialist State will have a whole arsenal of means at its disposal, including psychological means ranging from inducements and competition to deportation.

In addition to these opportunities for abuse provided by the organization of the means of production, there is the temptation to overcome irrational resistances by more expeditious means than those of education or discussion. In effect, the rational State encounters resistances of all kinds; some of these result from residual phenomena (described quite well by Chinese Marxists, in particular, and previously by Lenin in the *Infantile Disorder of Communism*). These resistances are typical of the peasantry and the lower middle class, demonstrating that the psychology of workers is not on the same plane as that of technocrats, but remains adapted to long standing situations. Thus we find resistances of a psychological character which do not spring from considerations of the general welfare of the people but from the habituation to outdated economic conditions. Yet all resistances are not subject to this explanation by backward mentalities. The socialist State has a more remote and more vast project than the individual whose interests are more immediate, limited to the horizon of his death or at the very most to that of his children. In the meantime, the State calculates by generations; since the State and the individual are not on the same wave length, the individual develops interests which are not naturally in accord with those of the State. We are familiar with at least two manifestations of this variance between the goal of the State and that of the individual: one concerns the division between investment and immediate consumption, the other the determination of standards and the rate of production. The micro-interests of individuals and the macro-decisions of power are in a state of constant tension, fostering a dialectic of individual demands and State constraint which is an occasion for abuse.

Thus we find tensions and contradictions which are not the remedies for the private appropriation of the means of production. Certain of these tensions and contradictions even derive from the new power of the State.

Lastly, the socialist State is more ideological than the "liberal" State. It may attribute to itself the ancient dreams of unifying the realm of truth within an orthodoxy encompassing all the manifestations of knowledge and all the expressions of the human word. Under the pretext of revolutionary discipline and technocratic efficacity, it can justify an entire militarization of minds; it can do it, that is to say, it has the temptation and the means to do so since it possesses the monopoly of provisions.

All of these reflections converge toward the same conclusion: if the socialist State does not abolish but rather revives the problematic of the State—if it serves to further its rationality while intensifying opportunities for perversion—the problem of the democratic *control* of the State is still more pressing in socialist regimes than in capitalistic regimes, and the myth of the *withering away* of the State stands in the way of a systematic treatment of this problem.

3. The third task of a critique of power in socialist regimes would then consist of coming back to the critique of the liberal state in light of this idea of democratic control. This would enable it to determine which institutional features of the liberal state were independent of the phenomenon of class domination and specifi-

cally adapted to the limitation of the abuse of power. No doubt
this critique could not be carried out within the specifically critical
phase of socialism; the liberal State had to appear almost inevitably
as a hypocritical means of perpetuating economic exploitation. Yet
today it is indispensable to discern between the instrument of class
domination and democratic control in general, at least after the
bitter experience of Stalinism. Perhaps it is the case that Marxism in
itself embodies the ingredients for this revision when it propounds
that a class in its ascending phase pursues a *universal* function. In
giving expression to the problem of democratic controls, the "philosophers" of the eighteenth century devised the true *liberalism*
which no doubt goes beyond the destiny of the bourgeoisie. It does
not follow that just because the bourgeoisie had need of these
controls in order to draw limits to monarchic and feudal power
and to facilitate its own ascension, that these controls therefore
exhaust their abiding significance within their provisory usage. In
its profound intention, liberal politics comprised an element of
universality, for it was adjusted to the *universal* problematic of the
State, beyond the form of the bourgeois state. This explains how a
return to liberal politics is possible within a socialist context.

I should like to cite a few examples of this *discernment* applied to
the structures of the liberal State, examples of the division between
the "universal" aspects and the "bourgeois" aspects of these structures. I shall present them in a problematic manner since we are
practically at the end of a critique of socialist power of which the
first postulates are scarcely certain:

a) Is not the independence of the "judge" the very first condition of permanent legal remedy against the abuse of power?

It seems to me that the judge is a personage who must be
voluntarily placed, by the consent of all, on the fringes of the
fundamental conflicts of society.

The independence of the judge, it will be objected, is an abstraction. Quite so. Society requires for its human respiration an "ideal"
function, a deliberate, concerted abstraction in which it projects
the ideal of legality that legitimates the reality of power. Without
this projection, in which the State represents itself as legitimate, the
individual is at the mercy of the State and power itself, without
protection against its arbitrariness. It stands to reason that the
proceedings of Moscow, of Budapest, of Prague, and elsewhere,
were possible because the independence of the judge was not

technically assured nor ideologically founded in a theory of the judge as a man above class, as an abstraction of human proportions, as the embodiment of law. Stalin was possible because there were always judges to judge in accordance with his decree.

b) The second condition of permanent legal remedy against the abuse of power is the citizen's free access to sources of information, knowledge, and science, independent of those of the State. As we have seen, the modern State determines the way of living since it orients economically all of man's choices by its macro-decisions, its global planning; but this power will become more and more indistinguishable from totalitarian power if the citizens are not able to *form, by themselves, an opinion* concerning the nature and the stakes involved in these macro-decisions.

More than any other, the socialist State requires the counterpart of *public opinion* in the strict sense of the word, that is to say, a public which has opinions and an opinion which is given public expression. It is quite plain what this involves: a press that belongs to its readers and not to the State, and a press whose freedom of information and of expression is constitutionally and economically guaranteed. Stalin was possible because no public opinion could launch a critique of him. But then again, the post-Stalin State alone has dared to utter that Stalin was evil, *not* the people.

The independent exercise of justice and the independent formation of opinion are the two lungs of a politically sound State. Without these, there is asphyxiation.

These two notions are so important that it was in virtue of them that the overthrow of Stalinism was accomplished; the notions of *justice* and *truth* gave birth to the revolt. This explains the role of intellectuals in the abortive revolution of Hungary and in the successful revolution of Poland. If intellectuals, writers, and artists played a decisive role in these events, it is because the stakes at issue were not economic and social, notwithstanding misery and low wages; the stakes were strictly political, or to be more precise, they were the new political "alienation" infecting socialist power. But the problem of political alienation, as we are well aware of since Plato's *Gorgias*, is the problem of untruth. We have also learned of this through the Marxist critique of the bourgeois State, situated, as it is, entirely upon the terrain of *untruth*, of being and appearance, of mystification, and of falsehood. It is just here that the intellectual as such becomes involved in politics. The intellectual is driven to the fore of a revolution, and not merely within its ranks, as soon as the incentive for this revolution is more political than economic, as soon as it touches upon the relation of power with truth and justice.

c) Next, it would seem to me that the democracy of work requires a certain dialectic between the State and labor councils. As we have seen, the long-term interests of the State, even apart from the consideration of money, do not immediately coincide with those of workers; this stands to reason in a socialist period, in the precise sense of the word, that is to say in a phase of inequality of wages, wherein professional specialization is in opposition to un-skilled and skilled laborers, directors, and intellectuals; this also stands to reason in a period of rapid or even forced industrializa-tion. Consequently, only a network of liaisons between the State and associations representing the diverse interests of workers can consolidate the groping quests for a viable equilibrium, that is to say at once economically sound and humanly tolerable. The right to strike, in particular, would seem to be the sole recourse of workers against the State, *even against the State of workers*. The postulate of the immediate coincidence of the will of the socialist State with all interests of all workers seems to me to be a pernicious illusion and a dangerous alibi for the abuse of State power.

d) lastly, the key problem is that of the control of the State by the people, by the democratically organized foundation. At this point, the reflections and experiences of the Yugoslavian and Polish communists ought to be consulted and analyzed very closely. The question is whether the pluralism of parties, the practice of "free elections," and the parliamentary form of government derive from this "universalism" of the liberal State, or whether they irremedi-ably pertain to the bourgeois period of the liberal State. We must not have any preconceived ideas: neither for nor against; neither for Occidental custom, nor for radical criticism; we need not be in a hurry to answer. It is certain that planning techniques require that the socialist form of production not be given over to the hazard of popular vote; that it be irrevocable, as is the republican form of our government. The execution of the Plan calls for full powers, a government of long continuance, a long-term budget. Yet our parliamentary techniques, our manner of interchanging the majorities in power, would not appear very compatible with the modern rationality of the State. And yet, on the other hand, it is just as certain that *discussion* is a vital necessity for the State;

through discussion it is given orientation and impetus; discussion curbs its tendency to abuse power. Democracy is discussion. Thus it is necessary that this discussion be *organized* in one way or another. Here we encounter the question concerning parties or the unique Party. What may argue in favor of the pluralism of parties is that this system has not only reflected tensions between social groups, determined by the division of society into classes, but it has also invested political discussion as such with organization, and it has therefore had a "universal" and not merely a "bourgeois" significance. An analysis of the notion of "party," on the sole basis of the socio-economic criterion, therefore seems to me dangerously inadequate and liable to encourage tyranny. This is why it is necessary to judge the theory of multiple parties and the theory of a single party not only from the standpoint of class dynamics, but equally from the viewpoint of the techniques of controlling the State. Only a critique of power in socialist regimes could further advance this question. Yet this critique has hardly been launched.

I do not know whether the term political "liberalism" can be saved from falling into disrepute. Perhaps its affinity with economic liberalism has compromised it once and for all, although of late, the label "liberal" tends to constitute a misdemeanor in the eyes of social fascists in Algeria and in Paris, and thus recovers its bygone freshness.

If the term could be saved, it would state rather well what ought to be said: that the central problem of politics is *freedom:* whether the State *founds* freedom by means of its rationality, or whether freedom *limits* the passions of power through its resistance.

The End of Belief

MALCOLM BRADBURY

Most of the thinkers represented in this anthology may be fairly classified as "believers." Whatever they reject or deny, they still "believe" in something, although it may be nothing more than Camus's rebellion or Popper's fallibilism. And yet many mid-century European intellectuals believe, strictly speaking, in nothing at all. The clamor of

SOURCE: *Eating People Is Wrong*, by Malcolm Bradbury (Knopf, New York, 1960), pp. 47–49 and 133–34. Reprinted by permission of Alfred A. Knopf, Inc., and Martin Secker and Warburg, Ltd. Copyright 1959 by Malcolm Bradbury.

the prophets for followers drowns out the quiet voices of the thousands who cannot commit themselves, in their anxiety or bafflement, to anything. A few novelists and playwrights have come close to articulating this radical noncommitment, but noncommitment by its very nature is extraordinarily difficult to expound in a technical treatise. In any purely verbal competition, the prophets will no doubt always prevail.

The most characteristic retreat of the noncommitted new intellectual is into the shelter of scholarly relativism. As an exhibit in evidence, consider the case of Professor Treece, head of the English department of a small provincial university in the Midlands and antihero of Malcolm Bradbury's comic novel *Eating People Is Wrong*. Now in early middle age, Treece ponders on the changes that have taken place in the British mental climate since his own student days. Emma is one of his graduate students, aged twenty-six. A university teacher of English himself, Bradbury belongs to Emma's generation rather than Treece's. See also his satire of American university life, *Stepping Westward*, published in 1965.

OF TREECE's formative years, which were the 1930's, of those busy days when to be a liberal was to be something; and people other than liberals knew what liberals were, of this period Treece had one sharp and pointed memory that cast itself up like a damp patch on the wall of an otherwise sturdy house, a memory of a time when late one night—indeed, at the two o'clock of one early morning—he had gone from the room he rented in Charlotte Street because he had had a row with the woman he was living with. On the night in question, Treece, then a research student with holes in his underpants and not a change of socks to call his own, was determined to leave Fay, in part because she did not like his poetry, but also because he knew that she did not trust him, since, with the cunning of females who know what faculties are of most or least worth in their prey, she had observed that he was a person without a firm, a solid centre; he was easily blown or altered. On this topic they had exchanged acrimonious words, and Treece had hurried forth into the dark street, pausing only to dress and snatch up his thesis, which reposed, well nigh completed, at the side of the bed. Coming along the Soho street, wearing a leather jacket and a most determined visage, Treece had met a friend of his, a speedway rider of strong and engrossing character. He was a communist, and, unlike Treece, took an active part in the political life. The two withdrew to an all-night café, and Treece, pressed to account for his presence abroad, told him of the row with Fay; he said that he was fed-up with her and didn't wish to go back. The speedway rider observed that severed links were the order of the day; he had finished his job and was going away, probably abroad, and he asked Treece to come with him. "I have no money," said Treece; whereat, from all over his leather jacket, the speedway motorcyclist produced wads of pound notes, all his savings, which he had withdrawn. But, as they talked, through the night, Treece began to think about Fay again, and how warm it was in bed. Finally, uncertainly, he went back to Fay, receiving a poor welcome; she had hoped, she said, that he meant it. Some time later Treece learned that his friend had, in fact, been on his way to Spain, where he had fought; and later still he heard that he had died heroically holding a solitary machine-gun position which had finally been wiped out accidentally by planes on his own side. When Treece heard all this, he felt that if only the man had said that it was to Spain that he was going, he would surely have gone. Afterwards he wondered whether he would; from time to time he certainly wished that he had.

It was against this sort of background that moments like the reception for foreign students, or Treece's responses to provincial life, took their shape. Being a liberal, after all *that*, meant something special; one was a messenger from somewhere. One was, now, a humanist, neither Christian nor communist any more, but in some vague, unstable central place—a humanist, yes, but not one of those who supposes that man is good or progress attractive. One has no firm affiliations—political, religious, or moral—but lies outside it all. One sees new projects tried, new cases put, and reflects on them, distrusts them, is not surprised when they don't work, and is doubtful if they seem to. A tired sophistication runs up and down one's spine; one has seen everything tried and seen it fail. If one speaks, one speaks in asides. One is at the end of the tradition of human experience, where everything has been tried and no one way shows itself as perceptibly better than another. Groping into the corners of one's benevolence, one likes this good soul, that dear woman, but despairs of the group or the race. For the mass of men there is not too much to be said or done; you can't make a silk purse out of a sow's ear. Persons tie themselves into groups, they attach to this cause and then to that, and, working with these abstracts and large emotions, they rush like a flock of lemmings into the sea to drown themselves. What can one do?

* * *

"It's a funny age, isn't it?" [Treece said.] "There are so many literatures, so many religions, so many cultures, so many philosophies, one doesn't know where to turn. Do you remember the thirties?"

"I'm not *that* old," said Emma. "I remember the forties, after the war. There were lots of grants for everybody and people used to sew leather patches on the elbows of perfectly new Harris-tweed sports jackets."

"I *am* that old," said Treece. "My goodness me, talking to you, I feel it. But the thing about the thirties was, you knew you were a socialist—there was nothing else to be—and there were all these socialist clubs, with people doing things about human quandaries. There were quandaries, too. I think that really, however pessimistic we were about the state of the world, we had a kind of Rousseau-esque belief in the perfectibility of man. It's such a paradoxical belief, of course—the evidence of ordinary experience is against it, and, as Rousseau himself admitted, wickedness is a source of considerable embarrassment. But we did think there was something to be done about the social order—that the human condition could be mended, that there was so much further to go. Now one doesn't. Do you have any hope for the future?"

"No," said Emma. "I don't."

"And I don't, none at all. If I see the future as anything other than an explosion, then I think of it as the present, only worse. But in those days . . . Take adult education. In those days it seemed really important work. One was evolving the new man. If you had in your class one of those old-style, working-class intellectuals who started in the mines and finished in Parliament, you felt really a part of the world's process. One was of the English scene. Now the classes are for middle-class ladies whose families are grown up, and there they come, a little lost, improving themselves and using the place as a kind of knitting-bee. Don't misunderstand me, I'm not contemptuous. . . ."

"No, I know," said Emma; Treece was never contemptuous of anything.

"But their prejudices are formed, and one teaches them nothing except facts. Not how to improve the world."

A Note on Recent Scholarly Sources

COMPETENT GENERAL surveys of European thought in the twentieth century are rare, not only because scholars lack perspective, but also because the intellectual life of the century is too various and inchoate to lend itself to the broad generalizations that the writer of synoptic history must impose on his material. Among recent works in English, the most enterprising and the most successful perhaps is Albert William Levi's *Philosophy and the Modern World* (Bloomington, Ind., 1959). Half the book is devoted to formal philosophy, from Bergson to Sartre; the other half includes chapters on Spengler and Toynbee, Freud and Rank, Leninism, and the revolution in theoretical physics. H. Stuart Hughes, *Consciousness and Society* (New York, 1958), focuses on the interaction of psychology, sociology, and philosophy in the period 1890 to 1930. The last ten chapters of George L. Mosse, *The Culture of Western Europe* (Chicago, 1961), offer a useful overview of twentieth-century social and political ideas. See also the last three chapters of Roland N. Stromberg, *An Intellectual History of Modern Europe* (New York, 1966), and the bibliographical notes on pp. 464–73. For a collection of major scholarly articles in the field, consult W. Warren Wagar, ed., *European Intellectual History since Darwin and Marx* (New York, 1967).

There is a similar shortage of synoptic treatments of the major intellectual movements and academic disciplines of the century. But one or two recent books in each field may be worth citing. Lincoln Barnett, *The Universe and Dr. Einstein* (New York, 1948), is a good popular treatment of contemporary physics. See also such works as Albert Einstein and Leopold Infeld, *The Evolution of Physics* (New York, 1938); Louis de Broglie, *The Revolution in Physics* (New York, 1953); and C. F. von Weizsäcker and J. Juilfs, *The Rise of Modern Physics* (New York, 1957). I. M. Bochenski offers a general account of twentieth-century European philosophy in *Contemporary European Philosophy* (Berkeley and

Los Angeles, 1956). The interaction of scientific thought and modern analytical philosophy is discussed in Philipp Frank, *Modern Science and Its Philosophy* (Cambridge, Mass., 1941), and Hans Reichenbach, *The Rise of Scientific Philosophy* (Berkeley and Los Angeles, 1951). Also worth consulting is J. O. Urmson, *Philosophical Analysis: Its Development between the Two World Wars* (New York, 1956). Existentialism is surveyed in James Collins, *The Existentialists* (Chicago, 1952), and Ernst Breisach, *Introduction to Modern Existentialism* (New York, 1962). William Barrett's *Irrational Man: A Study in Existential Philosophy* (Garden City, N.Y., 1958) includes several excellent chapters on the relationship between existentialist thought and contemporary Western culture. For the phenomenological movement and Edmund Husserl, see Pierre Thévenaz, *What Is Phenomenology?* (Chicago, 1962).

The best survey of twentieth-century European theology, despite its age, is still Walter M. Horton's *Contemporary Continental Theology* (New York, 1938). See also *Theologians of Our Time* (Notre Dame, Ind., 1964), a collection of essays by five scholars on twelve contemporary theologians, edited by Leonhard Reinisch. The impact of existentialism is usefully discussed in David E. Roberts, *Existentialism and Religious Belief* (New York, 1963). The later chapters of Franklin L. Baumer's *Religion and the Rise of Scepticism* (New York, 1960) bring deep insight to the study of twentieth-century religious longing and skepticism. In the philosophy of religion, the most comprehensive work is John Macquarrie, *Twentieth Century Religious Thought* (New York, 1963). For the contemporary history of the European churches, see Kenneth Scott Latourette, *Christianity in a Revolutionary Age*, Vol. IV (New York, 1961).

A helpful outline of modern psychoanalytical theory is provided by J. A. C. Brown in his *Freud and the Post-Freudians* (Harmondsworth, England, 1961), which summarizes the work of Freud, Jung, Adler, Rank, Fromm, and the chief British and American schools. Philip Rieff's *Freud: The Mind of the Moralist* (New York, 1959) is a superior study of special value to intellectual historians. See also the provocative essays by Kazin, Erikson, Herberg, Hyman, Kaplan, Niebuhr, Maritain, Bruner, and others in Benjamin Nelson, ed., *Freud and the Twentieth Century* (New York, 1957). Nicholas S. Timasheff surveys sociological theory since the nineteenth century in his *Sociological Theory* (revised edition, New York, 1957). Don Martindale, *The Nature and Types of Sociological Theory* (Boston, 1960), takes a somewhat ahistorical approach but offers useful summaries and bibliographies of the work of the chief modern sociologists both in Continental Europe and in America. An encyclopedic review of twentieth-century sociological theory is supplied by Howard Becker and Harry Elmer Barnes in their *Social Thought from Lore to Science*, Vol. III (third edition, NewYork, 1961).

There are a number of excellent histories of economic thought, such as Eduard Heimann, *History of Economic Doctrines* (New York, 1945), and Overton Taylor, *History of Economic Thought* (New York, 1960), although these devote comparatively little space to recent theorists. Joseph Schumpeter's *Ten Great Economists from Marx to Keynes* (New York, 1951) and *History of Economic Analysis* (New York, 1954) also compel respect. For Keynes, the best popularization of his General Theory is Joan Robinson's *Introduction to the Theory of Employment* (London, 1937); and there is a valuable symposium edited by Seymour Harris, *The New Economics* (New York, 1947).

Socialism receives more adequate treatment by scholars than any other variety of twentieth-century political thought. Alfred G. Meyer, *Leninism* (Cambridge, Mass., 1957), is a definitive study, and for the interaction of ideology and philosophy in the Soviet Union, the best account is Gustav A. Wetter, *Dialectical Materialism* (New York, 1958). All the varieties of twentieth-century socialism are treated synoptically in G. D. H. Cole, *A History of Socialist Thought*, Vols. III–V (New York, 1956–60). Cole is at his best in discussing British and French socialism; for the German and Russian schools, a more penetrating study is Carl Landauer's *European Socialism* (Berkeley and Los Angeles, 1959). Portions of Ernst Nolte's *Three Faces of Fascism* (New York, 1966) deal with the doctrines of the Action Française, Italian Fascism, and German National Socialism, but there is still no detailed investigation of fascism or Nazism as ideologies.

The other major ideologies and the technical development of European political science have received little synoptic treatment by recent scholars; but see Henry S. Kariel, *In Search of Authority: Twentieth Century Political Thought* (New York, 1964); Roy Pierce, *Contemporary French Political Thought* (New York, 1966); and W. J. Stankiewicz, ed., *Political Thought since World War II* (New York, 1964). Recent prophecies of a world civilization are discussed in W. Warren Wagar, *The City of Man* (Boston, 1963), with an emphasis on the prophetic contribution of Toynbee, who is also examined, together with Spengler and Freud, in the last chapters of Bruce Mazlish, *The Riddle of History* (New York, 1966). As yet there exists no satisfactory comprehensive study of twentieth-century European philosophy of history.

Among the many discussions of literature and the arts, those most helpful for the intellectual historian include Erich Heller, *The Disinherited Mind: Essays in Modern German Literature and Thought* (New York, 1957); H. V. Routh, *English Literature and Ideas in the Twentieth Century* (New York, 1948); Henri Peyre, *The Contemporary French Novel* (New York, 1955); Eric Bentley, *The Playwright as Thinker* (New York, 1946); Martin Esslin, *The Theatre of the Absurd* (Garden City, N.Y., 1961); Herbert Read, *The Philosophy of Modern Art* (New York, 1953); and Maurice Nadeau, *History of Surrealism* (New York, 1965).

Another way to approach the study of twentieth-century intellectual history is through the several anthologies of original sources now available. The best general collection of source materials is Part III of Franklin L. Baumer, ed., *Main Currents of Western Thought* (second edition, New York, 1964). Also valuable are Part III of Eugene C. Black, ed., *Posture of Europe, 1815–1940* (Homewood, Ill., 1964), and Adrienne Koch, ed., *Philosophy for a Time of Crisis* (New York, 1959). For the development of philosophy in particular, consult such works as Morton White, ed., *The Age of Analysis* (Boston, 1955); William P. Alston and George Nakhnikian, eds., *Readings in Twentieth-Century Philosophy* (New York, 1963); A. J. Ayer, ed., *Logical Positivism* (Glencoe, Ill., 1958); and Walter Kaufmann, ed., *Existentialism from Dostoevsky to Sartre* (Cleveland, Ohio, 1956). Religious thought is anthologized in Walter Kaufmann, ed., *Religion from Tolstoy to Camus* (New York, 1961), and Will Herberg, ed., *Four Existentialist Theologians* (Garden City, N.Y., 1958). Representative selections of modern sociological and political thought are offered in C. Wright Mills, ed., *Images of Man: The Classic Tradition in Sociological Thinking* (New York, 1960), and David Cooperman and E. V. Walter, eds., *Power and Civilization: Political Thought in the Twentieth Century* (New York, 1962). For the philosophy of history, see Hans Meyerhoff's excellent anthology, *The Philosophy of History in Our Time* (Garden City, N.Y., 1959).

One Hundred Great Books, 1900–1960

Editor's Note:

NOT ALL the landmarks in twentieth-century European intellectual history can be included in a chronological list of great books. Some of the most significant documents of our century are in the form of articles, lectures, manifestos, or short technical papers. In some instances, an important writer has exerted influence through many books, not one of which, however, can be described as "great." The contribution to thought represented by such major works of imaginative literature as *The Waste Land*, *The Magic Mountain*, *Nausea*, and *The Plague* also receives no notice here. But within these obvious limits, the list may have some value. By "great," of course, I mean seminal, representative, influential. Exceptional literary or intellectual power is not necessarily involved, nor is the appearance of any work below intended as an editorial endorsement of its ideas.

For works that appeared over a number of years, the date of publication of the first volume(s) only is given. In all cases the year shown is that of the edition in the language in which the book was first published. Several of the foreign-language titles have still not been translated into English, a remarkable tribute to the provincialism of Anglo-American publishers.

1900   Sigmund Freud, *The Interpretation of Dreams*
        Edmund Husserl, *Logical Investigations*

1901   Sigmund Freud, *The Psychopathology of Everyday Life*

1902   Benedetto Croce, *Philosophy of the Spirit*
        Peter Kropotkin, *Mutual Aid*
        Werner Sombart, *Modern Capitalism*

1903   George Moore, *Principia Ethica*

1907   Henri Bergson, *Creative Evolution*

1908   Georges Sorel, *Reflections on Violence*
       Graham Wallas, *Human Nature in Politics*

1909   V. I. Lenin, *Materialism and Empirio-Criticism*

1910   Bertrand Russell and Alfred North Whitehead, *Principia Mathematica*

1911   Robert Michels, *Political Parties*
       Hans Vaihinger, *The Philosophy of "As If"*

1912   Emile Durkheim, *The Elementary Forms of the Religious Life*
       Carl Gustav Jung, *The Psychology of the Unconscious*

1913   Sigmund Freud, *Totem and Taboo*
       Miguel de Unamuno y Jugo, *The Tragic Sense of Life*

1914   Wilhelm Dilthey, *Collected Works*
       Bertrand Russell, *Our Knowledge of the External World*

1916   Vilfredo Pareto, *The Mind and Society*

1917   Albert Einstein, *Relativity, the Special and General Theory*
       V. I. Lenin, *Imperialism, the Highest Stage of Capitalism*
       V. I. Lenin, *State and Revolution*
       Rudolf Otto, *The Idea of the Holy*

1918   Oswald Spengler, *The Decline of the West*

1919   Karl Barth, *The Epistle to the Romans*
       H. G. Wells, *The Outline of History*

1920   R. H. Tawney, *The Acquisitive Society*
       Max Weber, *Collected Works on the Sociology of Religion*

1921   Carl Gustav Jung, *Psychological Types*

1922   George Moore, *Philosophical Studies*
       Max Weber, *Economy and Society*
       Ludwig Wittgenstein, *Tractactus Logico-Philosophicus*

1923   Nikolai Berdyaev, *The Meaning of History*
       Martin Buber, *I and Thou*
       Ernst Cassirer, *Philosophy of Symbolic Forms*
       Sigmund Freud, *The Ego and the Id*
       Arthur Moeller van den Bruck, *The Third Reich*
       José Ortega y Gasset, *The Modern Theme*
       Albert Schweitzer, *The Philosophy of Civilization*

1925   Karl Barth, *The Word of God and the Word of Man*
       Adolf Hitler, *My Battle*
       Harold J. Laski, *A Grammar of Politics*
       Alfred North Whitehead, *Science and the Modern World*

1926   Ivan Pavlov, *Conditioned Reflexes*
       Joseph Stalin, *Problems of Leninism*

1927   Julien Benda, *The Betrayal of the Intellectuals*
       Martin Heidegger, *Being and Time*
       Karl Kautsky, *The Materialist Conception of History*
       Gabriel Marcel, *Metaphysical Journals*

1928   Rudolf Carnap, *The Logical Structure of the World*
       Arthur Eddington, *The Nature of the Physical World*
       Julian Huxley, *Religion without Revelation*

1929   Karl Mannheim, *Ideology and Utopia*
       Alfred North Whitehead, *Process and Reality*

1930   Sigmund Freud, *Civilization and Its Discontents*
       José Ortega y Gasset, *The Revolt of the Masses*
       Alfred Rosenberg, *The Myth of the Twentieth Century*
       Moritz Schlick, *Problems of Ethics*

1931   Nikolai Berdyaev, *The Destiny of Man*
       Karl Jaspers, *Man in the Modern Age*
       Karl Jaspers, *Philosophy*
       Carl Gustav Jung, *Modern Man in Search of a Soul*
       Pius XI, *Quadragesimo Anno*

1932   Karl Barth, *Church Dogmatics*
       Henri Bergson, *The Two Sources of Morality and Religion*
       James Jeans, *The Mysterious Universe*
       Leon Trotsky, *The History of the Russian Revolution*

1933   Alfred North Whitehead, *Adventures of Ideas*

1934   Rudolf Carnap, *The Logical Syntax of Language*
       Arnold J. Toynbee, *A Study of History*

1935   Kurt Koffka, *Principles of Gestalt Psychology*
       Karl Mannheim, *Man and Society in an Age of Reconstruction*
       Gabriel Marcel, *Being and Having*

1936   A. J. Ayer, *Language, Truth, and Logic*
       John Maynard Keynes, *The General Theory of Employment, Interest, and Money*
       Jacques Maritain, *True Humanism*

1937   Pitirim A. Sorokin, *Social and Cultural Dynamics*

1938   Benedetto Croce, *History as the Story of Liberty*
       Albert Einstein and Leopold Infeld, *The Evolution of Physics*
       Joseph Stalin, *History of the Communist Party of the Soviet Union*

1941   Erich Fromm, *Escape from Freedom*

1942   Albert Camus, *The Myth of Sisyphus*
         Joseph Schumpeter, *Capitalism, Socialism, and Democracy*

1943   Jean-Paul Sartre, *Being and Nothingness*

1944   Friedrich Hayek, *The Road to Serfdom*

1945   Karl Popper, *The Open Society and Its Enemies*

1947   Pierre Lecomte du Noüy, *Human Destiny*

1948   Rudolf Bultmann, *Theology of the New Testament*
         Jacques Maritain, *The Range of Reason*

1949   Richard Crossman, ed., *The God That Failed*

1951   Dietrich Bonhoeffer, *Letters and Papers from Prison*
         Albert Camus, *The Rebel*
         Paul Tillich, *Systematic Theology*

1952   Paul Tillich, *The Courage to Be*

1953   Ludwig Wittgenstein, *Philosophical Investigations*

1955   Pierre Teilhard de Chardin, *The Phenomenon of Man*

1959   C. P. Snow, *The Two Cultures and the Scientific Revolution*

1960   Jean-Paul Sartre, *Critique of Dialectical Reason*

Index

DOCUMENTARY HISTORY OF WESTERN CIVILIZATION
edited by Eugene C. Black and Leonard W. Levy

ANCIENT AND MEDIEVAL HISTORY OF THE WEST

Morton Smith: ANCIENT GREECE

A. H. M. Jones: A HISTORY OF ROME THROUGH THE FIFTH CENTURY
Vol. I: The Republic
Vol. II: The Empire

Deno Geanakopolos: BYZANTINE EMPIRE

Marshall W. Baldwin: CHRISTIANITY THROUGH THE CRUSADES

Bernard Lewis: ISLAM THROUGH SULEIMAN THE MAGNIFICENT

David Herlihy: HISTORY OF FEUDALISM

William M. Bowsky: RISE OF COMMERCE AND TOWNS

David Herlihy: MEDIEVAL CULTURE AND SOCIETY

EARLY MODERN HISTORY

Hannah Gray: CULTURAL HISTORY OF THE RENAISSANCE

Florence Edler De Roover: MONEY, BANKING & COMMERCE, 13TH-16TH CENTURIES

V. J. Parry: THE OTTOMAN EMPIRE

Ralph E. Giesey: EVOLUTION OF THE DYNASTIC STATE

J. H. Parry: THE EUROPEAN RECONNAISSANCE

Hans J. Hillerbrand: THE PROTESTANT REFORMATION

John C. Olin: THE CATHOLIC COUNTER-REFORMATION

Orest Ranum: THE CENTURY OF LOUIS XIV

Thomas Hegarty: RUSSIAN HISTORY THROUGH PETER THE GREAT

Marie Boas-Hall: THE SCIENTIFIC REVOLUTION

Barry E. Supple: HISTORY OF MERCANTILISM

————: IMPERIALISM, WAR & DIPLOMACY,1550-1763

Herbert H. Rowen: THE LOW COUNTRIES

C. A. Macartney: THE EVOLUTION OF THE HABSBURG & HOHENZOLLERN DYNASTIES

Lester G. Crocker: THE ENLIGHTENMENT

Robert Forster: EIGHTEENTH CENTURY EUROPEAN SOCIETY